A COLLECTION OF THEOLOGICAL ESSAYS FROM VARIOUS AUTHORS.

WITH AN INTRODUCTION,

BY

GEORGE R. NOYES, D.D.,
PROFESSOR OF SACRED LITERATURE IN HARVARD UNIVERSITY.

THIRD EDITION.

BOSTON:
WALKER, WISE, AND COMPANY,
PUBLISHERS FOR THE
AMERICAN UNITARIAN ASSOCIATION,
245 WASHINGTON STREET.
1860.

University Press, Cambridge:
Printed by Welch, Bigelow, and Company.

CONTENTS.

PAGE

Introduction. By George R. Noyes. v

Faith and Science. By M. Guizot. 1
The Law and the Gospel. By Rev. Baden Powell. 27
The Doctrine of Inspiration. By Dr. F. A. D. Tholuck. . 65
Holy Scripture. By Rev. Rowland Williams. 113
Servants of God speaking as moved by the Holy Ghost. By Rev. Rowland Williams. 127
The Spirit and the Letter, or the Truth and the Book. By Rev. Rowland Williams. 147
On the Causes which probably conspired to produce our Saviour's Agony. By Rev. Edward Harwood. 167
Of our Lord's Fortitude. By Rev. William Newcome. . . 197
The Doctrine of the Atonement. By Benjamin Jowett. . . 221
On Righteousness by Faith. By Benjamin Jowett. 239
On the Imputation of the Sin of Adam. By Benjamin Jowett. . 265
On Conversion and Changes of Character. By Benjamin Jowett. 273
Casuistry. By Benjamin Jowett. 299
On the Connection of Immorality and Idolatry. By Benjamin Jowett. 321
The Old Testament. By Benjamin Jowett. 325
On the Quotations from the Old Testament in the New. By Benjamin Jowett. 329
Fragment on the Character of St. Paul. By Benjamin Jowett. . 341

St. Paul and the Twelve. By Benjamin Jowett. 357
Evils in the Church of the Apostolical Age. By Benjamin Jowett. 383
On the Belief in the Coming of Christ in the Apostolical Age. By Benjamin Jowett. 393
The Death of Christ, considered as a Sacrifice. By Rev. James Foster. 403
The Epistles to the Corinthians, in Relation to the Gospel History. By Rev. Arthur P. Stanley. 415
Apostolical Worship. By Rev. Arthur P. Stanley. 437
The Eucharist. By Rev. Arthur P. Stanley. 443
Unity and Variety of Spiritual Gifts. By Rev. Arthur P. Stanley. 447
The Gift of Tongues and the Gift of Prophesying. By Rev. Arthur P. Stanley. 453
Love, the greatest of Gifts. By Rev. Arthur P. Stanley. . . . 472
The Resurrection of Christ. By Rev. Arthur P. Stanley. . . . 477
The Resurrection of the Dead. By Rev. Arthur P. Stanley. . 482
On the Credibility of Miracles. By Dr. Thomas Brown. . . . 485

Note A. 505
Note B. 512

INTRODUCTION.

The following collection of Theological Essays is designed for students in divinity, Sunday-school teachers, and all intelligent readers who desire to gain correct views of religion, and especially of the character, use, and meaning of the Scriptures. It was suggested by the recent excellent Commentary on the Epistles of St. Paul by Mr. Jowett, now Professor of Greek in the University of Oxford. Understanding that this work was not likely to be reprinted in this country, and that the high price of the English edition rendered it inaccessible to most readers, it appeared to me that a collection of Theological Essays, which should include the most important dissertations connected with that Commentary, would be a valuable publication. Mr. Jowett seems to me to have penetrated more deeply into the views and spirit of Paul, and the circumstances under which he wrote, than any previous English commentator. Some of the best results of his labors are presented in the Essays which are now republished in this collection. Mr. Jowett's notes might have been more satisfactory in some respects if, in addition to other German commentaries which he has mentioned, he had made use of those of De Wette and Meyer. But no illustrative dissertations in any German commentary with which we are acquainted are equal in value to those of Jowett. His freedom and independence are especially to be admired in a member of the Church of England, and Professor in the University of Oxford.

In the selection of the dissertations by other writers, regard was had partly to their rarity, and partly to their intrinsic value, and the light which they throw on important subjects which occupy the minds of religious inquirers at the present day. Three Essays are taken from Kitto's Journal of Sacred Literature, an English periodical conducted by clergymen of the Established Church, of which few copies are circulated in this country. The first, by M. Guizot, the eminent writer and statesman of France, presents the subject of Faith in an interesting point of view, and closes with an admirable lesson on the importance of the free discussion of religious subjects.

The second Essay, by Rev. Baden Powell, an eminent Professor in the University of Oxford, and author of several well-known publications, contains an able discussion of a very important subject, which appears to be now attracting some notice in this country; distinguished divines of the Baptist denomination taking the view of Dr. Powell, and some of the Orthodox Congregationalists opposing it. The prevalent opinion, which regards the Old Testament as an authority in religion and morals equally binding upon Christians with the New, appears to me to have had a disastrous influence on the interests of the Church and the interests of humanity. The history of the civil wars of England and Scotland, the early history of New England, and the state of opinion at the present day on the subjects of war, slavery, punishment for religious opinion, and indeed punishment in general, illustrate the noxious influence of the prevalent sentiment. A writer in one of the most distinguished theological journals in this country has been for some time engaged in the vain attempt to prove, in opposition to the plainest language, that the laws of the Pentateuch do not sanction chattel slavery. It was not thus that the great champion of the Protestant Reformation proceeded, when the authority of the Old Testament was invoked to justify immorality. When some of his contemporaries were committing unjustifiable acts against the peace and order of the community, and vindicated themselves by appealing to the Old Testament, Luther wrote a treatise entitled "Instruction on the Manner in which Moses is to be read," containing the following passage, which, in the clearness and force of its style, might have been imitated with advantage by some of his countrymen: "Moses was a mediator and lawgiver to the Jews alone, to whom he gave the Law. If I take Moses in one commandment, I must take the whole of Moses. Moses is dead. His dispensation is at an end. He has no longer any relation to us. I will accept Moses as an instructor, but not as a lawgiver, except where he agrees with the New Testament, or with the law of nature. When any one brings forward Moses and his precepts, and would oblige you to observe them, answer him thus: 'Go to the Jews with your Moses! I am no Jew. If I take Moses as a master in one point, I am bound to keep the whole law, says St. Paul.' . . . . . If now the disorganizers say, 'Moses has commanded it,' do you let Moses go, and say, 'I ask not what Moses has commanded.' 'But,' say they, 'Moses has commanded that we should believe in God, that we should not take his name in vain, that we should honor our father and mother, &c. Must we not keep these commandments?' Answer them thus: 'Nature has given these commandments. Nature teaches man to call upon God, and hence it is natural to honor God, not to steal, not to commit adultery, not to bear false witness, &c. Thus I keep the commandments which Moses has given, not because he enjoined them, but because nature implanted them in me.'..... But if any one say, 'It is all God's word,' answer him thus: 'God's word here, God's word there. I must know and observe *to whom* this word is spoken. I must know not only that it is God's word, but whether it is spoken to me or to another. I listen to the word which concerns me, &c. We have the Gospel.'"* I would not be understood to maintain every sentiment which Dr. Powell has advanced; but his views in general appear to me not only sound, but highly important.

The Essay on the subject of Inspiration, by Tholuck, is to be found in English only in the same foreign journal. The views of a biblical student who enjoys so great a reputation among Christians of various denominations in all parts of the world need no recommendation. The translation I have carefully compared with the original, and found to be made with great fidelity and accuracy.

The three Essays which follow on the use and character of the Scriptures are taken from a recent volume of sermons, entitled "Rational Godliness," by Rev. Rowland Williams, a clergyman and distinguished scholar of the Established Church of England, having been delivered before the Chancellor and

* See the passage in Luther's works, or as quoted by Bretschneider, Dogmatik, Vol. I. p. 181.

University of Cambridge. They appear to me sufficiently valuable to be reprinted. The writer may be thought by some to undervalue external authority, while maintaining the rights of intuition and experience as means of attaining Christian truth. But have not many Christians since the time of Paley paid too exclusive regard to the former? It seems to me that those who accept the New Testament records of miracles as genuine and authentic, will not fail to receive from them their due influence, and will be in no danger of attaching too great importance to intuitive faith and Christian experience. The older the world grows, the less must religious faith depend on history and tradition, and the more on the power of the human soul, assisted by the promised Paraclete, to recognize revealed truth by its own light.

The four Essays which follow relate to the great subject of the Atonement by Christ, and are designed to establish the true view of it, in opposition to certain false theories which human speculation has connected with it, dishonorable to the character of God, pernicious in their influence on man, and having no foundation in the Scriptures or in reason. The Essay on the Causes which probably conspired to produce our Saviour's Agony, is by a distinguished English scholar of the last century, the author of an Introduction to the New Testament, and of a translation of the same, which, though it departs too much from the simplicity of the Common Version, is highly creditable to the author as a critic and a man of learning. The Essay which is here republished is commended by Archbishop Newcome in his very valuable observations, which follow, on substantially the same subject, — the Fortitude of our Saviour. The two Essays appear to me to give a triumphant vindication of the character of our Saviour from the charges which have been brought against it by unbelievers, and, hypothetically, by some Christian divines, founded on certain expressions of feeling manifested a short time before his death, which his faithful historians have recorded for our instruction and consolation.

It so happens that that part of one of the speculative theories connected with the Christian doctrine of atonement which is most repulsive to the feelings of many Christians, is absolutely without foundation in the Scriptures, or in the faith of the Church for many centuries after the death of Christ. I refer to that opinion which represents him as receiving supernatural pain or torture immediately from the hand of God, over and above that which was inflicted by human instrumentality, or which arose naturally from the circumstances in which he, as God's minister for establishing the Christian religion, was placed, and from the peculiar sensibility of his natural constitution. The very statement of this theory by some distinguished theologians shocks the feelings of many Christians like the language of impiety. Thus Dr. Dwight says: "Omniscience and Omnipotence are certainly able to communicate, during even a short time, to a finite mind, such views of the hatred and contempt of God towards sin and sinners, *and of course towards a substitute for sinners*, as would not only fill its capacity for suffering, but probably put an end to its existence. In this manner, I apprehend, the chief distresses of Christ were produced." * What ideas! The omnipotence and omniscience of God are first

* Dwight's Theology, Vol. II. p. 214.

called in to communicate a sense of his hatred and contempt to a sinless man, and, secondly, the sufferings and even the death of Christ are represented as the immediate consequence of his sense of God's hatred and contempt!

Dr. Macknight, a theologian of considerable celebrity, gives a somewhat different view, but equally appalling. He says: "Our Lord's perturbation and agony, therefore, arose from the pains *which were inflicted upon him by the hand of God*, when he made his soul an offering for sin...... Though Jesus knew no sin, God might, by the immediate operation of his power, *make him feel those pains which shall be the punishment of sin hereafter*, in order that, by the visible effects which they produced upon him, mankind might have a just notion of the greatness of these pains...... His bearing those pains, with a view to show how great they are, was by no means punishment. It was merely suffering." * Such is the representation of Dr. Macknight, in a treatise entitled "The Conversion of the World to Christianity"!

Calvin, it is well known, represents our Saviour as actually suffering after death the pains of hell; a representation, however, which differs not materially from those of Dr. Dwight and Dr. Macknight, except in reference to time and place.

A recent work by Krummacher, which has been industriously circulated in New England, contains a representation similar to that of Dwight and Macknight, in language still more horrible. Other recent writers in New England have sanctioned the same view.

* See Macknight, in Watson's Tracts, Vol. V. p. 183.

Now to this theory a decisive objection is, that it has not the least foundation in the Scriptures, and that it is in fact inconsistent with the general tenor of the New Testament, which speaks of Christ's sufferings in connection with the obvious second causes of them, recorded in the history; namely, the reviling and persecuting of his enemies, the coldness and desertion of his disciples, the dark prospects of his mission,* his blood, his death, and the terrible persecution of his followers, which were to precede the establishment of his religion. Of the immediate infliction of pain by the Deity, over and above what Jewish malice inflicted upon him, we find not a word. There is not a particle of evidence to show that any of the sufferings of Christ were inflicted upon him by any more direct or immediate agency on the part of God, than those of other righteous men who have been persecuted to death in the cause of truth and righteousness. The text in Isa. liii. 10, — "Yet it pleased the Lord to bruise him; he hath put him to grief; when thou shalt make his soul an offering for sin," &c., — is often referred to. But such an application of this text can be shown to be wrong in two ways: — 1. It can be demonstrated, on principles of interpretation universally acknowledged, that the "servant of God," in this and the preceding chapters, denotes, at least in its primary sense, the Jewish church, the Israel of God, who suffered on account of the sins of others in the time of the captivity at Babylon. I cannot, for want of space, go into a defence of this view. But I fully believe it to be correct, and it is maintained by the most unbiassed and scientific interpreters of the Old

* Luke xviii. 8; Matt. xxiv. 24.

Testament.* 2. The language in question denotes no more direct and immediate agency of the Deity, than that which is everywhere, both in the Old Testament and the New, ascribed to the Deity in reference to the sufferings of the prophets and apostles. Comp. Ps. xxxix. 9, 10; Jer. xv. 17, 18; xx. 7, &c.; xi. 18, 19; Lam. iii. So in the New Testament, if St. Paul tells us that Christ was "set forth as a propitiatory sacrifice," he also says, "For I think that God has set forth us the apostles last, as it were appointed to death." Indeed, there is no idiom in the Scriptures more obvious than that which represents all the blessings and afflictions of life, by whatever instrumentality produced, as coming from God.

Modern speculative theologians, not finding in the sacred history, or in any Scripture statement, any authority for their supposition of a miraculous suffering or torment, inconceivable in degree, inflicted by the immediate agency of God upon the soul of Christ, resort to mere theory to support their position. If, say they, Christ was not enduring "vicarious suffering," inconceivable in degree, inflicted on his soul by the immediate exertion of Almighty power, then it follows that he did not bear his sufferings so well as many martyrs, — so well as "the thieves on the cross," so well as "thousands and millions of common men without God and without hope in the world." †

Without repeating the explanations of Dr. Harwood

---

* That the phrase "servant of God" is a collective term, denoting the people of God, comprehending the Jewish nation, or the better part of the Jewish nation, that is, the Jewish church, has been maintained by such critics as Döderlein, Rosenmüller, Jahn, Gesenius, Maurer, Knobel, Ewald, Hitzig; also by the old Jewish critics, such as Aben Ezra, Jarchi, Abarbanel, and Kimchi.

† See Stuart on Hebrews, Exc. XI. p. 575.

and Archbishop Newcome, it may be remarked, — 1. That at best this is only an argument *ad Christianum*. The sceptic and the scoffer are ready to accept the statement of the orthodox divine, and to tell him that, while the manner in which Christ endured his sufferings is matter of history, his way of accounting for them is pure theory.

2. It is very remarkable that the speculative theologians have not seen that a quality exhibited in such perfection by "thousands and millions without God and without hope in the world," "by the thieves on the cross," and, it might have been added, by any number of bloodthirsty pirates and savage Indians, was one the absence of which implied no want of moral excellence; that it was a matter of natural temperament, of physical habits, and of the firm condition of the nervous system, rather than of moral or religious character. Moral excellence is seen, not in insensibility to pain or danger, but in unwavering obedience to duty in defiance of pain and danger. The greater sense Jesus had and expressed of the sufferings which lay in his path, the greater is the moral excellence exhibited in overcoming them. In order to satisfy myself of the perfection of the character of Jesus, all I wish to know is that his obedience was complete; that his grief, fears, and doubts were momentary; that his most earnest expostulations and complaints, if so they may be called, were wrung from him by causes which are plainly set forth in the sacred history, while he was engaged without hesitation, without voluntary reluctance, nay, with the most supreme devotion of his will, in the greatest work ever wrought for man.

For my part, I am not ashamed to say, that I have a distinct feeling of gratitude, not only for the work which Christ performed, but for every expression of human feeling, whether of grief, or momentary doubt, or fear, or interrupted sense of communion with God, which he manifested. I should feel that I was robbed of an invaluable treasure of encouragement and consolation, if any one expression of feeling, whether in his words or otherwise, caused by such sufferings as all men, in a greater or less degree, are called to endure, should be blotted from the sacred record. In the midst of deep affliction, and the fear of deeper, nothing has given me greater support than the repetition of the prayer in Gethsemane, once uttered in agony of soul, "If it be possible, let this cup pass from me! Nevertheless, not as I will, but as thou wilt!" Now I know that "we have not a high-priest which cannot be touched with the feeling of our infirmities; but was in all points tempted like as we are, yet without sin."

3. Those who maintain that the character of Christ was imperfect or sinful, unless he received immediately from the hand of God inconceivably greater sufferings than were occasioned by human instrumentalities, and the second causes which are matters of history, do not make it clear how by their theory they relieve his character from the charges which they have hypothetically brought against it. If the manner in which Christ endured his sufferings was unworthy of him,— if it was faulty or sinful, — if his expressions in the garden of Gethsemane, or upon the cross, were wrong, — then no degree of suffering which the human imagination can conceive to have been endured by him can make them right. Strength of temptation can palliate what is wrong, but cannot make it right. Whatever was the nature of Christ's sufferings, however great in degree, and however immediately they

were inflicted by God, still, unless his memory of the past, as recorded in the Gospels, was wholly effaced, he had greater advantages than other men. He knew what testimonials and powers he had received from God. He knew that he was the object of Divine love. He knew that he had consented to his sufferings, and that they were a part of his work; he had no sense of sin to aggravate them; he knew that they were for a short time, and that they were certainly to be followed by a glorious resurrection, and by endless blessedness for himself and his followers. How then are what Dr. Dwight calls "the bitter complaints" of Jesus absolutely justifiable on his theory of the nature and causes of Christ's sufferings, if not on that view which has its basis, not in mere reasoning, but in the Scripture history, and which is set forth by Dr. Harwood and Archbishop Newcome in this volume? If all the mental and bodily sufferings naturally caused to Jesus by the malice of the Jews, the desertion of his disciples, and all the circumstances in which he was placed, cannot justify our Saviour's expressions, whether in language or otherwise, then no sufferings or torments the human imagination can conceive to have been immediately inflicted by God can justify them. In fact, the knowledge that they were inflicted immediately by the hand of God would have a tendency to make them more tolerable. Who would not drink the cup certainly known to be presented to his lips by the hand of his Almighty Father? I have no difficulty in the case, because I believe all the expressions of Jesus in relation to his sufferings, which have been supposed to indicate a want of fortitude, to have been momentary, extorted from him by overpowering pain of body and mind.

It is also to be observed, in connection with the preceding remarks, that what may be called the rich imagination of Jesus, as displayed in the beauty of his illustrations and his parables, as well as various expressions of strong feeling on several occasions in the course of his ministry, indicate an exquisite sensibility, which no debasement of sin had ever blunted.

Without anticipating what is said in the excellent Essays of Dr. Harwood and Archbishop Newcome, I may make one more remark. Injustice seems to me to have been done to Jesus by comparing his short distress of mind on two or three occasions with what may have been as short a composure of some distinguished martyrs, — Socrates for instance, — without taking into view the habitual fortitude of Christ. Now if any one believes that the feelings which Socrates exhibited when he drank the hemlock in prison, as described by Plato, were all which entered his mind from the time when he incurred the deadly hatred and persecution of the Athenians, and that no doubts or fears or misgivings occurred to him at any moment, in the solitude of his prison or elsewhere, I have only to say that his view of what is incident to human nature is very different from mine. Would Jesus have prayed, an hour before his suffering in Gethsemane, that his disciples might have the peace, and even the joy, which he possessed, had not the habitual state of his feelings been tranquil and composed? Panegyrists have described the bravery with which some martyrs have endured their sufferings before the eyes of their admirers. Jesus, who suffered not with a view to human applause, but to human consolation and salvation, was not ashamed or afraid to express *all* which he felt, and his faithful biographers were not ashamed or afraid to record it.

I have intimated that the view of the cause of our Saviour's principal sufferings, which I have endeavored to oppose, is not found in the Scriptures, nor in the general faith of the Church. It is the fruit of comparatively modern speculation. For proof of the last assertion, I refer to the standard works on the history of Christian doctrines. In regard to the principal utterance of our Saviour, to which reference has been made in relation to this subject, in the words of the first verse of the twenty-second Psalm, I cannot agree with those who find in them no expression of anguish or tone of expostulation, and who suppose them to be cited by our Saviour merely in order to suggest the confidence and triumph with which the Psalm ends; but which do not begin before the twenty-second verse. Under the circumstances of the case, the words appear to have had substantially the same meaning when uttered by Christ as when uttered by the Psalmist. They should not be interpreted as the deliberate result of calm reflection, but as an outburst of strong involuntary emotion, forced from our Saviour by anguish of body and mind, in the words which naturally occurred to him, implying *momentary* expostulation, or even complaint. But that the interruption of the consciousness of God's presence and love was only momentary, both in the case of the Psalmist and of the Saviour, is evident, first, from the expression, *My* God! *my* God! repeated with earnestness; secondly, from the expressions of confidence in the course of the Psalm, which might follow in the mind of Christ as well as in that of the Psalmist; and thirdly, from the usage of language, according to which the expression "to be forsaken by God" merely means "not to be delivered from actual or impending distress." The very parallel line in the verse under consideration, "Why art thou so far from helping me?" is, according to the laws of Hebrew parallelism, a complete exposition of the language, "Why hast thou forsaken me?" So Ps. xxxviii. 21, 22, "Forsake me not, O Lord! O my God, be not far from me! Make haste to help me, O Lord, my salvation!" Other passages are Ps. x. 1, xiii. 1, lxxiv. 1, lxxxviii. 14.

As the historical passages in which Christ expressed his feelings under the sufferings which he endured or feared, are of great interest, it may be satisfactory to many readers if I translate, and place in a note at the end of the volume,* the expositions of them given by men who are regarded by competent judges of all denominations of Christians as standing in the very first rank as unbiassed, learned, scientific expositors of the Scriptures. De Wette, Lücke, Meyer, Bleek, and Lünemann will be admitted by all who are acquainted with their writings to stand in that rank.

After the Essays on the nature and causes of the sufferings of Christ, and the manner in which he bore them, I have selected two on the design and influence of these sufferings in the atonement which he effected: one by that admirable writer, James Foster,† the most celebrated preacher of his day, of whom Pope wrote, long ago,

> "Let modest Foster, if he will, excel
> Ten metropolitans in preaching well";

and the other by Professor Jowett, of whom I have already spoken. The two dissertations, taken together,

---

* See Note A.

† By accident this Essay does not appear in its proper place in this volume, but will be found on page 403.

appear to me to give a very fair and Scriptural view of the Christian doctrine of atonement.

The great variety of theories which the speculations of Protestants have connected with the Christian doctrine of atonement is alone sufficient to show on what a sandy foundation some of them rest. As sacrifices of blood, in which certain false views of Christian redemption had their origin, passed away from the world's regard gradually, so one error after another has been from time to time expunged from the theory of redemption which prevailed at the time of the Protestant Reformation. Luther laid it down plainly, that the sins of all mankind were imputed to Christ, so that he was regarded as guilty of them and punished for them. Thus he says: "And this, no doubt, all the prophets did foresee in spirit, that Christ should become the greatest transgressor, murderer, adulterer, thief, rebel, and blasphemer that ever was or could be in all the world. For he, being made a sacrifice for the sins of the whole world, is not now an innocent person and without sin; is not now the Son of God, born of the Virgin Mary; but a sinner, which hath and carrieth the sin of Paul, who was a blasphemer, an oppressor, and a persecutor; of Peter, which denied Christ; of David, which was an adulterer, a murderer, &c. . . . . . Whatsoever sins I, thou, and we all have done, or shall do hereafter, they are Christ's own sins as verily as if he himself had done them. . . . . . But wherefore is Christ punished? Is it not because he hath sin, and beareth sin?" * Luther's theory was once the prevalent one in the Protestant Church.

It is also to be observed, as it contributes to the better understanding of the New England theories

* Luther on Gal. iii. 13.

which prevail at the present day, that the view of Luther was at one time almost universal in New England. In the year 1650, William Pynchon, a gentleman of learning and talent, and chief magistrate of Springfield, wrote a book in which, in the language of Cotton Mather, "he pretends to prove that Christ suffered not for us those unutterable torments of God's wrath which are commonly called hell torments, to redeem our souls from them, and that Christ bore not our sins by God's imputation, and therefore also did not bear the curse of the law for them."

The General Court of Massachusetts, as soon as the book was received from England, where it was printed, immediately called Mr. Pynchon to account for his heresy, dismissed him from his magistracy, caused his book to be publicly burned in Boston market, and appointed three elders to confer with him, and bring him to an acknowledgment of his error.* They also chose Rev. John Norton, of Ipswich, to *answer* his book, after they had condemned all the copies of it to be burned.† Mr. Norton's answer is now before us, in which he repeats over and over again the prevalent doctrine of the time: — "Christ suffered a penal hell, but not a local; he descended into hell virtually, not locally; that is, he suffered the pains of hell due unto the elect, who for their sin deserved to be damned." "Christ suffered the essential penal wrath of God, which answers the suffering of the second death, due to the elect for their sin, before he suffered his natural death." "Christ was tormented without any forgiveness; God spared him nothing of the due debt."

---

* See Records of Massachusetts Bay, Vol. IV. Part I. pp. 29, 30; also Holland's History of Western Massachusetts, Vol. I. p. 37, &c.

† See Note B.

Flavel, a Nonconformist clergyman in England, whose writings continue to be published by the American Tract Society, and who was contemporaneous with John Norton, thus writes: "To wrath, to the wrath of an infinite God without mixture, to the very torments of hell, was Christ delivered, and that by the hands of his own Father."* "As it was all the wrath of God that lay upon Christ, so it was his wrath aggravated in diverse respects beyond that which the damned themselves do suffer." †

In the Confession of Faith ‡ owned and consented to by the churches assembled in Boston, New England, May 12, 1680, and recommended to all the churches by the General Court held October 5, 1679, is contained the following (Ch. VIII. 4): "The Lord Jesus Christ..... underwent the punishment due to us, which we should have borne and suffered, being made sin and a curse for us, enduring most excruciating torments immediately from God in his soul, and most painful sufferings in his body." This was copied verbatim into the celebrated Saybrook Platform, adopted by the churches of Connecticut, September 9, 1708.

Some of the preceding views, for questioning which one of the wisest and best men in Massachusetts was so much harassed as to feel obliged to leave the Commonwealth, are now as universally rejected as

* Fountain of Life Opened, p. 10, Ser. IV. fol. edit.

† Ibid., p. 106.

‡ This Confession was taken, with a few slight variations in conformity with the Westminster Confession, from the "Savoy Declaration," that is, "A Declaration of the Faith and Order owned and practised in the Congregational Churches in England; agreed upon and consented unto by their elders and messengers at the Savoy [a part of London], October 12th, 1658," which may be seen in "Hanbury's Historical Memorials," p. 532, &c.

they were once received. But the most objectionable part of them, in a religious point of view, that which supposes supernatural sufferings or tortures to have been immediately inflicted by the Deity upon the soul of Christ, is still retained by many. The late Professor Stuart, as we have seen, supported this view on the ground that the character of Christ for fortitude would otherwise suffer. Many of the books industriously circulated by the Orthodox sects among the laity contain the doctrine in a very offensive form. The Assembly's Catechism, which declares that Christ "endured the wrath of God," evidently in the sense of Norton and Flavel, is scattered by thousands among the people, and made the standard of faith in the principal theological school of this Commonwealth. Vincent, whose explanation of the Assembly's Catechism has just been republished by the Presbyterian Board of Publication, says: "He, together with the pain of his body on the cross, endured the wrath of God, due for man's sin, in his soul."

With the progress of intellectual and moral philosophy, however, the doctrine of the imputation of sin to one who had not committed it, came to be held as a mere fiction by many, who yet retained that part of the old doctrine which maintains that Christ bore the *punishment* of the sins of all mankind. This view avoids the now evident fiction involved in charging the sins of the guilty upon the innocent; but it has no advantage over Luther's doctrine in reference to the character of the Deity. Luther's theory paid so much homage to the natural sentiments of justice in the human soul, as to make the attempt, though a vain one, to reconcile the conduct which his theology ascribed to God with those sentiments. Luther, with

John Norton and others of his school, felt as strongly as any Unitarian of the present day, that, where there is punishment, there must be guilt, and an accusing conscience.* They held, therefore, that Christ was punished because he was guilty, and "sensible of an accusing conscience." But the more modern theory, which holds that Christ bore the punishment of all men's sins without bearing their guilt, involves the idea of punishment without guilt in him who suffers it. It takes away the hypothesis which alone gave it even the show of consistency with the justice of God.

The perception of the incongruity involved in the supposition that one should receive punishment who is without guilt, has therefore led many theologians to give up this part of the old theory. It was abandoned by many in England as long ago as the time of Baxter. In New England, since the time of Dr. Edwards the younger, several theological writers have maintained that, as there can be no punishment without a sense of guilt and condemnation of conscience, but only pain, suffering, torment, it is erroneous to say that Christ endured vicarious *punishment* for the sins of mankind. Vicarious *pain* or *torment* might be endured by the innocent, but not vicarious *punishment.* Some, also, on the ground that the sufferings of Christ bear no proportion, in amount and duration, to the punishment which was threatened against sinners, have even rejected the term *vicarious* as inapplicable. Dr. Dwight says: "It will not be supposed, as plainly it cannot, that Christ suffered in his divine nature. Nor will it be believed that any created nature could in that short space of time suffer what would be equivalent to even a slight distress extended through

* See Norton's Answer, &c. p. 119.

eternity."* "When, therefore, we are told that *it pleased Jehovah to bruise him*, it was not as a punishment."† "It is not true," says Edwards the younger, "that Christ endured an equal quantity of misery to that which would have been endured by all his people, had they suffered the curse of the law...... As the eternal Logos was capable of neither enduring misery nor losing happiness, all the happiness lost by the substitution of Christ was barely that of the *man* Christ Jesus, during only thirty-three years; or rather during the last three years of his life."‡ Dr. Emmons says: "His sufferings were no punishment, much less our punishment. His sufferings were by no means equal in degree or duration to the eternal sufferings we deserve, and which God has threatened to inflict upon us. So that he did in no sense bear the penalty of the law which we have broken, and justly deserve."§

But this concession of the more modern New England theologians to the imperative claims of reason is not of so much importance as it may at first view appear. To say that Christ did not endure the punishment of the sins of mankind, nor indeed any punishment whatever, but only an amount of suffering or torment which, in its effect as an expression of the Divine mind, and in upholding the honor of the Divine government, was an equivalent to the infliction of the punishment threatened against sin, is of little avail, so long as it is maintained that the chief sufferings of our Saviour were of a miraculous character, inconceivable in degree, immediately inflicted upon him by

* Ser. LVI. Vol. II. p. 217.

† Ibid., p. 211.

‡ Sermons on the Atonement, Works, Vol. II. p. 43.

§ Works, Vol. V. p. 32.

the hand of God over and above those which he incurred from human opposition and persecution in the accomplishment of his work. The concession is made to philosophy, not to religion. So far as the Divine character is concerned, it is of little consequence whether you call the sufferings of Christ *punishment*, or only *torture immediately inflicted by God* for the mere purpose of being contemplated by intelligent beings.

Suppose that Christ had ordered the beloved Apostle John to be crucified, in order to show his displeasure at sin, when he forgave Peter, of what consequence would it be to say that John was not punished, but only tortured, for the sin of Peter? Would Christ deserve the more to be regarded as a righteous being, an upholder of law, a wise moral governor, for inflicting inconceivable anguish of body and mind upon John as the sole ground and condition of forgiving the sin of Peter?

How many of the theologians of New England at the present day retain this theory of miraculous suffering immediately inflicted by the Deity upon the soul of Christ, I have no means of ascertaining. It is not easy to see why the advocates of the governmental theory, after admitting that the sufferings of Christ were finite and of brief duration, that they were not the punishment, nor, as a penalty, equivalent to the punishment, of the sinner, should seek by mere ratiocination to magnify the sufferings of Christ beyond what the sacred history has recorded them to be, and to bring in the omnipotence and the omniscience of the Deity to inflict a pain which human malice and second causes could not inflict. The mere amount of suffering does not seem to be essential to this theory. The Scriptures contain, as we have seen, nothing for it. On the contrary, they seem to be positively against it, in insisting, as they do, on the *blood* of Christ, the *death* of Christ as a sacrifice, rather than on what he suffered before he died. It is just to state that I do not find, in the sermons on the atonement by Dr. Edwards the younger, Dr. Emmons, and Dr. Woods, reference to any sufferings of Christ, except those which were naturally incident to the discharge of his duty. True, they say nothing against the view held by Dr. Dwight, Dr. Macknight, and some recent writers. But it is to be hoped that they omitted the theory of miraculous suffering, immediately inflicted by the Deity upon the soul of Christ, because they had abandoned it. May the time soon come when all the advocates of the governmental theory shall cease to insist on a fragment of the old theory of penal satisfaction, which has no historical foundation, which is shocking to the feelings of many Christians, and strengthens the objections of the enemies of Christianity.

On the other hand, it appears to me that some writers, looking at the subject chiefly in the light of the principles of moral and religious philosophy, have given a somewhat imperfect view of the sentiments of St. Paul respecting the significance of the death of Christ, by maintaining that he limited the influence of it to its immediate effect in producing the reformation and sanctification of the sinner. This latter view is indeed prominent throughout the Apostle's writings. Christians are represented as being baptized to the death of Christ; that is, to die to sin as he died for it; to be buried in baptism to sin, and to rise to a new spiritual life, as he was buried and rose to a new life. But the Apostle regards the death of Christ, not only as exerting a sanctifying influence upon the heart, but as having a meaning and significance, considered as an event taking place under the moral government of God, according to his will. Its meaning serves, according to him, at the same time to manifest the righteousness of God, and his mercy in accepting the true believer. "Whom in his blood, through faith, God has set forth as a propitiatory sacrifice, in order to manifest his righteousness on account of his passing by, in his forbearance, the sins of former times." * It is true that the design of this providential event was still *manifestation*, and that the contemplation of the sacrifice, and the appropriation of it by faith, were regarded by the Apostle as leading to repentance and sanctification, as well as to peace of mind. But he contemplates it in this passage under another aspect. He has what may be called a transcendental, as well as a practical, view of this, as of all events. He contemplates the death of Christ, taking place according to God's will, as illustrating the mind of God; as manifesting his righteousness, though he forbore adequately to punish the sins of former times, and in mercy accepted as righteous the true Christian believer. His view seems to be that God, by suffering such a person as Jesus, standing in such a relation to him, having a sinless character, and sustaining such an office in relation to the world as Christ did, to suffer and die a painful and ignominious death, has declared how great an evil he regards sin to be, and how great a good he regards holiness to be; in other words, his hatred of sin, and love of holiness. The greatness of the evil of sin, and of the

* Rom. iii. 25.

good of righteousness, are to be seen in the greatness of the sacrifice which God, in his high providential government of the world, appointed, and which in the fulness of time Christ made. Why is not this view of St. Paul correct? God is surely to be seen, not only in the works of nature, in the intuitions of the soul, in immediate revelation, but also in the events of Providence. Especially the fact, that under the moral government of God the most righteous men, *those in whom the spirit of God dwells most fully and most constantly*, are willing to incur reproach and suffering in the cause of truth, righteousness, and human happiness, shows that the Giver of the Holy Spirit, the Source of all righteousness, regards sin as a great evil, and righteousness as a great good; that is, hates sin, and loves holiness. Much more, then, if Christ, in whom was the spirit of God without measure, who knew no sin, and who was in various ways exalted above the sons of men, becomes, according to the will of God, and by his own consent, a sacrifice for sin, does he illustrate his Father's hatred of sin, and love of holiness.

It appears to me that Edwards the younger, and other advocates of what is called the governmental theory, have connected with the view of the Apostle Paul two great errors. One consists in regarding that as the direct and immediate design of the death of Christ which was only incidental to it, as a providential event. This appears from the fact that the death of Christ is everywhere in the New Testament denounced as an evil and a crime. Of course, then, it was opposed to the direct revealed will of God. Everywhere in the New Testament we may learn that the direct design of God in sending his Son was that the Jews, as well as others, should reverence him. "This is my beloved Son, hear ye him." "He that honoreth not the Son, honoreth not the Father." "Woe unto that man by whom the Son of man is betrayed." It is admitted by all, that the direct will of God is declared in his commands rather than in his providence. Unless the Jews had acted against the will of God, it could not be said that by "wicked hands" they had crucified and slain the Saviour. But when, instead of hearing and reverencing Christ, they persecuted and crucified him, this event was overruled by Divine Providence, so as to convey a religious lesson concerning the attributes of God, and his government of the world. There is no more evidence that the Jews were instigated by God to crucify Christ, than to kill any prophet who had preceded him. There is no more evidence that this was according to the will of God, than any murder which ever took place. The Apostle Paul undoubtedly declares that Christ gave himself for us according to the will of God (Gal. i. 4); and that God had set him forth as a propitiatory sacrifice to manifest his righteousness (Rom. iii. 25). But he uses similar language in regard to many other events. Thus he declares that Pharaoh, the tyrant, was raised up to make known the power of God. (Rom. ix. 17.) But will it be pretended that God gave existence and power to Pharaoh for the direct and exclusive purpose of making known his power, and that his power could not be made known in any other way? Was it not the will of God that Pharaoh should be a just and beneficent sovereign? It is evident from the nature of the case, as well as from the current phraseology of the Scriptures, that the treachery of Judas, and the crucifixion of Christ, were not more immediately ordained by God, than any other case of treachery and murder which ever took place in the world. It is plain, then, that the manifestation of the righteousness of God by the sacrifice of Christ, referred to by St. Paul, was the incidental or indirect design of it, as an event taking place under the government of God, against his revealed will. The crucifixion of Christ declares the righteousness of God, just as the wrath of man in all cases is caused to praise him.

That the manifestation of the righteousness of God was only the incidental design of the sacrifice of Christ, appears also from this circumstance, that it is only when so regarded that it conveys to a rational mind an impression either of his righteousness or his wisdom. That God should so love the world as to send Christ to enlighten, reform, and bless it, though he foresaw that he would not accomplish his purpose without falling a sacrifice to human passions, gives an impression of his benevolence, and of his hatred of sin and love of holiness. But if he had immediately and directly commanded the Jewish priests to sacrifice him, or the Jewish rulers to insult, torture, and crucify him, simply that as an object of human contemplation he might manifest the righteousness of God, and his hatred of sin by his infliction of torture on an innocent being, then no such effect would be produced by it. The Jewish priests themselves would have said that such a sacrifice was heathenish, an offering such as the Gentiles used to make to Moloch. All the world would say, that such a God-commanded sacrifice, such a direct and immediate infliction of suffering by the Almighty upon an innocent being, for the main purpose of making known his dispositions, and maintaining the honor of his government, was a manifestation of any attribute rather than righteousness. We might believe an express verbal declaration, that such a direct infliction was designed to show God's righteousness; but in the fact itself of such torture, one could perceive neither righteousness nor wisdom. This may be clearly illustrated by an example.

If a human sovereign, the emperor of Russia for instance, being engaged in war with a rebellious province, and having a son distinguished by military skill, courage, and humanity above all his subjects, should send him at the head of an army, and expose him to all the casualties of war, in order to bring the province into submission, and this son should actually suffer death through the opposition of the rebels, who would not admire the self-denial and benevolence exhibited by the monarch?

Suppose now, on the other hand, that the rebels should, by the labors and sacrifices of that son, have been brought to repentance and submission, and should humbly sue for pardon, and that the monarch should say, "I will forgive you, but in order to express my feelings concerning the crime of rebellion, and to uphold the honor of my government, and maintain the cause of order, I must, as the condition of the forgiveness of your crime, inflict inconceivable anguish of mind and body upon my well-beloved son in the sight of all my subjects," and should actually do it with his own hands, would not the whole civilized world condemn such a monarch as guilty of injustice, cruelty, and folly? The consent of the son, could it be obtained, would only serve to deepen the cruelty and folly of the father.

The incidental effect of the sufferings of the Apostles is spoken of as designed, as expressly as that of the sufferings of Christ. Thus St. Paul says, "Whether we be afflicted, it is for your consolation and salvation."* Again, "Yea, and if I be offered up upon the sacrifice and service of your faith,"† &c. Again, he speaks of himself as "filling up what is wanting of the sufferings of Christ,"‡ thus implying that his own sufferings had the same general purpose as those of his Master. Again, the casting away of the Jews is represented by Paul in one verse as the reconciling or atonement of the world; in another, as the punishment of the Jews for their unbelief.§

It is readily conceded that a greater prominence, importance, and influence are assigned by Paul and other New Testament writers to the sacrifice of Christ, than to that of other righteous men. This is owing in part to his pre-eminent character, his supernatural powers and qualifications, the dignity of his office as head of the Church, and to the peculiar circumstances of his life and death. He had a greater agency than others in the work of the Christian atonement, of which, however, the Apostles were yet ministers.‖ He was the head of the Church.

The minds and feelings of the Apostles must have been in the highest degree affected by the ignominious death of their Master. It was the subject of the deepest gratitude that the blessings which they enjoyed were purchased by his blood. They had lost all hopes when he expired. His death was opposed to all their views of the Messiah. They had supposed that he would live for ever.¶ This expectation was

---

* 2 Cor. i. 6. † Phil. ii. 17. ‡ Col. i. 24. § Rom. xi. 15, 20.
‖ 2 Cor. v. 18. ¶ See John xii. 34; Matt. xvi. 22.

probably not wholly effaced from their minds till they saw him expire. When they preached the Gospel to the Gentiles, they preached the religion of one who had suffered like the vilest malefactor. The circumstance that the death of Christ was so ignominious was a strong reason for their insisting upon it the more, as the means through which they enjoyed the blessings of Christianity. The cross was a stumbling-block to the Jew, and folly to the Gentile. The oftener objections were made to it, the more would the Apostles be led to dwell upon it, and to present it in every light in which it could be presented. In reflecting upon the meaning of it as a providential event, the analogy between it and the sin-offerings of the Jews struck their imaginations forcibly. Certain passages in the prophetic writings, especially Isa. liii., which was originally spoken of the Jewish Church, were adapted to impart additional emphasis to this analogy.

It is also very possible that I may have too closely defined the meaning of Paul and other Apostles, in representing the death of Christ as a sacrifice. This idea having once taken full possession of their imaginations, they may not always have kept in mind the boundary which divides figurative from plain language. They may have connected certain sacrificial ideas or feelings with the death of Christ, which a modern cannot fully appreciate, or strictly define. Being born Jews, familiar with sacrifices from their infancy, and writing to those who, whether Jews or Gentiles, had been accustomed to attach the same importance and efficacy to them, it was natural that they should represent the death of Christ in language borrowed from the Jewish ritual, and that they should attach an importance to it which savors more of the religion which they had renounced, than of that which they had adopted. But so far as the question whether the atonement by Christ was effected by vicarious punishment, or vicarious suffering, is concerned, it is of no consequence how much importance the Apostles attached to the sacrificial view. For there is no reason to believe that in literal sacrifices vicarious punishment, or suffering, was denoted, or that the pain endured by the animals offered had anything to do with their efficacy or significance.*

The other error in the theory of Edwards the younger, and other advocates of the governmental theory, consists in representing the sufferings of Christ as absolutely necessary, as the ground of forgiveness, in the nature of things, or in the nature of the Divine government, or on account of the Divine veracity in reference to the declaration, The soul that sinneth, it shall die. Now in regard to this last consideration, that of the Divine veracity, it is certain that the threatened penalty of transgression is no more executed when the sinner is forgiven in consequence of severe suffering inflicted upon Christ, than if he were forgiven, without such an infliction, in consequence of the eternal mercy of God. For the penalty was never threatened except against the sinner. Of course it can never be executed except upon the sinner.

It has also been maintained by the advocates of the governmental theory, that to forgive sin on any other ground than that of the infliction of suffering upon Christ, equivalent, in the impression produced by it, to the eternal punishment of all the wicked, would

* See Christian Examiner for September, 1855.

operate as encouragement of wickedness. But it is not easy to see why those who would be encouraged in sin by the hope of being forgiven through the eternal mercy of God, would not also be encouraged in sin by the hope of being forgiven through the suffering inflicted upon Christ, or through any consideration founded on past historical fact. The forgiveness is certain to him who repents and becomes a righteous man on either theory, and may encourage an evil-minded person in one case as well as the other. He who can harden himself in sin in consequence of the infinite mercy of God in forgiving the penitent, can do the same thing in consequence of the exceeding love of Christ as manifested in his death.

That the advocates of some of the old theories should maintain the absolute necessity of vicarious suffering, does not appear strange. But that the advocates of the governmental theory should maintain its absolute necessity as the condition of the forgiveness of sin, so that the Divine mercy could not be exercised, and the honor of the Divine government maintained without it, is surprising. Having denied that the sufferings of Christ are in any sense the punishment of the sins of men, or that they are in any sense penal in their nature, it is singular that they should believe them to be absolutely necessary in order to vindicate the righteousness of God, and cause his government to be respected, so that, without these sufferings as a condition, the mercy of God could not and would not have been exercised in the forgiveness of sin. What! Have men no reason to believe in the righteousness of God, and to respect his moral government, unless they can be convinced of the historical fact that he immediately and directly caused inconceivable sufferings to Christ, as the indispensable ground of his forgiving a single sin? Have the unnumbered millions of the human race, who never heard of Christ, and yet believe in the forgiveness of sins, no reason to have faith in the righteousness of God, and to respect his moral government? Have the instinctive faith of the human soul in all the perfections of God, the condemnation of sin in the conscience, the retributions of Divine Providence, the intimations of a judgment to come in the human heart and in Divine revelation, no force to convince men that God hates sin and loves holiness, though he be long-suffering and ready to forgive? Would all these considerations lose their force with one who should believe that God could forgive a penitent, thoroughly regenerated transgressor for his own eternal mercy's sake alone? Cannot a father forgive a penitent son, without conveying the impression that he is pleased with sin?

It has been alleged by Edwards the younger, and others, that the very fact of the sufferings and death of Christ as means of manifesting the righteousness of God, and maintaining the honor of his government, implies their absolute necessity; because otherwise they would not have been allowed by the Deity to take place. I am wholly unable to perceive on what principle the mere occurrence of the crucifixion of Christ by the Jews shows its absolute necessity, more than the occurrence of the murder of any prophet or apostle shows its absolute necessity. But it will not be pretended that the purposes of God in the renovation of the world could not have been accomplished unless Stephen had been stoned to death, and James beheaded, and Peter crucified, however great may have been the actual influence of these cases of martyrdom in the regeneration of the world. Indeed, to argue the absolute necessity of the sacrifice of Christ from the fact of its actual occurrence, is to argue the absolute necessity of every murder that ever occurred in the world. Of course no one has ever denied the necessity of the sufferings of Christ in the same general sense in which the sufferings of all righteous men are necessary, or in which all the evil in the world is necessary. Bishop Butler, in the fifth chapter of Part Second of his Analogy, has shown that by the stripes of righteous men in general, under the government of God, the people are often healed; and of course that Christ might suffer in a similar way, and for similar ends. But he did not attempt to find anything on earth analogous to the theories on which I have been remarking. If he had made the attempt, he would have found such analogy only in the practice of the most barbarous Oriental despots. It appears to me that he is guilty of a gross violation of the common use of language when he says, that "vicarious punishment is a providential appointment of every day's experience." No one has ever doubted or denied the vicarious punishment of Christ in the sense in which vicarious punishment is matter of every day's experience. Every Unitarian, every Deist, would accept such a creed. But this paradoxical use of language has been generally rejected and condemned by modern theological writers of every name.* It serves only to confound things which differ.

Dr. Edwards and others have also argued the necessity of the sacrifice of Christ from the ancient sacrifices of the Jews. But as there was no absolute

* See pp. xxiv, xxv.

necessity for these sacrifices of animals, — as they were of human origin, and only tolerated, or at most sanctioned, by the Deity, — of course there could be no absolute necessity for the sacrifice of Christ; though when it was made, its good effects might be pointed out by the Apostle glancing his eye of faith over the events which took place under the government of God. As to the verse, "Without shedding of blood, there was no remission," the meaning is, that under the actual dispensation of the Jewish law, as permitted or appointed by God, there was no remission without a sacrifice.* The remark has no relation to the nature of things, or to the absolute necessity of the Divine government, but only to a usage which had passed away.

Some passages from the New Testament have also been adduced for the purpose of proving that the sacrifice of Christ was absolutely necessary, as the ground of Divine forgiveness, in the nature of things, or of the Divine government; such as Luke xxiv. 26, "Ought not Christ to have suffered these things, and to enter into his glory?" Also verse 46, "It behoved Christ to suffer," &c. But it is evident that the necessity here referred to by Christ arises simply from that of the fulfilment of prophecy. That he did not consider them absolutely necessary, is evident from his prayer to have the cup pass from him. See Newcome's remarks, pages 207, 210 of this volume.

Allowing, as we have done, that the sacrifice of Christ incidentally illustrates the righteousness as well as the love of God, its absolute necessity as a ground of Divine forgiveness is not more evident from

* On the subject of the Jewish sacrifices, in their bearing on the work of Christ, see Christian Examiner for September, 1855.

any language of Scripture, than the absolute necessity of such a tyrant and oppressor as Pharaoh. For the Apostle adopts similar language respecting Pharaoh: "Even for this same purpose have I raised thee up, that I might show my power in thee, and that my name might be declared throughout all the earth." Will it be pretended that the power and the name of Jehovah could not have been made known except by raising up just such a tyrant as Pharaoh? The Apostle is quite as explicit in declaring the design of the exaltation of Pharaoh to be that of manifesting the power of God, as in declaring the design of the sacrifice of Christ to be that of manifesting the righteousness of God.

My general conclusion is, that the Apostle Paul considers the death of Christ under two aspects:—1. He regards it as an event taking place under the providence of God, and according to the Divine will, and in some sense a sacrifice incidentally manifesting the righteousness of God in connection with the exercise of his mercy. See Rom. iii. 21–26. 2. He regards it in its immediate moral and religious influence upon the heart and life of the believer. See Rom. vi., vii., &c. He does not appear to regard it as an indispensable evidence of the Divine righteousness, without which it could not be seen, but only as a new and signal illustration of it in connection with his mercy. The latter view is the most prevalent. The first view relates to the enlightening influence of Christ's death; the second to its sanctifying influence. In both cases the influence of it is upon God's subjects, not upon God himself. Perhaps both views are united in the text, "He made him who knew no sin to suffer as a sinner in our behalf, that we through him might attain the righteousness which God will accept." *

I have preferred, for obvious considerations, to discuss the subject in the light of Scripture rather than of mere reason. But in regard to the sufficiency of the governmental theory to satisfy the reason, I cannot forbear quoting a few lines from a recent Orthodox writer, the author of the Sermon on the Atonement in the Monthly Religious Magazine, which has received some attention among us. "How could the suffering of one human being, either in amount, or as an expression of God's feelings towards his law, sin, and holiness, be equivalent to the eternal punishment of the wicked, to the smoke of their torment ascending for ever? The suffering of one created being for a few days or years would be, in comparison, as a drop to an ocean. . . . . . We are quite familiar with the answer which is made to reasoning of this kind, — with the argument, that the union of the Divine nature with the human gave a boundless dignity and worth to the sufferings of that human nature, though having no part in them. But we are constrained to say, that it never commended itself to our judgment, or gave us the least satisfaction. We cannot see how the Divine nature had, we think we see that it had not, any share in the atonement, if it had no share in *the sacrifice which constituted it;* nor how it could give dignity and worth to sufferings by which it was *entirely unaffected.* We have heard illustration after illustration upon this point; but to our mind it is like sailing in the face of the wind." † These remarks are the plain dictates of common sense. I have

* 2 Cor. v. 21.

† See the New Englander for July, 1847, p. 432.

no doubt that the time will come when the doctrine that a clear perception of the righteousness of God absolutely depended on the sufferings "of the man Christ Jesus during only thirty years, or rather during the last three years of his life," * will be regarded with greater wonder than the doctrine of Luther and Flavel and John Norton now is.

There are some other differences of opinion among New England theologians, which it will be sufficient only to mention. Thus, while some limit the sufferings necessary for the atonement to the death of Christ, others take in those of his whole life. Again, while some suppose his sufferings to have been only such as were inflicted by the instrumentality of man, and arose naturally out of his peculiar circumstances and character, others regard his chief sufferings as miraculous, inflicted by the immediate hand of God, independent of those inflicted by human instrumentality.

There is also a great difference of opinion among the New England theologians as to what constituted the atonement. Even among those who have rejected the doctrine of the imputed righteousness of Christ, some make the perfect obedience of Christ a constituent part of it; others not. Dr. Dwight and some recent writers have maintained, with much earnestness, that the obedience of Christ is an essential part of it. But Dr. Jonathan Edwards the younger, who seems to be followed by the majority, writes: "I venture to say further, that not only did not the atonement of Christ consist essentially in his active obedience, but that his active obedience was no part of his atonement, properly so called, nor essential to it." †

* Edwards the younger. See Works, Vol. II. p. 43.

† Works, Vol. II. p. 41.

On the other hand, the most distinguished New England writer in the Baptist denomination, Dr. Wayland, has expressed the opinion, that the perfect obedience of Christ was all that was essential to the atonement. "In what manner did Christ's appearing on earth have any effect upon our moral relations? To this various replies have been presented. It has been said that his unparalleled humiliation, or his lowly and painful life, his bitter death, were of the nature of a suffering of the penalty of the law. I, however, apprehend that this explanation has not always been satisfactory to those who have borne in mind the character of the law which we have violated, and the awful holiness of the Being against whom we have sinned. Besides, the sufferings of Christ, considered by themselves, were not severer, nor was his death itself more excruciating, than that of many martyrs, confessors, and missionaries...... His obedience had been so transcendent in virtue, he had so triumphantly vanquished all our spiritual enemies, and put to shame all the powers of darkness, that I know not whether anything more was demanded. 'The Lord was well pleased for his righteousness' sake' [his obedience], for he had magnified the law and made it honorable. That this was the case would seem probable, because there is no reference in the Scriptures to his suffering after death." *

There is also a difference of opinion among New England theologians as to the question whether the Divine, or only the human, nature of Jesus suffered and died. Thus a recent writer, the Rev. Mr. Dutton, whose Sermon on the Atonement has been thought worthy of being republished in the Boston Monthly

* Wayland's University Sermons, pp. 147, 160.

Religious Magazine, maintains the former opinion, — an opinion which strikes me as not only unchristian, but atheistic in its tendency. I have no more fear of its prevalence than of the prevalence of atheism, and therefore shall offer nothing in refutation of it. It is but just to say, however, that this view has found very few advocates. All the distinguished New England theologians, such as Hopkins, Edwards the younger, Dwight, Emmons, Woods, and others, limit the sufferings of Christ to his human nature.* Nor has a different opinion ever found its way, so far as I know, into the confession of faith of any church in Christendom. John Norton undoubtedly gave the orthodox or generally received opinion on this point when he wrote, " The second person of the Trinity, ... together with the Father and the Holy Ghost, did inflict the torments of hell *upon the human nature*." †

The dissertations selected from the Commentary on St. Paul's Epistles by Mr. Jowett are those which were thought to be most suitable for publication in this volume. I should have been glad to insert two other dissertations from the same work; namely, that on Natural Religion, and that on the Comparison of St. Paul with Philo. But the former, in setting aside some of the usual proofs of the existence of the Deity, did not appear to me to contain such explanations and qualifications as might make it useful to readers unacquainted with the writer's philosophy. The latter was omitted because, though learned and valuable, it was not likely to be useful to persons unacquainted with the Greek language.

---

* See page xxv.

† Norton's Answer to Pynchon, p. 122.

Several valuable Essays have been selected from the recent Commentary on the Epistles to the Corinthians, in two octavo volumes, by the Rev. Arthur P. Stanley, Canon of Canterbury, who is somewhat known in this country by his Life of Dr. Arnold. His work on the Epistles to the Corinthians manifests the same scholarship and independence, united with reverence, which distinguish the Commentary by Professor Jowett.

The closing Essay on the Credibility of Miracles, by Dr. Thomas Brown, the distinguished author of the well-known Lectures on the Philosophy of the Human Mind, has been for some time out of print. It appears to me to meet the objections of Mr. Hume in a far more satisfactory manner than they have been met by most writers on the subject.

It cannot escape the notice of the reader, that very few of the Essays in this volume were written by professed Unitarians. Most of them are by eminent divines and scholars of the Church of England. But in the circulation of books the great question should be whether they contain true and just views, and not by whom they were written. That we have been able to select so large a volume of Essays on very important subjects from writers of the Established Church of England in harmony with the views of Unitarians, is a fact highly encouraging in regard to the progress of truth, and at the same time highly creditable, not only to the independence of the writers, but to the practical freedom which at present prevails in that church. No one of them, I believe, has yet incurred any higher penalty on account of his publications than that of rewriting his name. It is to be hoped that the results to which several of the learned writers have arrived, notwithstanding the natural bias arising from their ecclesiastical connections, will secure for them, from different classes of readers, that candid and attentive consideration which their importance demands. The voice which comes from this volume is the united utterance of Episcopalians, Lutherans, and Unitarians.

CAMBRIDGE, May 7, 1856.

ESSAYS.

FAITH AND SCIENCE.*

BY M. GUIZOT.

ONE of the questions which theology has oftenest debated, — the foremost, perhaps, at least in the sense that it serves for a prologue to all others, — is the eternal antithesis of reason and faith. From the powerlessness of reason and the necessity of faith, certain writers make the point of departure and the termination of their works. The same idea at this time inspires and fills almost entirely a multitude of religious writings, whose object is to invoke faith, not to regulate, but to oppress, the reason. I shall not pretend to treat this question in all its extent, as it involves the entire problem of human nature and knowledge. I wish, in fact, rather to investigate the real and natural acceptation of the word *faith*, so powerful and so mysterious, and exercising such a different empire over the soul of man, sometimes illuminating, and sometimes misleading it; — here, the source of the most wonderful actions; there, the veil thrown over the basest designs. I wish to ascertain if, according to plain language and the common thought of mankind, there is, in reality, that opposition and incompatibility which certain writers endeavor to institute between faith and reason, between science and faith. Such an examination is, perhaps, the best means of solving

* Translated in Kitto's Journal of Sacred Literature, Vol. V., New Series, from *Méditations et Etudes Morales*, par M. Guizot. 2de édition. Paris.

the question which lies concealed under these terms,—of obtaining from them, at least, glimpses of the solution.

No one can doubt that the word *faith* (*foi*) has an especial meaning, which is not properly represented by *belief* (*croyance*), *conviction* (*conviction*), or *certitude* (*certitude*). Custom and universal opinion confirm this view. There are many simple and customary phrases in which the word *faith* (*foi*) could not be replaced by any other. Almost all languages have a specially appropriated word * to express that which in French is expressed by *foi*, and which is essentially different from all analogous words.

This word, then, corresponds to a certain state of the human soul;—it expresses a moral fact which has rendered such a word necessary.

We commonly understand by *faith* (*foi*) a certain belief of facts and dogmas,—religious facts and dogmas. In fact, the word has no other sense when, employing it absolutely and by itself, we speak of *the faith*.

That is not, however, its unique, nor even its fundamental sense; it has one more extensive, and from which the religious sense is derived. We say: "I have full *faith* in your words; this man has *faith* in himself, in his power," &c. This employment of the word in civil matters, so to speak, has become more frequent in our days: it is not, however, of modern invention; nor have religious ideas ever been an exclusive sphere, out of which the notion, and the word, *faith*, were without application.

It is, then, proved by the testimony of language and common opinion, first, that the word *faith* designates a certain interior state of him who believes, and not merely a certain kind of belief; that it proceeds from the very nature of conviction, and not from its object. Secondly, that it is, however, to a certain species of belief—religious belief—that it has been at first, and most generally, applied.

* In Greek νομίζειν, πιστεύειν; in Latin, *sententia*, *fides*; in Italian, *credenza*, *fede*; in English, *faith*, *belief*; in German (if I mistake not), *glauben*.

Thus, the sense of the word has been special, in fact and in its origin, although it is not fundamentally so; or rather, the occasion of the employment of the word has been special, although its sense is not so.

It would but be a fact without importance, and sufficiently common in the history of the formation of languages and ideas, if the true and general sense of the word *faith* was reproduced entire in its special employment; but it has been otherwise. The specialty of the usual acceptation of the word has profoundly obscured the general sense; the true notion of *faith* has undergone an alteration under the notion of *religious faith*. And from this disagreement between the historical senses, so to speak, and the philosophical sense of the term, have resulted the obscurity of the moral fact which it expresses, and the greater part of the errors to which it has given place.

In truth, the words which express an interior disposition, a certain state of the human soul, have almost always a fixed and identical sense, which is independent of the interior object to which the disposition refers, and of the external cause which produced it. Thus, men *love* different objects;— they have contrary *certitudes*;— but the words *love*, *certitude*, in ordinary language and common life, do not less preserve, always and for all, the same sense; their general acceptation remains and prevails, whatever be the specialty of their employment; and the passions, interests, and errors of those who make use of them do not want, nor have they the power, to alter it.

The destiny of the word *faith* has been different. Almost exclusively applied to religious subjects, what changes its sense has undergone, and still undergoes every day!

Men who teach and preach a religion, a doctrine, or a religious reformation, in making their appeal with all the energy of the freed human spirit, produce in their followers an entire, profound, and powerful conviction of the truth of their doctrine. This conviction is called *faith*; neither masters nor disciples, nor even enemies, refuse it this appellation.

Faith, then, is but a profound and imperious conviction of a religious dogma; it matters but little whether it has come in the way of reasoning, or controversy, or of free and liberal investigation: that which characterizes it, and gives it a claim to be called *faith*, is its energy, and the dominion it exercises, by this title, over the entire man. Such has been at all times — in the sixteenth century for example — the faith of great reformers and their most illustrious disciples, Calvin after Luther, and Knox after Calvin, &c.

The same men have presented the same doctrine to persons whom they were not able to convince by methods of reasoning, examination, or science, — to women and to multitudes incapable of long reflection: they have made their appeals to the imagination, to the moral affections, and to the susceptibility of being moved and of believing through emotion. And they have given the name of *faith* to the result of this work, as to that of a work essentially intellectual, of which I spake just now. Faith has become a religious conviction which was not acquired by reasoning, and which took its rise in the sensuous faculties of man. This is the idea which mystic sects attach to faith.

The appeal to man's sensuous nature, and the resulting emotion, have not always sufficed to bring forth this faith. Other sources have then been appealed to. They have enjoined practices, and imposed habits. It is absolutely necessary that a man should, sooner or later, attach ideas to his actions, and that he should attribute a certain meaning to that which produces in him a certain effect. The practices and habits have conducted the mind to the beliefs from which they themselves were derived. A new faith has appeared, which has had for its principal and dominant characteristic submission of the mind to an authority invested with a right to regulate the thoughts whilst governing the lips.

In short, neither the free exercise of the intelligence, nor the sentiment, nor practices, have elsewhere succeeded in producing faith. We have said that it is not communicated, and that it is not in the power of man to give it, nor to acquire it by his own peculiar endeavors; that it demands the interposition of God, — the action of grace; — grace has become the preliminary condition, and the definitive characteristic of faith.

Thus by turns the word *faith* expresses: —

1stly. A conviction acquired by the free labor of the human mind.

2dly. A conviction obtained by means of the *sensitivity* (*sensibilité*), and without the concurrence, often even against the authority, of the reason.

3dly. A conviction acquired by the very submission of the man to a power which has received from on high the right to command.

4thly. A conviction wrought by superhuman means, — by divine grace.

And according as the one or the other of these different *faiths*, if we may so speak, has prevailed, religion, philosophy, government, and the whole of society have been observed to vary, simultaneously and by a necessary correspondence.

How has the same word been able to subserve so many different, and even contradictory acceptations? What is that mysterious fact which presents itself to minds under such different aspects? Has the necessity of legitimating the fundamental principle, and the system of the government of different religious beliefs, alone caused the variation of the notion of *faith?* or rather, do all these definitions correspond, on some one side, with that state of the human soul; and have they no other irregularity than that of being partial and exclusive?

These are questions which cannot be solved, so long as men persist, as they have done to this day, in characterizing faith by its causes, or its external effects. It is in itself that the fact must be considered; we must search out what is the state of mind where faith reigns, independently of its origin and its object.

Two kinds of beliefs co-exist in man: — the one, which I will not call innate, — an inexact and justly-debated expression, — but natural and spontaneous, which germinate and establish themselves in his mind, if not without his knowledge, at least without the co-operation of his reflection and will, by the development solely of his nature, and the influence of that external world in the midst of which his life is spent. The others, laborious and learned, the fruit of voluntary study, and of the power which a man has, whether to direct all his faculties towards an especial object with the design of knowing it, or of reflecting upon himself, and of perceiving that which passes within him, and of giving himself an account of it, and thus of acquiring, by an act of the will and reflection, a science which he possessed not before, although the facts which it has for its object subsist equally under his eyes, or within him.

That there is *moral good* and *evil,* and that man is bound to avoid the evil, and to fulfil the good, — this is a natural, primitive, and universal belief. Man is so constituted that it develops itself in him spontaneously, by the course merely of his life, from the first appearance of the facts to which it must apply itself, very long before he could know himself, and could be able to *know* that he *believed.* Once originated, this belief acts on the soul of man almost as the blood circulates in his veins, without his willing it, and without his thinking of it. The greater part of mankind have never given it a name, nor formed for themselves a general and distinct idea of it: it does not, however, the less subsist in them, revealing itself every time that the occasion presents itself, by an action, a judgment, or a simple emotion. Human morality is a fact which does not stand in need of human science to throw light upon it.

Like every other fact, this also can become a matter of science. The moral being beholds itself, and studies itself: it renders account to itself of the principle of its actions, judgments, and moral sentiments: it assists at the spectacle of its own nature, and pretends not only to know, but to govern it, according to its acquired knowledge. Naturally and spontaneously, belief in the distinction of moral good and evil thus becomes reflective and scientific. Man remains the same; but he was self-ignorant, and acted simply according to his nature; nevertheless he knows himself, and his science presides over his action.

This is but an example; I could cite a thousand others of the same kind. Man carries within himself a multitude of beliefs of which he has the consciousness, but not the science; which external facts awaken in him, though they have never been the chosen objects and the special aim of his thoughts. It is by beliefs of this kind that the human race is enlightened and guided; they abound in the spirit of the most meditative philosophy, and direct it oftener than the reflective convictions to which it has arrived. Divine wisdom has not delivered over the soul and life of man to the hazards of human science; it has not condemned it to expect all its intellectual riches from its own proper work. It is, — it lives; that is enough: by this sole title, and by the progressive development of this fact alone, it will possess lights indispensable for guiding its life, and for the accomplishment of its destiny. It can aspire higher; it can elevate itself to the science of the world, and of itself; and, by the aid of science, can exercise over the world and itself a power analogous to creative power. But then it will be required that it should only build on the primitive foundation which it has received from Providence; for just as all natural and spontaneous belief can become scientific, so all scientific conviction received its source and its point of support in natural belief.

Of these two kinds of belief, which merits the name of *faith?*

It appears, at first sight, that this name agrees perfectly with natural and spontaneous beliefs; they are exempt from doubts and disquietude; they direct man in his judgments and actions with an imperial authority which he does not dream of eluding or contesting; they are natural, sure, practical, and sovereign. Who does not recognize in all this the characteristics of *faith?*

Faith has in effect these characteristics; but it has also

others which are wanting to natural beliefs. Almost unknown by the very man whom they direct, they are for him, in a certain way, as external laws, which he has received, but not appropriated, and which he obeys by instinct, but without having given to them an intimate and personal assent. They suffice for the wants of his life; they guide, warn, urge on, or restrain him, but without, so to speak, his own concurrence with them, and without awakening within him the sentiment of an interior, energetic, and powerful activity; and without procuring for him the profound joy of contemplating, loving, and adoring the truth which reigns over him. *Faith* has this power. It is not science, still less is it ignorance. The mind which is penetrated by it has never, perhaps, rendered, and perhaps never will render, an account of the idea which has obtained its faith; but it knows that it believes it; it is before it, present and living; it is no longer a general belief, a law of human nature, which governs the moral man, as the laws of gravity govern bodies; it is a personal conviction, a truth which the moral individual has appropriated to himself by contemplation, by free obedience and love. From that time this truth does much more than suffice for his life; it satisfies his soul; and still more than directing, it enlightens it. It is surprising how men live under the dominion of this natural belief that there is moral good or evil, without our being able to say that it has their faith! It is in them as a master to whom they belong and whom they obey, but without seeing him, and without loving or rendering him homage. That any cause whatever, revealing, so to speak, the consciousness to itself, should draw and fix their regards upon this law of their nature; that they acknowledge and accept it, as their legitimate sovereign; that their understanding should honor itself in contemplating it, and their liberty in obeying it; that they should conceive of their soul, if I may so speak, as a hearth where truth concentrates itself to spread from thence its light, or as the sanctuary where God deigns to dwell; all this is more than simple and natural belief, — it is *faith.*

The difference between these two states of the soul is so

real and so profound, that it has been at all times, and still is, one of the principal sources of the diversity of religions and the division of churches. The one is principally applied to spread, or to maintain, general beliefs, fixed and incorporated, in some way, in the habits and practices of life: in short, analogous, by the mode of their influence, to those irreflective and almost instinctive beliefs whereof God has made the moral condition of the human race. The others have had, above all, to awaken for the heart and in the soul of each individual, a personal and intimate belief, which should give him a lively feeling of his own intellectual activity and liberty, and which he might consider as his own peculiar treasure. The former have marched, so to speak, torch in hand, at the head of nations; the latter have sought to place within each man movement and light. Neither the one nor the other tendency ever could become exclusive; there have been facts beliefs profoundly individual in religions, which least of all provoke their development; there are, also, men governed by general and legal beliefs, external, in some sense, to their soul, in religions the most favorable to the interior life of the individual. It is not the less true, that, at all times, one or the other of these tendencies has ruled in various religions; and not only in various religions, but, by turns, in the same religion at various epochs of its existence; so that the difference of the two corresponding states of the soul, and the character of that to which truly the name of *faith* belongs, are clearly imprinted in the history of humanity.

Reflective and scientific beliefs, on the contrary, have this in common with faith, that they are profoundly individual, and give a lively feeling of interior and voluntary activity. Nothing belongs more to the individual than his science; he knows where it commenced, and how it has become enlarged, and what means and efforts have been used to acquire it; and what it has added, so to speak, to his intellectual worth, and to the extent of his existence. But if, by that means, scientific beliefs are nearer to faith than natural and irreflective beliefs, yet, on other sides, they remain much farther removed from them, and from the first they are confined to doubt and uncertainty. They measure, and almost admit, various degrees of probability; and even when they are confident of their legitimacy, they do not deny that they can be modified, and even overturned, by a wider and more exact science; — whilst the most entire and immovable certitude is the fundamental characteristic of faith. All science is felt to be bounded and incomplete; every man who studies, whatever be the object of his study, however advanced and assured he himself may be of his own knowledge, knows that he has not reached the boundary of his career, and that for him, as for every other, fresh efforts will lead to fresh progress. *Faith*, on the contrary, is in its own eyes a complete and finished belief; and if it should appear that something yet remains for it to acquire, it would not be faith. It has nothing progressive, — it excludes all idea that anything is wanting, and judges itself to be in full possession of the truth which is its object. From thence proceeds a vast inequality of power between the different kinds of conviction; faith, freed from all intellectual labor and from all study, (since, so far as knowledge is concerned, it is complete,) turns all the force of its possessor towards action. As soon as he becomes penetrated by it, only one task remains for his accomplishment, — that of causing the idea which has taken possession of his faith to reign and to be realized without. The history of religions — of all religions — proves, at each step, this expansive and practical energy of belief, with which the characters of faith have been converted. It displays itself even on occasions when in no way it appears provoked or sustained by the moral importance or the visible grandeur of results.

I could cite a singular example of it. In the course of our Revolution, the theoretical and actual superiority of the new system of weights and measures quickly became for some men, who were the subordinate servants of an administration charged with establishing it, a complete and imperious truth, to which nothing could be objected, added, or refused. They pursued from that time its triumphs with an ardor, an obstinacy, and sometimes a prodigious devotion. I have known a public officer, who, more than twenty years after the birth of the system, and when no one scarcely dreamed of disturbing himself any more about it, gave himself up, day and night, to extraordinary labors, letters, instructions, and verifications, which his superiors did not demand, and which he had often great trouble in causing to be adopted, in order to accelerate its extension and strength. The new system of weights and measures was for this man the object of a true faith; he would reproach himself for his repose, whilst anything remained to be done for its success. Scientific beliefs, even when they would admit of immediate application, rarely carry a man so to struggle against the outer world as to reduce it under his dominion. When the human mind is, above all, preoccupied with the design or the pleasure of knowledge, it there concentrates, and, so to speak, exhausts itself; and there remain for it neither desires nor powers to be otherwise employed. Scientific beliefs, accustomed to doubts, to groping in darkness, and to contempts, hesitate to command: without efforts and without anger, they make their appeals to ignorance, uncertainty, and even error, and scarcely know how to propagate themselves, or to act, but by methods which conduct to science; that is to say, by inciting to meditation and study, they proceed too slowly to be able to exercise outwardly an extensive and actual power.

Perhaps, also, the very origin of scientific beliefs might be counted amongst the causes which deprive them of that empire, and that confidence in action and command, which is the general characteristic of faith. It is to himself that man owes his science; it is his own work, the fruit of his own labor, and the reward of his own merit. Perhaps, even in the midst of the pride which such a conquest often inspires, a secret warning feeling comes over him, that, in claiming and exercising authority in the name of his science, it is to the reason and the understanding of one man that he pretends to subjugate men, — a feeble and doubtful title to great power; and which, at the moment of action, can certainly, without their own consciousness, cast into the soul of the proudest some timidity. Nothing like this is met with in *faith.* However profoundly individual it is, from the time it has entered into the heart of man, it signifies not by what means, it banishes all idea of a conquest which can be his own, or of a discovery the glory of which he can attribute to himself. He is no longer occupied with himself; wholly absorbed by the truth which he believes, no personal sentiment any longer raises itself with his knowledge, excepting the sentiment of the happiness it procures for him, and of the mission it imposes upon him. The learned man is the conqueror and the inventor of his science; the *believer* is the agent and the servant of his faith. It is not in the name of his own superiority, but in the name of that truth to which he has yielded himself, that the believer claims obedience. Charged to procure for it sovereignty, he bears himself, in reference to it, with a passionate disinterestedness; and this persuasion impresses upon his language and upon his acts a confidence and authority, with which the proudest science would in vain endeavor to invest itself. Let us consider how different is the pride which is produced by science, from that which accompanies faith: the one is scornful and full of personality; the other is imperious and full of blindness. The learned man isolates himself from those who do not comprehend what he knows; the believer pursues with his indignation or his pity those who do not yield themselves to what he believes. The first desires personal distinction; the other desires that all should unite themselves under the law of the master whom he serves. What can this variety of the same fault import, excepting that the learned man beholds himself, and reckons himself, in his science, whilst the believing man forgets and abdicates himself in favor of his faith? It is further necessary to explain how the same idea, the same doctrine, can remain cold and inactive in the hands of the learned man, and without any practical use even in men whose understanding it has illuminated; whilst, in the hands of the believer, it can become communicative, expansive, and an energetic principle of action and power.

Faith does not, then, enter exclusively either into the one or the other of these two kinds of beliefs, which, at first sight, appear to share the soul of man. It partakes of, and at the same time differs from, natural and scientific beliefs. It is, like the latter, individual and particular: like the former, it is firm, complete, active, and sovereign. Considered in itself, and independent of all comparison with this or that analogous condition, faith is the full security of the man in the possession of his belief; a possession freed as much from labor as from doubt; in the midst of which every thought of the path by which it has been reached disappears, and leaves no other sentiment but that of the natural and pre-established harmony between the human mind and truth. As soon as faith exists, all search after truth ceases; man considers himself to have arrived at his object; his belief is no longer for him anything but a source of enjoyments and precepts; it satisfies his understanding and governs his life, bestows upon him repose, and regulates and absorbs, without extinguishing, his intellectual activity; and directs his liberty without destroying it. Is he disposed to contemplation? his faith opens an illimitable field for his thoughts; they can run over it in all directions, and without fatigue, for he is no longer vexed by the necessity of reaching the object, and discovering the path to it; he has touched the boundary, and has nothing more to do but to cultivate, at his leisure, a world which belongs to him. Is he called to action? He throws himself wholly into it, sure of never wanting impulse and guidance, tranquil and animated, urged on and sustained by the double force of duty and passion. For the man, in short, being penetrated by faith, and within the sphere which is its object, the understanding and the will have no more problems to solve, and no more interior obstacles to surmount: he feels himself to be in the full possession of the truth for enlightening and guiding him, and of himself for acting according to the truth.

But if such is the state of the human soul, if *faith* differs essentially from other kinds of belief, it is evident at the same time that neither natural nor scientific beliefs have anything which excludes faith; that both one and the other can invest their characters with it; and, further still, that either one or the other is always the foundation on which faith supports itself, or the path which leads to it.

See a man in whom the idea of God has been nothing but a vague and spontaneous belief, the simple result of a course of life and of external circumstances,—an idea which holds a place in his mind and conduct, but on which he has never fallen back and fixed his intellectual regards, and which he has never appropriated to himself by an act of voluntary and briefly-sustained reflection. Let any cause whatsoever—as a great danger or sorrow—strike him with a powerful emotion, and present to him the misery of his condition and the weakness of his nature, and awaken within him this need of superior succor,—this instinct of prayer, often lulled to sleep, but never extinguished in the heart of man. All at once the idea of God, till then abstract, cold, and proud, will appear to this man, living, urgent, and particular; it has attached itself to him with ardor,—it will penetrate into all his thoughts,—his belief will become faith; and Pascal will be borne out when he said, "Faith is God sensibly realized by the heart."

Another has lived in submission to religious practices, without having associated with them any truly personal conviction; as an infant, others might make a law for him; as master of himself, he has retained the habit of obedience, docile to a fact rather than attached to a duty, and not dreaming of penetrating farther into the sense of the rule than to verify its authority. A time has arrived when occasions and temptations to offend against this law have presented themselves; a contest has arisen between the habits and tastes, between the desires, and, perhaps, the passions. What this person could practise without thought has now become a subject of reflection, anxiety, and inward sorrow. To preserve its empire, it becomes necessary that the rule, until then mistress only of the exterior life of the man, should penetrate and establish itself within his soul. It has succeeded in that;

and to remain true to his practices, he has been required to make sacrifices for them; and he has made them. The state of his soul is changed: habit is converted into conviction; practice into duty; and observance into moral want. In the day of trial, the long submission to a general rule, and to a power clothed with the right to prescribe, has brought forth a particular and individual adhesion of *thought* and *will*, — that is to say, what was wanting to faith.

For scientific beliefs this transition to the state of faith is more difficult and more rare. Even when, by meditation, reasoning, and study, any one has attained to conviction, he remains nearly always occupied with the labor which has conducted to it, his long uncertainties, the deviations by which he has been misled, and the false steps he has made. He has arrived at his object, but the remembrance of the route is present to him, with all its embarrassments, accidents, and chances. He has come into the presence of light, but the impression of the darkness, and the dubious lights he has crossed, are yet present to his thoughts. In vain his conviction is entire; there are yet to be discovered traces of the labor which has presided over its formation. It wants simplicity and confidence. There is a certain fatigue connected with it, which enervates its practical virtue and fruitfulness. He finds trouble in forgetting and overthrowing the scaffolding of the science, in order that the truth, of which it is the object, may wholly belong to his nature. We might say, the butterfly is restrained by the shell in which it was born, and from which it is not fully disengaged.

Nevertheless, although the difficulty is great, it is not insurmountable. More than once, for the glory of humanity, man, by the force of his intelligence and scientific meditations, has reached to beliefs, to which there has been wanting none of the characteristics of faith, — neither fulness nor certainty of conviction, nor the forgetfulness of personality, nor expansiveness and practical power, nor the pure and profound enjoyments of contemplation. Who would refuse to recognize in the belief of the most illustrious Stoics in the sovereignty of moral good, — in Cleanthes, Epictetus, and Marcus Aurelius, — a true faith? And was not the religious faith of the principal Reformers, or Reformed, of the sixteenth century, Zwingle, Melancthon, Duplessis Mornay, the fruit of study and science, as well as the philosophical doctrines of Descartes and Leibnitz? And lately, under the idea that falsehood is the source of all the vices of man, and that at no price, in no moment, and for no cause, can it be necessary to swerve from the truth, did not Kant arrive, by a long series of meditations, to a conviction perfectly analogous to faith? The analogy was such, that the day when his certainty of the prinple became complete and definite constituted an epoch in his memory and life, as others call to mind the event or the emotion which has changed the condition of the soul; so that, dating from that day, according to his own testimony, he lived constantly in the presence, and under the empire, of this idea; just as a Christian lives in the presence, and under the empire, of the faith from which he expects salvation.

Reflective and scientific beliefs can be converted into faith: the difficulties of the transformation are much greater, and the success much more rare, than when natural and spontaneous beliefs are concerned. Nevertheless, the transformation of science into faith can be, and sometimes is, accomplished; and if more frequently science stops far short of faith, it is not because there exists something opposed and irreconcilable in their nature, but because faith is placed at the boundary of that course which science is not in a condition wholly, and of itself, to accomplish.

Nevertheless, it is easy, if I mistake not, to observe the fault of these theories which I enumerated at the commencement, and which men and the world so ardently dispute. It is their fundamental error, that they have not regarded *faith* in itself, and as a special state of the human mind, but in the mode of its formation. They have been thus induced to assign for its essential and exclusive characteristic such and such origins, from which it is possible that faith may be derived, not admitting it as legitimate, however, or even real, but when it had a certain especial power; and rejecting and denying all faith when derived from a different source, although it should place the soul of man in the same disposition, and produce the same effects. It is true that faith often receives its origin from an emotion, as the mystics contend; but it is also produced by submission to authority, as the Roman Catholic doctors with reason say; and also from reflection, science, and a full and free exercise of the human understanding, although both the one and the other refuse their assent to this. In his liberal wisdom, God has offered more than one way for arriving at that happy state when, tranquil at length in the possession of his belief, man dreams of nothing but of enjoying and obeying what he regards as the truth. There is faith in knowledge, since it has truth for its object; and man can reach it by the faculties which he has received for *knowing*. There is also love in faith; for man cannot see the fulness of truth without loving it. The sensuous faculties and the emotions of the soul are sufficient to engender faith. In short, in faith there are respect and submission; for truth commands, at the same time that it charms and enlightens. Faith can be the sincere and pure submission to a power which is regarded as the depository of truth. Thus the variety of the origins of faith, of which human pride would make a principle of exclusion and privilege, is a benefit bestowed by the Divine will, which, so to speak, has placed faith within reach of all, in permitting it to take its origin from each of the moral elements which constitute faith, — namely, *knowledge*, *submission*, and *love*.

As for those who, rejecting every kind of explanation and origin of faith merely human, will see nothing in it but the direct and actual interposition of God and especial grace, their notion, if apparently more strange, is at bottom more natural; for it touches the problems which do not belong to man to solve. In the external and material world, when a powerful, sudden, and unexpected phenomenon appears, which, at a stroke, changes the face of things, and seems not to attach itself to their ordinary course, nor to explain itself by their anterior state, man instantly refers it to a real and particular act of the will of the Master of the World. The presence of God can alone explain for man that which strikes his imagination and escapes his reason; and where science and experience cannot reach, there he assigns an especial and immediate act of God. Thus the thunderbolt, the tempest, earthquakes, vast floods, concussions, and extraordinary revolutions of the globe, have been taken for signs and effects of the direct action of God, up to the time when man has discovered for them a place and an explanation in the general course of facts and their laws. The same want and the same inclination rule man in the ideas he has formed about the interior world, and the phenomena of which he himself is the theatre and the witness. When a great change and moral revolution have been accomplished in his soul, when he perceives himself to be illuminated by a light, and warmed by a fire, hitherto unknown, — he has taken no notice of the mysterious progress, the slow and concealed action, of ideas, sentiments, and influences which were probably for a long time preparing him for this state. He cannot attribute it to an act of his own will; and he knows not how, so to speak, to trace back the course of his interior life for the purpose of discovering its origin. He refers it, therefore, to a divine will, special and actual. Grace alone could have produced this revolution in his soul, for he himself did not make it, nor does he know how it was produced. The birth of faith, above all when it proceeds from natural and irreflective beliefs which pass, without the intervention of science, to this new state, often bears this character of a sudden revolution, unforeseen and obscure for him who undergoes it. It is, then, very plain that the idea of the direct interposition of God has been invoked on this occasion. In the sense which people have commonly attributed to this idea, it withdraws itself and retires, here as elsewhere, before a more attentive study and a more complete knowledge of facts, their connection, and their laws. We are led to acknowledge that this state of the soul, which is called *faith*, is the development — differently conducted, sometimes sudden and sometimes progressive, but always natural — of certain anterior facts, with which, although essentially distinct, it is connected by an intimate and necessary tie. But supposing this recognized, and faith thus conducted to the place which belongs to it in the general and regular course of moral phenomena, a grand question always remains, the question lying hid at the bottom of the doctrine of grace, and which indirectly this doctrine attempts to solve. In ceasing to see God in the tempest and thunder, narrow and weak minds figure to themselves that they shall no more meet with him, and that they shall nowhere any more have need of him. But the First Cause hovers over all second causes, and over all facts and their laws. When all the secrets of the universe shall have unveiled themselves to human science, the universe will yet be a secret to it; and God appears to withdraw himself from before it, only to invite and constrain it to elevate itself more and more towards himself. In the science of the moral world the same thing happens. When people shall have ceased every moment to invoke grace, and grace alone, to explain faith, it will always remain to be learnt what power presides over the life of the soul; how truth reveals itself to man, who is unable either to seize or reject it, according to his own will; from whence comes that fire whose hearth is evidently external to himself; what relations and communications exist between God and man; what, in short, in the interior life of the human soul, is the share of its own activity and freedom, and what it must attribute to that action which proceeds from without, and to that influence from on high which the pride or the levity of the human mind endeavors not to know. This is the grand problem, the problem that presents itself the moment we touch that point where the things of earth and man are joined to that higher order on which man and the earth so clearly depend. The doctrine of grace is one of the attempts of the human mind to solve it. The solution, at least in my opinion, is beyond the limits assigned to human knowledge.

I have endeavored to determine with precision what faith

is in itself, independently of its object; I have laid down the characteristics of this state of the soul, and the different paths by which man can be conducted to it, whatever may be, so to speak, its *materials*. By this means we may be able to succeed in ascertaining the true nature of faith, and in bringing it into clearer light, disengaging from every foreign element the moral fact concealed under this name. I hasten to add, nevertheless, that this moral fact is not produced indifferently in all cases; that all human beliefs, whether natural or scientific, are not equally susceptible of passing from the condition of faith; and that, in the vast field where human thought is exercised, there are objects especially calculated to awaken a conviction of this kind, to become materials for faith.

This is a fact which is attested even by the history of the word, and which I noticed at the beginning; its common acceptation is also special. At first sight, it seems to be exclusively consecrated to religious belief; and although it lends itself to other uses, and although, even in our own days, its sphere seems to be enlarged, it is evident that, in a multitude of cases where it is concerned (for example, with geography, botany, technology, &c.), the word *faith* is out of place; that is to say, the moral state to which this word corresponds is not produced by such subjects.

As faith has its peculiar interior characteristics, so it has also its exterior necessary conditions; and it is distinguished from other modes of belief of man, not only by its nature, but by its object.

But what are the conditions, and what is the external sphere, of faith?

Up to a certain point we can determine and catch glimpses of them, from the very nature of this state of the soul, and its effects. A belief so complete, so accomplished, that all intellectual labor seems to have reached its termination, and that man, wholly united with the truth of which he thinks himself to be in possession, loses all thought of the path which has conducted him to it, — so powerful, that it takes possession of the exterior activity, as well as of the human mind, and makes submission to its empire in all things a passionate necessity, as well as a duty,—an intellectual state, which can be the fruit, not only of the exercise of the reason, but also of a powerful emotion, and of a long submission to certain practices, and in the midst of which, when it has been once developed, the three grand human faculties are actively employed, and at the same time satisfied,—the *sensibility*, the *intelligence*, and the *will;*—such a condition of soul, and such a belief, demand in some sort occasions worthy of it, and must be produced by subjects which embrace the entire man, and put into play all his faculties, and answer to all the demands of his moral nature, and have a right, in turn, to his devotedness.

Intellectual beauty, and practical importance, appear then, *à priori*, to be the characteristics of the ideas proper for becoming the materials of faith. An idea which should present itself as true, but at the same time without arresting by the extent and the gravity of its consequences, would produce certitude; but *faith* would not spring from it. And so practical merit—the usefulness of an idea—would not suffice for begetting faith; it must also draw attention by the pure beauty of truth. In other words, in order that a simple belief, natural or scientific, should become *faith*, it is necessary that its object should be able to procure the pleasures of activity, as well as of contemplation, that it may awaken within the double sentiment of its high origin and power; in short, that it should present itself before man's eyes as the mediator between the moral and the ideal world,—as the missionary charged with modelling the one on the other, and of uniting them.

Facts fully confirm these inductions, drawn from the mere nature of the moral phenomenon I am studying. Whether we regard the history of the human race, or whether we penetrate into the soul of the individual, we see faith throughout applying itself to objects in which the two aforesaid conditions are united. And if sometimes the one or the other of these conditions is wanting,—if, on some occasions, the object of faith should appear in itself denuded of ideal beauty or practical importance,—we may hold it for certain, that it is not so in the thought of the believer. He will have soon discovered, from the truth which is the object of his faith, consequences and applications which for others are obscure and distant, but for him clear and infallible. Before long his ideas, which appear to have but one aim and one useful merit, will be elevated in his mind to the rank of a disinterested theory, and will possess in his eyes all the dignity and all the charm of truth. It is possible that the believer is deceived, and that he exaggerates the practical worth or intellectual beauty of his idea; but even his error, agreeing in this with the reason and experience of the whole human race, is but a new proof of the necessity of these two conditions for the production of faith.

We can understand, however, why the name of *faith* is almost the exclusive privilege of religious beliefs: these are, in fact, those whose object possesses in the highest degree the two characters which excite the development of faith. Many scientific notions are beautiful and fruitful in their application; political theories may forcibly strike the mind by the purity of their principles and the grandeur of their results; moral doctrines are yet more surely and generally invested with this twofold power; and either has often awoke faith in the soul of man. Nevertheless, in order to receive a clear and lively impression, sometimes of their intellectual beauty and sometimes of their practical importance, there is almost always required a certain amount of science, or sagacity, or, at all events, a certain turn of public manners and the social state, which are not the portion of all men, nor of all times. Religious beliefs have no need of any such aids; they carry with themselves, and in their simple nature, their infallible means for effect. As soon as they penetrate into the heart of man, however bounded in other respects may be the development of his intelligence, however rude and inferior may be his condition, they will appear to him as truths at once sublime and common, which are applicable to all the details of his earthly existence, and open for him those high regions. and those treasures of intellectual life, which, without their light, he would never have known. They exercise over him the charm of truth the most pure, and the empire of interest the most powerful. Can we be astonished that, as soon as they exist, their passage to the state of faith should be so rapid, and so general?

There is yet another reason more hidden, but not less decisive, and which I regret I can only refer to;—the object of religious beliefs is, in a certain and large measure, inaccessible to human science. It can verify their reality; it can reach even to the limits of this mysterious world, and assure itself that there are facts to which the destiny of man infallibly attaches itself; but it is not permitted to reach these facts themselves, so as to submit them to its examination. Struck by this impossibility, more than one philosopher has concluded that there was nothing in them, since reason could perceive nothing, and that religious beliefs address themselves but to the fancy. Others, blinded by their impotence, have tardily sprung forward towards the sphere of superhuman things, and, as though they had succeeded in penetrating into it, have described facts, solved problems, and assigned laws. It is difficult to say which mind is the most foolishly proud, that which maintains that what it cannot know *is not*, or that which pretends to be capable of knowing all that *is*. Whatever may be the case, neither the one nor the other assertion has ever obtained for a single day the avowal of the human race; its instinct and practices have constantly disavowed the *nothing* of the incredulous, and the *confidence* of theologians. In spite of the first, it has persisted in believing in the existence of an unknown world, and in the reality of those relations which hold mankind united to it; and notwithstanding the power of the second, it has refused to admit that they have attained the object, and lifted the veil; and it has continued to agitate the same problems, and to pursue the same truths, as ardently and laboriously as at the first day, and as if nothing had yet been done.

See, then, what, in this respect, is the situation of man. Natural and spontaneous religious beliefs are produced in him, which, by reason of their object, tend at once towards the state of faith. They can arrive at it by means foreign to reasoning and science, — by the emotions and by practices; and the transition is often thus actually brought about. One other way appears open before man. Religious beliefs naturally awaken within him the want of science, which not only desires to render an account of them, but aspires to go much farther than they can conduct it, to know truly this world of mysteries, of which they afford it glimpses. Oftentimes, though, if I mistake not, wrongly, it flatters itself it has succeeded; and thus theology, or the science of divine things, is formed, which is the origin of that rational and learned faith, of which so many illustrious examples do not permit us to contest the reality. Often, also, man, by his own confession, fails in his enterprise; the science which he has pursued after resists his most skilful endeavors, and then he falls into doubt and confusion, — he sees those natural and irreflective beliefs darkened, which served him for his starting-point; or, in fact, despairing of the variety of his attempts, and always tormented by the want of that faith which he has promised himself to establish by science, he returns to his early beliefs, and requires of them to conduct him to faith, without the help of science; that is to say, by the exaltation of his sensuous faculties, or by submission to a legal power, the depository of the truth which his reason cannot seize.

Theology itself, from the moment when it announces itself as a science of the relations of God with man and the world, and presents to the human mind its solutions of the religious problems which besiege it, proclaims nothing less than that these problems are impenetrable mysteries, and that this science is interdicted to human reason; and that faith, born of love, submission, or grace, is alone able to open the understanding to truths, which, however, theologians undertake to reduce to systematic doctrine, in order to be able to teach or demonstrate them to the reason. To such an extent does a feeling of the powerlessness of human science, in this matter, remain imprinted upon him in fact; although everywhere man appears to boast himself of having escaped it.

Thus, also, is explained that obscure physiognomy, if I may so express myself, which appears to be inherent in the word *faith*, and which has so often made it an object of a kind of distrust and dislike to strict and free minds. Frequent above all within the religious domain, and there oftentimes invoked by the powerful and learned, sometimes for the purpose of making up for the silence of the reason, and sometimes for the purpose of constraining the reason to be silent, faith has been considered only under this point of view, and judged only after the employment to which it lends itself on this occasion. People have concluded that this belief was essentially irrational, blind, and the fruit of ungoverned imaginations; or else imposed by force, or fraud, on the weakness or servility of the mind. If I have truly observed and described the nature of that which bears the name of *faith*, the error is evident. On the contrary, *faith* is the aim and boundary of human knowledge, the definite state to which man aspires in his progress towards truth. He begins his intellectual career with spontaneous and irreflective beliefs; at its termination is *faith*. There is more than one way — but none certain — for leaping over this interval; but it is only when it has been leaped over, and when belief has become *faith*, that man feels his nature to be fully satisfied, and gives himself up wholly to his mission. Legitimate faith, that is to say, that which is not mistaken in its object, and addresses itself really to the truth, is then the most elevated and most perfect state to which, in its actual condition, the human mind can arrive.. But faith may be illegitimate; it may be the state of mind which error has produced. The chance of error (experience at every step proves it) is here even much greater, as the paths which lead to it are more multiplied, and its effects more powerful. Man may be misled in his faith by feelings, habits, and the empire of the moral affections, or of external circumstances, as well as by the insufficiency or the bad employment of his intellectual faculties; for faith can take its origin from these different sources. And, nevertheless, from the time of its existence, faith is hardy and ambitious; it aspires passionately to expand itself, to invade, to rule, and to become the law both of minds and facts. And not only is it ambitious, but bold; it possesses and displays, for the support of its pretensions and designs, an energy, address, and perseverance, which are wanting to almost all scientific opinions. So that there is in this mode of belief, far more than in any other, chance of error for the individual, and chance of oppression for society. For these perils there is but one remedy, — liberty. Whether man believes, or acts, his nature is the same; and to avoid becoming absurd or guilty, his thought stands in need of constant opposition and constraint, as well as his will. Where faith is wanting, there power and moral dignity are equally wanting; where liberty is wanting, faith usurps, then misleads, and at length is lost. Let human beliefs pass into the state of faith; it is their natural progress and their glory; and in their effort towards this object, and when they have reached it, let them constantly continue under the control of the free intellect; it is the guaranty of society against tyranny, and the condition of their own legitimacy. In the coexistence and mutual respect of these two forces reside the beauty and the security of social order.

THE LAW AND THE GOSPEL.

By the Rev. BADEN POWELL, M. A., F. R. S., F. G. S.,

SAVILIAN PROFESSOR OF GEOMETRY IN THE UNIVERSITY OF OXFORD.

Ὁ γὰρ Χριστιανισμὸς οὐκ εἰς Ἰουδαϊσμὸν ἐπίστευσεν ἀλλὰ Ἰουδαϊσμὸς εἰς Χριστιανισμόν, ὡς πᾶσα γλῶσσα πιστεύσασα εἰς Θεὸν συνήχθη. — Ignatius *ad Magnes.* § x.

"For Christianity hath not believed in Judaism, but Judaism in Christianity; — that every tongue having believed in God might sound forth together." *

Introduction.

Among persons professing to receive the Bible as the authentic record of what in general they believe is Divine Revelation, it is remarkable how little attention is commonly given to the obvious diversity of nature and purport in those very distinct portions of which the sacred volume consists. To any one who does but for a moment reflect on the widely remote dates, the extremely diversified character of the contents, the totally dissimilar circumstances and occasions of the composition, of the several writings, it must be obvious how essentially they require to be viewed with careful discrimination as to the variety of conditions and objects which they evince, if they are to be in any degree rightly understood, or applied as they were intended to be. But manifest as these considerations are, and readily admitted

---

* I should translate the last clause of this quotation, "that every tongue which believed might be gathered together unto God." — G. R. N.

when simply put before any reader of the most ordinary attainments and discernment, it is singular to observe how commonly they are practically lost sight of in the too prevalent modes of reading and applying Scripture.

In this point of view it must be allowed a matter of the most primary importance, as bearing on the whole purport and design of the Bible, to apprehend rightly the general relation, but at the same time the characteristic differences, of the Old and New Testament, the Law and the Gospel, the distinctive character to be traced and the sort of connection actually subsisting between them. Nor does this turn on considerations of any nice or critical kind, demanding extensive learning to appreciate, or deep study to judge of; it implies a mere reference to matters of fact, which require but to be indicated to be understood, so that it is the more remarkable how commonly they are overlooked.

Yet on no subject, perhaps, are more confused and unsatisfactory ideas more commonly prevalent; not only among ordinary, careless, or formal readers of Scripture, but even among many of better information and more serious religious views, a habit is too general of confounding together the contents of all parts of the sacred volume, whether of the old or new dispensations, of the Hebrew or of the Christian Scriptures, into one promiscuous mass, regarding them, as it were, all as one book, or code of religion, and of citing detached texts from both, and promiscuously taking precepts and institutions, promises and threatenings, belonging to peculiar dispensations, and applying them universally, without regard to times, persons, or circumstances. And such a mode of appealing to Scripture is sometimes even defended, as evincing a meritorious reverence for its divine character, and upheld as a consequence from the belief in its *inspiration*. Yet in whatever sense that belief be entertained, adopting even the strictest meaning of the term, it surely by no means follows but that inspired authority may have a reference to one object and not to another, — a precept or declaration may have been addressed to one party or in one age, and not designed for another, — without any disparagement to its divine character.

From a thoughtless, desultory, or merely formal habit of reading the divine Word, it is not surprising that there should result an adoption of those low and unworthy notions which prevail so commonly as to the character and genius of the Christian religion; and which especially arise from the confused combination of its principles with those of older and less perfect dispensations. That such ideas should obtain ready acceptance with the many will not surprise those who consider the various causes in different ways operating to lower and degrade the exalted purity and simplicity of the Gospel to the level of the corrupt apprehensions of human nature, especially among the mass of the ignorant and unthinking nominal professors of a belief in its doctrine.

But it must be a matter of more astonishment that such notions should find encouragement with some who professedly look at Christianity in a more enlightened sense, and avowedly seek to receive it in no blind, formal manner, but in the spirit of its *evangelical* purity. Yet such unhappily is the case. And whether from mere want of thought on the one hand, or from preconceived theories on the other, or even in some cases (we must fear) from more mixed motives, so unprepared are men to entertain more distinct views, that the very announcement of them is commonly altogether startling and even painful to their prepossessions, and especially when these questions are found to be mixed up with certain points of supposed practical obligation and religious observance; it follows, that when a more explanatory view of the subject is presented, the hearers too generally turn away with impatience, or even with disgust and offence.

Without indulging the hope of being able to remove or conciliate such opposing feelings in all instances, it will be at least the endeavor, in the following exposition, to avoid giving offence by the assumption of a polemical tone; yet to state the case of Christianity as independent of previous dispensations, simply in reference to the matter of fact, with that plainness which the cause of truth demands, according to the tenor of the evidence furnished by Scripture, and in the desire to maintain and elucidate the pure and enlightening principles of the New Testament, according to what appears, at least to the author, their unadulterated and evangelical simplicity.

I. *The Primeval Dispensations.*

The general nature, character, and connection of the successive divine dispensations recorded in the Bible, as briefly described by the writer of the Epistle to the Hebrews (i. 1), — the announcements in various measures and "portions," and under various "forms" or "aspects,"* made in times past to the fathers by the prophets, — fully accords with what we collect in detail from the writings of the Old Testament, and affords the only simple and satisfactory clew to the interpretation of them.

The view presented to us is that of successive revelations, systems, covenants, laws, given to different individuals, families, or nations, containing gradual, progressive, and partial developments of the truth, and intimations of the Divine will for their guidance, accompanied with peculiar positive institutions, adapted to the ideas of the age and the condition of the parties to whom they were vouchsafed.

Thus peculiar revelations are represented as having been made — each distinct from the other, though in some instances including repetitions — to Adam, to Noah, to Job, to Abraham, to Isaac and Jacob, to the Israelites, first by Moses, afterwards by a succession of prophets, as well as in some instances to other people; as, for example, to the Ninevites (if the book of Jonah be regarded as historical); — while, *in contradistinction to all these*, we are told, "in *these last days* God hath spoken *unto us* by his Son" (*ib.*), in a universal, permanent, and perfect dispensation; — the earlier and more partial were *not* made "*to us*," or designed "*for us*."

Yet it is important to trace the history and character of

---

* This is clearly the force of the original, πολυμερῶς καὶ πολυτρόπως. Heb. i. 1.

these former dispensations, in order more fully to elucidate the distinct nature and independence of the last; and especially to remove prevalent misconceptions from a subject which, however plain when historically and rationally considered, has been involved in much difficulty from gratuitous and often visionary theories.

When we consider the very imperfect intimations, often mere hints and allusions, given in the Hebrew records, as to these early religious institutions and the design of them, as well as the obvious and wide differences in the circumstances of those people and times from our own, the discerning reader at once sees how little they can have been intended to be understood as containing any permanent elements of a universal religion, as seems to have been sometimes imagined. In the plain terms of the narrative we discover nothing of the kind, and in the comment on it which the New Testament supplies, we have direct assurance to the contrary.

In general, we find only that the servants of God in those ages were accepted in walking each according to the lights vouchsafed to him; while in other respects we see peculiar institutions and announcements specially adapted to the peculiar ends and purposes of the dispensations. Thus we trace from the first the approach to God through sacrifices, offerings, and formal services.

Some infer from the account of the Divine rest after the creation, that there was a primeval institution of the Sabbath, though certainly *no precept* is recorded as having been given to man to keep it up. But since, from the irreconcilable contradictions disclosed by geological discovery, the whole narrative of the six days' creation cannot now be regarded by any competently informed person *as historical*,* the *historical* character of the distinction conferred on the seventh day falls to the ground along with it. Yet even without reference to

* I do not here pretend to enter on the *evidence* in support of this conclusion. It will be found fully discussed in my work, *On the Connection of Natural and Divine Truth,* 1838, and in my article "Creation," in Kitto's *Cyclopædia of Bib. Lit.*

this consideration, some of the best commentators have regarded the passage as proleptical, or anticipatory.

Afterwards we find the distinction of clean and unclean animals introduced, and the prohibition of eating blood, in the covenant with Noah (Gen. ix. 1), of which the Sabbath formed no part; nor can we find any indication of it in the history of the other patriarchs: a point particularly dwelt upon by the early Christian divines, who adopted the belief of the Jews of their age in interpreting their Scriptures.* Some have dwelt on the mention of the division of time by weeks † in several parts of the early Mosaic history: yet

---

* Justin Martyr (*Dial. c. Trypho,* 236, 261) says, "The patriarchs were justified before God not keeping Sabbaths," and "from Abraham originated circumcision and from Moses the Sabbath," &c. Irenæus (IV. 30) and Tertullian (*Ad Jud.*, II. 4) both declare that "Abraham without circumcision and without observance of Sabbaths believed in God," &c.

† The early and general adoption of the division of time into *weeks* may be obviously and rationally derived from the simple consideration, that among all rude nations the first periodical division of time which obtains is that of lunar months, while those conspicuous phenomena, the phases or quarters of the moon, correspond to a week nearly enough for the common purposes of such nations.

The universal prevalence of this division by weeks among Eastern nations from a very remote period is attested by various ancient writers. Dio Cassius ascribes the invention of it to the Egyptians, and assigns the origin of the planetary names of the days. (*Hist. Rom.*, XXXVII. 18, 19.) Oldendorf found it in the interior of Africa. (Jahn, *Archæol. Bib.*, art. "Week.") The Brahmins also have the week distinguished by the planetary names. (*Life of Galileo,* 12; Laplace, *Précis de l'Hist. d'Astron.* 16.) The Peruvians divide lunar months into halves and quarters, i. e. weeks, by the phases of the moon, and besides have a period of nine days, the approximate third part of a lunation: thus showing the common origin of both. (Garcilasso, *Hist. of the Incas,* in Taylor's *Nat. Hist. of Society,* I. 291, 292.)

So also the Romans had their "Nundinæ." On the other hand, the Mexicans have periods of five and of thirteen days, with names to each day. (Norman on *Yucatan,* i. 85, and *Trans. of American Ethnog. Soc.,* I. 58.) And the week is not known to the Chinese, nor to the North American Indians (Catlin, II. 234); facts opposed to the idea of any universal primitive tradition.

Allusions to a sanctity ascribed to the seventh day by the early Greek

it by no means follows that, because the historian adopts a particular mode of reckoning, it was *therefore* used by the people of whom he is writing: but were it so, this would not imply the institution of the Sabbath.

In all the early dispensations religious truths are conveyed under figures, and obligations enforced by motives, specially adapted to the capacities and wants of the parties addressed. Thus temporal prospects are always held out as the *immediate* sanctions; and the *mode* of announcement adopted is always that in which God is represented as vouchsafing to enter into *a covenant* with his creatures; — the form is always that of a

---

poets, such as the ἑβδομάτη δ' ἔπειτα κατήλυθεν ἱερὸν ἦμαρ of Homer, and like expressions of Callimachus, Hesiod, &c., are quoted by Clemens Alexandrin. (*Strom.*, V.), and expressly described by him to have been derived from the Jews, with whose Scriptures so many parallelisms are found in the classic authors.

Generally, however, the universal superstition of the sacredness of the number 7, combined with the equally common propensity to attach sanctity to particular periods and days, are sufficient elements out of which such ideas would naturally take their rise.

Among the ancient Romans festivals were held in honor of Saturn, with a reference to commemorating the Saturnian or Golden age, and with this idea it was unlawful on the day sacred to Saturn to go out to war (Macrobius, Lib. I.; *Saturn.*, c. 16), and it was held unlucky to commence a journey or undertake any business: a superstition alluded to by Tibullus (*Eleg.* I. 3, v. 18), "Saturni aut sacram me tenuisse diem."

What particular feast is here referred to there is nothing to show. The supposition of some of his commentators, that it meant the seventh day of the week, is wholly gratuitous. But if it were so, the idea would be naturally and obviously borrowed from the Jews, whose customs, especially the Sabbath, are so frequently alluded to by the Roman writers; and, from their wide dispersion, must have been generally familiar, as in fact we learn from the boast of Josephus (*Adv. Ap.*, II.) and of Philo, that "there is no place where the Sabbath is not known," and the testimony of Theophilus Antiochus (Lib. II., *Ad Arist.*) to the same effect, as well as others often cited: which show the strict preservation of the observance among the scattered Jews; and it may possibly have been conformed to by others, or the occasion laid hold of as convenient for other purposes: as, e. g., we are told by Suetonius (Lib. XXXII.), "Diogenes grammaticus disputare sabbatis Rhodi solitus."

stipulation of certain *conditions* to be fulfilled, and certain blessings or punishments to be awarded as they are fulfilled or not; — and these conditions, always of a precise, formal, positive kind, not implying merely moral obligations. The spirit of all these covenants was that of "touch not, taste not, handle not" (Col. ii. 21), involving a ground and motive of obedience precisely adapted to the very infancy of the human race. Such was the very covenant with Adam in Paradise: "Eat not of the tree, — or thou shalt die." Nor can it be denied that, if the Sabbath had formed a part of that covenant, it was an institution exactly in keeping with it: Eat not of the tree, — keep holy the seventh day. The same idea of a covenanted stipulation of *positive* observances, in which sacrifice was the most prominent, characterizes all the succeeding announcements, — from the covenant of circumcision with Abraham down to the more detailed and complete scheme of the Mosaic Law.

In these early and imperfect dispensations it is idle to look for any great principles of universal moral application, as has been sometimes fancied: — for instance, finding authority for capital punishment in the precept given to Noah (Gen. ix. 6), or for tithes in the example of Melchisedec (Gen xiv. 20). So far from perceiving any support for the idea, that because a precept or institution was from the beginning, it was *therefore* designed to be of universal and perpetual obligation, on the contrary, we rather see in its very antiquity a strong presumption that it was of a nature suited and intended only for the earliest stage of the religious development of man.

But apart from these peculiarities, we trace all along the announcement of "*the promise*" (Gal. iii. 19), which was before the covenant, and to which the fathers looked *as not transitory*. Christianity, by fulfilling the promise, supersedes all previous imperfect dispensations: itself emphatically a *New* covenant, the very reverse of a *recurrence* to a primitive religion (as fancied by some). The patriarchs, and especially Abraham, are set forth as examples of *faith in the promise;* and in this respect Christian believers are called children of

Abraham (Gal. iii. 7): but manifestly not in the sense of their retrograding to an older and less perfect state of things: the whole tenor of the Divine revelation is clearly stamped with the character of *advance*.

II. *The Judaical Law.*

The manifest design of the book of Genesis was *not* to teach *us* a primitive religion, but to form an *introduction to the Law* for the Jews. It has been well observed, that "to understand Genesis we must begin with Exodus"; from the actual history and circumstances of the people we can best appreciate what their books spoke to them.

Those events in the *previous* history are always selected and enlarged upon which have a direct reference to points in the *subsequent* institutions, or were *anticipations of the Law*, or the rudiments out of which its ordinances were framed.

Thus, the narrative of the six days' creation, first announced in the Decalogue, and afterwards amplified in Genesis, as has been already observed, can *now* only be regarded as an adaptation of a poetical cosmogony (doubtless already familiar to the Israelites) to the purpose of enforcing on them the institution of the Sabbath. And in like manner the other institutions of primeval worship (already adverted to) — the sacrifices, the distinctions of clean and unclean animals, the prohibition of blood, and afterwards the appointment of circumcision, the choice of a peculiar people, the promise of Canaan — form the prominent topics, as being the beginnings of the Mosaic covenant, and approximations towards the system of the Law.

The object of the Law was declared to be, in the first instance, to *separate* the people of Israel by peculiar marks and badges from all other nations, as a people *chosen* for the high ends and purposes of the Divine counsels (see especially Exod. xix. 5; xxxi. 13 – 17; Deut. xiv. 1; xxvi. 16; Ezek. xx. 9 – 12). This was to be effected especially by such distinctions as those of circumcision, the prohibition of intermarriages, or any participation with idolaters; by all their exclusive usages and ceremonies, but chiefly by the marked singularity of the Sabbath, which, along with the Passover, was appointed earlier than the rest of the Law, and was emphatically declared (Exod. xxxi. 16; Ezek. xx. 12; Neh. ix. 14, &c.) to be a distinctive *sign* between God and the people of Israel, which they were always to *remember* to keep up; a peculiarity further evinced by its being always prominently coupled with the sanctity of the temple, the new moons and other feasts (Lev. xix. 30; Isa. i. 13; lxvi. 23; Hos. ii. 11; Ezek. xlv. 17), and one of the pledges by which the proselyte was to *take hold of the covenant* (Isa. lvi. 6). The directions for the *mode* of observing it were minute and strict; and the precepts always precisely regard the observance, not of one day in seven, but of *the seventh day of the week* as such, in commemoration of the rest after the Creation,* though in one respect also it is afterwards urged as reminding them of their deliverance out of Egypt (Deut. v. 14). These distinctions constituted at once their security and their motives of obedience. The Law throughout is a series of adaptations *to them* and their national peculiarities.

Yet it is often spoken of as something general, as "a preliminary education of the human race"; † but the plain history discloses nothing but the training of one single people for a specific purpose.

We see continued exemplifications of wise adaptation to the Jewish national mind in the entire *mode* of the delivery of the Law amid terrors, signs, and wonders; and especially in the oral announcement of the Decalogue from Sinai; while its consignment to tables of stone is expressly stated to be for

---

* The Jewish Rabbis have always understood the institution to belong *to the particular day* of the cessation of the Creation, enjoined on the people of Israel, as they say, "that they might fasten in their minds the belief that the world had a beginning, which is a thread that draws after it all the foundations of the Law or principles of religion." (Rabbi Levi of Barcelona, quoted by Patrick, on Exod. xix.) The same idea occurs in a Jewish form of prayer quoted also by Patrick.

† See Pusey on *Rationalism*, I. 156.

a memorial or "testimony" (Exod. xxxi. 18; xxxiv. 29) to the covenant, of which these precepts constituted some of the more primary stipulations. And throughout the whole Law we trace equal adaptations in the form and manner of the precepts and injunctions: all minute and literal, not rising to any broad principles, which the Israelites at that time would have been incapable of comprehending.

The distinction adopted by many modern divines between the "*ceremonial*" and the "*moral*" law appears nowhere in the books of Moses. No one portion or code is held out as comprising the rules of *moral* obligation distinct and apart from those of a *positive* nature: such a distinction would have been unintelligible to them; and "the Law" is always spoken of in Scripture as *a whole*, without reference to any such classification; and the obligations of all parts of it, as of the same kind.

In particular, what is termed the moral law is certainly in no way peculiarly to be identified with the Decalogue. Though moral duties, are specially enjoined in many places of the Law, yet the Decalogue certainly does not contain *all* moral duties, even by remote implication, and on the widest construction. *It totally omits many such*, as, e. g., beneficence, truth, justice, temperance, control of temper, and others; and some moral precepts omitted here are introduced in other places.

Equally in the Decalogue and the rest of the Law, we find precepts referring to what are properly moral duties scattered and intermixed with those of a positive and formal kind, and in no way distinguished from them in authority or importance; but both connected with the peculiarities of the dispensation, expressed in a form accompanied with sanctions and enforced by motives precisely adapted to the character and capacity of the people, and such as formed part of the exact stipulations of the covenant.

Their duties were urged more generally in some passages (as, e. g., in Deut. xi. 21, 22; iv. 27, &c.) on the consideration of national blessings; in others on more particular grounds, such as the motives assigned for filial obedience (Exod. xx. 12) in a long life; the recompense for beneficence and equity (Prov. xix. 17; Ps. xli. 1; xxxvii. 25, &c.); the appeal to the dread of Divine vengeance (Exod. xxiv. 17; Deut. iv. 24; Isa. lxvi. 16; Deut. iv. 31); and the remembrance of benefits conferred. In general their reward was to be found in obedience: to keep the statutes and ordinances was to be "their wisdom and their righteousness"; and the great maxim and promise was, "He that doeth these things shall live in them" (Deut. iv. 6; vi. 25; Lev. xviii. 5).

The Law conformed to many points of human infirmity: it offered splendid rites and ceremonies to attract popular reverence, and wean the people from their proneness to the gross ceremonies of idolatry. It indulged the disposition to observe "days, and times, and seasons" by the Sabbaths and feasts, and by occasional fasts, originally only a symbol of ordinary mourning, but afterwards invested with a religious character (Isa. lviii. 5; Joel ii. 12). It commended avenging and sanguinary zeal, especially in the punishment of blasphemers (Lev. xxiv. 14; Deut. xiii. 9). It sanctioned the "*lex talionis*" (Exod. xxi. 23), — "life for life, eye for eye, tooth for tooth," — that most perfect idea of retributive justice to the uncivilized mind; and in general it connected the idea of *punishment* with that of *vengeance*, the most congenial to a barbarous apprehension. If it restricted marriages within certain degrees of kindred, it at least connived at polygamy; and allowed a law of divorce suited "to the hardness of their hearts" (Matt. xix. 8). The Law altogether was established with a regard to the infirmity and blindness of the people, "*in consideration to transgressions*" * (Gal. iii. 19).

While it prohibited idolatry, it represented the Deity under human similitudes, with human passions and bodily members,

---

* This appears to me to be the proper force of the adverb χάριν here used by the Apostle. From its etymology it must be supposed to imply "because of," in a *favorable* or *indulging* sense. It seems to correspond to πρός in Matt. xix. 8.

as, e. g., weary and resting from his work, angry, repenting, and jealous of other gods; and designated more particularly as "Jehovah," the national God of Israel, &c. It is not one of the least remarkable of these anthropomorphisms that (as in former instances) the disclosure of the Divine purposes is made under the figure of Jehovah entering into a *covenant* with his people, an idea specially adapted to a nation of the lowest moral capacity. All points of duty were proposed under the form of precise stipulations, (just as in other times religious vows, temperance pledges, subscriptions to creeds, &c. have been adopted,) to keep a stronger hold on those incapable of higher motives. The immediate appeal to divine sanctions sensibly present, and the enforcement of moral duties under the form of a positive engagement, were precisely calculated to influence those who had no apprehension of pure principles of moral obligation, or of a higher spiritual service.

Again, obedience was to be rewarded and sin to be visited by blessings or judgments on the *posterity* of the offender (Exod. xx. 5), not merely in the sense of the ordinary consequences of good or bad conduct in the parents naturally influencing the fortunes of the children, but by a peculiar providential interposition. And in connection with this was another striking peculiarity of the covenant, that obedience and disobedience were both regarded as *national*, for which *national* rewards and judgments were to be awarded; the *whole people in the aggregate* being represented as possessing a *collective* and common responsibility. These peculiarities were obviously connected with the absence of those higher motives and sanctions which would be derived from the doctrine of a future state; which clearly *formed no part of the covenant*, even if believed by some pious and enlightened individuals, and in later times hinted at by the prophets.

The obligations of the Law were strongly declared to be *perpetual* (as, e. g., Exod. xxxi. 17; Lev. xvi. 34; xxiv. 8; 2 Kings xvii. 37, &c.; Isa. lv. 3), and the covenant *everlasting*, — expressions which cannot now be taken literally.

Its privileges might at all times be extended to strangers by their undergoing the initiatory rite. This was in later ages extensively realized (see Exod. xii. 48; comp. with Isa. lvi. 6; and Deut. xxix. 11).

The prophecies of the future extension of the Mosaic religion might in a first sense apply literally to this extension of proselytism, — the coming in of remote nations to the Jewish church and worship, resorting to its temple, adopting its rites and offerings, and keeping its festivals and Sabbaths: as we know was in fact largely fulfilled before the introduction of the Gospel (Isa. lvi. 3; lxvi. 11, 12, 19 – 23; Micah iv. 1; Zech. viii. 21; Amos ix. 11; comp. Acts ii. 5, &c.).

These predictions are, however, also figuratively interpreted of the spread of the Gospel and the glories of the spiritual Zion. If so, *all* the particulars in the description must be interpreted by the *same* analogy; if Israel and the temple be metaphorical, then the sacrifices, new moons, and Sabbaths must be so likewise; if these latter are taken literally, we can only understand the whole literally, or we violate all rules of interpretation and analogy.

The precision and formality of the *Law* were in some degree extended and spiritualized by the *Prophets*. The words of Ezekiel (xviii. 3) have been understood as positively abrogating the punishment of the posterity for the sins of the father; and Isaiah (i. 13, &c.) strongly decries the sacrifices and Sabbaths. They also gave intimations that the Law was to come to an end, or rather to be superseded by a better and more spiritual covenant (Isa. ii. 2; Jer. xxxi. 31; Ezek. xxxvi. 25; Mal. iv. 2 – 6). Malachi, the last, connects the two dispensations, — looking backwards to Moses and forwards to Christ and his forerunner.

John the Baptist was the minister of an intermediate or preparatory dispensation. He accordingly recognized all existing obligations, but reproved hypocrisy and formality, and urged repentance and its practical fruits (Luke iii. 10 – 14; Matt. iii. 7). He more especially announced the kingdom of heaven as at hand, and pointed to Jesus as "the Christ," "the

Lamb of God" who should bring it in (John i. 27, 29), and "take away the sin of the world."

III. *The Teaching of Christ.*

In the teaching of Jesus we find *no repeal* of an old dispensation to introduce a new; but a gradual method of preparation by spiritual instruction for a better system.

During his ministry on earth, the kingdom of heaven was still only "at hand" and "to come" (Mark i. 15; Matt. vi. 10). Serious misconceptions often arise from applying his instructions without remembering that he was himself emphatically "made under the Law" (Gal. iv. 4), and addressing those under it as still in force.

To the Jews in general he inculcated moral and spiritual duties; not any *change* in existing *grounds* and *principles*, but reform in *practice*. He censured severely the hypocrisy and ostentation of the Pharisees and their followers; their excessive minuteness even in matters ordained, and their "making of none effect" the divine law by human additions (Mark vii. 13). Yet he offered no disparagement to the Law as such. While he insisted on its weightier matters, he would not have its lesser points neglected (Matt. xxiii. 23). He enlarged its spirit, yet acknowledged its letter as the rule still in force on the Jews. His own example was emphatic. His plain declaration implies none of those refined distinctions which have been sometimes drawn as to the meaning of the terms "destroy" and "fulfil" (Matt. v. 17); to quiet the apprehensions of the Jews as to his having a design hostile to the Law and the Prophets, he assures them that the very aim of his life was to obey it in every particular, "to fulfil," in their phrase, "all righteousness" (Matt. iii. 15). And so his Jewish followers were exhorted to "keep the commandments" if they "would enter into life" (Matt. xix. 17); and doing so, they were "*not far* from the kingdom of God" (Mark xii. 34), though not yet in it. Not the least of the commandments was to be broken; no part of its force to fail during that age or dispensation (Matt. v. 18).

Thus far in general: in more special instances we find him upholding the authority of the existing church and its teachers, and the appeal to its tribunals (Matt. xxiii. 1; xviii. 17). He recognized the Mosaic law of marriage and divorce, and though he limited the latter more strictly (Matt. xix. 8), it was to repress the gross abuse of it which then prevailed; and this only under an express reference to what was the original design of the institution from the authority of the books of Moses.

He referred to fasting as an existing rite under the Law, though sternly reproving the hypocritical and ostentatious performance of it (Matt. vi. 18; comp. Isa. lviii. 5). In the same terms he censured formality and ostentation in almsgiving and prayer (Matt. vi. 1 – 5); and taught that offerings at the altar were not to be omitted, though reconciliation was of more importance (Matt. v. 23).

He particularly and repeatedly reproved the Pharisaical moroseness in the observance of the Sabbath: himself wrought cures on it, and vindicated works of charity and necessity (Matt. xii. 1); yet only by such arguments and examples as the Jewish teachers themselves allowed, and their own Scriptures afforded authority for. But he did not in any way modify or abolish it, or substitute any other for it, though he fully asserted his power to do so; and expressly urged upon them the consideration that it was made for "the man" * (i. e. those to whom it was appointed), and not "the man" for it; as an institution of a permanent kind connected with the moral ends of man's being; adapted to the parties for whom it was designed, but having nothing in its nature of unchangeable or general obligation to which mankind were to conform.

He defeated insidious questions by an appeal to the Law itself: "What is written?" (Luke x. 26; Mark x. 3, &c.); and taking occasion from a point disputed among them, he enforced the *two great commandments* (Matt. xxii. 37;

---

* This is clearly the force of the original (Mark ii. 27), διὰ τὸν ἄνθρωπον.

comp. with Deut. vi. 5 ; Lev. xix. 18 ; Matt. vii. 12 ; Tobit iv. 15) as the sum of the Law and the Prophets, and in general urged obedience on the very principle and promise of the Law itself: " Do this, and thou shalt live " (Luke x. 28 ; Rom. x. 3 ; Gal. iii. 12 ; comp. with Lev. xviii. 5 ; Ezek. xx. 11 ; Neh. ix. 29).

He took the Decalogue as the text of his instructions to the Jews (Mark x. 19 ; Matt. v. 21, &c. ; xix. 16, &c.) ; and made many enlargements upon it : giving them new precepts expressly *in addition* to it, and not as *unfolding* anything *already contained* or *implied in it*, and expressly contrasting his own teaching with what " was said of old." But we find *no modification or softening of the Law, no repeal of one part and retaining another*, as is often imagined.

Christ's teaching during his ministry was plainly but *preliminary* and *preparatory* to the establishment of the new dispensation. His general discourses were simply practical, yet with an obvious peculiarity of adaptation to the ideas of the Jewish people. " The mysteries of the kingdom " were veiled in parables to the multitude, explained to the disciples in private, and understood only by those who " had ears to hear " (Matt. xiii. 9 – 17). During his ministry " the kingdom of heaven suffered violence " (Matt. xi. 12), the more enlightened partially understood it, and the strong in spirit forced an entrance.

He pointed to the necessity of a new beginning from first principles (Matt. ix. 17 ; xviii. 1), for becoming as little children ; holding out the prospect of a progressive enlightenment (John viii. 31), urging the Jews especially to search their own Scriptures (John v. 39), (those in which *ye* think ye have eternal life,) in support of his claims, and insisting especially on a new and higher " regeneration " than that acknowledged by the Rabbis (John iii. 3).

He repeatedly declared his mission to be *only* to the House of Israel. In some few instances, indeed, Gentiles came to him ; but no distinct instruction was given, except in the one remarkable case of the woman of Samaria, which is peculiarly important as being the *only distinct* reference in Christ's teaching to the new dispensation *as extending to the Gentiles*, and the *termination of the old* with respect to the *Jews* (John iv. 21).

According to the whole system disclosed in the New Testament, it is clear that Christ's kingdom could not properly begin till after his death and resurrection (Luke xxiv. 46). Its extension to all nations, though more than once *hinted at* in his discourses (Matt. viii. 11; John x. 16, &c.), and indirectly *figured out* in several of the parables, was not *positively announced* till the final charge was given to the Apostles (Matt. xxviii. 19; Mark xvi. 16; Luke xxiv. 47; Acts i. 8).

IV. *The Teaching of the Apostles.*

The preaching of the Apostles in the first instance was confined to Jews and proselytes, who continued under the Law and in the worship of the synagogue, simply adding the belief in Jesus as the Messiah, and joining in Christian communion.

The Apostles themselves conformed to the Law in all particulars, even St. Paul, while he claimed the liberty of doing otherwise; and St. Peter was reproached with inconsistency in deviating from it even in one point (Acts xxi. 24; Gal. ii. 11).

The first great step was the announcement of the *abolition of the separation* between Jew and Gentile, commenced in the commission to Peter to convert Cornelius (Acts x. 34). Yet in fact Christianity was long confined chiefly to Jews or proselytes, or Gentile converts from among those who had previously in some degree conformed to the Law. In addressing such parties the appeal would be naturally made to the Old Testament as furnishing proofs of Christianity.

Of the preaching to the Samaritans nothing is recorded, but it was doubtless accordant with the words of Christ to the Samaritan woman, and could involve little reference to Jewish obligations.

When purely Gentiles, or heathens, were addressed, there is no evidence or instance of any reference being made to

Old Testament authority, *to the Law as preliminary to the Gospel*, or to any supposed *primitive religion*, as to a sort of prior, but forgotten, obligation. The appeal was (in all the few cases recorded) to the *natural* evidences of one God, to the moral law of *conscience*, and then directly to the fact of Christ's resurrection and its consequences. Such was the tenor of St. Paul's discourse at Lystra and at Athens (Acts xvii. 22; xiv. 17), and such the purport of his whole elaborate argument in the beginning of the Epistle to the Romans (Rom. i. 18; ii. 14, &c.), where he positively and pointedly makes his appeal to the Gentiles, *not* on the ground of the *revealed law*, but solely on that of *natural* reason and conscience. And just as he referred the Jews to their Scriptures, so, to enforce his argument with authorities to the heathen, he quotes their own poets (Acts xvii. 28; 1 Cor. xv. 33; Tit. i. 12).

The omission of any reference to *previous obligations* (which, if they had existed, were certainly unknown) is *emphatic*. Any supposed universal law given to the Patriarchs would clearly have required to be revived, but no intimation or even allusion of the kind is to be found in the records of the Apostolic teaching. Such a reference, for example, was manifestly requisite for any revival of a primeval Sabbath, had it been contemplated; but it is needless to say, no such intimation can be found. The only allusion to the subject at all is addressed to the Hebrews (Heb. iv. 4), and the turn of the allusion is figurative and obviously quite different.

The very natural belief of the Jews, that the Gentiles were incapable of justification, except through conformity to the covenant of circumcision, at a very early period led to attempts to impose the Law on Gentile converts (Acts xv. 1 – 28), until the Apostolic decree finally settled the question, in which certain observances *only* are retained and prescribed, described as practically "necessary" from the circumstances of the times: the omission of all others, as meats, Sabbaths, &c., is emphatic, as well as the absence of any recognition, whether generally of the Law as such, or of any previous dispensation, or of any part of it, or an enlarged or modified view of its precepts to be made the rule of Christian obedience. But so inveterate were the prepossessions of the Jews, that later attempts of this kind were continually made, which called forth the special censures of St. Paul, and the strongest arguments against these notions so destructive to the real spirit of the Gospel, such as form the main purport of his Epistles to the Galatians and Colossians, of material portions of those to the Romans, and the Second to the Corinthians (as, e. g., 2 Cor. iii., &c.), and of scattered declarations in nearly all.

Hence the expression *Christian "liberty"* obviously applies only by way of *contrast* to the particular instance of Judaizing, while the assurance "ye are not under the Law, but under grace," (the necessity for which arose solely from the same cause,) is most carefully guarded against any such misapplication as would sanction sin, any tendency to the preposterous doctrine of Antinomianism (Rom. vi. 1, 14). No such language need have been used with respect to Gentile converts but for such attempts at enslaving them. The Apostle addressed distinctly both those "under the Law,"—the Jews,—and those "not under the Law,"—the Gentiles; the former generally were still under it, though they might have been released from it. But the latter *could not be released from that to which they had never been subject.* To say that they were *free from the law of the Hebrews* was indeed true, but *superfluous;* they needed not to be told so; what was to bring them under it? certainly not the Gospel.

The strong feeling of the Jews with respect to the distinction of circumcision appears, however, very reasonable; it was not a mere national prejudice, but arose purely out of the belief in the Divine authority of the covenant, and to them seemed to involve all the other obligations of the Law, not to be abrogated without the loss of that distinction. Hence the difficulty of the argument with them. It is, however, conducted with consummate skill by the Apostle, directing his reasoning with admirable effect, so as at once to bear on the case of the Gentiles, and with equal force on that of the Jews, in a way which they must acknowledge as conclusive on their own principles (as in Rom. xi. 13, &c.).

He maintained himself a compliance with the ordinances yet subsisting: "to the Jews he became a Jew," as "under the Law"; to the Gentiles as "without the Law" (1 Cor. ix. 20): but this was no deceptive assumption, since he *actually was* in one sense both.

The distinction of meats, clean or unclean, of days to be kept holy or not, remained actually in force to the Jewish Christians until their convictions became sufficiently enlightened to see the abolition of those distinctions. To the Gentile it was equally clear that they were not obligatory *on him*, while his service was a spiritual one in faith. In Sabbaths and meats each might judge for himself (Rom. xiv. 5, 6); there was no moral immutable obligation, but neither was to judge the other. Both acting in faith were exhorted to mutual charity, a line of conduct pre-eminently recommended by the Apostle's own example (1 Cor. x. 23; viii. 13, &c.). But there was no compromise of essential truths; we cannot but be struck with the contrast of the Apostle's liberality of sentiment with his strenuous assertion of Christian freedom. "Christ crucified" (1 Cor. i. 25) was preached alike to Jew and Greek, the Author of Salvation equally to those under the Law and those without it (Rom. xv. 8, 9).

To both parties it was argued that they stood equally *condemned* in the sight of God. The Gentiles were expressly shown to be in this state of condemnation from their own moral depravity, *not* from any sentence of a covenant which their remote forefathers had broken, as some have fancied. Setting aside the total unreasonableness of such an imagination, nothing can be more clear or positive than the argument of St. Paul, that they stood condemned expressly *without* any such *revealed law*, and *solely by their violation of the law of conscience*, written by natural light in their hearts (Rom. ii. 15). Still less were they to be awakened by any terrors of the law of Sinai given to the Jews.

On the other hand, the Jew stood condemned because he

had transgressed the law of revelation, which he acknowledged to be holy, and just, and good, and in which he believed himself justified. St. Paul therefore expressly argues, that he was *not only not justified, but positively condemned*, by that very Law in which he trusted and made his boast, which "he approved" and "served with his mind"; yet in truth, "with his flesh he served sin" (Rom. vii. 25, &c.).* The difficulty was to convince the Jew, that *he stood condemned by his own law;* that "by it he had the knowledge of sin," that "the strength of sin was the Law," but the victory in Christ.

Both being thus *alike under condemnation*, though *by different laws*, it followed that both were to be accepted and justified on another, a new and common ground, that of faith in Jesus Christ; and the grand point thus was, that the line of separation was removed; all distinctions were merged and lost in the greater privilege now conferred by the Gospel, "of the twain was made one new man" (Eph. ii. 11–22; 1 Cor. vii. 19; Gal. vi. 15; Col. iii. 11), Christ was to be *all and in all.*

Christ redeemed the Jews "from the curse of the Law" (Gal. iii. 15; iv. 3); the Gentile "from all iniquity" (Tit. ii. 14). Both were called to repentance and faith, but on different grounds; both led, though by different ways, to moral duties; to the Jew obedience was "the fulfilment of the Law" (Gal. v. 14; Rom. xiii. 8), "the end of the commandment" (1 Tim. i. 5), "the pure service" (James i. 27 [θρησκεία]), "the royal law according to the Scripture" (James ii. 8); to the Gentile without any such reference it was simply "the things just, and pure, and true" (Phil. iv. 3), in accordance with the natural moral sense; to "live soberly, righteously, and godly" (Tit. ii. 12); to walk "honestly" (Rom. xiii. 13); but all this based on the high and peculiar motives of Christian faith.

To the Jews the grounds of Christian obligation were often

* Such at least appears to me to be the real and plain tenor of this chapter, so often imagined difficult to rescue from the eager grasp of the Antinomian.

represented and enforced by *analogies* drawn from the Old Testament. Thus the Gospel itself is by *analogy*, and with especial reference to the words of the Prophets, called a *covenant* (Heb. viii. 6; comp. Jer. xxxi. 31): not implying that there was *really* any covenant, but only that it stood in *the same relation* to Christians as *the covenant* did to the Jews; since it is expressly distinguished (indeed the whole argument of the Apostle turns on the distinction, Gal. iii. 18)* as *not really a covenant*, BUT A FREE PROMISE AND GIFT; *not* the act or deed of *two parties* as a compact, but of *one* as a gift or a testament.

The Jew was to be brought gradually to see his deliverance from the "bondage" (Gal. iv. 25; 2 Cor. iii. 6–14; Heb. xii. 18) of Sinai, effected by his increasing faith and knowledge, supported by the arguments from Abraham (Gal. iii. 6; Rom. iv. 1), and the Prophets (Hab. ii. 9; Heb. vii. 18); "the Law being his schoolmaster to bring him to Christ" (Gal. iii. 24). The Law ceased at no one time, but to each individual as his belief and enlightenment progressively emancipated him (Rom. xiv. 1–6).† It was never formally rescinded: it died a natural death.

Wherever the cessation of the Law is spoken of, it is *as a whole*, without reference to moral or ceremonial, letter or spirit. We find no such distinction as that "the Law, as being of Moses, was abrogated, yet, as the Law of the Spirit, still binding";‡ the language of St. Paul is utterly opposed to any such idea.

But if all this had been otherwise, it would little concern *us;* the Law should be contemplated as a *national and local*,

---

* The obscurity of the passage is admitted; but what I have here stated appears to me to be the real tenor of it, though fully aware of the existence of difference of opinion among commentators.

† The Rabbis held that distinctions of meats and even the Law itself were to cease when the Messiah came, as also the Sabbath, *arguing expressly from* Isa. lxvi. 23. (R. Samuel, in Talmud, in titulo *Nidr.* Cited by Grotius *de Ver.*, V. 9, 10.)

‡ See *Life of Dr. Arnold*, I. 355.

rather than as *a temporary* dispensation; for, had it *not* been *temporary*, it would still have been restricted *to one people:* the Gentiles would have had no part or concern in its *continuance* (unless as becoming proselytes to it), nor had they in its *cessation.* Christianity as addressed to the Gentiles *was not founded on Judaism:* * nor does it imply any *substitution of one obligation for another:* it stands simply on its own ground: the essential character of its institutions is independent. Its few observances were in fact at first adopted *along with* those of Mosaism, by the churches "of the circumcision," who formed so large a part of the early Christian community.

From this circumstance the teaching of the Apostles would necessarily exhibit a large infusion of Judaical ideas; and we accordingly find them introducing a multitude of adaptations of passages from the Old Testament; besides maxims and proverbial sayings (e. g. Rom. xii. 20; James v. 20; 1 Pet. iv. 8) and forms of expression, habitual among the Jews, which sometimes, mistaken for original sentiments, lead to serious misconceptions. Their reasonings would naturally be built upon opinions currently received, and on appeals to the Jewish Scriptures, of undeniable force to those who recognized its authority; and the introduction of analogies and applications of the incidents and language of the Old Testament (e. g. Rom. vii. 1; Eph. vi. 1; 1 Pet. iii. 10; 1 Tim. v. 18) for the instruction of converts who could only be convinced through such associations of the new truths with the old.

* See the whole paragraph in Ignatius (partially quoted at the beginning of this essay) for an eloquent exposition of this idea. It includes a passage which, as I think most unnecessarily, has been the subject of much discussion, as supposed to allude to the Lord's day; but it appears to me that the simple sense of *κυριακὴ ζωή* is "the Lord's life," which was to become the pattern of the spiritual life of those Jewish converts who saw their emancipation from the Law, and therefore lived *μηκέτι σαββατίζοντες,—ἀλλὰ κατὰ κυριακὴν ζωὴν ζῶντες.* See my article "LORD'S DAY," in Kitto's *Cyclopædia of Biblical Literature.*

It is in this way only that the Apostle Paul sanctions any use of the Old Testament Scriptures; as in the practical and typical accommodation of passages to points of Christian instruction (Rom. xv. 4; 1 Cor. x. 1, &c.). It was thus that even to Timothy the Old Testament was still to be "profitable," but only when applied "through faith in Jesus Christ" (2 Tim. iii. 15). And thus St. Peter (the very Apostle of the circumcision) commends the use of the prophetical writings, *only as* preparatory and auxiliary to the Gospel (2 Pet. i. 19).

The more we consider the nature of the precise points of analogy dwelt upon, the more we perceive the independent spiritual characteristics of the Gospel to which they point; as in the typical application of the temple to the body of Christ, and thence to the community of Christians (1 Cor. iii. 16); of Jerusalem to that which is above (Gal. iv. 26; Heb. xii. 22); the laver to regeneration (Tit. iii. 5, λουτρόν; Exod. xxx. 18, &c.); the altar and sacrifices primarily to the death of Christ (Heb. xiii. 10; x. 1, &c.); and thence in a lower sense to almsgiving (Heb. xiii. 16; Phil. iv. 18); to praise; to the reasonable service of Christians (Rom. xii. 1; Heb. xi. 20); the priesthood primarily to the person and office of Christ, though, in a secondary sense, to all Christians (1 Pet. ii. 9); circumcision to purity of heart (Deut. x. 16; xxx. 6; Jer. iv. 4; Rom. ii. 29; Col. ii. 11); the anointing to grace (1 John ii. 20); the Sabbath to the rest reserved for the faithful (Heb. iv. 9). In after times the same desire of adaptation without apostolic warrant, and carried often to extravagant lengths, led to a larger use of the Old Testament among Christian writers, and the spirit of allegorizing and evangelizing all parts of it. The Apostles' arguments and representations, misunderstood from want of consideration of the circumstances, and appeals *ad hominem* taken positively, in modern times have become subjects of endless mistake and confusion.

But in the Apostles' teaching we find no dependence recognized of the one system on the other; no such idea as that of a *transference* of Old Testament ordinances to Christianity; or the fulfilment of one in the other: for example, we find no appeal to the Old Testament for the basis of *marriage*, the reference of St. Paul (Eph. v. 31; 1 Cor. vii. 2) to the primeval precepts being made only incidentally, and the Christian institution essentially grounded on a different principle; we perceive no carrying on of the priesthood in the Christian ministry (which was derived from the officers of the *synagogue, not of the temple*) *; no continuation of sacrifices in the Lord's supper, or of the Sabbath in the Lord's day (charitable collections were made on the first day of the week,† 1 Cor. xvi. 2), precisely because it was *not* the Sabbath, on which they were unlawful.

Yet, from a misconception of points of analogy in such cases, often directly at variance with the express words of the Apostles, opinions have prevailed on these and the like points tending not a little to perplex and impair the simplicity of the Gospel.

All the essentially Christian institutions were independent and simple. We must carefully distinguish from the more essential and permanent, some minor ordinances of a purely temporary and occasional character, which certainly bear a more formal appearance; but were evidently adopted for the sake of peace and union, and especially for the great objects of mutually conciliating the Jewish and Gentile converts, or from a wish not abruptly to violate existing customs; as, e. g., the injunctions in the apostolic decree (Acts xv.), already referred to; and some of those given by St. Paul to the church at Corinth (as throughout 1 Cor. v., vi., and vii.), and to Timoty (1 Tim. v., &c.).

The same may be said of the practice of fasting (see Acts

---

* See Vitringa, *De Synagogâ*, of which valuable work an excellent abridged translation has been published by the Rev. J. L. Bernard. London. 1842.

† Cocceius, quoted by Vitringa, says: "This was ordained on the first day of the week, as being regarded non ut festum sed ut ἐργάσιμον." See Bernard's *Vitringa*, pp. 75 and 167.

xiii. 2) ; there does not exist a single precept or hint for its general adoption by Christians, much less is there any sanction for other ascetic observances, which soon claimed an availing merit utterly at variance with the spirit of the Gospel. So far as they had begun to prevail, they met with unequivocal censure (Col. ii. 18 – 23 ; 1 Tim. iv. 3, 8) from St. Paul. Of other institutions of Christian worship, very little can be collected from the New Testament. At first the disciples met *daily* for prayer and communion (Acts ii. 26). In one instance afterwards it *may be implied* that they assembled peculiarly on the first day of the week (Acts xx. 7) ; and in the latest period of the New Testament age " the Lord's day " is spoken of once, but wholly without explanation (Rev. i. 10).

The ministry and form of church government were borrowed directly from the synagogues, which were actually the churches of the Jewish converts. Certain peculiar regulations also were connected with the extraordinary gifts (Mark xvi. 17), as temporal visitations (1 Cor. xi. 30, &c.), and the power of inflicting them (1 Cor. v. 5), and the anointing of the sick (James v. 14, comp. with Mark xvi. 18, and vi. 13).

Christianity, as indeed it is hardly conceivable should have been otherwise, was at first communicated and established in the way of adaptation in its *outward form* to existing ideas and conditions. Thus it won its way at first according to the economic dispensations of divine grace; while its spiritual essence asserted its internal influence over the disciple who had the capacity to receive it; and under whatever outward aspect, the words of Christ were verified, "The kingdom of heaven is within you."

V. *Subsequent Views of the Law and the Gospel.*

The tendency to engraft Judaism in a greater or less degree on Christianity in the early Church, the steps by which such a system advanced and gained ground, and the extent to which it was carried, are not difficult to trace or to explain. But the peculiar turn which has been given to somewhat similar ideas in modern times is, apparently, much less easy to justify or account for on any rational principles.

The constant appeals of the Apostles to the Old Testament in their arguments with the Jews were doubtless of the most primary importance and convincing cogency with those they addressed; to the Gentiles they would not have been so; yet the peculiar character and result of the appeal was, no doubt, felt to be precisely that of valuable testimony extorted from an adverse party, and brought to support our cause, and therefore in constantly exhibiting which a sort of triumph is felt.

Hence the more general introduction in the early Church, even among the Gentiles, of the Old Testament Scriptures, and the prominence given to them, which continued by custom long after the original occasion had ceased.

But, for the Gentile converts, with the broad distinction between themselves and the Jewish churches before their eyes, this reference to the Jewish Scriptures could not by possibility degenerate into such inconsistent notions of their application as would suppose Gentile Christians brought under the obligations of the old precepts.

Without direct Judaizing, however, the gradual adoption of some Judaical forms in Christian worship naturally arose out of the synagogal model on which all the first churches were framed. And it would not be a matter of surprise if, occasionally, Judaical ideas should have been thus mixed up with Christian doctrines, institutions, and practices, even to a greater degree than we find was the case.

The Jewish converts continued, along with their other peculiarities, to observe the Sabbath, which, it is hardly necessary to say, the Gentiles did not. From an early period it seems probable that both Jewish and Gentile churches had begun to hold religious assemblies on the first day of the week. But it is from Justin Martyr * (A. D. 140) that we

* Justin., *Apol.* i. § 67. For other authorities on this point the reader is referred to my article, "LORD'S DAY," in Kitto's *Cyclopædia of Biblical Literature.*

first learn the regular establishment of this practice, as well as its professed ground and object; as being the day on which the work of creation was begun, and on which also the new spiritual creation was commenced by the resurrection of Christ. Other writers * adopt more fanciful analogies, referring to the Mosaic creation; yet always distinctly such as to exclude all idea of any reference to a primitive Sabbath (had they believed in it), which would have been an entire confusion of ideas between the day of the commencement of the creation and that of its cessation.

In the course of the first few centuries many corruptions had crept in; and we then for the first time trace some increasing precision in the observance of the Lord's day, upheld in certain expressions of Tertullian † (A. D. 200), Dionysius of Corinth (somewhat later), Clement of Alexandria,‡ Hilary,§ and others.

These writers speak of the Lord's day in conjunction with the Sabbath, but always in the way of contrast, and as obviously distinct institutions. And doubtless, with the view of conciliating the Judaizing churches it was that the celebration of both days was afterwards enjoined, both in the so-called Apostolic Constitutions ‖ (a forgery of the fourth century), and by Constantine,¶ who first prohibited business on the Lord's day,

* In the spurious Epistle of Barnabas (which, as generally allowed a forgery of the second or third century, may be taken as evidence of views then held) the writer makes out a comparison of the six days of the Creation with six ages of the world, followed by a seventh of rest under the Gospel, to which is to succeed an eighth of final triumph, and "therefore," he adds, "we keep the eighth day with joy, on which also Jesus rose from the dead." (*Ep.* I. 15.)

† *De Orat.* § 23.

‡ *Strom.* VII. 744.

§ *Comm. in Psalm. Prol.*

‖ *Apost. Const.* VII. 24.

¶ Euseb. IV. *De Vit. Const.* 18. See also Jortin's *Remarks*, III. 326. A singular exemplification of the continuance of this twofold observance, carried out even to a great degree of rigor, and preserved to modern times, has been presented in the discovery by Major Harris of an ancient Judaized Christian church in the interior of Ethiopia. Something similar has also been noticed by Mr. Grant among the Nestorians in Armenia.

with a special exception in favor of the labors of agriculture. The Council of Laodicea,* however, took an opposite tone, and censured the Sabbath, while it enjoined the Lord's day.

But though a certain kind of assimilation between the two institutions was carried farther by some later writers, yet neither was the observance itself pushed to the extent which has since been sometimes contended for; nor was it possible for that confusion of ideas between the two institutions to arise which in modern times has occasionally prevailed; and still less was such a notion as that of any transfer of the obligations of the one to the other, or any change in the day, ever conceived.†

Down to later times we trace some remains of the observance of the Sabbath in the solemnization of Saturday as the eve or vigil of the Lord's day.

The constant reference to the Old Testament law on the part of the Jewish converts not unnaturally led to the disposition to find for it at least some sort of allegorical application to the Gentiles. Thus, guided possibly by the figurative language of the Apostle (Heb. iv. 4), and the fondness for what they termed evangelizing the Old Testament, some of the Fathers adopted the idea of a metaphorical interpretation of the fourth commandment (where, of course, the literal sense could not apply) in the case of Gentile converts, as meaning the perpetual service of a Christian life. ‡

More generally, the practice of introducing even thus indirectly the sanctions of the Old Testament in later times

---

* *Counc. of Laodicea*, Can. XXIX.

† Yet so inveterate has this absurd idea become in the minds of modern divines, that even so acute and independent a writer as Bishop Warburton, arguing too expressly against the Sabbatists, speaks incidentally of "*a change in the day* having been made by the primitive Church," which it most assuredly never was. (*Div. Leg.* IV. 34, note.)

‡ Thus Justin Martyr (*Dial. cum Trypho*, 229) says, *Σαββατίζειν ἡμᾶς ὁ καινὸς νόμος διαπαντὸς ἐθέλει.* And later, to the same effect, Augustine (*Ep.* 119) observes, "Inter omnia decem præcepta solum ibi quod de sabbato positum est figurate observandum præcipitur."

began to assume the character of a more direct habitual acknowledgment of its authority. And in the earlier stage of the Reformation, some more precise theories of this kind found ready support in the extravagant notions of the literal applications of Scripture into which the violent reaction of opinions carried a portion of the Reformers, involving very peculiar notions of what was termed "the moral law" of the Old Testament, and the obligation of the Sabbath as a chief point and instance of it: a phrase, the very use of which betrays some confusion of thought, and has been at the root of all the popular errors on the subject.

The main outline of the theory seems to have been this: it was held that the Old Testament, and more especially the Decalogue, was designed to convey a revelation of the moral law to all mankind; that this law, without reference to any anterior distinctions of natural morality or the like, derives its whole force and obligation from the sole will of God positively declared, and is to be found specially summed up in these precise commandments; that all men are really subject to it even though in ignorance of it, whether Jews or Gentiles; but all, even when endeavoring to live by it, are in a state of bondage and stand condemned by it: from this bondage and condemnation the Gospel by grace and faith releases them, and they are then free from the law of works, and enjoy "Christian liberty." And there are not wanting some who pushed this idea still further, and would in fact make this freedom involve a release from the obligations of morality; which is indeed no more than a direct consequence, if moral obligations are derived from no other source than those positive commandments. Such was the consistent theory of Antinomianism, a theory which might appear startling to those not versed in theological systems, but which received obvious proof from the literal application of Scripture texts.

But against such tenets of legal and sabbatical formalism, Luther, with his accustomed masterly grasp of the breadth and depth of evangelical principles, most strenuously contended,* as did also Calvin,† especially denouncing the notion of the *moral* obligation of the Sabbath as one of the "follies of false prophets" (nugæ pseudo-prophetarum), more forcibly still in his French version, as "mensonges des faux docteurs."

Calvin also appears once to have had an intention of fixing the day of Christian worship on Thursday, as he said, "to evince Christian liberty"; and in a similar spirit Tindal says, "We are lords of the Sabbath, and may *change it* to Monday or any other day, or appoint every tenth day, or two days in a week, as we find it expedient." ‡ The idea of *changing* a Divine institution, if obligatory at all, still shows some of the common confusion prevailing in the Reformer's mind.

The complete doctrine of an identification of the Lord's day with the Sabbath seems to have been first formally propounded by Dr. Bound (1595), — a divine of great authority among the Puritans, — from whom it was adopted by the Westminster Assembly in their Confession, and thence has become a recognized tenet of the Scottish and other Presbyterian communions in Great Britain and America, though as wholly unknown to the Continental Protestants as to the old unreformed Church.

In later times this idea has been variously modified. Some, acting up to the *commandment* in strictness, consistently keep holy the seventh day of the week. Many adopt the distinction of the *Jewish* Sabbath, though we can find but one Sabbath mentioned in the Bible, or speak of the *Christian* Sabbath, — an institution wholly without warrant in the Christian Scriptures. Some turn away from all such distinctions, as mere questions of words and names. It is indeed wholly unimportant by what name we choose to designate anything; but it is important that we are not *misled* by the *name* to *mistake* the *thing*.

It is, however, a tenet nowhere inculcated in the authorized formularies of the Church of England. The Decalogue in-

---

* *Comm. on Gal.* iv. 8 – 11. † *Instit.*, II. c. 8, § 28 – 34.

‡ Reply to Sir T. More. See Morer on *Lord's day*, 216.

troduced into the Communion Service is of course to be fairly interpreted by the Catechism; where the explanation of the fourth commandment is simply, "to serve God truly all the days of my life," and that such a continual service is the only Christian Sabbath accords with the ideas of the Fathers before referred to.

It is true, among the divines of most approved reputation in the English Church there has been all along a division of opinion on the subject, not unmixed probably with the continued struggle between the Puritanizing and the Catholicizing extremes of the Reformation. They nearly all, however, even those most opposed to the Puritanical views, more or less seem intent rather on endeavoring to moderate between opposing opinions and attempting a middle path of compromise, than on grasping firmly the broad principle and maintaining a clear consistency in their own views.

With many the plea of *utility* prevails: they allege that the restraints of the Law are still requisite *for the many:* that "a preparatory discipline is as needful now as formerly"; * that the terrors of the Law are necessary to prepare men for the mercies of the Gospel. Yet in the case of a *divine appointment*, what right have we to model its application according to our ideas of the *necessity* of the case, or our conceptions of *utility?* Again, it is often elaborately argued, on the other hand, that such or such institutions are in their nature ceremonial, or would be burdensome or impracticable for general adoption, and *on that account* are to be believed not generally obligatory.

But the real question is, Supposing they were not so, were they *intended* to apply to us? In a question of divine obligation it is not the supposed excellence of an institution which would make it obligatory, any more than its inconvenience or inutility would annul it were it really enjoined.

Many who argue in support of the *abrogation* of the Law in fact take unnecessary trouble to prove the *abolition* of

* See Pusey on *Rationalism*, I. 134.

obligations of which they have not shown the *existence.* Others, contending for the *repeal* of *some parts* of the Law, labor to defend the *exceptions* before they have established the *rule.* The *onus probandi* lies on those who would *impose* the obligation, not on those who contend that it never existed.

It might be thought that the great natural principles of right and wrong evinced by reason would be too plain to admit of misapprehension or question. Yet when the reference is made to such principles of moral sense implanted in our nature, there are many who object to such a view of moral obligation as carnal and unevangelical.

It is, however, on all hands admitted, that when we turn to the pages of the New Testament, *in point of fact* all duties which can come under the denomination of *moral,* on any theory, *are distinctly included* and laid down even in literal precepts, (though certainly nowhere exhibited in any one code or summary,) but, much more, implied and involved in the whole spirit and tenor of the doctrine of Christ and the Apostles. This then to all parties may suffice to furnish a simple unassailable basis of Christian moral obligation.

It is no doubt true *also* that *some* of the same moral duties (though by no means all of them) were enjoined in particular precepts of the Mosaic Law and the prophetical books.

But those who receive the Gospel simply as the universal revelation of God's will will surely acknowledge the obligation of those duties, not *because* they may be found prescribed in the Old Testament, but *because* they form part of the spirit and principles of the New.

On any intelligible view of the principles of moral obligation, it is perfectly clear that a precept to *consecrate* any portion of time is in its nature a *positive,* not a *moral* injunction: that on no *moral* grounds can we regard *one day* as more sacred than another; and practical reasons for devoting set portions of time to religious purposes cannot apply to one seventh more than to any other portion of time. If so, just in the same way it might be argued, for example, cleanliness is a virtue; hence the ablutions and purifications of the Law are moral precepts perpetually binding.

But though there is no foundation for Sabbatism in natural *morality*, yet there is a deep-seated one in natural *formalism.* No moral or religious benefits, however, can justify a corruption of Christianity or the encouragement of superstition.

The plea of civil and social benefits derivable from such observances has been the favorite argument with many who take up the question rather on the ground of external policy than of religious truth, — and especially as maintaining a convenient hold on the minds of the multitude, which they are desirous to secure even by legislative coercion. In a word, their Sabbatism is precisely that of the legislators and philosophers of the heathen world, who by the very same arguments upheld their religious festivals.* Nor can we fail to trace precisely the same spirit in the Jewish Rabbis, who, well knowing human nature, avowed the maxim, doubtless most acceptable to the many, — "The Sabbath weigheth against all the commandments." †

Such, however, are the views which, in one form or another, have become very general among our countrymen, who, under the narrow prepossessions of an exclusive education, (in which the Decalogue, in its letter, wholly unexplained, too often forms the main religious instruction,) are commonly surprised and scandalized when they find in other Christian countries those tenets wholly unknown in which they have been kept studiously blindfolded by religious teachers, many of whom, too, know better.

Increased intercourse and information, however, it may be hoped, is now opening the eyes of many to the peculiarly

---

* Thus Seneca speaks of the practice of all legislators to enjoin public festivals and periods of relaxation as essential to the good of the state (*De Tranq. Anim.*); and Plato, carrying the matter higher, says, "The gods, pitying mankind born to painful labor, appointed for an ease and cessation of their toils the recurrence of festival seasons observed to the gods." (*De Leg.*, II. 787.)

† Midrash, in Exod. xxvi.

national prejudices on these subjects; an object to which nothing seems more likely to contribute than attention to the simple matter-of-fact view of the whole question here attempted to be followed up.

Conclusion.

To recapitulate and conclude: — "God spake in times past in sundry portions and under divers forms to the fathers"; but "in these last days unto us by his Son." All the Divine declarations are to be understood according to their manifest purpose, and with reference to the parties addressed. It may be true, that "God spake these words," but not *therefore* TO US. Our concern is not with what was *at first*, but with what has been revealed "in these *last* days." The Old Testament is to us nothing, except as applied in the New. *Temporary* dispensations have *passed away*, and with *national* dispensations *we have no concern.* We Gentiles are "not under the Law," *not* because it has been *abolished*, but because to us it *never existed.* The New Testament does not bring us under the Old. If we were not "under grace," we should only be under nature, not the Law.

Meats and days, ordinances and Sabbaths, if primeval, have ceased; if Judaical, are national. To introduce such observances under the plea of utility and policy, is to disparage Divine authority. Expediency is not to be set up against truth. Our sole rule must be that of Gospel truth: to adopt any other is to pretend to know more of the will of God than is revealed in the Gospel. Christianity recognizes the universal and eternal moral law; but exalts and enlarges it, and sets it on a firmer basis. Distinctions of days have no connection with morality; under the Gospel no one day is more holy than another; its service is a perpetual one, "in spirit and in truth."

Christianity is not the religion of Moses, nor of Abraham, nor of Adam, but something far better. To mix it with extraneous additions, even from those dispensations, is to pervert its very nature and object, which is to supersede and crown them all; — to impair its efficacy by ingrafting on it an unevangelic formalism most alien from its spirit; — to lay it open to the attacks of the objector, and give the strongest handle to scepticism. And to instil such principles in education in these times is but to lay the train for a fearful reaction; when, on the contrary, it ought to be the more peculiar endeavor of every sincere and enlightened advocate of the Gospel to vindicate its spiritual and rational character, and the practical simplicity of its principles, — at once the source of its power, the test of its truth, and the ground of its stability and perpetuity.

THE DOCTRINE OF INSPIRATION.

By Dr. F. A. D. THOLUCK,

PROFESSOR OF THEOLOGY IN THE UNIVERSITY OF HALLE.*

Part I. — HISTORICAL.

Sect. 1. — *Introductory. — The Reformers and their Immediate Successors. — Origin, in Modern Times, of the rigid View of Inspiration.*

The older form of doctrine concerning the Inspiration of the Scriptures furnished Rationalism with one of its chief points of attack upon the teaching of the Church. This older doctrine, however, does not reach so far back as the age of the Reformation. As regards the great witnesses of the Reformation, so mightily had the word of God in the Scriptures made good to their hearts the "demonstration of the spirit and of power" (1 Cor. ii. 4) belonging to it, that, without feeling any necessity to account in detail for those constituent parts of Scripture, in which that word of God was not contained, they bore this testimony as with one voice, — "Here is the word of God, the standard of all Truth."

But, in proportion as matters drew near to the close of that first Protestant period, in which, through the testimony of the Holy Spirit in the soul and the Holy Spirit in the Scriptures reciprocally, the direct evidence of Evangelical truth was sus-

---

* Translated from the German for Kitto's Journal of Sacred Literature.

tained in life; and in proportion as controversy, sharpened by Jesuitism, made the Protestant party sensible of the necessity of an externally fortified ground of combat; in that same proportion did Protestantism seek, by the exaltation of the outwardly authoritative character of the sacred writings, to recover that infallible authority which it had lost through its rejection of inspired councils and the infallible authority of the Pope.

In this manner arose, amongst both Lutheran and Reformed divines, not earlier, strictly speaking, than the seventeenth century, those sentiments concerning the inspiration of Holy Scripture which regarded it as the infallible production of the Divine Spirit, not merely in its *religious*, but in its *entire* contents; and not merely in its *contents*, but also in its very *form*. In both Protestant churches (the Lutheran and the Reformed) it was taught that the writers of the Bible were to be regarded as writing-pens wielded by the hand of God,* and amanuenses of the Holy Spirit who dictated,† whom God uses as the flute-player does his instrument; ‡ not only the *sense*, but also the *words*, and not these merely, but even the *letters*, and the *vowel-points*, which in Hebrew are written under the consonants, — according to some, the very *punctuation*, — proceeded from the Spirit of God.§ It is true, that there are modes of conception and expression, and individual diversities, apparent in the sacred authors; but these were to be regarded only as the effect of the Holy Spirit's adaptation. ‖ It might be further submitted as a question, whether the Holy Spirit descended to grammatical errors, barbarisms, and solecisms. By *Musaeus* and some others, indeed, this was asserted to be the case: but by the greater number such an assumption was considered blasphemous; and by Quenstedt and others the difficulty was so far disposed of, that what to the Greeks was

* "Dei calami." † "Spiritus sancti dictantis notarii."

‡ *Quenstedt*, Theol. Didact. Polem., P. I. 55. *Heidegger*, Corp. Theol., II. 34.

§ *Calovius*, I. 484. *Maresius*, Syntag. Theol., p. 8.

‖ *Quenstedt*, Theol. Didact. Polem., P. I. 76.

a barbarism, was not necessarily such in the eyes of the Church.* By some, again, the thorough purity and classical character of the New Testament language were asserted.†

With greater or less consistency and strictness, this opinion is still adhered to by the Kirk of Scotland [and the Free Church]. It has also found in Professor Gaussen,‡ of the Evangelical Academy at Geneva, a devout and rhetorical defender, causing even a violent breach in the bosom of that institution. In Germany it has been advocated by Rudelbach, whose treatise, however, in the *Lutherischen Zeitschrift von Rudelbach und Guericke*, from 1840 till the present time (1850), has been occupied solely with the historical part of the question. But among the great majority of German theologians, the defenders, too, of an orthodox theology, in consequence of the historico-critical biblical investigations introduced since the middle of the last century, the rigidity of the system which prevailed during the seventeenth century has been more and more relaxed; and the Protestant theology of foreign countries also, such as that of the Church of England and of the Dissenters, as also that of the French, Danish, and Swedish churches, has given to the dogma of inspiration a more liberal construction.

In the succeeding historical part of this Essay, which, by the way, makes no pretension to scientific fulness and completeness, it shall be shown, first of all, that the more liberal aspect referred to has no unfriendly bearing upon Evangelical doctrine. So far from its being open to the suspicion of being the fruit of modern Rationalism, it has, on the contrary, *found advocates in all ages of the Church*, and, at least, was involuntarily developed as soon as a person reflected upon the peculiarities of the text. By the Lutheran historian of the doctrine, mentioned above,§ witnesses of *this* kind are for the most part passed over in silence, especially those in the early

* Ibid., p. 84.

† *H. Stephens*, *Seb. Pfochen*, *Hollaz*, *Georgi*, and others.

‡ In his work, "La Theopneustié, ou l'Inspiration Plénière," &c.

§ Rudelbach.

Church. The present Essay will supply this defect. But although this be so, not only is it impossible on this account to consider it *un-Christian,* it cannot even for once be shown to be *un-Lutheran.* Of course, we say this on the assumption that we do not regard the rigorous propositions of Lutheran divines, any more than the more liberal individual expressions of Luther, as constituting the measure of what is Lutheran, but confine our attention solely to the Lutheran *confessions of faith.* For, while the more rigid definitions of inspiration above alluded to are omitted in some Reformed symbols,* for instance, in the *Formula Consensus,* the Lutheran symbols contain no express declaration whatever upon the inspiration of the Scriptures. The expressions which have a bearing upon the question in the symbolical books are found collected by Köllner in his *Symbolic der Lutherischen Kirche,* p. 612.

SECT. 2. — *The Inspired Word distinguished.*

The word *inspiration,*† borrowed from 2 Tim. iii. 16, characterizes the contents of the sacred writings as having proceeded from the *breath,* the *spirit* of God. In what manner arises in the minds of the readers of a theopneustic ‡ writing this conviction of its origin? We answer: It arises from the certainty that the *effects produced* by the contents of the writing upon the intellect, the will, and the feeling, are capable of leading to a religiously moral self-satisfaction, — as that passage expresses it, they are able "*to make the man of God perfect.*" Now the truth is, that, properly speaking, the Scripture is for those contents — for the divinely efficacious facts, expressions, and truths — only *the vessel which contains them;* but the immediate consciousness, by metonymy, transfers what may be predicated of the *contents,* to the containing *vessel* itself. A clear illustration of this is supplied by Gal. iii. 8: "And the Scripture, foreseeing that God would justify the heathen by faith, preached before the Gospel unto

---

* Standards, or doctrinal creeds. — TR.

† "Eingeistung" = inspiriting.

‡ Divinely inspired.

Abraham, saying, In thee shall all nations be blessed." Here the gift of prophecy is ascribed to the writing itself, because it *contains* predictions. Those parts of the contents of Scripture, however, from which the effects above referred to do *not* directly flow, such as a genealogical table, a list of encampments, and the like, stand more or less in *indirect* connection, at least, with the rest.

As long, then, as the immediate religious consciousness has not developed itself into reflection, it extends the idea of inspiration to these portions of Scripture also, although not without the slumbering acknowledgment that the Divine breath, or spirit, does not exercise an equal control throughout the whole: in proportion as it is external and incidental is it less in degree. That this acknowledgment does slumber in the background is evident as soon as reflection is directed to such incidental externalities. Let us suppose it to be proved to the simple-minded Christian that Paul, in 1 Cor. x. 8, where he writes, "There fell in one day twenty-three thousand," must have committed an error of memory, inasmuch as in the Old Testament narrative recording the fact,* the number twenty-four thousand is given; or, that Matthew commits an error of memory when he ascribes the passage concerning the thirty pieces of silver to Jeremiah,† while it really occurs in Zechariah xi. 12, 13. What condition would he be in? At first, doubtless, he would confidently declare that no error of memory could exist, — that there might be some other solution of the difficulty; although to all learned men such solution were unknown. But suppose that upon this it should be explained to him that Paul, in 1 Cor. i. 16, while writing an inspired Epistle, does really not lay claim to infallibility of memory in such details.‡ What would be his reply to this? From his own religious necessity, he would have no objection whatever to offer to such (supposed) failure of memory; only he would still be unable to suppress the fear, that, by conced-

* Numb. xxv. 9.

† Matt. xxvii. 9, 10.

‡ "And I baptized also the household of Stephanas: besides, *I know not that I baptized any other*."

ing failure of memory in one place, other and more material truths of Scripture might lose their certainty and infallibility. If one could only set him at rest on *this* matter, — by making it manifest to his mind that the evidence of no material truth would be thereby impaired, — he would doubtless willingly abandon the accuracy of those statements, as a thing not essential to his religious wants.

Sect. 3. — *The Fathers.*

With this kind of unreflecting reverence for the Sacred Scriptures as records proceeding from the Spirit of God, and pervaded by him, we find the ancient Church Fathers also filled. We discover amongst them no *searching exposition,* no *elaborated theory.* Nay, what is altogether remarkable, we do not find these things even during the lapse of succeeding centuries, until, after the Reformation, we reach the doctrinal theology of the Lutheran and Reformed churches. Men were satisfied with general and occasional expressions. Where the Church Fathers, without reflecting more precisely upon details, give us the sum total of their *impression* concerning the Holy Scripture, they acknowledge their belief in its inspiration, and designate it by the names, "Divine writing," "divinely inspired writing," "Instrumentum divinum," "Cœlestes Literæ," &c.

Justin Martyr, about the middle of the second century, says: "Such exalted things could not be known by human reflection, but only by means of a heavenly gift which descended upon holy men. These men needed no artificial eloquence, — no skilful art of disputation: but they merely yielded up their pure souls to the inward operation of the Divine Spirit. As a bow upon a lyre evokes tones of music, so the Deity used these pious men as instruments to make known to us heavenly things." *

"The Holy Scriptures," says Origen, in the third century,

* Cohort. ad Gentes, c. 8. [For his views on the inspiration of the Prophets, see his Apol. I., 56, 57, ed. Paris, 1815. — Tr.]

"are penetrated throughout as by the wind by the fulness of the Spirit; and there is nothing therein, either in the Prophets, or the Law, or the Gospels, or in the Apostolical writings, which does not proceed from the Divine Majesty." *

Eusebius, in the fourth century, commenting on Psalm xxxiii. 34, declares: "I hold it to be presumptuous for any man to say that the Holy Scripture has erred." †

Augustine, also, in the fourth century, declares it as his "most settled belief, that none of the writers of the books called canonical committed any error whatever in writing." ‡

At the same time, however, they may have had in view the sense of Scripture more than the words; for so carelessly were verbal citations then made, that the writers who flourished up to the end of the second century quote the language of Scripture sometimes from oral traditions, but for the most part merely from memory, and, at times, with the greatest deviations from our text. Besides, the Old Testament was known to them only in the Alexandrian Greek translation (Septuagint), and they must, therefore, if they claimed for the Book a *literal* inspiration, extend it, without any warrant for so doing, to that translation also. This Justin Martyr does; but none else.

At the same time, it is important to bear in mind that many of their expressions give far more explicit proof that their general statements concerning the divinity of the sacred writings are not to be understood absolutely. At all events,

---

* In Jerem. Hom. II.

† Also his Eccles. Hist., Lib. III. cap. 24.

‡ "Ego solis eis scripturarum libris, qui jam canonici appellantur, didici hunc timorem honoremque deferre, ut nullum eorum auctorem scribendo aliquid errasse firmissime credam."

[At the same time, it cannot be denied that passages are also to be met with, especially in Augustine and Jerome, from which it is evident that there were occasions on which they were compelled to modify their views. Thus Augustine accounts for the variations found in many parts of the Gospels on the principle that each writer exercised freely his mental faculties, and presented his own peculiar aspect of facts and circumstances, &c. Henderson, Div. Insp., 2d ed., p. 50. — Tr.]

they did not refer to it in the sense in which it has been taught by the post-Reformation divines.

We begin with a man who was an immediate disciple of our Lord, — the Presbyter John. Far from entertaining the idea that the contents of their writings were supernaturally delivered to the Apostles, — and, by the way, the passage in Luke i. 1 – 3 would not agree with such a supposition, — he relates concerning the composition of the Gospel of Mark as follows: "He (Mark) was the interpreter of Peter, and carefully recorded all that he retained from him in his memory, without binding himself to the chronological order of the words and deeds of Christ." *

In like manner, Irenæus, about the end of the second century, cannot have held the opinion that the contents of Paul's writings had been imparted to him while in a purely passive state. A treatise was composed by this Father "On the Peculiarities of the Pauline Style," in which he acknowledges the unsyntactic construction of the Apostle, and accounts for it on the ground of "the rapidity of his utterances, and the impulsiveness of spirit which distinguished him." † Such an influence of his personal peculiarity upon his expressions would be incompatible with the assumption that the Apostle at the time of inspiration was in a purely passive state.

Origen, although in other respects an advocate of the most rigid theory of inspiration, boldly makes a distinction between the words of the Lord and those of the Apostles. He says: "Those who are truly wise in Christ are of opinion that the Apostolical writings have indeed been disposed wisely, credibly, and with reverence for God; but, nevertheless, not to be compared with such declarations as 'Thus saith the Lord Almighty.' And on this account we must consider whether, when Paul says, '*All Scripture is inspired by God and use-*

---

* Eusebius, Eccles. Hist., III. 39.

† "Velocitas sermonum suorum, et propter impetum, qui in ipso est, spiritûs."

ful,' * he includes his own Epistles, and whether he would exclude some parts of them, such as those where it is said, '*That which I speak, I speak not after the Lord*'; † and this, '*As I teach everywhere in every church*'; ‡ and again, '*At Antioch, at Iconium, at Lystra, what persecutions I endured*'; § and other like things which here and there he has written of his own knowledge, and by authority (κατ' ἐξουσίαν), but yet which have not flowed forth purely and entirely from divine inspiration." ‖ He declares, also, that, according to the *historical* sense, an insoluble contradiction exists between John and Matthew in relation to our Lord's last Passover journey. "I believe it to be impossible," he says, "for those who upon this subject direct attention merely to the external history, to prove that this apparent contradiction is capable of being harmonized." ¶

Augustine, who, on the one hand, is unwilling that it should be said that Christ wrote nothing, since the Apostles were only his hands in writing,** declares, nevertheless, on the other hand,†† that each of the Evangelists has written, sometimes more and sometimes less fully, as each remembered, and as each had it in his heart: ‡‡ and asserts §§ that the words

---

* Dr. Tholuck's rendering: "Alle Schrift ist von Gott eingegeben und nützlich." Gr. Πᾶσα γραφὴ θεόπνευστος καὶ ὠφέλιμος, κ. τ. λ. 2 Tim. iii. 16. — Tr.

† 2 Cor. xi. 17. Also comp. 1 Cor. vii. 40.

‡ 1 Cor. iv. 17.

§ 2 Tim. iii. 11.

‖ In Johann., Tom. I. p. 4, ed. 1668.

¶ Ibid., Tom. I. p. 183. — Tr.

** De Consensu Evangel., I. 35.

†† Ibid., II. 12.

‡‡ "Ut quisque meminerat, et ut cuique cordi erat."

§§ De Consensu Evangel., II. 28. "Quæ cum ita sint per hujusmodi evangelistarum locutiones varias, sed non contrarias, rem plane utilissimam discimus et pernecessariam, nihil in cujusque verbis nos debere inspicere, nisi voluntatem, cui debent verba servire, nec mentiri quemquam, si aliis verbis dixerit quid ille voluerit, cujus verba non dicit: ne miseri aucupes vocum apicibus quodammodo literarum putent ligandam esse veritatem, cum utique non in verbis tantum, sed etiam in cæteris omnibus signis animorum non sit nisi ipse animus inquirendus."

of the Evangelists might be ever so contradictory, provided only that their *thoughts* were the same.

Jerome, who was an accomplished grammarian, so fully recognized the diversities incident to the style of the Apostles, that he often imputes solecisms to their language, and writes of Paul that he had used "*sermone trivii,*" *street language.**

The great bishop and expositor, Chrysostom, who declared such confidence in the Scripture as to say that all the contradictions (enantiophonien) found there are, after all, only *apparent* contradictions (enantiophanien),† has nevertheless taken the liberty to remark upon the words of Paul in Acts xxvi. 6: "He speaks humanly, and does not throughout enjoy grace, but it is permitted him even to intermix his own materials." ‡

We see, then, that even amongst the ancient Church Fathers, although they had a general impression of the divinely inspired character of Scripture, the opinion that its language was human and imperfect was held to be unmistakable; that verbal contradictions, nay, contradictions even in matters of fact, were ascribed to it without hesitation; and that the authority of the Apostolical writings was regarded as secondary to those which were said to have proceeded immediately from God himself.

SECT. 4. — *Views of Inspiration in the Roman Catholic Church. — The Scholastics.*

The Catholic Church, since the time when the dogma of the infallibility of ecclesiastical tradition as the interpreter of

---

* Ad. Fol., 3. 1. "Jerome, when commenting on the passage Gal. v. 12, finds no difficulty in supposing that St. Paul, in the choice of an expression, is governed by the vehemence of an emotion, arising, however, out of a pure temper of heart. 'Nec mirum esse, si Apostolus, ut homo, et adhuc vasculo clausus infirmo, vidensque aliam legem in corpore suo captivantem se et ducentem in lege peccati, semel fuerit hoc loquutus, in quod frequenter sanctos viros cadere perspicimus.'" Neander, Church Hist., IV. p. 12, ed. Clark. — TR.

† Opera, Tom. VII. p. 5.

‡ Ibid., Tom. X. p. 364. Ἀνθρωπίνως διαλέγεται καὶ οὐ πανταχοῦ τῆς χάριτος ἀπολαύει, ἀλλὰ καὶ παρ' ἑαυτοῦ τὶ συγχωρεῖται εἰσφέρειν.

Holy Scripture was developed, must still less have felt a desire to give any extension to the doctrine of Inspiration. The Scholastics, when they treat of any principle of theological science, certainly give expression to the idea that the latter has a principle different from philosophy, — the *revelatio* laid down in Holy Scripture; but into the question concerning the *extent* of its inspiration, they do not, at least more closely, enter. Expressions marked by liberality transpire even during these dark times. Thus Bishop Junilius,* in the sixth century, to the question, "How is the authority of the sacred books to be considered?" returns the answer, "Some are of perfect authority, some of partial authority, and some of none at all." Amongst the second class (those of *partial* authority) he included the book of Job, the books of Chronicles, Ezra, and others; and amongst the last class (those of *no* authority whatever), those which are properly Apocryphal.

In the ninth century, Agobard, Archbishop of Lyons, writes: "What absurdity will follow if the notion is maintained, concerning the Prophets and Apostles, that the Holy Spirit inspired them not only with the *sense* of their predictions, and the forms or arguments of their phraseology, but also that he fashioned in their lips the very words themselves bodily and outwardly." †

In the works of the Greek Catholic expositor Euthymius Zigabenus, in the twelfth century, the following words are found upon Matt. xii. 8: "It is not to be wondered at if one Evangelist relates this, and the other passes by that; for they did not write down the Gospels immediately from the lips of Christ, so as to be able to give a perfect impression of all his words, but many years after he had spoken. And since they were men, they were liable to omit many things through forgetfulness. This will explain to you how one may have recorded what another may have omitted. Oftentimes they have made large omissions, simply for the sake of brevity; sometimes because they thought the matter to be unnecessary."

* De Partibus Div. Legis, 1. 8.

† Adv. Fredegisum, c. 12.

The Scholastic theology introduced a distinction between what *directly*, and what *indirectly*, belongs to faith; a distinction which is pertinent to our subject, and may also serve as a basis for a theory of inspiration. "Those things belong *directly* to faith," says Thomas Aquinas, in the thirteenth century, "which to us are pre-eminently of *Divine origin*, as, that God exists in a Trinity of persons; and to hold a false opinion concerning these is the very cause of heresy. On the other hand, things belonging to faith *indirectly*, are those from which *follows* anything contrary to faith, as if, for example, any one should assert that Samuel was not the son of Elkanah; for from this it would follow that the Scripture is false." *

From the interest here mentioned there arises also, amongst ourselves, ever afresh, the practical need of an unexceptionable and uniform inspiration of the Scripture. How this need is to be judged of will be the subject to be handled in our second part. Here the language of the great Church Father just quoted (Aquinas), may only serve as a testimony that the religious consciousness in man, when it reflects upon itself, *makes a distinction* between the several parts of Scripture, agreeably to which the necessity also for its inspiration is a *mediate* or an *immediate* necessity. Besides, the Scholastics, in contending for the exclusion of all error, have been so far from maintaining strict consistency, that we find at least in Abelard a concession of individual doctrinal errors. He says ("Sic et Non," ed. Cousin, p. 11): "It is certain that the Prophets themselves were at times destitute of prophetic grace, and that in their official capacity as Prophets, while believing that they were in possession of the *spirit of prophecy*, they declared, *by their own spirit*, some things that were *fallacious;* and this was permitted them in order to preserve their humility, — in other words, that they might more truly know the difference between themselves as persons receiving Divine assistance, and as relying solely upon the guidance of their

* Summa Theol., I. Qu. 32, art. 4. (Ed. Antw. 1585.) — TR.

own spirit." He then cites the instance of Peter, who on account of a deviation from the truth had been so severely censured by Paul, and adds: "What wonder is it, therefore, seeing that it is certain that even Prophets and Apostles were not entirely free from error, if amongst so great a number of Church Fathers a few writings appear to have been issued containing mistakes."

The Catholic Confession of the Council of Trent has given no more direct explanation of the sense in which the Sacred Scripture is to be considered as divinely inspired than the Lutheran symbols.* In Sessio IV. the canonical writings are mentioned, and it is there only incidentally stated that the Apostles wrote as it was dictated to them by the Holy Ghost.† The opinions of Catholic theologians have so moved between two boundary lines, that by some, in the same manner as by the Protestants, the strictest literal inspiration has been advocated, ‡ while by others inspiration has been restricted to those portions only which contain doctrinal matter; § but the decisive authority of the Church interfered not with their differences. By the most eminent authorities, — the Jesuit Bellarmine, the Dominican Camas, the learned Bonfrère, the jesuitically famous Cornelius à Lapide, and others, *revelatio* proper was distinguished from divine assistance (*assistentia*); the latter being an influence which kept those from error who wrote by the force of their own minds. ‖ Many amongst them make no scruple in conceding that the Evangelists fall into errors. The celebrated Canus supposes an error of memory in Stephen in the passage Acts vii. 16.¶ Erasmus treats in like manner some passages in Matthew.

* Creeds.

† "Spiritu sancto dictante."

‡ Vide *Casp. Sanctius*, *Salazar*, *Huet*, and *Este*.

§ *Antonius de Dominis*, *Richard Simon*, *Henry Holden* in the *Analysis Fidei*, 1685, &c.

‖ *Quenstedt*, I. ch. 4, p. 67 et seq.; *Rich. Simon*, in his Criticisms on the New Test., I. c. 24.

¶ Where Ephron the Hittite is called "Ephron the father of Sichem." Comp. Gen. xxiii. — Tr.

Maldonatus, in referring to Matt. xxvi. 28, "For this is my blood of the New Testament," &c., declares his belief that the words of the institution of the Lord's Supper have been more correctly given by Matthew and Mark than by Luke and Paul.* Antonius de Dominis judges as follows concerning such defects: "Mistakes of this kind, which touch not the substance of the fact, neither do, nor can do, any injury to the faith; nor do they relate to any portion of the Divine Faith which demands belief, but to that which carries with it a knowledge which is merely human, and thought out by the mind." †

SECT. 5. — *Lutheran and Reformed Divines.*

The leading dogmatical works of the two Protestant churches, ‡ the *Loci Theologici* of Melancthon, and the Christian Institutes of Calvin, like the *symbolical* writings of the Lutheran Church, propound no doctrine of Inspiration. They convey a general impression of the divinity and credibility of the Biblical writings, and nothing more. With many strong expressions, Luther bears testimony to the Bible as a book whose entire contents are useful and salutary; § in which are no contradictions; ‖ and every letter, nay, every tittle, of which is of more significance than heaven and earth together; ¶ and so on. And yet he has not hesitated to utter the well-known offensive declarations concerning the Canon of Holy Scripture. It is true that at a later period he considerably softened down his opinions on these points, but he still freely ascribed to the Scriptures imperfections or logical errors. In his preface to Linken's "Annotations on the first Five Books of Moses," ** he says: "Doubtless the Prophets studied the writings of Moses, and the last Prophets studied the first, and wrote down in a book the good thoughts which the Holy Spirit

* *Quenstedt,* I. ch. 4, p. 75; *R. Simon,* I. p. 185.

† *R. Simon,* I. p. 525.

‡ The Lutheran, and the Reformed or Calvinistic Church. — TR.

§ Walch, I. 1196. Ibid., II. 1758.

‖ Ibid., VIII. 2140. ¶ Ibid., VIII. 2161. ** Ibid., XIV. 172.

excited (vom H. Geiste eingegeben) within them. But allowing that these good, faithful teachers and searchers of the Scripture sometimes build with a mixture of hay, straw, and stubble, and not entirely with silver, gold, and precious stones, the foundation nevertheless remains unshaken; as for the other, the fire will consume it." Luther also took the liberty to understand Old Testament words in a sense different from that which is given them as they are explained in the New Testament. This passage from Isa. viii. 17, 18, — "And I will wait upon the Lord, that hideth his face from the house of Jacob, and I will look for him. Behold, I and the children whom the Lord hath given me are for signs and for wonders in Israel," &c. — is understood, as quoted by the author of the Epistle to the Hebrews (ii. 13), as a declaration made by Christ; but Luther, in his Commentary upon Isaiah, explains it as a declaration by the Prophet himself.* Concerning the argument of Paul, conducted on the ground of a typical apprehension of the history of Hagar and Sarah,† he frankly declares that it "is too unsound to stand the test, and yet it throws a clear light upon the question of faith." In relation to the sections forming the twenty-fourth chapter of Matthew, and the twenty-first chapter of Luke, where commentators have had much disputation as to what portions refer to the destruction of Jerusalem, and what to the end of the world, he is of opinion that Matthew and Mark have mixed both events together indiscriminately, and do not observe the order which Luke has observed.‡ According to Genesis xii. 1 – 11, God first appeared to Abraham in Haran; according to Acts vii. 2, he had already appeared to him in Mesopotamia. Luther observes upon this: "It appears to me that Moses narrates this history carefully and accurately: not so Stephen, who has only borrowed it from Moses. Now, it often happens that, when one gives a plain, hasty narration of anything, he does not pay such close attention to all the circumstances, as

* Walch, VI. 121 et seq.

† Gal. iv. 22 et seq.

‡ Walch, XI. 2496.

they must do who wish to write faithfully a history of past occurrences, for the benefit of posterity. Moses is an historian: Stephen relies upon the fact that the history stands written by Moses" [and that hence his hearers, perusing that history, were in no danger of being misled by his cursory detail of facts]. In Gen. xv. 13, the duration of the Egyptian bondage is given as four hundred years; Exod. xii. 40, gives it at four hundred and thirty years; while Paul, on the contrary, in Gal. iii. 17, following the *Septuagint* and the *Samaritan* (Pentateuch) reckons the time from the period *when the promise was given to Abraham* until the end of the Captivity, at four hundred and thirty. Now, Luther first endeavors, under the guidance of Lyra, by unnatural wresting, to reconcile this calculation of Paul with the text, and then, at Gen. xv. 13, he makes the admission that here the historian "does not very closely and accurately calculate the time." *

With him, however, such questions are generally insignificant. Of mistakes in answering questions concerning matters purely historical, he says: "These mistakes are of such a nature as to do no damage to the faith, nor do they prejudice our cause; concerning Truth alone must we firmly adhere to the Sacred Scripture, and rigidly defend it, while we leave to others things that are darker, to be settled by their own judgments." † Giving his opinion on the book of Job in his "Table Talk," he observes: "This book, excellent as it is, was not written by him (Job), nor concerning him only, but all the afflicted. Job did not actually utter the *words* ascribed to him; but his *thoughts* were such as are there represented. The book unfolds itself before us, both in matter and execution, much after the manner of a comedy, and the strain of its argument is almost that of a *fable*." ‡

The same liberal mode of viewing the verbal fidelity and the chronological accuracy of the history, presents itself in

---

* Walch, XI. 1448. † Ibid., 1089.

‡ Colloquia, ed. Frankf. 1571, II. 102.

Calvin's Harmony of the Gospels. Luke — to give an instance — has related that temptation of Christ as *second*, which in Matthew is the *third*. Upon this Calvin remarks: "It signifies nothing at all, for it was not the intention of these Evangelists so to weave the thread of history as always to preserve exactly the order of time, but to collect, as they would present in a mirror or on a tablet, a *summary* of those things which it is most advantageous for us to know concerning Christ."

Luke * differs from Matthew † in his manner of stating the command of our Lord concerning that high manifestation of patient endurance, where a man, after being deprived of one garment, yields up again another. Calvin, referring to this, simply observes, "Diverse readings in Matthew and Luke change not the sense." In the Epistle to the Hebrews, chap. xi. 21, the passage found in Gen. xlvii. 31 is quoted according to the Greek version (Septuagint), ‡ which follows a reading different from the Hebrew text. § Calvin briefly remarks, "We well know that the Apostles were not, in this matter (of quotation), so very precise; but in reality there is little difference." Concerning 1 Cor. x. 8, where Paul mentions twenty-three thousand instead of twenty-four thousand, Calvin says, "It is not a new thing, where it is not intended to present a minute enumeration of individuals, to give a number which substantially approximates the actual truth." Upon Matthew xxvii. 9, he says it is clear that Zechariah must here be read instead of Jeremiah; and adds, "How the name of Jeremiah crept in here, I confess I do not know, nor am I anxious about the matter." In that candid way does Calvin judge concerning the more external errors of memory. And as to the *doctrinal* contents of Scripture, he speaks as follows: "Seeing that heavenly oracles are not of every-day occurrence, they obtain complete authority among believers

* Chap. vi. 29. † Chap. v. 40.

‡ Καὶ προσεκύνησεν ἐπὶ τὸ ἄκρον τῆς ῥάβδου αὐτοῦ.

§ Eng. Vers. from Hebr.: "And Israel bowed himself upon the bed's head."

only when they prove themselves to have proceeded from heaven, as if the very living words of God themselves are distinctly heard therein."

Zuinglius, in treating of the Church Fathers, has given a canon which accords infallibility to Christ alone, so withholding it from the Apostles. These are the words: "It is not true that the writings of all holy men are infallible; nor is it true that they do not err. This pre-eminence must be given to the Son of God alone out of the whole human race." *

The immediate followers, also, of the German Reformers, as well as those of the Swiss Reformers, speak of certain imperfections in the Biblical writers, in a manner not consistent with very extreme notions of Inspiration. Bugenhagen, † in the scheme he drew up for harmonizing the narratives of our Lord's passion, remarks: "Consider that the Evangelists wrote each for himself what they saw, and oftentimes while they record what occurred, they are heedless of the *order* of occurrence." He also takes especial care to expose the errors of the Alexandrine translation (Septuagint), which have sometimes been transferred to the New Testament.

Likewise Breuz, upon Rom. ix. 25, ‡ remarks, "that the quotation does not give the true sense of the Old Testament text, but that the purport is the same.

Bullinger, the Swiss, very ingenuously allows that the sacred penmen were liable to *errors of memory*. In reference to 1 Cor. x. 8, he writes: "Transcribers easily fall into error in stating numbers; but sometimes the *writers* also were led *by treacherous memories into the commission of mistakes.*"

Castellio, another Swiss theologian, complains that Paul, in

---

* Schriften von Usteri und Vögelin, II. 247.

† Bugenhagen was a distinguished promoter of the Reformation in Denmark. Vide Münter's Kirch. Geschichte von Danemark und Norwegen. — Tr.

‡ "As he saith also in Osee, I will call them my people which were not my people; and her beloved, which was not beloved." Quoted from Hos. ii. 23.

Rom. ix., has not expressed his meaning more fully and openly; and brings against the Apostle's logic the charge, that it confounds together two comparisons which ought to have been kept distinct,* &c.

Moreover, after Melancthon, the Lutheran Church had no knowledge of such definitions concerning inspiration as represent it affecting minute details. The "Loci Theologici" of Chemnitz, 1591, leave the dogma of the Holy Scriptures † entirely undiscussed; and even John Gerhard, at the commencement of the seventeenth century (1610 – 25), while indeed in his "Loci Theologici," that most important dogmatical work of the Lutheran Church, he has definitions of great strictness upon the *authority* of Scripture, and its *perfection*, nevertheless said nothing in his *earlier* writings upon the subject of its inspiration. ‡ Definitions that go into detail first occur in "Systema Theologicum" of Calovius, § in the second half of this century (1655 – 77). As to what opinions the Reformed Church adopted on the subject, we may say that its earlier confessions confine themselves entirely to the mere assertion of the inspiration of the Bible as a dogma. The "Formula Consensus Helvetici," which appeared not earlier than 1675, declares in detail concerning the Old Testament: "It is divinely inspired (*θεόπνευστος*), equally as regards the consonants, the vowels, and even the vowel-points, or at least as it regards the force of the vowel-points, both as to matter and as to words." ‖ To this position most of the divines of the Reformed Church adhere. Inspiration, in the widest extent of the idea, is especially vindicated by the erudite Professor Voetius, of the University of Utrecht, in a

---

* Dial. II. De Electione, pp. 103, 107, 132.

† The dogma concerning the nature and authority of Scripture. — Tr.

‡ By direction of Dr. Tholuck in a recent communication the translation here varies slightly from the original text. — Tr.

§ Calovius died 1686. It is said that he daily offered up the petition, "Imple me, Deus, odio hæreticorum!" — Tr.

‖ "Tum quoad consonas, tum quoad vocalia, et puncta ipsa, sive punctorum saltem potestatem, et tum quoad res, tum quoad verba, *θεόπνευστος*."

treatise entitled "Quousque se extendat Auctoribus Scripturæ Inspiratio." * "Not a word," it is here said, "is contained in the Holy Scriptures which was not in the strictest sense inspired, — the very interpunctuation not excepted: even what the writers previously knew was given them afresh by inspiration; and this was the case, not indeed as it regards impressions of things intelligible by the exercise of their natural faculties, but as it regards formal conception and actual record." In direct contradiction to Luke i. 1 – 3, to the question, "Whether ordinary study, inquiry, and premeditation were necessary for writing (the Scriptures)," it is replied (p. 47): "No; for the Spirit immediately, extraordinarily, and infallibly moved them to write, and both inspired and dictated the things to be written."

Besides the two great Protestant Churches, the adherents of Luther and Calvin, we must also take into consideration the followers of Socinus. Agreeing with the Reformers respecting the inspiration of the Scriptures, it was nevertheless maintained by Socinus, in his treatise "De Auctoritate Scripturæ," † that into things "which are of small moment," the Evangelists and Apostles have allowed slight errors to enter; and agreeably with such a notion, the commentators of this party, here and there, acknowledge errors of memory in the Biblical writers.

But, even amongst the great Protestant Churches, there went forth in the seventeenth century, side by side with that extreme theory already mentioned, another of a more moderate character. This, however, met with great opposition. In the Reformed Church (followers of Calvin), we find learned theologians, of the French Academy at Saumur especially, unhesitatingly admitting here and there an incorrect apprehension of the Old Testament by the writers of the New, or errors of memory. We also find German Reformed theologians, such as Junius, Piscator, and others, equally free in their sentiments. The liberal tendency of opinion thus

* "Disputationes Selectæ," p. 1.

† Chap. I. p. 15.

manifested was reduced to more general exegetico-dogmatical principles by the Arminian party, who were thrust out of the Dutch Reformed Church. Grotius, in his "Plea for Peace," * avows his belief that the historical books of Scripture, in distinction from the prophetical, can lay claim to nothing beyond credit for the ability of the writers, and their sincere desire to communicate the truth.† In the treatise "Riveti Apologia Discuss.," p. 723, it is asked, by way of affirmation to the contrary, "Has Luke said, The word of the Lord came to Luke, and the Lord said to him, Write?" A thorough remodelling of the earlier theory of inspiration, and its reduction to some such form as has been defended by the supranaturalists of more recent times, is found in the Eleventh Letter in the works of the Arminian Le Clerc. ‡ Episcopius § ascribes to the Apostles only an *assistance of the Divine Spirit* in the composition of works which proceeded from their own determination; and allows that in such passages as the genealogy in Matthew ch. i. errors may possibly have crept in.

In the Lutheran Church it was Calixt, ‖ in the middle of the sixteenth century, who gave forth a more liberal theory of inspiration. The distinction between *revelatio* and *assistentia* or *directio divina,* which had widely prevailed in the Catholic theology, he adopted, and maintained "that God did not reveal in a peculiar manner to the sacred writers those things which naturally struck their senses, or were otherwise known to them; but still that he so directed and aided them as that they should write nothing contrary to the truth." Nay, more, he even limits the *revelatio* to those truths only

* "Votum pro Pace Ecclesiastica."

† Opera Theol., ed. Amsterd. 1679, III. 672. — Tr.

‡ "Sentimens de quelques Théologiens de Hollande sur l'Histoire Critique du V. Test." Composée par Rich. Simon. 1685.

§ "Instit. Theologiæ," III. 5. 1.

‖ For an account of this remarkable divine and controversialist, see Möller, "Cimbra Literata," and Mosheim by Murdoch, Cent. 17, S. 2, p. 2, ch. 1. Schlegel's note to sect. 21. — Tr.

which Thomas Aquinas had fixed upon as the peculiar and direct objects of faith.

These sentiments were still more widely diffused by the school of the Helmstädt theologians. In the Swiss and French Reformed Churches, the sentiments of Le Clerc met with a welcome reception. In the "Théologie Chrétienne" of the celebrated Pictet, Professor in Geneva (1702), the inspiration of Scripture is limited to the truth which was knowable by Revelation alone. From this were distinguished — while based upon it — those conceptions which were peculiar to the Apostles themselves. Revelation was restricted to those things which by natural means were not known to them. As to all other things a divine guidance in preventing error was adopted.

Sect. 6. — *State of Opinion in England.*

A freer treatment of the question — namely, the limitation of inspiration to the subject-matter — has from the first, along with individual advocates of a more rigid view, found place in the English Church.* Several Dissenters, also, eminently distinguished for their exemplary piety, occupy the same liberal ground.† The Presbyterian Church of Scotland alone has continued up to the present day to adhere to the straitest acceptation of the idea of inspiration. The free spiritual insight of Baxter in that celebrated work, "The Reformed Pastor," is especially surprising. He says: "As the glory of the Divine Maker shines more brilliantly in the whole frame of nature than in an individual grain, stone, or insect; and in the whole man, more than in any particular part of least comeliness; so also the authority of God shines forth more visibly in the whole system of Holy Scripture and holy doctrine than in any minor part. Nevertheless, for the advan-

* Vide Lowth's Vindication of the Old and New Test., 1692; Williams's Boyle Lecture, 1695; Clarke's Div. Authority of Holy Script., 1699, &c.

† Baxter's Method. Theol. Christ. 1681; Doddridge's Dissertation on Inspiration of N. Test., &c.

tage of the whole system, these parts are not wanting in beauty any more than the others, such as the hair and nails. But their *authority* is to be seen more from their agreement with the whole of Scripture, and from their more distinguishing portions, than from themselves separately." Here alone in an orthodox divine of the seventeenth century does the question meet with a complete treatment, in which, on the one hand, the conception of Scripture as an organism, and, on the other hand, the argument from the testimony of the Holy Spirit, stand forth as fundamental ideas.

Sect. 7. — *Progress of Opinion in Germany, &c. in the Eighteenth Century.*

With the beginning of the eighteenth century, in Germany, the firmly built fabric of the traditional ecclesiastical system began, upon this question as upon others, to totter. The following circumstances were instrumental in bringing about this result. The peculiarity of the Calixtine efforts has been pointed out in a recent Monograph upon George Calixt, as follows: "There lies therein the opposition of *religious* to *dogmatic* salvation,* together with an appeal to the nature and foundation of the early Apostolic Church. To such an extent had exclusive zeal in attaching importance to dogmas been carried, that the body of dogmatic declarations, separately and conjointly, had nearly been exalted to the position of an arbiter respecting the reception or non-reception of eternal life. Against this domination over, and entire absorption of, faith by mere dogma, Calixt raised his voice." † In a

---

* That is, we suppose, Salvation through the *possession of religious principle* was opposed to salvation (so called) through the mere *reception of certain dogmas.* — Tr.

† Gasz: George Calixt, und der *Synkretismus*, p. 11. "Syncretism." — This term, in the seventeenth century, marks the great controversy between Calixt and the more bigoted sections of the Protestant Church. This divine had travelled much abroad, and intercourse with different churches had given him a liberalized tone of feeling which led him to propose a cessation of hostilities between Protestants and Romanists,

manner purely practical, the same necessity made itself felt in the pietism which arose at the end of the seventeenth century. Led on by the exclusively practical power of inward religion, this pietism was indifferent to the dogmatical system of the day, and attended solely to the fundamental *truths*, by means of which the religious life in man is awakened. The established doctrine of inspiration was not even touched upon by Spener, except that he impugns the notion of the pure passiveness of its recipients, and maintains the influence of human peculiarities upon the *form* of the discourse or writing.* As, however, traditional reverence for the earlier dogmatical system gave way, and as the spiritual tone of pietism was again corrupted into mere externalism, — in that proportion was preparation made, as soon as scientific appliances could be so directed, to combat as erroneous and dangerous those decisions which had hitherto been considered as indifferent.

In addition to this, there came an impulse from without. Earlier even than in Germany, a relaxed notion of inspiration, nay, indeed, a notion reducing it to its very *minimum*, had spread itself in England. From the beginning of the eighteenth century, the writings of the laxer English clergy, of the Dissenters as well as of the Deists, had found an ever-increasing reception amongst the theologians of Germany. Besides, about the middle of the century, orthodox culture, and the inward spiritualism promoted by the pietists, had been superseded amongst many of the German divines by a purely *literary interest*. From the scrutiny of this new

---

and — "not to unite together and become one body, as his opponents interpreted him to mean, but — to abstain from mutual hatred, and cultivate mutual love and good-will." He was an Aristotelian in Philosophy, as a theologian had strong sympathy with the Fathers, and wished to find in the "Apostles' Creed" and the usages and doctrines of the first five centuries a common ground of union for the three great sections of German Christians, the Roman Catholic, the Lutheran, and the Reformed or Calvinist Churches. This doctrine was branded as "Syncretism." Mosh. Eccl. Hist., Cent. 17, Sect. 21. Notes by Schlegel. — Tr.

† Consilia Theologica, I. p. 46 et seq.

power, those contradictions which had been discovered — indubitable fruits of historico-critical inquiry during the dominancy of the more rigid theory of inspiration — could not remain concealed. The history of the middle of the eighteenth century gives us the impression that that was a period of general mental indolence, not only in theology, but also in philosophy, in the arts, and in politics. Even that which had been retained from the earlier theory of inspiration, moved on now with difficulty only as a dead tradition, in respect to which living faith was quite as much wanting as courage for a total negation of it. Upon this age of indolence, about the middle of the century, there follows, in the second half of it, in the province of Theology as in others, an energetic striving to beat out new paths. The spirit of the age had been already alienated from the kernel of the earlier doctrines of faith; it now began to break in pieces and cast away what yet remained of the shell, and to seek a new kernel. Thus the diminution of the dogma of inspiration, which had hitherto been ever advancing, at last degenerates into its complete negation. As one of the earliest representatives of the incipient insecurity, who were still, through reverence for ecclesiastical tradition, shy in taking bolder steps, the theologian Matthew Pfaff of Tübingen may be mentioned, whose leaning towards the position occupied by Calixt and the Arminians but ill concealed itself behind a cautious phraseology.*

The aim of this first part of our treatise has now been attained. It has been proved that the assumption of an inspiration extending to the entire contents, to the *subject-matter* and *form* of the sacred writings, has so little claim to the honor of being the only orthodox doctrine, that it has only been the opinion of, comparatively speaking, an exceedingly small fraction. Since now the symbolical writings of the Lutheran Church have not so much as once erected a barrier in the way of a freer construction of the doctrine, the Lu-

* Introduction to his "Notæ Exeget. in Evangel. Matt." 1721. Also his "Institutiones Theol. Dogm. et Moral." 1719. He died 1760.

theran, who is true to his symbols, can take no umbrage at the establishment of such a free construction.*

Part II. — EXEGETICO-DOGMATIC.

Preliminary.

We have submitted, that belief in an absolute (*schlechthinnige*) inspiration of the Scripture was by no means first abandoned by Rationalism. So far from this being the case, we may say that at no period whatever was such an opinion generally entertained. During the period of ecclesiastical faith, first from the age of the Fathers up the Middle Ages, and then again from the Reformers to the beginning of the eighteenth century, we have observed an increasing *restriction* put upon those liberal definitions which had been received from the very beginning. If, then, a growing *limitation* might take place in the interest of Faith, there may be also a growing *freedom from limitation* in the same interest. This will occur as soon as Faith has become more conscious of its peculiar nature, and has been distinguished from that which forms the peculiar business of *science.* After such earnest conflicts of science with the earlier forms of theology, in the midst of which Christendom became still more conscious of the foundations of faith, we in modern times have arrived at a point where a deeper apprehension of the doctrine of inspiration, derived from the nature of faith, should result as one of the fruits of those conflicts.

Let us more accurately define the subject of inquiry. The question is not whether the Holy Scripture includes inviolable

---

* The reader will remember that Professor Tholuck is a member of the Lutheran Church. Hence his justification. In England, also, we are in the main free from authoritative declarations on this point. While the Bible is firmly held to be of paramount authority as embodying the will of God to man, the rule of faith and practice, none but the ill-informed or bigoted will trench upon the inquirer's peace. — Tr.

divine contents, a *revelation* from God. We profess faith in the contents of the Law, as revealed; so of the Prophets; and so of the teachings of Christ, and of the Apostles. Thus much any one may profess, and yet feel himself urged to abandon the inspiration of the Bible in the current sense of the term.

By *inspiration*, as distinguished from *revelation*, is customarily understood, since the time of Calovius, and especially since the time of Baumgarten,* the communication by God † of *the entire written contents of Scripture*, whether the matter written down was previously known to the writers or not. The most recent advocate of the more rigid theory, Professor Gaussen, says expressly that the Holy Spirit by inspiration did not at all aim at the illumination of the writers, — *they* were nothing more than transient instruments, — a view was had rather to their books. ‡

Now we can well imagine the believer's heart, when predisposed to take a side in favor of the more narrow theory, turning away with displeasure from any lax notions on the subject. *Certainty* in matters of faith depends upon a believing disposition; properly, indeed, only certainty concerning the true doctrine of salvation; but still it may be asked, Can this certainty be sufficiently stable, if everything which stands, not only in *direct*, but also in *indirect* connection with this doctrine of salvation be not also true? That absolute inspiration of the Holy Scriptures advocated by Professor Gaussen thus appears clearly to the Christian mind as a religious necessity. We must, however, first of all, draw atten-

---

* "De Discrimine Revelationis et Inspirationis." 1745.

† "Die göttliche Eingebung."

‡ "It is of consequence for us to say, and it is of consequence that it be understood, that this miraculous operation of the Holy Ghost had not the sacred writers themselves for its object, — for these were only his instruments, and were soon to pass away; but that its objects were the holy books themselves, which were destined to reveal from age to age to the Church the counsels of God, and which were never to pass away." *Theopneustia.* — Tr.

tion to the fact that this external certainty is not wholly given therewith. Consider the position of the unlearned reader. What does it avail you, says the Roman Catholic, to have an infallible *document*, unless you have also an infallible *translation?* And what could an infallible translation avail you, without an infallible *interpretation?* Nay, verily, your learned men themselves, who abide by the original text, — whence derive they certainty concerning its correctness? Does not the number of various readings in the New Testament alone, according to modern calculation, exceed fifty thousand? One can and must yield to our pious friend, Professor Gaussen, and confess that, essentially, the great majority of these readings are immaterial. But this is by no means the case with them all. That it is not indifferent, for example, whether the passage concerning the Trinity in 1 John v. 7, 8 be genuine or not, Professor Gaussen so decidedly acknowledges, that he believes the defence of the received reading must at all risks be undertaken, notwithstanding the passage is found in no Greek Codex except the *Codex Britannicus* * of the sixteenth century; in the *Codex Ravianus*, which is a copy partly from the *Complutensian Polyglot* and partly from the third edition of Stephens; and in the Vulgate only since the tenth century. If *one* credible testimony in reference to this subject were not of equal weight with many, a host of others might easily be added; but this instance must now suffice.

The Christian who can feel his faith certain and out of danger only in a diplomatic attestation derived *from without*,† can find peace only by repairing to the (so-called) infallible

---

* *Codex Brit.* — Otherwise called *Codex Montfortianus* or *Dublinensis.* This is one of the cursive manuscripts, and belongs to the library of Trinity College, Dublin. It closely resembles the Vulgate in the much disputed passage referred to in the text, and in many others. Dr. Tholuck uses the title given it by Erasmus. Dr. Davidson is of opinion that it could not have originated earlier than the fifteenth century. (Kitto's Cyclop., Art. Manuscript. Bibl.) — Tr.

† An external written authority. — Tr.

Roman pontiff.* But it is not well for us to prescribe to Divine wisdom the mode in which it may best and most safely conduct men to their object of pursuit (i. e. certainty of faith). Consider how former apologists for this strict theory of inspiration acted; and, indeed, how its most recent apologist, already mentioned, acts. Their manner throughout, for example, of giving prominence to the passage, "All Scripture is given by inspiration of God," 2 Tim. iii. 16, is as if their theory depended entirely upon the testimony of the Bible concerning itself. But, in truth, their argument all through depends simply upon what, in their estimation, is the demand of the *religious necessity* in man. Are we so much as conscious whether it is not from this religious exigency that we sometimes even wish that the Scripture itself were quite differently arranged? Who does not feel the need of possessing an indubitable record *from Christ's own hand?* Who does not wish that the New Testament were equal in extent to the Old? Who, moreover, would not deem it a wiser arrangement, if, instead of giving us the first three Evangelists with similar contents, one of them had been directed carefully to record those passages in the life of Christ which they have now, all of them, entirely omitted? Rightly has it been objected by Thiersch to Möhler's † construction of the

* Comp. Tholuck's "Gespräche über die vornehmsten Glaubensfragen," p. 176.

† Möhler (died 1838) is one of the ablest writers of the Roman Catholic Church. He was once an adherent of Schleiermacher's views, but afterwards opposed them, and took a prominent part in the controversy against Protestantism. He, in company with Hermes, sought to base the Romish dogmas upon a more profound and philosophical basis, not by reference to Scripture and the practice of the early Church, but to the nature of man, and the exigencies of his position, considered *à priori*. In short, he removed the data of the controversy entirely from the external to the internal or subjective. In this manner, much against their intention, the writings of Hermes and Möhler, by promoting a virtually Protestant spirit, namely, that of private judgment, did much towards undermining the authority and infallibility of the Pontiff and the Church. Vide Möhler's *Patrologie;* also his *Symbolik.* Mainz, 1832. — Tr.

Church, that the whole argument rests upon an *à priori* accommodation of historical facts, upon a *presumed* divine necessity; but that history, and even the history of the Church and of its corruption, takes shape, *not according to opinions antecedently established* in the mind of the student, *but must be received in the fashion in which it unfolds itself.* What can we say when we hear Bellarmine representing a divine infallible translation of the Bible as a necessity on the ground of this fact, namely, that the great majority of those prelates who form the decrees of Councils *are ignorant of Hebrew!* * Which were the more Christian wish, that the prelates, since the Old Testament has been written in Hebrew, should learn that language, or that, since the prelates have no inclination to do this, the sun should regulate itself according to the clock, and an infallible Latin Bible be added to the Hebrew? It were wise for men not to prescribe the way for satisfying their religious wants, but rather submissively to seek to apprehend the wisdom of God in that which has been given us by it.

Granted that a theory of inspiration of a less rigid kind would abate in some measure the stringent proofs of our faith: how, then, would Pascal be right when he perceives divine wisdom in the fact that faith is not established by external evidences? And is it not true that modern conviction, arrived at through doubt and internal conflict, is the possession of the believer much more fully than would have been the case by any divine contrivance by virtue of which, whenever a question arose, an external oracle instantly supplied an answer?

We may therefore readily lend an ear, when so great a number of witnesses for the faith, after conscientious examination, assure us that that religious necessity to which men appeal in support of an absolute (*schlechthinniges*) inspiration of the Scriptures cannot possibly be right, *since in the very Scripture itself* there are found decisive facts which stand opposed to it. We shall pursue our inquiry in the following order: —

---

* Opera, I. De Verbo Deo, 2. 10.

Sect. 1. — Arguments against the absolute* inspiration of Scripture derived from *the condition of the Biblical writings* themselves.

Sect. 2. — Arguments to the same effect derived from *the declarations of the Biblical writers concerning themselves.*

Sect. 3. — Alleged proofs *from Scripture itself* of its absolute inspiration.

Sect. 1. — *Arguments against the Absolute Inspiration and the Infallibility of Scripture, derived from the Nature of the Document itself.*

Were the Biblical writer, in the strict sense of the word, nothing more than an instrument of utterance through which God speaks to men, must we not also expect that no human imperfection in any respect should be contained in Scripture? Not only must eternal truths be free from all error, and from all former imperfection; but also the ordinary historical, geographical, and other facts must be correctly reported throughout. Nay, we might even demand the absence of all lingual imperfections. We have seen that a belief in inspiration to this very extent has been actually demanded by many. On the contrary, in relation to the *language* a Divine accommodation has been conceded by others. That the language of the New Testament in no respect varies from the Hellenistic Greek current at the time, is clear as daylight. It is true that it might be reasonably maintained that the Deity, in order to become intelligible to that generation, must speak to them not in classic Greek, to which they were not accustomed, but in the more corrupt dialect with which they were familiar.

---

* From the general tenor of our author's language, it would appear that the original word, *schlechthinnig,* — a word not yet in very common use among German writers, — may be fairly represented by the word "absolute." By this term Professor Tholuck designates a theory which errs by excess of strictness and credulity, — such as that of Professor Gaussen. — Tr.

But then in the language of the New Testament books, not only dialectic, but also *individual** characteristics of language appear. The style of Paul, and that of John, correspond entirely with what we know from other sources of the individual characters of these Apostles respectively. If herein also one should wish to find a Divine accommodation to the manner of speech peculiar to these Apostles, such an assumption would be the less satisfactory, since no adequate ground for any accommodation of the kind can be discovered.

But in addition to this, especially in Paul, there are certain imperfections of style,† imperfections, too, founded in his own peculiarities. For example, his vivacity very frequently occasions him to leave a sentence unfinished, through forgetting the conclusion. If the Divine accommodation is to be extended to these individual defects, then we must say that such a caricature of Divine accommodation is not only aimless, but, in so far as such defects actually embarrass the understanding, positively self-defeating. Assuredly, therefore, we have no choice but to abandon this position, and to admit the influence of human peculiarity upon the contents of Scripture. But even this must be farther extended, namely, *to the form of the thoughts recorded.* That is to say, the peculiarity of a Paul, of a John, or of a James, is to be understood as seen in *the mode of putting forth* Christian truth. The life of our Lord in the fourth Gospel, for example, is recorded in a manner different from that exhibited in any of the other three Gospels, — a manner, indeed, which, from the personality of John, is quite conceivable.

As unto persons who from different elevations view the general mass of a town, the houses group themselves in various forms, and present different centres; so the above-

---

* That is, wherein the idiosyncrasies of the individual writers are apparent. — Tr.

† It is regretted that a passage on the defects of the Pauline style, to which Dr. Tholuck in a private communication refers us, cannot here be cited, — the work containing it, *Redepennig über Origenes,* not being within reach. — Tr.

mentioned Apostles present Christian truth under diversified points of view, according to their personal peculiarity, and according to the progress of their inward development. To Paul, the interposition of a righteousness by faith, acquired through Christ, — to John, the communication of a true eternal life, — to James, the illustration of the law as a law of freedom, — are the ground ideas respectively. And must this peculiarity, too, be nothing more than the product of a Divine imitation? * We cannot forbear inserting here the words of a profound writer, who has become an intellectual polar star to many inquiring minds in England and America, — I mean Samuel Taylor Coleridge. †

"Why should I not [believe the Scriptures throughout to be dictated, in word and thought, by an infallible intelligence]? Because the doctrine in question petrifies at once the whole body of Holy Writ, with all its harmonies and symmetrical gradations, — the flexile and the rigid, the supporting hard and the clothing soft, — the blood *which is the life*, the intelligencing nerves, and the rudely woven, but soft and stringy, cellular substance, in which all are imbedded and lightly bound together. This breathing organism, this glorious *pan-harmonicon*, which I had seen stand on its feet as a man, and with a man's voice given to it, the doctrine in question turns at once into a colossal Memnon's head, a hollow passage for a voice; a voice that mocks the voices of many men, and speaks in their names, and yet is but one voice and the same; and no man uttered it, and never in a human heart was it conceived. *Why* should I not? Because the doctrine evacuates of all sense and efficacy the sure and constant tradition, that all the several books bound up together in our precious family Bibles were composed in different and widely distinct ages, under the

* "Divine imitation," — *göttlichen Mimik.* By these terms our author means, God interposing to produce effects similar to those which would naturally follow the idiosyncrasies of the writers: which, being unnecessary, and contrary to the analogy of the divine proceedings, is not to be admitted. — Tr.

† *Confessions of an Inquiring Spirit*, pp. 31 – 36. Lond. 1840.

greatest diversity of circumstances and degrees of light and information, and yet that the composers, whether as uttering or as recording what was uttered and what was done, were all actuated by a pure and holy spirit, one and the same, — (for is there any Spirit pure and holy, and yet not proceeding from God, — and yet not proceeding in and with the Holy Spirit ?) — one Spirit, working diversely, now awakening strength, and now glorifying itself in weakness; now giving power and direction to knowledge, and now taking away the sting from error! Ere the summer and the months of ripening had arrived for the heart of the race, — while the whole sap of the tree was crude, and each and every fruit lived in the harsh and bitter principle, — even then this Spirit withdrew its chosen ministers from the false and guilt-making centre of self. It converted the wrath into the form and organ of love, and on the passing storm-cloud impressed the fair rainbow of promise to all generations. Put the lust of self in the forked lightning, and would it not be a spirit of Moloch? But God maketh the lightning his ministers; fire and hail, vapors and stormy winds, fulfilling his words.

"'Curse ye Meroz,' said the angel of the Lord; 'Curse ye bitterly the inhabitants thereof,' sang Deborah. Was it that she called to mind any personal wrongs, rapine or insult, that she or the house of Lapidoth had received from Jabin or Sisera? No: she had dwelt under the palm-tree in the depth of the mountain. But she was a mother in Israel; and with a mother's heart, and with the vehemency of a mother's and a patriot's love, she had shot the light of love from her eyes, and poured the blessings of love from her lips, on the people that had *jeoparded their lives to the death* against the oppressors; and the bitterness awakened and borne aloft by the same love she precipitated in curses on the selfish and coward recreants who *came not to the help of the Lord, to the help of the Lord against the mighty.* As long as I have the image of Deborah before my eyes, and while I throw myself back into the age, country, circumstances, of this Hebrew Boadicea, in the not yet tamed chaos of the spiritual creation, — as long as I contemplate the impassioned, high-souled, heroic woman, in all the prominence and individuality of will and character, — I feel as if I were among the first ferments of the great affections, — the proplastic waves of the microcosmic chaos swelling up against, and yet towards, the outspread wings of the Dove that lies brooding on the troubled waters. So long all is well, all replete with instruction and example. In the fierce and inordinate I am made to know, and be grateful for, the clearer and purer radiance which shines on a Christian's paths, neither blunted by the preparatory veil, nor crimsoned in its struggle through the all-enwrapping mist of the world's ignorance; whilst in the self-oblivion of these heroes of the Old Testament, their elevation above all low and individual interests, above all, in the entire and vehement devotion of their total being to the service of their Master, I find a lesson of humility, a ground of humiliation, and a shaming, yet rousing, example of faith and fealty. But let me once be persuaded that all these heart-awakening utterances of human hearts, — of men of like faculties and passions with myself, mourning, rejoicing, suffering, triumphing, — are but as a *Divina Commedia* of a superhuman — O, bear with me, if I say — Ventriloquist; that the royal Harper to whom I have so often submitted myself as a *many-stringed instrument* for his fire-tipped fingers to traverse, while every several nerve of emotion, passion, thought, that thinks the flesh and blood of our common humanity, responded to the touch, — that *the sweet Psalmist of Israel* was himself as mere an instrument as his harp an *automaton*; — poet, mourner, and suppliant, all is gone; all sympathy at least, and all example. I listen in awe and fear, but likewise in perplexity and confusion of spirit."

[Coleridge proceeds as follows: —

"Yet one other instance, and let this be the crucial test of the doctrine. Say that the book of Job throughout was dictated by an infallible intelligence. Then reperuse the book, and still, as you proceed, try to apply the tenet; try if you can even attach any sense or semblance of meaning to the speeches which you are reading. What! were the hollow truisms, the unsufficing half-truths, the false assumptions and malignant insinuations of the supercilious bigots, who corruptly defended the truth, — were the impressive facts, the piercing outcries, the pathetic appeals, and the close and powerful reasoning with which the poor sufferer, smarting at once from his wounds, and from the oil of vitriol which the orthodox *liars for God* were dropping into them, impatiently but uprightly and holily controverted this truth, while in will and in spirit he clung to it, — were both dictated by an infallible intelligence? Alas! if I may judge from the manner in which both indiscriminately are recited, quoted, appealed to, preached upon, by the *routiniers* of desk and pulpit, I cannot doubt that they think so, or rather, without thinking, take for granted that so they are to think; the more readily, perhaps, because the so thinking supersedes the necessity of all afterthought."]

But, what is of still greater importance, we also find throughout the Old and New Testaments numerous proofs of inaccuracy in statements of fact. An anxious orthodoxy has of course endeavored to rebut these accusations, and everywhere to maintain absolute accuracy. This has been accomplished, however, only by so many artificial and forced supports, that the Scripture set right after this fashion wears more the appearance of an old garment with innumerable seams and patches, than of a new one made out of one entire piece. It is quite true that the adversaries of Christianity have professedly fallen upon many discrepancies where none are really to be found; but in many places, where we can compare Scripture with Scripture, we meet with difficulties where either the contradiction will not admit of removal at all, or but very imperfectly. In proportion as the reader is destitute of the skill which learning gives, in that proportion will he be unconscious of these facts, and be prepared confidently to boast in his defence of a verbal inspiration, for "What one does not know, gives him no annoyance." * This

* "Was ich nicht weiss, macht mich nicht heiss." — *Prov.*

remark is applicable, too, to our excellent friend Professor Gaussen, who, in his book already quoted, has given such an eloquent vindication of plenary inspiration.

By way of proof, we must enter into some details. Out of numberless instances, however, we shall select only a few: for if by one or two proofs the matter appears beyond dispute, there is no need to multiply arguments. Entire accuracy throughout can no longer be maintained. We make a distinction between *errors in translation* and *errors in fact*, which occur in the Biblical writers.

1. The New Testament authors have made abundant use of the Greek translation executed in Alexandria, called the Septuagint.* This was natural, since this translation was not only generally known to the Jews who spoke the Greek language, but, at the time of the rise of Christianity, was also in high repute in Palestine. Now there are found in several books of that Greek translation, especially in the Book of Psalms, not a few material misapprehensions of the proper sense; or, at least, readings differing from our Hebrew text. † Notwithstanding this, however, the writers of the New Testament, here and there, even when the argument depends upon particular words, go not to the original Hebrew text, but follow the Greek translation. This Professor Gaussen admits in page 236 of his work. ‡ He assumes, however, through the whole of his defence, that he has made good the position that the Apostolical writers in all those places where stress is laid on the quotation, have actually made their quotations from the original Hebrew. This judgment is in this general sense incorrect. It is true in reference to Paul and Matthew; but our author forgets the Epistle to the Hebrews, in which the original (Hebrew) text is never attended to, not even in those places where the author argues from passages which, as

* On this version see Dr. Davidson's article in Kitto's Cyclop. of Bibl. Liter., sub voce.

† Comp. Davidson's Sacred Hermeneutics, pp. 334, 338, et seq. Also Dr. Henderson's Lect. on Div. Insp., p. 375, 2d ed.

‡ Engl. Transl., p. 84.

they are translated, exhibit material errors.* We admit that many of the older orthodox interpreters attempted, at least with some of these passages, to explain the Old Testament text in the sense adopted by the author of this Epistle.† But the passage (chap. ii. 13) quoted from Isa. viii. 17, 18, Luther explains, and the rest Calvin explains, in the sense demanded by their Old Testament connection, without any regard to the manner in which they are quoted in our Epistle. From the author's way of arguing from Old Testament passages, it can scarcely be maintained that they were merely *applied* for hortatory purposes. This would not readily be conceded even by the advocates of strict orthodoxy. If this solution then is rejected, we are not aware that any others remain to help us to avoid the concession, that passages of Scripture quoted incorrectly, and in a way not altogether corresponding with their proper original meaning, have been used by way of argument.

2. We leave this part of our subject, and pass on to *inaccuracies in matters of fact.* When such inaccuracies must be proved by instances of collision between the Biblical and extra-Biblical witnesses, the Christian, having faith in the Bible, will hesitate to admit their existence. But he can hardly persist in his hesitation, if cases are adduced where the writers report either the very words of our Lord, or matters of pure fact, with irreconcilable variations the one from the other. It is true that here also many charges of contradiction have been proved to be groundless. Some, however, remain, where the Christian critic cannot with the most candid mind disown discrepancies, — discrepancies in which one only of the reports given can be faithful. The Sermon on the Mount, according to Luke vi. and Matt. v. – vii., presents, in this twofold narration, such manifold variations, that many of the older commentators assumed the

---

* Comp. chap. ii. 6, 12, 13; x. 5; xii. 26.

† Dr. Tholuck controverts the Pauline authorship of the Epistle to the Hebrews, and deems the weight of evidence to be rather in favor of Apollos. — Tr.

delivery of two separate Sermons on the Mount, and to this solution of the difficulty Professor Gaussen still adheres. The opposite view, however, was adopted by Chemnitz and Calovius, and is also received by all the more recent writers of the present century. If we grant this, then the confession appears unavoidable that the same ideas are reproduced by the two Evangelists in different forms. The ideas expressed by Matt. v. 40 and vii. 16, are in those places given forth in a different form from what they assume in Luke vi. 29, 44. Matt. vii. 12 differs from Luke vi. 31. Now when Chemnitz, in order to establish the thorough correctness of the narrations, assumes that the same thought in the same discourse may have been twice expressed by our Lord in a different form and position, he only introduces a makeshift, which, while it removes from the reporters the charge of discrepancy, reflects no little discredit upon the method of discoursing adopted by Christ himself. With Luke vi. 29 and Matt. v. 40 he has not been bold enough to use this expedient, although he was compelled to admit that by the two Evangelists the violence supposed to be committed is *represented under different forms.**

Stier also, who deems it altogether objectionable to admit that in Matthew, who was an Apostle, there is found any departure whatever from historical accuracy, has been compelled to allow in Luke what in Matthew he has protested against.† He has even given up generally the defence of *verbal* truth and correctness. "The Spirit of God," he says,

* Luke vi. 29. "And him that taketh away thy cloak, forbid not to take thy coat also."

Matt. v. 40. "And if any man will sue thee at the law, and take away thy coat, let him have thy cloak also."

These and many other similar variations must be fatal to any theory of *verbal* inspiration; but since on either side the *ethical principle* enforced is the same, the value of the Bible as the depository of moral and religious truth is not necessarily affected. Comp. also Luke vi. 20 – 23, and Matt. v. 3 – 12; Luke vi. 30, and Matt. v. 42; Luke vi. 27, 28, 35, and Matt. v. 44, 45. — Tr.

† Stier's Reden des Herrn nach Matt., pp. 170, 308.

"so put the Evangelists in mind of the discourses of our Lord, that they might write them, not *word for word*, or with *entire fulness* according to the letter; but the Spirit of Truth has withal permitted no *essential* untruth whatsoever to occur." * Professor Gaussen alone persists in maintaining that such formal diversities, where found, must have as their originator the Holy Spirit himself, to whom (he says) it is permitted to express the same thought in various forms of language. Certainly. Only it must be remembered that along with this is also given up the strictly faithful recording of the *discourses of our Lord, who actually delivered them only in one of two ways.*

If, now, by an examination of the Scripture in detail, we discover a human side, on account of which the Bible is not to be declared free from defects and errors, then the question is, How can a theory of inspiration, which shall be consistent with these phenomena, be established? The historical part of this treatise has proved how by a great number of theologians, both Protestant and Catholic, a positive Divine cooperation was asserted only in relation to that portion of the contents of Holy Writ which was *revealed*, or the truths which were the proper objects of faith; † from which position it follows that *revelation* and *inspiration* are identical. As it regards the remaining contents, it was held that a negative Divine efficacy was present, serving as a defence against vital error, i. e. error damaging to the doctrine of faith. To this, as we have seen above, amounts the language of Stier even, if we take into account certain portions of his writings; although, judging from others, he approximates more nearly than any other German theologian to the older idea of inspiration; so also the views of the more recent English theologians, among the Dissenters as well as among the clergy of the Episcopal Church. Dr. Henderson designates it as the fruit of prejudice to say that the Holy Scripture in all its

* Stier's Reden des Herrn nach Matt., p. 74.

† "Den eigentlichen Glaubenswahrheiten."

parts alike has been inspired by the Spirit of God in such a manner as that thereby human co-operation was superseded.*

The prevailing doctrine, even in the strictest form of it, both in the Catholic and in the Protestant Church, makes such a distinction between the separate contents of Scripture, as must necessarily lead, at least, to a charitable judgment of the difference of opinion which has obtained upon the subject. We have already seen how Thomas Aquinas made a distinction between that truth which is given by God *principaliter*, as the proper object of faith, and those other portions of Scripture which belong to faith only *indirectly*.† The most rigid writers upon dogmatic theology amongst the Lutherans,‡ make a similar distinction between that which belongs to *faith generally*, and that which belongs to *faith specially* considered: to the latter belong only the dogmas of faith; to the former, all the remaining contents of Scripture. The opinion of the Jesuit Tanner, that all things whatsoever which the Bible contains, "even the account of the fox-tails of Samson, and the building of the tower of Babel," &c., belong to the articles of religious faith, is nothing less than ridiculous.

It is therefore clear, that when these theologians feel constrained to draw the fence of inspiration around the *entire* written word, it is only from the apprehension that, if this were not done, the portion which properly belongs to faith would thereby be made insecure. In one place this fence cannot be completed. Even by the most stringent defenders of inspiration no means have been discovered whereby they could evade the confession that it does not lie before us diplomatically certain; but that the decision concerning it must be left to the *scientific investigations of the learned.* The consequence which results from this is one of importance. The Bible, as it appears *to us*, can in no case pass as verbally inspired; *therefore also its contents cannot in all their details*

* Lect. on Div. Insp., p. 296 et seq., 2d ed.

† Vide p. 76, ante.

‡ Quenstedt, Theol. Didact. Polem., Tom. I. 4, 2, 5; and König, Theol. Posit. Proleg., Sect. 133.

throughout be considered as externally guaranteed. Professor Gaussen himself is forced to allow this; and he rests satisfied with admiring that Divine guidance whereby things are so brought about, that, notwithstanding the great uncertainty which surrounds individual "readings," yet no Scripture truth which is an object of faith (*Glaubenswahrheit*) is unsettled, since each rests upon more than one passage, and even the various readings only give shades, and not real diversity of meaning. Now if this consideration suffices here to give comfort to the mind, why should it not avail also if failure of memory, and errors in certain historical, chronological, geographical, and astronomical details must be admitted? and if here and there a passage appears to be spurious? or if, amongst the canonical books, a few are found that are uncanonical? It is an undeniable fact, that hundreds of the most distinguished Christians, who have brought forth fruit in joyful faith, and have stood forth in that respect prominently as Christian exemplars, have thus judged concerning the Scriptures, and have nevertheless been ready to lay down their life for the Gospel.

We proceed upon the same ground as that upon which, with the Christian, the *Divine* evidence of an inspiration of the Scripture rests, and say: *This belief entirely coincides with, and stands entirely in relation to, belief in the Divine contents.** Faith in a Divine inspiration of Scripture relates, first of all, to that truth witnessed by the "demonstration of the Spirit and of power," by which (according to 1 Cor. ii. 4) the Apostle established belief in his preaching in the hearts of the Corinthians; that is, *the Christian doctrine of salvation.* This doctrine approves itself to us as truth, when the man becomes conscious that his intercourse with God is re-estab-

---

* That is, we have Divine evidence of the inspiration of Scripture only from those parts which have been derived from God. The further question, *what* parts have been thus derived, must be determined by a variety of considerations, but principally by that which our author proceeds to consider; i. e. the fitness to produce moral effects — towards making perfect the man of God. — Tr.

lished; that for time and for eternity he enters into proper relation to his God; that thus, and thus alone, he can become a true *man of God.** "If the Spirit of God," he may ask, "had not exerted a ruling power over the recording of this saving truth, and of the facts upon which the truth is founded, how could the recorded word have this effect upon me?" If we Christians of the present day ascribe to the written word of the Lord what those servants of the High-Priest ascribed to the word then spoken to them, † must not the written be substantially the same as the spoken word? If we also exclaim, after reading the Scripture about the holy sufferings and death of the Lord, as that centurion did after he had witnessed them, "Truly this man was the Son of God!" ‡ must not these sufferings and this death, in all their essential features, have been faithfully recorded to us? We are speaking of fidelity of record with respect to words and facts *essentially.* It may be a matter of dispute, a hundred times over, where the line of demarcation between the essential and non-essential is to be drawn; but that such a distinction, although subject to uncertainty, does really exist, is witnessed by the speech and logic of every nation where the question has been entertained. There is much that is non-essential, which still in *some respects* touches the essential; but there is also that which does not touch it *at all.* The words, like the facts, of Scripture, have a kernel and a shell. To the former, the witness of the Holy Spirit is direct and absolute; to the latter, only indirect and relative. The great idea that the disciple of the Lord, in so far as his own selfish interest alone is concerned, — suppressing the slightest tendency to vindictiveness, — should seek by kindness to subdue his enemy, remains entirely the same, whether Christ uses the example of him who, when sued at law, yields up his *cloak* in addition to his *coat,* as Matthew puts it, § or that of him who on the highway is robbed of his cloak, and yields up his coat also, as Luke puts it. ‖ The fact of our Lord's resurrection remains

* 2 Tim. iii. 17.

† The allusion is probably to John vii. 46. — Tr.

‡ Mark xv. 39.

§ Chap. v. 40.

‖ Chap. vi. 29.

equally certain, whether he first appeared to these persons or to those. The Evangelists have even passed over in entire silence the important appearing to the five hundred, of whom Paul speaks in 1 Cor. xv. 6.

This belief in saving truth and fact leads us on still farther. The word of the Lord makes us certain that the Apostolical writers of New Testament books must have written by the Spirit of God, because as bearers of this his word, and as promoters of his work, they received from him the promise of the Holy Ghost.* If this Spirit inspired † them during their *oral* report, how could he fail them in their *written* report? Always, indeed, holding fast that distinction already mentioned of *essential* and *non-essential*, we shall still feel convinced of this, that neither upon the communication of historical knowledge, gained by their own experience, nor upon the revelation which they had received from God, could their natural subjectivity exercise any obscuring influence. And faith in Christian truth and fact, thus confirmed, like faith in their inspiration, will now also determine our convictions concerning the *Old Testament religion*. That the Mosaic economy according to its ritual part was in a symbolico-dogmatical respect, according to its ethical part in an ethical respect, a preparative to the Christian economy, even the imperfectly enlightened but ingenuous inquirer cannot deny. But the luminous eye of that dispensation, through which preeminently the preparing Spirit, which diffuses itself throughout all, gleams upon us, is the prophetic part. The more clearly we perceive this in the documents written a thousand years before, the more unquestionable does it appear that there is a Divine co-operation in the production of the record.

If moral and religious perfection, if the kingdom of God in Christ upon earth be the highest aim of humanity, must not that document which is the most powerful agent in promoting this, and in which Christendom has had, and still has, the fertilizing spring and the guiding rule of faith, be an especial

* Comp. John xiv. 26; xv. 26, 27; xvi. 12 – 14.

† *Beseelen*, to animate, to quicken.

object of that Providence which controls the events of the world? In other words, must not far other than ordinary means have been used for the purpose of its record and preservation? Suppose that of the written monuments of classical antiquity no authors had been preserved except those of the iron and brazen ages, or that the works of the silver and golden ages had come down to us only in copies which were thoroughly corrupt and unrestorable by any criticism, what then had become of our classic culture? In like manner, what had become of our Christian culture if nothing had been handed down to us from Christian antiquity except perhaps the Apocryphal books of the Old Testament, or the General Epistles of the New, or even the Gospels, in a state at once mutilated and no longer capable of being deciphered? It were presumption to declare upon mere *à priori* grounds what Providence ought to have *done*, or ought to have *prevented*, in order to have secured for us a record answering to all the conditions of a sufficing certainty. But that Providence must be eminently active in this respect is an unavoidable supposition to every one to whom the religio-moral significancy of this record in history has become manifest. And have we not in this collection of books, embracing a period of more than *three thousand years*, the clearest proofs of a controlling Providence? We have already mentioned that, in spite of the fifty thousand various readings found in the New Testament, the sense of it in the main remains steadfast.* Further, a criticism, which in part has been led on by a decidedly negative interest, has for a hundred and fifty years submitted the books of both Old and New Testaments, in a body, to the most fiery *ordeal*. And with what result? In as far as it pertains to the principal books of the *New* Testament at least, — if we omit a very small minority of German

* "It has been truly said, that such is the character of the New Testament Scriptures, that the worst copy of the Greek text, and the worst translation, represent the original with sufficient accuracy to secure all the highest ends of Christian instruction." Rev. S. H. Godwin, Introd. Lect. at opening of New Coll. — Tr.

theologians who are of a contrary opinion, — a growingly strong conviction among learned men of their authenticity. This Bible, written by kings, herdsmen, priests, fishermen, and tent-makers, and entirely as if by accident bound together into a whole, does it not nevertheless produce the impression of a collection of documents put together with the most careful deliberation? From the creation of man and his fall, to the apocalyptic proclamation, "Behold, I make all things new," one book, stretching thus over the entire field of the history of mankind, leads them on in their journey from its very beginning to its close. In the Old Testament, as in the New, we have first of all the divine facts presented, then such books as exhibit the faith and spirit of the community which by those facts have been confirmed, and lastly, the prophetical writings which conduct from the Old Testament to the New, and from this again to the "new heaven and new earth" where the consummation of redemption shall be realized!

We have now come to the close. We have declared what, with respect to inspiration, is certain to *faith*, — what, even to every common Christian reader, admits of certainty, — upon the ground of the testimony of the Spirit and of power. What is *not* here embraced belongs more properly to *scientific research*. The faith which has become conscious of its own nature will readily yield to science its due province in this respect. A sound condition of the Church cannot be thought of without science; for though it be granted that science has, in the service of human over-curiousness and unbelief, a hundred times brought injury to the Church, still we are bold to aver that in the service of truth, morality, and faith it has quite as frequently brought life and blessing to the Church. We know well that timid minds will be frightened to find that upon so many points they are dependent on the investigations of learned men. If this does not satisfy that these points are by no means essential, there is no help for them. There are suspicious souls who, if celestial spirits made their appearance to them, would not believe unless they brought authorized written certificates from another world. We Christians, however, who occupy a higher platform than that of written certificates as vouchers, must learn to believe in the witness of the Spirit. What would a Paul say to him whose faith in the Son of God would be doubtful, because he did not know whether, in Acts xx. 28, the correct reading was "the Church of God" or "the Church of the Lord"; or because he could not feel certain whether "vinegar," as Matthew says,* or "wine mingled with myrrh," as Mark says,† was offered to the Saviour on the cross; or whether Christ healed the blind man on his *entrance into*, or on his *departure from* Jericho;‡ or whether the passage, John xxi. 24, 25, was subjoined by John himself, or by a friend of his? To such a doubter, I say, what would a Paul answer? He would tell him, "*Man, thy hour is not yet come!*"

---

* Matt. xxvii. 34. † Mark xv. 23.

‡ Comp. Matt. xx. 29; Mark x. 46; Luke xviii. 35.

HOLY SCRIPTURE.

By ROWLAND WILLIAMS, B. D.,

FELLOW AND FORMERLY TUTOR OF KING'S COLLEGE, CAMBRIDGE, AND PROFESSOR OF HEBREW AT LAMPETER.

"Whatsoever things were written aforetime, were written for our learning, that we, through patience and comfort of the Scriptures, might have hope." — Romans xv. 4.

The study of history has always been allowed to be one of the happiest means of awakening and improving the mind. It has even been called wisdom, teaching by instances. For, if it rise in any degree to its high vocation, it summons the men of past times to move before us as they lived; it enables us to hear them, though dead, yet speak; to appreciate, perhaps, the difficulties which surrounded them; and, by the unconscious effect of sympathy, to ingraft on our own minds the power of confronting with no less manliness any similar trials which may possibly beset our path. So eminently is this true, that the man who has traced with throbbing heart the career of great patriots, stricken down perhaps by overwhelming odds, or of great thinkers, who have either embodied their wisdom in legislation, or bid the eloquent page glow with its record for ever, has in all probability *assimilated* himself in some measure to the mighty of whom he has read: for he has lived over in thought what was their life in act: he has thus drunk into their spirit, and by breathing a kindred atmosphere has become partaker of their very nature.

10*

But if such assertions may be ventured of great men and deeds in general, they more emphatically apply to such records as we have inherited of the earnest aspirations of good men, in any time or country, to the eternal Source of their being, and the mysterious Controller of their destiny. That solemn ritual of Greek tragedy, which our own Milton did not disdain to recommend as a repository of "grave, sententious wisdom"; those orators who could tell an incensed multitude, that they rejoiced in having brought down on their country a disastrous defeat (if Heaven so ordered it), rather than see her forfeit her old character for honor, and her consciousness of self-respect; those still loftier teachers, to whom their country's mythology was only the fanciful expression of a far higher and more remote, yet ever-present principle; and he, who declared the world to bear as clear a testimony to its Author, as a finished poem does to the existence of a poet, while no really great man, he thought, could be without a certain divine inspiration,—all these, I say, and other records of kindred meaning, stir us with an emotion of sympathy far deeper than is inspired by the ordinary subjects of the historian. We watch with intense interest such men groping their way towards an eminence of light, on which not our own arm has placed us; we sigh at the weakness of our race, as we occasionally see them wander in some hopeless maze of speculation; and we can scarcely refrain from an exulting cry, when some pure conscience and reaching intellect seems almost to lay hands "unknowingly" upon the very mercy-seat of the unsearchable I AM THAT I AM.

Yet after all, the result accruing from such teachers among the Gentiles is rather touching our hearts with wholesome emotion, than furnishing our minds with any groundwork on which doctrine may be reared. We read them as sympathizing critics, but cannot sit at their feet as pupils. We have need therefore to look elsewhere for more definite teaching. And if we seek such aid in the Hebrew Scriptures, we soon find reason to believe, that He who nowhere kept himself without witness yet *gave the Spirit in larger measure* to those who knew him by his name Jehovah, and worshipped him on Sion, the mountain of his holy place. Nor is it necessary here to dwell on that mere external evidence, which in itself is not unimportant. The space which custom allots me may be more profitably employed in directing your thoughts to some of the characteristic features of the books themselves.

We are speaking now of the Hebrew Scriptures. Perhaps the first thing to notice is the manifest fidelity of the writers, both as respects the manners of their country, the character of the people described, and the infirmities, nay, the very crimes even, of men whom they delight to honor. We read in their pages of life as it now exists in the East; and as it may be believed with partial variation to have existed for many ages. We find no attempt to represent king, or prophet, or priest, as perfect: the tyranny of one, the passion of another, the weak connivance of the third, are set forth in their naked simplicity. And this ingenuous character is the more striking, because it is directly opposed to the usual genius of Oriental narrative, which delights rather in pompous and inflated exaggeration. It is also opposed more especially to the writings of the later Scribes and Rabbins, which abound in laborious trifling and transparent fable. Nor can any reason be given for this superiority of the older books more obviously true, than that the writers conceived themselves to be acting under a responsibility of a strictly religious kind. They took up the pen to celebrate events which were not merely the triumphs of their race, but the manifestations of the power and the truth of the Lord God of Israel. They had heard that he abhorreth the sacrifice of lying lips, and they would not blot the Scriptures animated by his Spirit with any lying legend, or cunningly devised fable. Hence arises (what, as far as the East is concerned, seems to have been then unprecedented) the strictly historical and trustworthy character of Hebrew literature. Growing up under the shadow of the temple, superintended by those who worshipped a God of truth in the beauty of holiness, yet read every seventh year in the ears of all the people, it has that double guaranty which is derived from intelligent and sacerdotal authority, and from exposure to the contemporaneous criticism of masses of mankind. Even those books, such as Kings and Chronicles, which dwell chiefly on the outward history of the nation, have hence no common interest. They carry us as it were behind the scenes of an important part in the great drama of the history of the world. They show us events happening, and the subtle causes which produced them; man proposing, but God disposing; Israel rebelling, and Jehovah smiting; Cyrus rearranging his conquests, and Jehovah (whom the conqueror knew not) wielding him as an instrument to restore his people Israel.

Yet a still higher interest attaches itself to this collection of records, when we consider them as a history emphatically of religion: that is, in the first place, of the aspiration of the human heart to its Creator.* For we then read of men of like passions with ourselves, treading a course which resembles in its great analogies our own; men now striving, and now at peace; now sinning, and (as a consequence) suffering; now crying unto the Lord, and the Lord hearing them, and delivering them out of all their trouble. It is from this point of view, that the Book of Psalms, in particular, may come home to every one of our hearts. Who cannot trace, in the vivid delineation of the Psalmist's personal experience, in his humiliation, his strong crying, and his tears, his trust in God, his firm assurance of the final triumph of the right, a type, as it were, and a portrait by forecast, alike of the struggles of whatever is noblest in the whole human race, and especially of Him, its great Captain and its Head, who was to cherish the almost expiring flame, until he made the struggle end in victory? Do we fret, as it were, in uneasy anxiety at our

* If any one supposes such a sentence as this either to exclude the preparations of the heart by God's providence and grace, or to imply indifference or despair as to truth (as if thoughts and inferences were less trustworthy than sensations), I can only wonder at his ingenuity in misunderstanding. What would such a person think of the first and second books of Hooker?

short life, and its ever-threatening end, — the Psalmist teaches us to make such fear an instrument of spiritual growth. "Lord, let me know mine end, and the number of my days, that I may be certified how long I have to live." "Teach me to number my days, that I may apply my heart unto wisdom." Yet, notwithstanding such appeal, do our spirits sink within us, either for our own backsliding, or for the blasphemy of the multitude on every side? How is such a feeling expressed better than in the words, "My heart panteth, my strength hath failed me: and the sight of mine eyes hath gone from me. My lovers and my neighbors did stand looking upon my trouble; . . . . and they that went about to do me evil talked of wickedness, and imagined deceit all the day long"? Would we have some one, alike righteous and friendly, to whom we may appeal with confidence? "Lord, thou knowest all my desire, and my groaning is not hid from thee. O Lord my God, be not thou far from me." Or does the consciousness of our own unworthiness bow us down, so that almost we say with St. Peter, "Depart from me, O Lord, for I am a sinful man"? Again, we may adopt the piteous cry, "Innumerable troubles are come about me; my sins have taken such hold upon me, that I am not able to look up; yea, they are more in number than the hairs of my head, and my heart hath failed me." "O Lord, let it be thy *pleasure* — that is, let it be the will of thy free grace — to deliver me; make haste, O Lord, to help me."

But, again, are such hopes and aspirations the jest of the ungodly, and do the drunkards make songs upon us, because we mourn in our prayer, and are vexed? "Fret not thyself," says the same faithful monitor, "because of the ungodly; neither be dismayed at the proud doer: yet a little while, and the ungodly shall be clean gone: hope thou in the Lord, and keep his way: when the ungodly shall perish, thou shalt see it." Yet does the kingdom of Heaven tarry, and the foundations of the earth seem out of course? "Tarry thou the Lord's leisure," is still the precept; "be strong, and he shall comfort thine heart": let the man of the earth leave much substance for his babes; but as for us, we will behold the presence of God in righteousness: the day cometh for us to be satisfied with his presence, when we wake up transformed according to his likeness.

What is it, then, brethren, which afflicts us? Sickness, and pining, of the body or of the heart, shrinking from the sneer of the wicked, remorse for our own sin, fear of again offending, fear of death, and of the dim unseen which is behind death? In all these things the Psalmist persuades us we are more than conquerors; for in the light which God shed upon him in the valley of shadows we too see light: we too have a share in the songs of faith, which God his maker gave him in the night of his affliction. Said not the Apostle well, therefore, "Whatsoever things were written aforetime, were written for our learning; that we, through patience and comfort of the Scriptures, might have hope"?

It may be interesting to remark here, that, although a very rigid criticism would find slender grounds for determining how many of the Psalms were absolutely written by David the son of Jesse, there is a sufficient consonance between the events of his life and the sentiments of a large portion of the number, to countenance decidedly that belief, which was the tradition alike of the Jewish Church and of our own. There is the same contrast in the life between David innocent and David guilty, as in the Psalms between his joyful exuberance of trust and his deep cry of remorse. Contrast in your memories the shepherd stripling, with his heart yet unstained, going forth to do battle with the giant warrior, and the guilty king ascending the hill with downcast brow, not daring to let his mighty men scourge the Benjamite, who had cursed the Lord's anointed. "Let him curse; the Lord hath said unto him, Curse David." Now this is the difference between innocence and guilt. Even so, how jubilant the cry of communion with his God: "The Lord is my strength: whom then shall I fear?" And how sad the agony of penitence: "Deep calleth unto deep at the noise of thy waterspouts; all thy waves have gone over me; my soul is full of trouble, and my life draweth nigh unto hell."

May we not learn there, brethren, the eternal and ineffaceable difference between doing the thing which is right, and forsaking the law of Him whose name is Holy? And was not such a lesson one of the principal reasons for which Scripture was written? Yet even in such dark depths we find Scripture still written for our consolation: since a way of sighs and tears, but still a way of hope, is pointed to in the words: "Thou shalt make me hear of joy and gladness, that the bones which thou hast broken may rejoice."

On turning forward to the Prophets, we find their general character is very much the same. One of their most striking features is their evidently intense perception of spiritual truths. This is the more remarkable, because mere religion (as taught by a priesthood) has been thought sometimes to blunt the moral sense, by making the Deity an arbitrary being, who acts apart from the eternal laws of right. Whereas it is apparent on the face, that neither the Psalmist nor the Prophets had any low or mean conception of the services of that sanctuary where the honor of Jehovah dwelt. The Psalms were in fact the main part of the Jewish liturgy; for the strains which now sweep through Westminster Abbey are the same as were chanted of old in the temple of Sion; and the Prophets never burst out into such indignant strains, as when their hearts burn within them at the sight of altars thrown down, the ark taken, or the temple defiled. Yet with all this, they ever lay most emphatic stress upon the weightier matters of the Law; upon the moral dispositions, and mental being, which are both the graces of the Holy Spirit and the processes by which we grow up into the full stature of the children of God.

If the hands are full of unjust gain, "bring no more incense, it is an abomination." If the feet are swift to evil, "who hath required it of you to tread my courts? saith the Lord." Will your solemn assemblies at new moons, and your Sabbaths, atone for a double heart, and for adding sin to sin? Can you by passionate prayers and ceremonial observances make a covenant with death? That is indeed to make *lies* your refuge. Judgment and righteousness are the line and the plummet with which the Lord layeth his sure foundation-stone. "Come now, let us *reason* together, saith the Lord: if your sins be as scarlet, *shall they** be as white as snow? if they be red like crimson, shall they (at the same time) be as wool?" *Think it not*, is the inexorable answer implied in the original: but "if ye be willing and obedient, ye shall eat the good of the land." "Wash you, make you clean: cease to do evil." "Let the wicked forsake his way, and the unrighteous man his thoughts: and let him return unto the Lord, for he will (then) have mercy upon him; and to our God, for he will abundantly pardon."

We have in such texts, which might be multiplied indefinitely, distinct intimation of the irreconcilable aversion of the Almighty to any form of moral evil, yet of his abundant readiness to pardon and save the sinner returning from his sin. Now it is this truly spiritual character of the Bible which fits it to be a book for all nations. Hence we do not fear to put it in the hands of the most ignorant, not indeed disparaging other means of grace, or forgetting that Scriptural language may be made the vehicle of the worst passions, and alleged to support the most dangerous errors: but we do so in the conviction, that to the pure all things are pure, and in the trust that He whose word came of old to prophets and teachers of righteousness, will not suffer even the record of the same word which then came to return altogether empty. Hence also our anxiety to place the same record of many a divine message to guilty man in the hands of the heathen: not from any bigoted dogma that the God and Father of all consolation will burn his children for not knowing what they were never taught; but from a perception, that the record of the holy words of prophets and evangelists has a natural tendency to awaken whatever is good in man, and so (if prop-

* This interrogative rendering is grammatically as probable as the common one, and, in sequence of thought, more so. [The common version of this text seems to me more correct; the condition of repentance being implied. — G. R. N.]

erly used) to help forward the moral restoration of a fallen nature. Thus then we believe with the Apostle, that whatever things were written aforetime, were written for our instruction.

There is, yet further, however, a distinct (but kindred) feature in the Hebrew prophets, which stamps their writings with peculiar value. It is that dim yet undoubting anticipation of a more perfect way than any commonly known in their age, which was to be revealed when the Hope of Israel should come. In other words, it is that foreboding of One anointed with the Holy Spirit and with power, which may especially be termed the spirit of prophecy; and in virtue of which we ascribe to its possessors a more than ordinarily large measure of (that sacred impulse, which may be described as) inspiration. We do not indeed assert, that the Hebrew prophets knew precisely what manner of salvation they foretold; for they often shadow it forth under such temporal deliverances, as to make the literal or Jewish interpretation of their predictions not altogether unreasonable. Nor, indeed, do they themselves make any claim to omniscience. The word of the Lord comes to their heart or conscience for a particular purpose, and they speak it; but where their own faculties and usual means of information can come into play, they naturally exercise them. Thus their language is simple Hebrew, and only when they reach Babylon, Chaldaic; the countries which they describe are those adjoining their own; their general range of knowledge is that of their age; in short, the circumscribed limits of their horizon stand out at every turn. Still amidst this imperfect knowledge we find those accents which stir the heart like the sound of a trumpet, foretelling with the strongest confidence the ultimate triumph of pure religion, the springing of a righteous Branch out of the stem of Jesse, and the reign of a King who should execute justice and mercy. New virtues, they say, shall flourish with this new dispensation; the nations shall not learn war any more; the sacrifice of the (human) heart shall be counted above that of bulls and oxen.

Although then some circumstances in the description of God's First-born and Elect, by whom this change is to be accomplished, may primarily apply to collective Israel, [many others * will admit of no such application. Israel surely was not the child whom a virgin was to bear; Israel did not make his grave with the wicked, and with the rich in his death; Israel scarcely reconciled that strangely blended variety of suffering and triumph which was predicted of the Messiah.]

But however that may be, it is indisputable that a change has partly come about, and is still partly proceeding; such as these ancient seers foretold. There is a growing society in the world, which, though ever lashed by stormy waves, seems still founded on a rock. Its members own as their Head one whom they hail as Prince of peace; an anointed one, a first-born, and an elect, — a Person, in whose mysterious unity they are able to combine things which might have been deemed incompatible: majesty and weakness, grace and awe, suffering and conquering, death and immortality, frail man and perfect God. † In him the mystery is unveiled, the riddle is read aright. In his kingdom men are exalted by humility, triumphant by patience, immortal by death: and to this his city not built with hands we are now taught by the interpreting revolution of events to apply what Isaiah spake of his ideal Sion: "Arise, shine; for thy light is come, and the glory of the Lord is risen upon thee. For, behold, the darkness shall cover the earth, and gross darkness the people: but the Lord shall arise upon thee, and his glory shall be seen upon thee. And the Gentiles shall come to thy light, and kings to the brightness of thy rising."

Thus, after the lapse of centuries, the world has seen the grand anticipations of those who worshipped Jehovah in a little corner of the world, fulfilled in a sense more magnificent

* I no longer feel confident of the assertion in brackets; but now believe that *all* the prophecies have primarily an application nearly contemporaneous. — *February* 11, 1855.

† This appears to me to be true only in the sense that the moral character of the Deity is discerned in "the face of Jesus Christ." — G. R. N.

than they themselves expected. Perhaps indeed this gift of foresight is not really more excellent or desirable than such a keen perception of the truths which concern our peace as we have already found in the Old Testament. Nor dare I say that the one has not been sometimes confounded with the other. Yet this gift of prediction, as distinct from predication, is so remarkable a quality as to invest the prophetical writings (according, at least, to the more received view of them) with a character almost unique, and to furnish a distinct ground for the Apostle's holding, that "whatever things were written aforetime were written for our instruction."

But if for *his instruction*, brethren, who had seen the Lord Jesus, much more for that of those whose lot is cast in later days. We, too, like St. Paul, may have our hearts warmed by whatever is glowing and excellent in the older writers; we, like him, may trace the great stream of Divine Providence, and admire the unconscious prefigurements of the great Teacher of the world; we, moreover, unlike him, may gather corresponding instruction from his own writings also, and from those of his companions in the ministry of the word. For though these later writings are scarcely comprised in the Scriptural canon to which our Saviour appealed, yet they come from men who had the best opportunities of information; who had seen the Son of God incarnate, and had been animated by the Holy Spirit of God descending; who also, in the power of what they believed, either from eyesight or from credible testimony, converted kingdoms, and built up the Church of Christ on the ruins of the gigantic power which they overthrew. Either the Apostles therefore understood Christianity, or else no one did. And now, suppose St. John or St. Peter were at present to reappear on earth, with what eager and devout curiosity should not we appeal to either of them in our controversies, and entreat him to clear up our difficulties! Who would deny his narrative of some miracle of our Lord's, or dispute his opinion as to what was pure and undefiled religion? But then may we not say, that such a power of appeal is already in our hands? St. John writing cannot be less trustworthy than St. John preaching. In neither case could he be termed omniscient; in both cases men might carry away a wrong conception of his meaning; yet surely in both we ought (as Christians) to award him and his fellows a respectful and candid hearing. On this ground then, that the Apostles generally saw our Lord, and had the best means of information as to his religion, their writings seem to be properly added to those of the Old Testament which they explain. They were men, indeed, compassed with infirmities like ourselves, and they professed only to know in part, and to prophesy in part. Yet God has not given us any higher written authority, and the highest which he has given must be sufficient for our salvation. But why reason from theory? Search rather their writings in practice, brethren, and you will find them sufficient for your peace. If indeed you disdain rational and proper helps, such as a competent knowledge of the original tongues, and of the customs, manners, and modes of thought of the persons using them, you may stumble grievously in this, as in any other inquiry. You may then, if both unlearned and also unstable, wrest the Scriptures to your own destruction. But if you are content to start with such a key as the Church puts into your hands in the form of the three primitive creeds, or of the English prayer-book generally, you cannot go greatly wrong, even in speculation. And if you use the Scriptures, as they were intended to be used, chiefly for warning, for encouragement, for consolation, you will find them the Book of books, — a shrine from whence light will stream on your path, and an oracle whose words will be comfort to your soul.

For, after all difficulties which may be raised, and all distinctions which must be made, these Hebrew and Christian Scriptures seem likely ever to constitute the book dearest to the downcast and the contrite, — to the bereaved, the outcast, and the Magdalene, — to all them that are stricken or afflicted in mind, body, or estate. So Collins, a man of the rarest genius and largest endowments, solaced the lucid intervals of an overwrought and shattered intellect with *one* book, — "*it was the best*," he said, — and it was the Bible. So many a soul stricken with remorse has been lured back to the way of life; and so (what after all, believe me, is far better) many a pure spirit has been strengthened to preserve its garments of fine linen unspotted through life, and so entered *without doubt* into an inheritance undefiled.

Lastly, from the same source, we ever may derive strength to resign those whom we love best into the hands of a merciful Creator and Redeemer; not fearing also ourselves, when God shall call us, to answer, "Even so, Lord: for so it seemed good in thy sight. Now therefore into thy hands we commend our spirits; for thou hast redeemed us, O thou God of Truth."

SERVANTS OF GOD SPEAKING AS MOVED BY THE HOLY GHOST.*

By ROWLAND WILLIAMS, B. D.,

FELLOW AND FORMERLY TUTOR OF KING'S COLLEGE, CAMBRIDGE, AND PROFESSOR OF HEBREW AT LAMPETER.

"Holy men of God spake as they were moved by the Holy Ghost." — 2 Peter i. 21.

So long as the religion of Christ is recommended only by the inherent weight of its ideas, it stands on nearly the same ground as the sentiments of justice or of right, if considered prior to their being exemplified in history, or embodied in law.

Few minds, we may hope, are so brutishly depraved as not to acknowledge their neighbor's right to his own life, to the fruit of his labor, and to fair dealing in all social transactions, if only the conceptions of those things are brought calmly and deliberately within cognizance of their thought. But yet the naked idea of justice is not found powerful to restrain men's actions with anything like the dominion which it is capable of acquiring when its principles have been embodied in law, transgression of them forbidden by penalty, and instances of their operation in all the transactions of life

---

* Preached before the University of Cambridge [Eng.], on the Second Sunday in Advent, December, 1854.

recorded and set forth in the history of a nation. So far, indeed, as the subjects of a realm are concerned, the authority which practically binds them is not that of the abstract sentiment of justice, but the positive law of the land.

A man is not permitted to argue that his conception of justice gives him a social claim; it is law which must ratify that claim, define its measure, and lay down the method of enforcing it. There is nothing in our own land so lofty, and not many things so minute, as not to fall within the range of positive and written law. But yet this law, which gives majesty to the sceptre, and edge to the sword, extending its ample shield over the lives of subject millions, and enforcing even for its own errors a sacredness which the wisest are the slowest to dispute, has behind it and underneath it a power greater than its own. For it is itself the creature of human thought; the ever-growing and often-varying embodiment of the conceptions of mankind; and although legislators, judges, and reformers, or even martyrs in the cause of freedom, may have spoken it of old, as they were moved by the providence and the Spirit of God, teaching them either through experience or through impulse, yet it is often marked by the imperfections of its time. The vessels in which the great treasure of the desire of justice was embodied, may have been vessels of earth; and if it is to retain its hold upon advancing generations, it must purify itself ever by contact with the living fountains of justice; must adapt its interpretation to new exigencies of social life; and must beware lest, by superstitious tenacity of the letter, any violence be done to the spirit, — even to that sense of righteousness in man, which is ever being trained upward, to realize the unwritten word of God.

Now we may very reasonably say, that to ourselves, as members of the Church of England, the great standard of theological doctrine must be that volume of Holy Scriptures which embodies the experience of the Church of old; the record of her revelations, and the tradition of her spiritual life; the transfusion, as it were, of her spirit into writing; which also the Church of our own land has stamped with authority, by adopting it as her written law. There are many obvious advantages in having so easy a court of appeal: an authority which teaches by example as well as by precept; a judge not biassed by our controversies of the day; and a record extending over a sufficiently ample range of time for questions of all kinds to have found in it a practical solution, — for the blessings of innocence, and for the judgments which wait on crime, to have been each very signally exemplified; and for the often-contending (though they ought to be harmonious) claims of king and priest and people, of power and weakness, of wealth and poverty, to have each had a limit assigned to them; — a sentence, as it were, having been passed upon them by that experience of generations which expresses the verdict of the great Ruler of the world. Moreover, it must be noticed, that Scripture will have a greater sacredness than law, because it deals with a subject-matter still more sacred; and although the relations which the two bear to the thing written about may be the same, yet since the subjects are different, the writings will also differ.

Yet it ought ever to be acknowledged, that this Holy Scripture, which all members of our Church so justly regard with veneration, has also something behind it deeper* and far holier still; and if that spirit by which holy men spake of old is for ever a living and a present power, its later lessons may well transcend its earlier; and there may reside in the Church a power of bringing out of her treasury things new as well as things old.

If it had been the will of Almighty God, we cannot doubt his power to have instructed mankind by pouring before their gaze from the beginning all the treasures of his providence, and all the wonders of his grace. But it has pleased Him, who doeth all things well, to train up his Israel as a child, and to make the experience of bygone generations a landmark for

* To deny this, is to deny Christ far more utterly than the Galatians did; and for any one to call such sayings an inversion of the groundwork of Christianity, only shows the urgent need there is for servants of God to preach them.

those who were to come. There was a time when as yet the Bible was not, and we must not think that it was necessary to salvation. For the Spirit of God may have then striven with men; possibly even his Eternal Offspring, the not yet Incarnate Word, may have preached through the movements of conscience, and through words of warning, in the days of Noah. Certainly Enoch may have walked with God; Melchisedec may, in the sanctity of a Gentile priesthood, have blessed Abraham; the faith of the patriarch in One who was his shield and his exceeding great reward, may have been counted to him as righteousness; and all these, and others whom no man can number, may have been gathered to the spirits of just men made perfect, if not before any records existed, at least centuries before the earliest of our sacred books took their present form.

But when the patriarchs have grown into twelve tribes, they are become a nation, and a nation must have a history; when they come out from the house of bondage, and conquer a new land, the Author of their deliverance, and the Giver of their conquest, must have his wondrous works recorded; when they have law, which is to be enforced by human rulers, though with reference to the Divine Ruler, it must be written in some express form; or, just as man, because he has the gift of reason, will utter speech with meaning, so the nation, because thoughts are stirring in its breast, must have a voice to speak forth the national mind; and if the life which animates its thoughts be truly religious, the words which are their utterance must be sacred words. Thus, where there is a church, there must be a Bible or a liturgy; where there is a true temple, there will be solemn psalms; where decay or formalism creeps over the servants of the sanctuary, if the spirit of God has compassion on his people to awaken them, there will arise prophets, whose protest will be couched in accents pregnant with eternal truth; who will say to the dry bones, "Live," and to the prostrate Church, "Stand upon thy feet."

Thus, although man is gathered to his fathers, yet, as

nations and churches represent, throughout fleeting generations, the everlasting providence and spirit of God, so it is probable they will strive to prevent their best thoughts from being swept into forgetfulness; and they will, by writing, give a permanent shape to their record of things temporal, and to their perception of things divine.

Then, again, if the destined course of the world be really one of providential progress, if there has been such a thing as a childhood of humanity, and if God has been educating either a nation or a church to understand their duty to himself and to mankind; it must follow, that, when the fulness of light is come, there will be childish things to put away. Not (indeed) that any part will have been useless in its day; perhaps a certain *unalterableness of spirit* may run through every link of the chain. Yet, if the chain is one of living men, each link must have a freedom of expansion, and there will be a power of modifying mere circumstance very different from the bare continuity of inanimate things. Hence, if the religious records represent faithfully the inner life of each generation, whether a people or a priesthood, they will all be, in St. Paul's phrase, *divinely animated*, or with a divine life running through them; and every writing divinely animated will be useful; yet they *may*, or rather they *must*, be cast in the mould of the generation in which they were written; their words, if they are true words, will express the customs of their country, the conceptions of their times, the feelings or aspirations of their writers; and the measure of knowledge or of faith to which every one, in his degree, had attained. And the limitation, thus asserted, of their range of knowledge, will be equally true, whether we suppose the short-coming to be, on an idea of *special* Providence, from a particular dictation of sentiment in each case; or whether, on the more reasonable view of a *general* Providence, we consider such things permitted rather than directed; the natural result of a grand scheme, rather than a minute arrangement of thoughts and words for each individual man. It may be that the Lord writes the Bible, on the same principle as the Lord builds the city; or that he teaches the Psalmist to sing, in the same sense as he teaches his fingers to fight; thus that the composition of Scripture is attributed to the Almighty, just as sowing and threshing are said to be taught by him;* for every part played by man comes from the Divine Disposer of the scene.

By some such process, however, as has above been sketched, it has pleased the Giver of all wisdom to bring about for us through his providence the writing of these sacred books, which comprehend (1.) the literature of the Hebrew people, (2.) the oracles of Jehovah's priesthood, and (3.) the experience of the apostles of Christ.

For such seems to be a division under which we may naturally class those many voices of the Church of God, or those records of the spiritual convictions of the great society in which the fear of the Lord has been inherited from generation to generation, the aggregate of which books we call the Bible. Shall we venture to glance at each of these divisions in turn? We claim for the oldest of our sacred books an antiquity of perhaps fifteen hundred years before the Christian era. But the external evidence for their existence can hardly be said to extend over more than half that period. For all the earlier half, we rely chiefly upon the contents of the books themselves. Nor can we even appreciate this kind of evidence without a certain freedom of investigation, which proceeds upon what Hooker assumes as the primary revelation of the human understanding. Yet from this kind of evidence we are able, for a large part of the earlier books, to prove an origin of very high antiquity. Partly, the language agrees with what the date requires; as in the earlier books of the Pentateuch there are Egyptian words; partly, the manners agree, whether we glance at the ancient castes of Egypt, as attested by her monumental stones, or at the wandering tents of the patriarchal tribes; partly, again, the general scenery is true in character; and,

---

* Isaiah xxviii. 23 – 29.

still more decisively, the general tone of feeling, and the mental horizon, as it were, of the writers, is exactly what we should expect, as in due proportion to the age in which their lot was cast. Only, it must be added, that all these proofs of genuineness are also equally proofs of a positive limitation to the range of knowledge. We cannot in one moment say, these books were written in such an age because they have the knowledge of that age, and in the next moment argue that they have a divine omniscience, and therefore were *dictated*, or, as it were, dropped from heaven; for this would be, with the greatest inconsistency, to destroy our own argument and to introduce miracle, where we have been assuming the faithfulness of God's providence; as if we said, that the rain * and the sunshine are a contradiction to those laws of the Author of Nature which seem intended expressly to guide them.

Here, therefore, both for the above reasons, and for others to be mentioned hereafter, let me in all humility protest against that unwise exaggeration which makes the entire Bible a transcript of the Divine omniscience, or a word of God for all time, without due reference to the circumstances and to the range of knowledge of those holy men who spake of old. The writers, after all, are *men;* and the condition of mankind is imperfection. They were *holy* men and servants of God; but yet all human holiness and all human service is only comparative, and a thing of degree. They *spake;* but speech is the organ of thought; therefore there is nothing in the Scripture but what was first in the mind of the scribe. *Nihil est in Scripto, quod non prius in Scriptore.* They spake *of old;* but all old times represent, as it were, the childhood of the human race, and therefore had childish things, which we must put away. The *Holy Ghost* was their teacher; but the province of this eternal Agent in our redemption is not to give knowledge of earthly facts, which we know by the providence of the Father, nor yet to give a new revelation of things heavenly, which we know by the positive

* Dr. Powell of St. John's.

incarnation of the Son; but the province of the *Holy Ghost* is rather to quicken our conceptions of things otherwise known; to hallow our impulses, restrain our wanderings, and guide our steps in those paths which the Father and the Son have already laid down for us to walk in.

But let no one therefore suppose that this limitation of the knowledge of the sacred writers should lessen the sacredness, or destroy to us the usefulness, of that literature which, according to the measure of its time, the Church of God spake of old. We may receive the message of the servants as true without for a moment dreaming that the great Master had communicated to them all the knowledge of his eternal plan. We may acknowledge the history a very wonderful one, because the events which it records were first wonderful. On the same principle as the very structure of the Hebrew sentence is a written echo of the chant of the temple, so that acknowledgment of the living God, which they whom the nations despise, and Christians often misrepresent, have held fast amidst a thousand persecutions, runs throughout their history as a memorial of the mighty works of Jehovah in the land of Ham, and by the Red Sea.

Without here venturing upon the very debatable ground of where miracle begins and where providence ends, or without determining (what perhaps is by no means so important as many may suppose) how much we ought strictly to assign to each, we may safely say, the entire history, or literature, is one which seems destined to be the handmaid of true religion in the world. Just as the ancient Greek manifested the sensitiveness of his organization and the activity of his mind by a literature moulded in beauty and full of speculation; and as the Roman, whose mission it was to civilize the world with law, spoke the firm language of history and of manly virtue; so the Hebrew, having been wonderfully trained, laid the wisdom of the Egyptians at the feet of Jehovah; he looked upon the earth and its fulness, and he said aloud, "It is the Lord's"; he saw kings reign, and he felt that One mightier than they had set fast their thrones; he heard of his fathers migrating, and marrying, and burying their dead in a strange land; and he felt that not one of these things was disregarded in the sight of Him who teacheth the wild-fowl their course through the heaven, and who upholdeth also our steps in life: or he bowed in the sanctuary on Mount Zion; and, as the question arose, "Who shall ascend into the hill of the Lord, or stand in his holy place?" the Spirit of God within him made answer, "He that hath clean hands and a pure heart; that hath not spoken the name of Jehovah over falsehood, nor sworn to deceive his neighbor."

Thus, in short, the spirit which runs through the literature of the Hebrews is eminently a religious spirit; in their history, and in their proverbs, and in the common stories of the people, though these may have been moulded somewhat in Oriental form, there is a true reference of all things to the will of a righteous Lord.

But, still more emphatically, the same character applies to the direct utterances of the great teachers of righteousness; to the oracular songs of the Temple, and to the kindling accents in which the prophets woke the conscience of their compatriots, as they denounced the fierce anger of a Judge long provoked by incurable sin. There priest and prophet go harmoniously hand in hand; so that the attempts of the assailants of church polity to sever their functions are but vain. It is the province of the priest, not only to teach the difference between the holy and the profane, but also that his lips should keep knowledge; and again, however earnestly the prophet may cry aloud for reformation of heart, he yet never ceases to maintain the sacredness of whatever has had spoken over it the holy name of the Most High.

Only we cannot judge either one or the other truly, unless we regard them in the closest connection with the history of the people among whom they are written. For they are not so much a word of God, externally dropping from heaven, as a true confession to God, responding from the heart of man. Both the deep sighing of passionate devotion, and the fervent trust in a deliverer out of national bondage, would lose half their value, unless we believed that they came from men who prayed earnestly for themselves; who had tasted the rod of the oppressor; and who were concerned about the realities of their own mind and their own time. But why should not their devout sayings, and all the heroic deeds of trust, or love, or magnanimity, serve to the same end in religion, as the history of kingdoms in politics, and the strains of poetry in education, without our presuming to assign to the writers an infallibility which they never claim for themselves? We may read Moses, not for his physical geography, but for his ten commandments and his history. We may read the book of Joshua, not for its astronomy, but for a tremendous example of the law by which God sweeps corrupt nations from the earth; we may find in Kings and Chronicles, not imaginary and faultless men, but subjects of Divine providence, instances of Divine teaching, and all that blending of interest with instruction, which the history of a devout people, told with reference to the Judge of the whole earth, is ever calculated to afford. We may also fully admit the unalterableness of Scripture, in the sense that deeds truly done cannot be undone, and fixed principles cannot be changed; nor would it be modest, to weigh the personal authority of even the most spiritual teacher now, against that of the Apostles who followed Christ; but yet we need not suppose that the arm of the Eternal is shortened, or that his Holy Spirit ever ceases to animate the devout heart. Above all, let no man blunt the edge of his conscience, by praising such things as the craft of Jacob, or the blood-stained treachery of Jael; nor let the natural metaphor, by which men call a sacred record "the word of God," ever blind us to the fact, that no text has been found, from Genesis to Revelations, in which this holy name is made a synonyme for the entire volume of Scripture; but rather, the spirit is often, especially in the New Testament, put in opposition to the letter, and the living word, as for instance it was spoken by the Apostles, is constantly distinguished from the written tradition of the days of old. Most commonly in the New Testament, the phrase *word of*

God means the gospel of Christ, or the glad tidings of the Messiah being come. It should also be noticed, that, while the discoveries of modern travellers do so far confirm the books of the Old Testament, as to show their historical character, they give no countenance to any exaggerated theory of omniscience, or dictation, but rather contravene any dream of the kind. When men quote discoveries as confirmations of the Bible, they should consider in what sense and how far it is confirmed by them.

And now, if we pass on to the experience of the apostles of Christ, we shall find ample means for enabling us to fix its true value upon the record of Holy Scripture. However true it may be, that we know less of the individual writers, and of the precise dates of the three earlier Gospels, than our fathers took rather for granted, yet it is certain that they express the belief and the preaching of the Church in the first century of the Christian era. Thus, instead of three men, we may rather appeal to the united testimony of the hundred and twenty persons who constituted the infant Church before the day of Pentecost.

And although some few books, such as the Epistle from which our text is taken, have their authorship reasonably called in question, yet modern criticism does, on grounds of internal evidence, agree very closely with that belief as to the genuineness of the Apostolic writings in general, which the primitive Church adopted, from traditions of her own. (This, by the way, is an instance in which our modern freedom of investigation has added a fresh argument to our evidence.)

In these books, then, we find traces of a new spirit in the world. We have the thoughts of those who walked with Christ, and heard the gracious words which he spake. We have the simple fervor of one apostle; the despondent diffidence of another; the angelic loveliness and the love of a third; and, above all, we have the Judaic learning, the awakened mind, the passionate zeal, the practical energy, and the combining wisdom of St. Paul. The Epistles of this one writer will alone prove that, whenever our Gospels may have been, perhaps, moulded out of the familiar converse of the Apostles into their present form, the belief in our Lord's resurrection from the grave was at least current long before the destruction of Jerusalem.

Now, all these writers of the New Testament appear partly as antagonists of the Old, and partly as witnesses who confirm it. Partly they are antagonists, for even the doctrines of Christ find fault with much that had been spoken of old. He appeals from the law of Moses about marriage to the purer instinct of the heart, as that which had been from the beginning; he refuses to confirm the law of retaliation; and both he and his apostles, but especially St. Paul, turn men's thoughts from the tradition of the wisdom of old time, which was principally enshrined in the Bible, to that life of the soul which comes of the Holy Ghost, and to the ever-expanding law which is both written in the heart, and which accumulates enactment from experience. For St. Paul's "tradition" contains his Hebrew descent, and his circumcision on the eighth day, with many other things which had been purely scriptural. They had all been written in the volume of the Book, and yet he repudiates them all.

Whereas, on the other hand, the Scribes and Pharisees call the followers of Jesus accursed for not knowing the law; by which they mean the Scripture. They even pride themselves on searching the Scriptures, for they thought that therein they had eternal life. Yet our Lord does not hesitate to blame them, as searching the Scriptures in vain.

So again, St. Paul calls the Galatians foolish for desiring to be under the law, under which term he includes the book of Genesis. He is quite in accord with Jeremiah, who had prophesied a time under Christianity when the word of God should be written, not in book or stone, but on the fleshly tables of the heart, or in the conscience of reasonable beings. Yet, it is true, the same Apostle thinks that the Divine Teacher of mankind had never ceased to warn his Church of old; and that by the great principle of trust in an unseen but all-righteous Guide, he had led its members from the beginning; and hence all the utterances of that Church, or the traditions of the Old Testament, are divinely animated; they are written for our instruction; for who would not listen to the lessons of a great history of thought, or would spurn the inheritance of his ghostly fathers? And thus their tendency is to make the servant of God wise, putting him, through the medium of an enlightened understanding, on the track as it were of Christian salvation.

Again, while the writings of the apostles of Christ represent chiefly the principle of the living spirit, they are themselves the utterance of the Church, or of that society which is the habitation of the ever-present Spirit of God; and, when duly preserved, they are capable of being themselves handed down as an inheritance or a tradition; yet, as being a tradition of a spiritual age, they may become witnesses, either for sober history against vague mysticism, or for the lively inspiration of the heart against the more lifeless tradition of a grosser and more formalized age.

What blessed lessons, then, may we not derive, if we are wise, from those holy books? What evidences do they not afford of our faith! They do not merely record, so much as absolutely *talk* of the inspired lives of the men who indited them. What warning do they not utter, as with a trumpet's sound, when we, forgetful of the Rock from whence we are hewn, become negligent in the work of the Lord! What comfort do they not breathe, in all our sorest distress,—in our perplexity of mind, in our pain of body, and in our lowliness of estate! By cherishing their words we assimilate our thoughts to the minds of apostles, and saints, and martyrs; casting, as it were, our earth-bound affections over again in a holier mould, and so drinking of the deep fountains which have their source in the well of life beneath the throne of the majesty of God our Saviour.

Let no man be ashamed, if the page on which such words are written is often wet with his tears; or if their fashion, though in many things it be temporal, give shape and voice to his deepest thoughts of things eternal. Neither intellect, nor humanity, nor devotion, can anywhere be better purified and strengthened than in the homely page either of our familiar Prayer-book or of our Bible. There our sorrow and our guilty alarm will almost inevitably flee for comfort; and there, if we are wise, we shall learn in time to discipline our youth, and to purify our joy.

But yet, brethren, let no inconsiderate exaggeration, and no polemical reaction from overstrained claims of the Church of Rome, induce us to mistake the spirit of the Gospel or of the Cross for the letter of the Bible. A man may know his Bible by heart, and yet turn a deaf ear to the word of God. He may lay stress on temporary accidents, such as *anointing with oil;* and may be blind to eternal principles, such as faith, hope, charity. He may even express the most malignant passion in Scriptural phrase, as if truth were more true, or malice were less hateful, because the vehicle in which it is conveyed may be of Aramaic form. Thus some have defended *slavery* because they truly observe that St. Paul's epistles do defend it, and even condemn attempts to abolish it as the work of men "proud, knowing nothing." * Yet it is evident, that God had destined slavery to flee away in time before the principles with which the Gospel is pregnant. Thus our religion is one thing, and the books which record it are another. Some, again, have laid unreasonable stress upon the accidental opposition of Christianity to the governments and religions of the corrupt generation in which it was first founded; and hence many irrational arguments against kings and priests; yet it is evident that the sacredness of the office of governor, and of teacher, and of rightful minister in the sanctuary, must last as long as this world endures. How many, again, with most unfair sophistry, distort various texts of Scripture in order to force them unnaturally into a harmony which they suppose needful; whereas the very idea of a divine teaching, which lies at the bottom of the Bible, implies also the idea of progress, and makes it natural for the

---

* 1 Tim. vi. 2 – 4.

newer sentences to differ from the old. So, again, every new science has to run the gauntlet of opposition, until, after forcing its way through bitter searchings of heart, it is at last pretended to be in harmony with those texts which were once (more truly, but yet quite irrelevantly) alleged to oppose it. Time would fail me to tell of Puritan perverseness, of fanaticism passing into tyranny, of science persecuted, reason insulted, morality depraved, and the Gospel of Christ congealed, mutilated, and clipped, as it were, of its wings, because men have assumed what the Bible does not assume, that inspiration means omniscience, or that the All-gracious Father, who taught men of old, has his unsleeping eye blinded or his arm shortened, so that he can teach us now no more. But perhaps no single study has suffered so much from this cause as the interpretation of the Bible itself. It may, however, be suggested, whether devotion also has not suffered somewhat. For although the Psalms and other sacred writings are a treasury of expressions which harmonize admirably with the deepest breathings of our hearts; yet, when men compile prayers from these with servile imitation, as schoolboys take verses from the poets, the spirit of devotion is apt to be exorcised. And this is one reason why modern prayers are so inferior to the ancient liturgies; for so long as the Church of old believed in the real presence of the Holy Ghost, she waxed mighty in prayer as she grew rich in experience; then the storehouse of her liturgies became heaped with things old, and yet her heart ever indited good matters that were new; and from those fountains the stream of prayer has flowed into all lands, until, at last, our bishops and pastors, as if they despaired of the promise of Christ, would take no weapon in hand that had not been hammered on the Jewish anvil. And so, many of our modern prayers have become a lifeless patchwork of texts; * a disquisition to the

* Compare Jeremy Taylor, Preface to *Golden Grove*. Would that those who in our own time have right manfully endeavored to heal the disease of unreality in our devotional compilations, did not too often

people, instead of a crying to God; and, as there is little affection in them which might even savor of the spirit, so there is often something which offends the understanding. We have fallen, in this respect, far below the level which the genius and the piety of Hooker had attained three centuries ago. That illustrious champion, both of the purity of the Gospel of Christ and of the freedom of the human mind, shows clearly, in the second book of his immortal work, how Scripture may become "a *misery*," and "a *torment*," and "a *snare*"; and his counsel is most truly judicious, that we should beware, lest, by claiming for Holy Scripture more than we ought, we provoke men to deny it its due; lest, in fact, we pervert the Bible itself, and either destroy the spirituality of our faith, or give occasion to many perverse delusions; or, again, provoke till we almost justify a most dangerous reaction into scoffing infidelity.

But if such was Hooker's counsel in his own time, how much greater need is there that some one, either in his spirit, or in that of the incomparable Jeremy Taylor, should speak words of even bolder counsel now! For it hath pleased the Giver of our thoughts, and the Disposer of our lot, to enlarge on all sides the boundaries of human knowledge. There is no science of the heavens above, or of the earth beneath, or of the waters under the earth, which has not revealed mysteries of its own; or which does not refuse to be limited by the brief range of the Hebrews, who in all such things were learners rather than teachers. Again, our more extended familiarity with other literatures daily shows us that aspirations congenial to those of the Hebrews had been taught elsewhere by the God of the spirits of all flesh. But, above all, the critical interpretation of the sacred volume itself is a

---

bring their own remedies from the dregs of the Middle Ages: and often, by assembling merely the dolorous portions out of Scripture, make work in feminine and sensitive natures for physicians of the body, (I speak from sad observation,) rather than do the work of the Physician of souls. But the true kingdom of God brings peace and joy in believing, with childlike confidence.

study for which our generation is, by various acquirements, eminently qualified. Hence we have learnt that neither the citations usually made in our theological systems, nor even those adduced from the Old Testament in the New, are any certain guide to the sense of the original text. The entire question of prophecy requires to be opened again from its very foundation. Hence, to the student who is compelled to dwell on such things, comes often the distress of glaring contradictions; and with some the intellect is clouded, while the faith of others has waxed cold. If the secret religious history of the last twenty years could be written, (even setting aside every instance of apostasy through waywardness of mind, or through sensuality of life,) there would remain a page over which angels might weep. So long, indeed, as such difficulties are thought absolutely to militate against Christianity, the strong necessity which the best men feel for Christian sentiment will induce them to keep the whole subject in abeyance. Yet surely the time must come when God will mercifully bring our spirit into harmony with our understanding. Perhaps a greatness and a place not far from the Apostles in the kingdom of heaven may be reserved for some one, who, in true holiness and humility of heart, shall be privileged to accomplish this work. We can almost sympathize with that romantic though erroneous faith, which has made some men attempt to roll back the stream of human knowledge, and to take refuge from doubts in a dream of living infallibility. But all such attempts must fail; for the God of truth will make them fail. He who dwells in light eternal does not promote his kingdom by darkness; and He whose name is Faithful and True is not served by falsehood. If knowledge has wounded us, the same spear must heal our wound.

Nor can I close without humbly asking the grave, the reverend, and the learned, whether all this subject does not call for greater seriousness, tenderness, and frankness. Who would not be serious on observing how many men's hope of heaven is bound up with belief in the infallibility of a book, which, every day convinces us, expresses, as regards things of earth, the thoughts of fallible men? Or who would not pity rather than blame, when the very inquiries in which the love of God and zeal for his honor first engaged us seem to introduce (according to popular theories) the most distressing contradictions? Or who is so blind as to think the cause of eternal truth should be defended by sophistries, of which a special pleader would be ashamed? One would make large allowance for the conscientious anxiety of those eminent persons, whose position makes them responsible as bulwarks of the faith; and who are ever dreading the consequences to which the first outlet of the waters of freedom may tend. But may God in his mercy teach them, that nothing can be so dangerous as to build on a false foundation. The question, *how far we would go*, will best be answered by experience. Only it never will be safe to stop short of the Truth.

But, in fact, almost everything doubtful, or, at least, everything transparently erroneous, in our sacred books, might be surrendered to-morrow with little or rather no detriment to the essentials of the Christian faith. It is strangely unreasonable for men to argue that they cannot believe God ought to be worshipped in spirit and in truth, unless they are also convinced that Cyrenius was president of Syria, or that the Cretans were always liars. Nor ought any one to doubt whether God made sea and land, because it may fairly be questioned how far the poetry in Joshua about the sun standing still (or the allegory in Jonah about the whale) ought to be interpreted literally.

Almost all difficulties which are fairly raised belong to those things of earth, about which well-meaning Martha was unnecessarily cumbered; while the life and the power and the salvation are the inalienable inheritance of Mary, while she sits in calmness at the feet of the Saviour.

Let not then exaggerations, or polemical inferences, frighten us in vain. We may grant to the Romanist, as well as to many Anglicans, that the Church was before the Bible, as a speaker is before his voice; and that Holy Scripture is not the foundation of the Christian faith so much as its creature, its expression, and its embodiment. But it will not therefore follow that this Holy Scripture should be sealed in dead languages, or withheld from men thirsting for the words of life. Nor ought any modern mystic to persuade us that the history of the Divine dealings of old is ever useless to the human mind; and yet we may concede that the two things from which Scripture sprang are for ever in the world, — I mean the conscience of man, and the Holy Spirit of God. From these two, meeting in the Church, the Bible derives its origin, its authority, and its power to persuade.

I exhort, therefore, every soul who hears me to value highly the Bible; to read it, pray over it, understand it. But yet beware of lying for God; or of ascribing infallibility to men of like passions with ourselves; or of sacrificing the spirit which enlivens to the letter which deadens.

So may you deserve the praise of those ancient Berœans, who are ever honored because they were *more ingenuous* (εὐγενέστεροι), or because their minds were candid in receiving the truth. So too will you be, not infidels, but believers in Holy Writ, when it tells you that its authors knew only in part, and prophesied only in part; so will you avoid attributing blasphemy to them, by calling the word of God that which they profess to speak as *men;* and even to speak as fools; so will you not make them, as writers, more than they were as speakers; nor will you sever, as they did not sever, their inspiration from that of the congregation at large, when they exclaim, "I think that I too" (δοκῶ δὲ κἀγώ), that is, "I, as well as others, have the Spirit of God." But above all, so will you be blessed, as servants of that living God who is never weary of creating, and whose promise is that he will dwell among us; and so too disciples of Jesus, who prayed, not for his Apostles only, but for all who should believe through their word; whose most precious testament was, not, I give you the Bible, but, "I send you the Comforter, even the Spirit of truth"; and whose binding promise is, not, I am with the first generation of Christians, and possibly with the second, but, "Lo, I AM WITH YOU ALWAY, EVEN TO THE END OF THE WORLD." *

---

* Abundant proofs of the non-Petrine origin of the Epistle called St. Peter's Second, are given in the second edition of Bunsen's *Hippolytus*, from whence, however, I did not learn it. Even Eusebius had said, "Of the writings named as Peter's, I know only one Epistle genuine." *Hist. Eccl.* III. 3. The internal character of the Epistle corresponds with this external disavowal. But if any one asks me, Why then take your text from it? such a questioner, I presume, thinks that a sentiment cannot be true, or worthy of commentary, unless it be a particular Apostle's; that is to say, he thinks things are true because they are written, instead of being written because they are true; or again, he thinks that the Church has not authority sufficient to persuade even her own ministers what books they shall lecture upon. But to no one of these propositions am I able to assent; nor again do I feel any difficulty in adopting the sentiment of my text, whoever may have written it.

Having said positively that *nowhere* in Holy Scripture is the term "word of God" made an equivalent or synonyme for the Bible, I may refer to the Sermon on the Kingdom of God for an explanation of some texts usually misapplied. I did not make up my own mind on this specific point until after a consideration extending over many years. The two texts most favorable to the vulgar Pharisaism are perhaps St. Mark vii. 13 and vii. 7; but in the one, the thing intended is the fifth commandment, as we see from St. Matthew xv. 4, 9, where also we find things both Levitical and Scriptural condemned by our Lord (see ver. 10, 11): and in the other, the antithesis is not between written and unwritten, but between divine will and human precept. Perhaps παράδοσις means *precept* oftener than *tradition*.

It should, however, be clear, that I know of no tradition, ecclesiastical or other, worthy to be named in the same day with St. Paul's Epistles; and I admit κατὰ συμβεβηκὸς the approximate coextensiveness of our New Testament Scriptures and of Apostolic doctrine; only I cannot violate the first principles of Christianity itself, as well as of human reason, by putting the letter before the spirit, or the books before the religion, as our popular tradition does. We are rightly taught that "all Holy Scripture is written *for our instruction*." Whenever, therefore, it is used to stunt our knowledge, or fetter our spirits, it must be misapplied; as we read that it was by the great Tempter.

THE SPIRIT AND THE LETTER, OR THE TRUTH AND THE BOOK.*

By ROWLAND WILLIAMS, B. D.,

FELLOW AND FORMERLY TUTOR OF KING'S COLLEGE, CAMBRIDGE, AND PROFESSOR OF HEBREW AT LAMPETER.

"After the way which (they) call heresy, so worship I the God of my fathers." — Acts xxiv. 14.

THERE certainly was a time when to be a member of the Society of Friends implied something greater than more or less harmless peculiarities; for they bore witness before princes and people, in bonds and persecution, for the great principle of the spirit of the living God, and were not ashamed. If then one of them had been asked, Do you not worship the God of battles? he might possibly have answered, No; and again, if he were told that the Almighty is called in the Old Testament the Lord of hosts, it is conceivable that he might have rejoined, But we have better oracles. Immediately upon this might have been raised a cry, This man is an infidel, for he denies the Scriptures; or rather an atheist, for he disowns the Lord of hosts. Yet the Quaker again might plead, that he had learnt to know God, not so much by might, or by power, as by the spirit wherewith he has taught us to call him, "Our Father which is in heaven."

---

* Preached before the Vice-Chancellor and University of Cambridge [Eng.], in King's College Chapel, on March 25, 1855.

He might go on to affirm, that, in thus recognizing the eternal I AM under his more blessed character as the Prince of Peace, he did not for a moment deny the same Lord to have been known as Almighty by the patriarchs, and as Eternal by the Jews; but still, that the sundry times and divers manners of ancient revealing had somewhat melted in the brightness of the revelation of that Spirit, which cometh forth from the Father and the Son. Thus, that many things "said of old time," * in the rigor of the letter, must now be interpreted, or rather expanded, in the freedom of life; and so, after a manner which, even if it were called heresy, was yet the manner of Christ and his apostles, he worshipped the God of his fathers.

Nor would such an answer be unlike in spirit to those which the great Apostle of the Gentiles often urges in vain upon the attention of his irritated countrymen. For it is not only at Athens that he is called an introducer of new divinities; but at Jerusalem he is denounced as one who taught apostasy from the sacred place, and the Book of the Law, and the worship of the God of the Hebrews.† Difficult as it may be, with our scanty information, to reconcile some parts of his conduct — such as the "being at charges" in participation of sacrifice in the temple — with his argument in the Epistle to the Galatians, we are yet able to observe a wonderful blending of courage with delicacy in his management of the many intricate questions which are proposed to him. He does not think that the Father of the spirits of all flesh was a God of the Jew only, and not also of the Gentile, yet he concedes there may have been great advantage in those opportunities of enlightenment, and in that faithfulness of the Divine promises, which belonged to the

* Compare the running antithesis, St. Matt. v. 21 - 27, 31, 43, with Jer. xxxi. 31, 32; Heb. viii. 8 - 10; 2 Cor. iii. 4 - 14; 1 Cor. ii. 7; iii. 1; 1 John ii. 20 - 27.

† The common charge against the early Christians was, with Jews, infidelity; with Gentiles, atheism. The word *heresy* had not yet acquired its technical sense.

chosen people of old. So he admits even the Law of Moses to have been in its idea holy and pure, yet he contends that this sanctity was not from the fact of its being imposed with penalties at the Exodus, but from its participation in those older and holier principles of which Abraham had the promise, and even the Gentiles a scripture in their heart. The Law, then, so far as it is Mosaic, and penal, or even outwardly preceptive, can never be the highest guide of those who have the mind of Christ, — yet its ancient records may still be useful; and not only would he quote them largely, in addressing Jews who "desired to be under them," as he quotes even Gentile prophets in addressing Athenians, but his own mind was evidently imbued with reverential affection towards those songs of Zion which (as the liturgy of his race) he must often have sung in solemn services, and to those deeply searching prophets whose fervent spirit, ever penetrating from the form of godliness to its power, was so often a type of his own.

Again, the Apostle does not seem able to contend, that the entire scheme of Christianity is legible in the Old Testament with that perfect clearness which some modern interpreters would compel us to acknowledge; and our favorite citations of prophecy find in him little place; but yet he thinks there was always a unity in the Divine dealings; the predestination of the Gospel may have been veiled, but yet it must have been predestined * as a scheme for calling men to repentance from all eternity; and though this veiled design had lurked under the choice of temporal Israel, and under the offering of slain beasts, and the form of written precepts, yet its meaning (mystery) would be revealed in the uncovering to all men of the face of the Father, — in the lively sacrifices of men saying by the spirit of Christ, "Lo, I come to do thy will," † — and in the purified vision of consciences quickened by a faith which should draw life from love, and thereby be the fulfilment of the highest law.

* First chapter of Ephesians.

† Compare Psalm xl. 8 and Hebrews x. 7 – 9.

Thus is St. Paul a servant, faithful to Christ, and yet wise in the wisdom of Moses; bringing out of his treasury things new, without dissociating them rudely from things old.

Now we cannot say that any change so great as that heralded by the first preachers of Christ is to be expected in our own time. For certainly the words of Christ, in their highest meaning, do not pass away. May there not, however, be something sufficiently analogous for the great Apostle's example in this, as in other respects, to have been written for our instruction, though upon us the last dispensation is come? Even in the same generation, there are many persons who may claim alike the designation of Christians, yet whose conceptions of the Gospel differ so widely, that no one of them could adopt the views of any other one without a change of mind so sweeping as to be painful. Even in our own lives, if we have made it our business to study religion, either as a matter of thought or of practice, we cannot but be conscious of passing through certain changes of apprehension. When we are children, we think as children; and when we are men, we put away childish things. But, much more, in a succession of generations, very great differences may be expected to prevail in the mode of holding a truth essentially the same.* The Christianity of the early Fathers of the Church is hardly that of St. Augustine; still less is it that of St. Anselm, † or of Calvin. The great object of our faith remains the same yesterday, to-day, and for ever; but those reflections from his thoughts, which are thrown figuratively ‡ on the mirror of our understanding, may be darker or more distinct, from day to day. Perhaps even the very truth which saves the soul,

---

* See some admirable remarks on this, needed now more than when they were written, in Professor Hey's Norrisian Lectures, edited by Bishops Kaye and Turton.

† A sufficient notion of St. Anselm may be got from some recent Bampton Lectures by Mr. Thompson; but the accomplished author seems to be hardly aware how much more profound what the Fathers meant was than the supposed improvement of St. Anselm.

‡ ἐν αἰνίγματι. 1 Cor. xiii. 12.

whether it be called faith, or love, or Christ, or the Holy Ghost, may be held with more or less clearness. Or, if this be thought necessarily simple and uniform, still there is a point, which may be difficult to define, — but there is a point, at which the truth of things eternal comes in contact with our experience of things temporal, and there the knowledge, the manners, the favorite studies, of every generation of Christians may indefinitely vary, and give a bias in proportion to their mode of conceiving of some of the associations of their faith.

Thus, in our own time, our wider acquaintance with both nations and languages, our habit of scrutinizing ancient records and comparing different faiths together, as well as the cultivation of those mental inquiries which approach, if they do not touch, upon religion, have all tended to awaken a spirit which some condemn, and others welcome, but which most observers will admit to exist. Even if discoveries which must affect the general shape of our conceptions as regards Divine Revelation are not now made for the first time, yet a knowledge of such discoveries, confined perhaps once to a few scholars, is now diffused amongst masses of men; and the real significance, or the import, with which some characteristics of our sacred literature are pregnant, is far more clearly discerned, from the opportunities which we enjoy for comparing such things with similar phenomena elsewhere. There is a leaven which may have been in the world before, but which is now fermenting through the three measures of meal. Hence arises the question, how a growing spirit of scepticism in some quarters, and of perplexity in others, ought to be met by those who are responsible both to God and man for the stability or the progress of religion in the world. And if it be now, as ever, the abiding sentence of the Almighty, that whoso rejects knowledge shall be rejected from being priest before him, a few suggestions on this subject may well claim your attention, brethren, in these walls, which were consecrated to be a nursery of the faith of Christ, and upon this our solemn Feast-day.

There are some persons who look on all the tendencies

above alluded to with undisguised alarm; and others who do so with hope, or at least with perfect tranquillity of faith. Does not this difference of view imply, that there are also two sets of persons, one laying exclusive stress upon the evidences of the body, the other regarding rather those of the mind? It is obvious to remark, that these two aspects ought to be combined rather than separated; but we find that a tendency in either one direction or the other is apt to preponderate so much as to give a practical impress to a man's character, and to the cast of his belief.

The first set consider man as a mere animal, and divorce him by nature from God and from immortality. They may do this, either from a materializing philosophy of the senses, or from an ultra-Augustinian emphasis on the fall of Adam; but in either case, they leave as wide a gulf between God and mankind, as that which Mahomet was unable to fill. As to any pure voice of conscience, or better aspiration of the heart leading us upward, they almost boast of considering all such things utterly untrustworthy; they cast a disdainful glance over the great history of the Gentile world, and find in it no traces of the finger of the God of the spirits of all flesh; and if they are asked, How then does God teach man? they answer, By Moses on Mount Sinai, and by our blessed Lord in Jerusalem; and these two revelations are so attested by miracles, that we cannot doubt their truth, while on account also of the same miracles we have our attention imperiously arrested by the Book which records them; and are then led to regard that Book as not only true, but exhaustive of truth, and unquestionably the very word of God. Thus only, as they conceive, can we arrive at the satisfaction of certainty; for as to any agreement of the contents of the Book with our moral and intellectual being, that is at best a secondary and an untrustworthy kind of evidence; our great foundation is miracle, and our only result is the Bible.

On the other hand, our second set of thinkers look upon mankind as something different from the beasts that perish. They regard him rather as the child of God; fallen indeed, or falling ever, below that which his Maker calls good, and his own earnest expectation groans for; yet still trained by Providence; appealed to, however indiscernibly, even from childhood upwards, by something of spiritual experience; and, from the mould in which he was formed, not destined to find rest or happiness apart from that Being whose image he bears. Nor is this, as they contend, a fanciful conception, but one to which all history bears witness, — the greatest men, and the noblest nations, and the most enduring virtues, having been everywhere sustained by some vestige of such a belief; nor ought it to be allowed, according to all human analogies, that the admixture of various errors is any argument against a truth, which may yet survive, as the redeeming principle, among them. So that just as Christianity had the Law as its schoolmaster among the Jews, it may also have had a preparation of men's minds by training for it, from the great teachers of righteousness in Hellas, and from the masters of polity at Rome. And just as these to the ancient Gentile, so our conscience with all our experience of history may be to us now, what Moses and the Prophets were to the Jews, in respect of the great Teacher and Saviour to come.

Here then is a tone of thought very different from the one first described. If we attempt to illustrate the two from ancient heresies, we might say the first has an Ebionite tendency; the second is in danger of some form of Gnostic error. Or, if we consider them both as interpreting things connected with Scripture, the one would say, that the phylacteries of the Jews, with texts, were worn in obedience to express revelation; the other would see in them a strong figure * of exhortation corrupted into a formal usage. So by *Urim and Thummim*, one would understand, that a light, grossly physical, and yet supernatural, falling on the high-priest's breastplate, made its stones oracular; while the other

* Compare Exodus xiii. 9 – 16 with Numbers xv. 38, 39. Does the greater literalness of the later book (considering also the signs of compilation in its twenty-first chapter) betray an interval of some generations?

would imagine rather a symbol of that light which God gives to his upright ones in the clearness of understanding. Perhaps, again, the Shechinah of the temple (or even of the tabernacle) might admit of a similar variety of interpretation.

Again, if we ask the followers of the two tendencies we are describing for their watchwords, one will reply, the infallibility of the Bible; but the other will say, the truth of Christ. So, the one would define Christianity as the religion contained in the Bible; whereas the other would call it the Gospel, as being good news; or the doctrine of the Cross, as being self-sacrifice; or, in short, the religion of Christ. The one, then, pays its principal allegiance to the Scripture, which is true; but the other to the Truth, which is also written. Again, the one finds a duty, and even takes a pleasure, in opposing the Bible, by means of the sharpest conceivable contrasts to all the whispers of natural equity, to the purest yearnings of our affections, and to the presentiments of our conscience; whereas the other never hesitates to say, that the Bible itself is either a providential embodiment of those very things, which are the witness of God in man, and cannot be disparaged without blasphemy; or else at least it is a result, for which, under the good guidance of God, they had been preparing the way.

It is now easy to understand why the advocates of our first manner of thinking are so disquieted by anything which tells, I do not say against the general truth, but against the infallibility of the Sacred Records, which they make not only the symbol, but the foundation, of their faith. For they have, as it were, desecrated life and all its experiences; they have in effect, if not in intention, removed God from it as far as they can; they think all its fair humanities, whether art, or music, or literature, have at best little to do with religion, and are perhaps dangerous to it. Hence they survey their progress with indifference, diversified only by fits of panic; while as for the deep sense of things eternal, wherewith our Maker encompasses us, — the crying out of the heart and the flesh for the living God, the instantaneous response of every uncorrupt conscience to the sayings of our Saviour upon the mount, and the calm happiness which comes of well-doing, —they have either so materialized * their own souls that they are not conscious of such experiences, or else they think, that, apart from a particular fashion of speech, such things are utterly untrustworthy, and possibly may be of the Devil. In short, they have staked their cause upon one argument. It may be doubted if that is the one St. Paul would have recommended, or if it would have been chosen by those who had been longest at the foot of the Cross. "Except they see signs and wonders, they will not believe." When, then, their tendency of opinion reaches its full result, such men's religion becomes neither a leaven fermenting through human nature, nor a vine rooted and growing, nor a living and a moulding power; but it is as an image fallen down once for all from heaven, with no analogy in nature, with no parallel in history, with no affinity among the Gentiles, and (except for some special reasons) with no echo to its fitness from the human heart. Hence, however, it is only natural for any encroachment on the solitary ground of such persons' faith to appear "dangerous"; and since the great recommendation of all their cast of sentiment was its fancied safety, they are in proportion alarmed. Thus it is painful to them even to be told of little discrepancies in our sacred books; they cannot understand that a true teacher of religion may be imperfectly informed in other things, though analogous instances might strike them every day; even the idea of religious growth, which pervades the whole Bible, is not kindly accepted by them, or is confined to one or two great epochs of dispensation; and as for the many inquiries of great literary and historical interest, which the criticism of the Sacred Volume involves, they have so prejudged such questions, that they either will not acquire the knowledge requisite to answer them, or they shut their eyes to any fresh form of the answer,

* That is, in St. Paul's language, "made carnal."

as it appears in the light of to-day; or they even raise an outcry against the investigation of any more consistent student, as if it were a triumph of "infidelity," — and thereby they most unwisely make it so. Certainly, their heart does not stand fast; for they are afraid when any fresh tidings come, either from general knowledge, or from fervent and self-sacrificing devotion, or from a critical study even of the Bible.

But turn we now to those who, reverencing the letter at least as deeply as St. Paul did, have yet grounded their faith mainly on the spirit, without neglecting the aids of the understanding. They are persuaded that they may justify the ways of God by rendering to the intellect its own, and yet render to faith the things that are faith's. Nay, rather, they think that doing the one is a condition necessary to the other.* Clearly, then, it does not disturb them to learn that the purpose of God, though veiled from the Jews (μυστήριον), had made the Gentiles, even of old, heirs of a certain salvation of the soul. Hence they approach with calmness such questions as how far Moses took anything from the wisdom of the Egyptians, or whether Hellenizing Hebrews † had used language adopted by St. Paul and St. John; they can even welcome any fresh instances that God has left himself nowhere without witness; and, since both providence and grace have ultimately One Giver, they can easily believe that the one has been a cradle for the other. Perhaps, indeed, the wonderful correspondence between the spiritual judgments of the Gospel and of the purest searchers after godliness elsewhere,

---

* The saying, *Believe, that thou mayest understand,* belongs more to principles than to facts, and may be as much misused as its opposite, *Let me understand, that I may believe.* For it has been applied to darkness as often as to light. Hence it might be better to say, *Love the truth, that thou mayest know it.* For this would give nearly the same lesson, and be less liable to abuse.

† Good Jacob Bryant wrote a book to prove that Philo resembled St. John; and although his chronology requires to be inverted, his proof of the resemblance holds good.

is not one of the least arguments for the true divinity of Christ. For it shows that the Wisdom which took flesh in him came from the Supreme and Universal Teacher of mankind. Nor, again, do Christians, such as I now speak of, require a great gulf between the experiences of devout men to-day and those of the servants of God in the days of old. One of their great reasons for believing things written in Scripture is, that they experience the same. They are persuaded of the comfort of prayer, the peace of trustfulness, the joy of thanksgiving, the rightful rule of holiness, the necessity of repentance, and the wholesomeness of a discipline of conscience; and they gladly welcome the forgiveness of sins. Because God teaches such things now, they more easily believe he taught them of old. Nor have they any desire to doubt, that He who thus fashioned the hearts of his people, may also have exhibited great wonders of old to their external sense. The great majority of them, indeed, implicitly believe the letter of every miracle in the Bible; yet they would never be so illogical as to make these remote and often obscurely attested events the proof* of things being true which they know by experience, and which are so far more important in saving the soul alive. Hence many of them believe the miracles for the sake of the doctrines; and this order is more truly Christian than the converse. Some of them, however, would remark, that the modern definition of a miracle is far too technical; in the old Hebrew mind, everything was a great wonder which caused a present awe of the great Governor of the world. Thus the morning roll of the tide, and the stormy wind arising, were great wonders; and though other things, to which the same name is applied, may seem more extraordinary, yet we can believe the Divine agency in them to have marched along the silent path of forethought rather than with the Cyclopean

* This is almost too forcibly put in the striking *wish* of Mr. Maurice, that persons, resting their faith as Christians on the ten plagues of Egypt, might find all Egyptian experiences tend to shake it. See his Sermons on the Lessons from the Old Testament.

crash of strength and force. As to our Saviour's miracles, indeed, they are even wrought generally with the concurrence of the receiver's faith; and they are all signs of mercy, or parables full of meaning; and, again, so far as the element of power is brought out in them, it is rather as exemplifying the rule of a very present God over nature, than as "evidence"* for truths which are themselves far more evident. Hence, whether an event should be considered as more or less miraculous, is always a question to be decided by the probabilities of the particular passage, whether prose or poetry, contemporaneous or remote; and is never to be prejudged as if it affected either way the foundations of our faith.†

From such a tone of thought as regards miracles, we may expect those who entertain it to approach the more important

---

* Has not the ambiguity of the term *evidence* somewhat misled our modern apologists? It may have meant clearness, or *visibility*, as of Truth and Justice; but they take it in the sense of legal testimony, and so entangle themselves in special pleading.

† Suppose any one brought up to understand as literal prose Cowper's hymn,

> He plants his footsteps in the sea,
> And rides upon the storm, —

would it be an utter loss to him to discover that the terms were figurative? or might they still express to him a truth? Apply the same idea to many of the Psalms, such as the eighteenth, which the Hebrew title makes a description of David's deliverance from Saul. May it not also apply to other poetical parts, such as part of Habakkuk, and to such fragments as are expressly quoted from the book of Jasher (I do not say all that have been conjecturally ascribed to it), especially if some of them closely resemble the ode in Habakkuk? But it will be said, here was a *poetical intention;* and it is a wide leap to interpret plain prose on such principles. This distinction should have its weight. Still the fondness of some nations for apologue or parable, the tendency of *ideas* to clothe themselves in narrative, and the possibility of traditions, once oral or poetical, having subsequently taken form in prose, are all things which may suggest themselves to critical readers, and should weigh for what they are worth in each case, and for no more. But if scholars wantonly exaggerate difficulties, or state them with indecency or scoffing, the case is different. I have never intended doing so, and have no sympathy of feeling with any one who does.

subject of prophecy, without suffering their reverential prepossessions to take an undue form of prejudice, or any disappointment of them to be a cause of overwhelming alarm. Suppose that what Bishop Butler said hypothetically on this subject should now be come actually upon us, — suppose that things often treated as direct literal predictions of Christ should have been spoken primarily of some king, or prophet, or nation. Such a result may cause great distress, and even desolation of mind, to those who make theology a mere balance of texts, and make the peace of God, which passeth all understanding, depend upon the critical accuracy of illustrations borrowed in the New Testament from the Old. But no such grievous consequence follows to men who have been so born of the Spirit, that they believe Christ's words because they are spirit and truth. They are no more surprised that their Saviour should appear under earthly images in the Old Testament, than that he should be called "the carpenter's son" in the New. Their conception of him is not formed by balancing the imperfect utterances of childhood against those of the full-grown stature of the servants of God; but it rather takes in the height of that great idea at which the Church arrived when she stood as it were by the goal; for then she looked back with understanding on the race of Him who,* though manifested in the flesh, had been justified in the spirit, and who, though seen only by Apostles, had been preached to nations; and whom she found so believed upon, as a king, throughout the world in which he once had not where to lay his head, that she felt, surely God must have received him up into glory. For they all along admit the idea of training; and so, the principle of life and of growth. It was natural for the people of Nazareth to see in Jesus only Joseph's son;

* 1 Timothy iii. 16, where I have ventured to paraphrase that reading of the Greek which seems on the whole best attested. It should be compared, for the sense of *angels*, with ch. v. ver. 21 of the same Epistle; and for the general sentiment, with Romans, ch. i. vv. 3, 4. On this, as on other questions of *text*, I am glad to fortify myself with the authority of Dr. Tregelles.

it was natural for the old Hebrews to think of the righteous king, and the afflicted prophet, and the chosen people, before they rose to the conception of a verily Divine wisdom and love, uncovering itself in substance, and pervading the conceptions of all nations.

But where, then, some one will ask, are our "evidences"? It may be answered in two words, the character of Christ and the doctrine of Christ. Or to say the same thing in the words of St. Paul, we preach Christ the power of God, and Christ the wisdom of God. If priests embody the idea of consecration, he is holy, — if prophets that of knowledge or vision, he is the great speaker of truths which touch the heart, — if kings imply rightful rule, he, or his spirit, is that which should sway our thoughts, — if the poor and afflicted are the special care of God, was ever affliction like his? — if teachers do a sacred work, if martyrs throw a fire upon the earth which is not quenched, if the shepherd to his flock, and the husband to his wife, and the pastor to his people, have all some office of beneficence, and so something of sacredness from their having been designed in the love of God; — all these things are, as St. Paul says, "brought to a head in Christ"; he concentrates and exhibits in his life, in his doctrine, in his death, and in the holy spirit whereby he ever lives, and wherewith he animates the whole body of his Church, the Divine perfection of those excellences, of which fragments, and shadows, and images, are scattered throughout the world elsewhere. And however true it may be, that our religion is in its essence attachment to Christ as a person, this can never mean to his name, or to his power, as if he were jealous or arbitrary; but rather * to that goodness and that truth which he embodies, and which commend themselves by their excellence to the faith of the pure in heart.

Those then come to Christ who believe in the spirit of Moses and of Isaiah, and who would have listened to each prophet of truth from time to time among the Jews, — who

* The issue raised in this sentence is vitally critical, and pregnant.

would stand by Socrates as he drank his hemlock among the Greeks, — and who, in short, in all times and places, would acknowledge the authority of whatsoever things are pure, whatsoever are lovely, whatsoever are of good report. Now this kind of free allegiance, from love, and for the excellence of the object's sake, is perhaps not exactly that of those who, starting with the Bible, — or even with the Divine authority of our Lord, — infer from thence dogmatically the excellence of his precepts; but it is more like that of the Apostles, who saw the superhuman beauty of our Lord's truth and patience, and his majesty made perfect through sufferings; and then reasoned * upward, Surely this was the Son of God.

Such a mode of thought has also the advantage of starting more from the purer moral instincts of our nature. Yet it is so far from fearing reason, that it finds, in a way, confirmations everywhere. It is under no temptation to wrest texts into conformity with systems; or to congeal the outpourings of passionate penitence into materials for syllogisms; or to make traditional applications of prophecy, whether due to the devout rhetoric of the early Church, or to the very imperfect criticism of St. Jerome † in his Vulgate, either parts of the faith, or perilous supports of it. It can readily welcome with hearty gratitude whatever discovery in science, or language, or history, may so far dissociate from the Jews those who may yet, like the Jews, remain children of a Divine promise; nor is it with dismay, but with thanksgiving, that it sees many of their temporal images, time after time, give way to that eternal pattern which Moses saw in the Mount, and which the servants of God may now see more

* The Apostles felt goodness, and inferred God. We assume God, and demand acknowledgment of goodness. Which of these is the more wholesome argument? The answer may somewhat depend upon what conception of Deity we start with.

† In Haggai ii. 7, the Hebrew says *desires*, or *desirable things*, and the context shows silver and gold to be intended. But St. Jerome said, *Veniet desideratus omnibus gentibus*, and we have followed in his track. But are those who clamorously make such things proofs of Christianity its friends?

clearly revealed to them in conscience, and experience, and understanding. For that which is written in the nature of things is shown us by God.

But if persons thus thinking are less restrained from the free adoption of whatever consequences the mind may work out, so long as it works in righteousness, they are far more bound to purge their mind's eye, and to keep the whiteness of their soul unspotted from evil. For their faith has only ceased to be a congeries of human propositions, that it may better become a divine life. And although some of them may meditate with Butler, how far the mysterious grace of God is given us on a system, so that, if we saw the whole range of things, it would appear to us regular and natural, rather than contra-natural, yet the belief in that "Spirit which is holy, supreme, and life-giving,"* is far more a governing principle of their lives, than can ever be the case with men who substitute the bonds of system for those of truth, and the letter for the spirit.

Hence it will be found, all great reformers, either of life or institutions, have had something in them of the spirit we now speak of. Nor has it been quite unknown even to men in other respects of most opposite views: it has burst forth, now in that earnest preaching which rent the veil of the invisible world, and made men tremble or exult at the present realities of judgment or salvation; and it has wrought again in those who reared once more the standard of the Cross as a thing to live by, in a luxurious and garrulous age; it allies itself most eminently to the Gospel, but it can also flow along the channels of the Church; its more prominent advocates in England have been men whose eccentricity somewhat marred their usefulness, but it may well harmonize with the affectionate soberness of that Prayer-book, which it should forbid us to sever, so widely as we do, from the inspiration of our Bible. It woke in Reginald Pecock some presage of the Reformation, when as yet this College was

* Nicene Creed.

not; it found no obscure utterance in Hooker, when he taught that "the rules of right conduct are the dictates of right reason"; it is assumed, either tacitly or expressly, in the grand discourse of Jeremy Taylor; it is more formally put forward by Barclay, whose broad and unqualified propositions are yet on more than one account well worthy of being studied; it moves, though in fetters, across the pages of the more learned Puritans, and especially of Milton; it takes a form of wisdom, toleration, and faith, amidst the vast learning of Cudworth, and his kindred teachers of a godly humanity;* it is not alien to the Evangelical Platonism of Leighton; nor is it quite quenched by the arrogant temper of Warburton, whose learning and whose courage alike led him to acknowledge some light in the Gentile world; but with greater fondness it loved to linger amid the deep reasonings of Butler, prevented only by his Laodicean age from bearing in him its full fruit; it took a form of subtle idealism, and allied itself to "every virtue" in Berkeley; it had no mean representative in this place, in the thoughtful candor of Professor Hey, over whose moderation any brief triumph of zeal in our time may only pave the way for a dangerous reaction; it sounds, not ineloquently, but too uncertainly, from the deep struggles of Coleridge; and it found a happier expounder in him whose recent loss we may well deplore, the Guesser at Truth, and the preacher of the Victory of Faith. *Est et hodie, nunc tacendus: olim nominabitur.* In our own time, indeed, those who entertain it at all have felt themselves urged alike on the negative side by the necessities of historical criticism, and on the positive by the deep hunger of men's spiritual affections, to cross over more and more from the scribe to the apostle, from the letter to the spirit, from the formula to the feeling which engendered it.

How many questions now arise before me which time will not permit to handle at due length! Will this freedom, which even the highest controller of our destiny is in some measure

* E. g. John Smith, who has been praised in such opposite quarters.

awakening among us, always know where to stop? It will be led, perhaps, by the inexorable laws of historical criticism to alter our modes of conceiving of some portions of Hebrew literature, which are comprehended in our Bible; and even questions apparently barren may sometimes, to the scholar, be fruitful in inferences.* It may also observe so much of local or sensible imagery, † in describing things which eye hath not seen, nor ear heard, that it may almost indefinitely lessen the field of intellectual definition, though sparing that of conscientious expectation. It may, for instance, somewhat merge the doctrine of a resurrection in the idea of immortality; ‡ and it may lay not so much stress on a day of judgment, as on a Divine retribution. But will it also apply St. Paul's idea of our Lord's laying down his mediatorial kingdom, § not to any one moment hereafter, but to that period, whatever it may be, in each man's life, when he has been brought by the Son to the Father, — so that it shall be no longer necessary for the Son to pray for men ‖ so enlightened, since the Father himself loves them, because they have conceived of him according to the picture revealed of him in his well-beloved Son? How far will this be a dangerous intensification of what is yet a true feeling of the *economic* nature

* It is morally certain, that the books of Joshua and of Daniel are each *four hundred* years later than the date ordinarily ascribed to each; and this fact leads to inferences which it would be wise to meet practically, by either modifying our cycle of Old Testament lessons, or by giving the clergyman at his discretion a liberty of doing so.

† If any one considers the various opinions on the state of disembodied souls before the day of judgment, he will find them turn on a clash of conflicting metaphors, or on a balance of allusions, each borrowed from some temporal usage.

‡ As Bishop Butler evidently did, but Isaac Taylor's Physical Theory of a Future Life may be read on the other side.

§ Read carefully 1 Corinthians xv. 24–28; but compare Pearson on Sitting on the Right Hand, in the Creed. It was reckoned a peculiarity in the profound Origen that he prayed only to the Father through the Son; but, at the altar, the whole African Church, and perhaps the Church Catholic, did so.

‖ St. John's Gospel xvi. 25–27; Colossians i. 15.

of the office of the *Mediator?* Or will the same spirit go so far with any, as to think it unimportant through what imagery God may frame in us thoughts of things ineffable; so that whether memory or fancy lend the shadow, and whether faith* be nourished more from fact or from thought, still the real crisis of our souls shall hang upon our ever holding fast that eternal substance of the Divine Light, the radiance of which is wisdom, and truth, and love, and which enlighteneth every man, both at its coming into the world in the flesh, and also long before? This last would sound like a dangerous revival of Gnostic imaginations. Yet would even the wildest flight of such aberrations be so dangerous to the spirit of religion, as that secular-minded Ebionitism into which the opposite tendency, the mere sifting of the letter, is ever apt to drift, the moment it escapes from the influence of tradition? To answer all such questions would require a prophet rather than a preacher. One thing, however, is clear, and that I desire to say very seriously: the spirit of inquiry is most likely to go hand in hand with reverence, if no other checks be imposed upon it than such as come of conscience and of truth. This also, brethren, let us be unshakably persuaded of, whatever other things fail, the attempt to realize in ourselves the mind which was in Christ Jesus has never been found to fail any man. This, after all, seems to be what constitutes a Christian.

The prospects of an attack must depend very much upon the conduct of the defenders. If those who have leisure, learning, and authority encourage persons less informed, not merely in entertaining as opinions, but in asserting as foundations of the faith, things which scholars are ashamed to say, there must come a crash of things perishable, in which also things worth preserving may suffer shipwreck. Whereas, if the same persons were wise to distinguish eternal meaning from temporal shape, it would still prove that, though the Church is beaten by waves, yet she is founded on a rock.

---

* Compare Hebrews, tenth and eleventh chapters.

ON THE CAUSES WHICH PROBABLY CONSPIRED TO PRODUCE OUR SAVIOUR'S AGONY.*

By EDWARD HARWOOD, D. D.

ADVERTISEMENT.

THE following Dissertation was composed about fourteen years ago. Upon reviewing it, I saw no reason to depart from the theory and sentiments it advances. The *manner* in which it is compiled requests the reader's candid and favorable censure. The reason which originally induced me to write it was my dissatisfaction with the schemes which gloomy and systematic divines have devised to account for our Lord's agony; some ascribing it to the unappeased wrath of Almighty God, now hurled in all its tremendous vehemence upon this illustrious sufferer; others, to the temptation and onset of the Devil, into whose tyranny, during this hour of darkness, he was freely delivered; and others to the whole accumulated weight of the sins of the whole world, which the wisdom and justice of God appointed that he should now sustain, in order that he might experimentally feel their infinite demerit, and, by supporting in his own person the oppressive load, accomplish the proper atonement and expiation of them. I hope an attempt to vindicate the equity, rectitude, and goodness of God, and to justify the conduct of our Lord on this

* First published in London, 1772.

occasion, by evincing that there is nothing in this transaction which eclipses, or in the least diminishes the lustre of his divine character, will be deemed laudable, however I may have failed in the execution of my design. I had not seen, till within these few weeks, Mr. Moore's excellent pamphlet on this subject, which was published by Doctors Lardner and Fleming, and printed by Noon, 1757. It gives me great pleasure and satisfaction, as it is no small confirmation of this Essay, to find that the reflections and sentiments of this ingenious writer on this subject have so happily coincided and harmonized with my own.

DISSERTATION.

By the adversaries of our divine religion it has often been suggested that the concluding scenes of our Redeemer's life are attended with circumstances which reflect no great honor upon his character. From that expression, *My God! my God! why hast thou forsaken me?* one of the most eminent of the Deists asserteth, that our Saviour, a little before his death, publicly renounced the cause in which he had been engaged, and even died in that renunciation. How injurious and false this aspersion is, need not be evinced, since the whole tenor of our Saviour's history contradicts it, and everywhere displays a most exalted and consummate virtue. It is in the highest degree absurd to suppose that our Lord should publicly abjure his religion, and yet die to confirm it and give it its last sanction. He came to bear witness to the truth, and he gave the strongest proof of the justness of his pretensions to the character he assumed, that he was the Messiah and Lawgiver of the world, and that the cause in which he had embarked was the cause of God and Truth, for he sealed this cause with his blood.

His agony in the garden of Gethsemane has been very undeservedly the subject of calumny and detraction. It has not infrequently been intimated, that during this scene of sufferings our Lord's behavior was very far from being consistent with the rest of his life, and that he meanly and abjectly shuddered at the prospect of calamities which, notwithstanding, it was his destiny to meet.* Persons, who have rejected Christianity, and alleged the causes of their rejecting it, have insinuated, among other things, that this agony of grief hath all the appearance of a dishonorable timidity, that our Saviour in a dispirited manner sunk under the afflictions which he had rashly brought upon himself, by assuming the character of a Reformer, — whereas, if he had been conscious that his doctrines were true, and that his mission was divinely authorized, he would have sustained them with an heroic fortitude and magnanimity worthy such a cause. Instead of this, in the prospect of his last sufferings, he is overwhelmed in despondency, and betrays a pusillanimity unworthy a common philosopher. Instead of embracing with virtuous transport so noble an occasion, now offered him, of attesting the truth of his mission and ministry by sufferings, he shrinks back at the view of them, falls into dishonorable tremors, is plunged into the last terror and confusion, and with vehement importunity implores Almighty God to extricate and save him from them. *Let this cup pass from me!*

But if we impartially consider the history in which this agony of distress and sorrow is recorded, we shall be convinced that it was not want either of virtue or of fortitude to sustain his impending sufferings, which dictated these words. There is nothing in them inconsistent with the general tenor of his conduct, — nothing in them that can make us suspect the truth of his pretensions, or that in the least diminishes the divine worth and dignity of his character. Our Saviour was clothed with human nature, and is he to be censured for having the sensibilities of human nature? Is his conduct to be loaded with reproach and contumely, because he was not a proud, unfeeling Stoic,† and did not manifest an entire

* See Voltaire's late treatise *Sur la Tolerance.*

† "Was there not something pusillanimous and inconstant in this part

apathy and insensibility in his sufferings? Is it any disparagement to our blessed Lord, any imputation on his wisdom or his virtue, that he was affected with the sorrows and sufferings of humanity? "Jesus," as a judicious writer has well observed, "was sensible of his own and others' sufferings, and conceived a dread and horror at them. He was so *sore amazed and full of grief*, as earnestly to pray, that, if it were possible, the cup might pass away from him. A true picture this of genuine humanity in distress. It is natural to us to hate pain, and to have an abhorrence of misery. The constitution of our beings requires it should be so. It is the first and strongest principle the Creator hath cast into the human frame. The philosophy taught in the heathen world by Zeno and his followers, that pains and afflictions are no evils, and that a wise man should be hardened against all sense of them, was truly perversive, not perfective of the nature of man. To feel calamities when they come upon us,

---

of our Saviour's conduct? I answer, No. Those expressions are far too narsh, and cannot be applied to our Lord without manifest injustice. He had not, indeed, that intrepidity, for which the rude heroes of history are celebrated, who were fearless and undaunted in their greatest dangers. What then? Was a character expected in him that required a peculiar warmth of the blood and juices, and the impetus of some criminal passion, to form and exhibit? Natural courage is well known to be mechanical, and to rise and fall with a certain temperature of the body. The passions, says Mr. Grove, which have most filled the world with *heroes*, are *vainglory*, and a dread of the reproach of cowardice. Moral Philosophy, Vol. II. p. 259. What is to be looked for in the blessed Jesus is a perfectly moral character. Now a manly, virtuous courage is so far from being incompatible with, that it supposes, fear. For as that is inspired with a sense of what is just and honorable, the fear of infamy to one's self, or of injury to others, must needs take place, inasmuch as the objects are evils that ought, if possible, to be avoided, and when and in whomsoever those fears shall coincide with the natural fear of death, a passive fortitude is all that can be expected.

"And as to *inconstancy* of mind, I ask, Who is there among the sons of men, or what are they, whom the circumstances of time and place, in respect to a cruel and ignominious death, will not sensibly affect? A person, doomed to suffer as a state criminal, may indeed put on the *stoic* on such an occasion, and in point of prudence, as it is called, or for the

or upon others, and to give vent to our tears,* is much more congruous and suitable to our frame and station, than the apathy and rant of the Stoics. We are connected with flesh and blood, made with selfish and social affections and passions, and placed here in a state of discipline; and a tender, susceptible temper better becomes us, and will sooner perfect our virtue, than insensibility and foolhardiness. This consideration alone, if there were none other, should make us not ashamed of Jesus in his agony in the garden, or on the cross." †

The following account of this awful scene is exhibited by the four Evangelists. "When Jesus had spoken these words [that consolatory discourse recorded in the fourteenth, fifteenth, and sixteenth chapters of St. John's Gospel] he went forth with his disciples over the brook Cedron, where was a garden [Gethsemane], into which he entered and his disciples. And he saith to the disciples, Sit ye here, while I go and

---

sake of his honor, stifle his passions from the view of others. And no doubt but that this has often been the case. But our Lord acted upon no such mean motives. He felt things to impress him differently, and he told what he felt. The mind is not answerable for these different impressions. They are unavoidable to it, and the result of the human frame. Had not Jesus shown a reluctancy to the evils now before him, the reality of his sufferings might justly have been called in question. And so far was he in this his behavior from acting an *inconsistent* or *inconstant part*, that, notwithstanding he felt a greater uneasiness to himself than at any other time, he stood firm to the noble resolution he had formed, of an entire submissive obedience to the Divine Will. There is then no impeachment of the courage and constancy of our Lord. His character remains unsullied, yea, shines through the darkest cloud that ever passed over him." — Moore on our Saviour's Agony, pp. 88 – 90.

* They who of all writers undertake to imitate nature most, oft introduce even their heroes weeping. See how Homer represents Ulysses, Od. I. ver. 151 ; II. ver. 7, 8. The tears of men are in truth very different from the cries and ejulations of children. They are silent streams, and flow from other causes ; commonly some tender, or perhaps philosophical, reflection. It is easy to see how hard hearts and dry eyes come to be fashionable. But, for all that, it is certain the *glandulæ lachrymales* are not made for nothing. Religion of Nature Delineated, p. 139, note.

† Moore on our Saviour's Agony, pp. 102, 103.

pray yonder. And he took with him Peter and the two sons of Zebedee, and began to be sorrowful, to be sore amazed, and very heavy. And he saith to them, My soul is exceeding sorrowful, even unto death: tarry ye here and watch. And he was withdrawn from them about a stone's cast, and fell on the ground and prayed, saying, O my Father, if it be possible, let this cup pass from me! nevertheless, not my will, but thine, be done! And he cometh unto the disciples, and findeth them fast asleep, and saith unto Peter, What, could ye not watch with me one hour? Watch ye and pray, lest ye enter into temptation; the spirit is willing, but the flesh is weak. He went away the *second* time, and prayed, O my Father, if this cup may not pass away from me, except I drink it, thy will be done! And he came and found them asleep again, for their eyes were heavy, neither wist they what to answer him. And he left them and went away again, and prayed the *third* time, saying the same words. And there appeared an angel unto him from heaven, strengthening him. And being in an agony, he prayed more earnestly, and his sweat was, as it were, great drops of blood falling down to the ground. And when he rose from prayer, and was come to his disciples, he found them sleeping for sorrow; and he saith unto them, Sleep on now and take your rest: it is enough, the hour is come: behold, the Son of Man is betrayed into the hands of sinners." * Let the reader figure to himself our Lord's situation at this time, and consider what images must necessarily obtrude upon his mind. His ministry was now closed, — he was in a few moments to be apprehended and treacherously delivered into the power of those who had long thirsted for his blood, — his beloved disciples were going to abandon him in his adversity, — and in two days' time, by wicked hands, he would be crucified and slain. Jesus now had a strong conscious perception of all these impending calamities. Let the reader's imagination represent to him

* I have formed the *several* circumstances related by *different* Evangelists into one continued narrative.

the state of our Saviour's mind in this awful crisis; and with the full idea of his situation before him, let him consider, whether the *following* painful reflections crowding into his soul, in this melancholy hour, might not naturally produce that scene of distress and horror the sacred writers have recorded.

Section I.

One cause which no doubt greatly contributed to distress our blessed Saviour, now his ministry was concluded, was the distressing reflection that his painful labors and benevolent attempts to convert and reform the Jews had proved generally unsuccessful. In the fulness of time God the Father had sent him from heaven among men, and empowered him to work many stupendous and beneficent miracles in confirmation of his divine mission and character. In the space of three years and a half, he had in person visited the cities, towns, and villages of Judæa, and in all of them had effected such astonishing operations and supernatural cures, as could evidently be ascribed to nothing but to the immediate power and agency of God. He had delivered to his country a perfect system of religion and morals, enforced by the strongest encouragements, and recommended by his own virtuous and irreproachable conduct. And yet his conduct, his doctrines, his precepts, his miracles, had been able to make little impression on the hearts of this depraved people. They despised the meanness of his birth and the obscurity of his family. They were prejudiced against the place of his education, and declared it impossible that a prophet should ever arise out of Nazareth. So averse had they been from all conviction and instruction, and so deliberately determined to shut their eyes against the clearest light, that they attributed the most amazing displays of Divine power to a compact and intercourse with Beelzebub. This man doth not work miracles, but by Beelzebub the prince of the devils. Instead of attending his public ministry with minds sincerely disposed for the reception of truth, they contrived low clandestine arts to ensnare him, and hoped, from some incautious expressions into which they might betray him, to accuse him as a traitor to the Roman government, and effectuate his condemnation and death as an enemy to Cæsar. These were the illiberal and dishonorable expedients they employed to murder the Messiah. Are such principles and dispositions as these friendly to truth and virtue? Is a nation, which manifests such a character as this, and frames such measures as these against the life of a holy and good man for remonstrating against their superstition, bigotry, and immoralities, to be convinced by the force of evidence, and moved by the charms of an amiable example? So far were they from examining his doctrines and pretensions to the high character he assumed, with coolness and candor, that they practised every method to prevent them from being admitted, and excluded those from their synagogues who openly professed them. How determined and inveterate their virulence was against our Lord's person and usefulness, we may judge from this single most egregious instance of it, their solemnly deliberating in council to destroy Lazarus, merely for being the subject of one of his miracles.* Impossible, therefore, was it for our Saviour to propagate his religion in a nation so prejudiced and depraved. All his attempts to make them virtuous and everlastingly happy proved ineffectual.

Now this wrung his benevolent heart with the acutest anguish. The consideration that his country should have rejected that system of divine truths he had been delegated from God his Father to deliver to them, overwhelmed him in the deepest sorrow and distress. When he *now* reviewed the past years of his ministry, it filled him with great and painful concern, that his miracles had been so numerous, but his success so very inconsiderable. He had made it the uniform study of his life to diffuse happiness around him, to do good to the souls and bodies of men, had performed

---

* "But the chief priests consulted that they might put Lazarus also to death." John xii. 10.

the most benevolent cures, taught the most excellent doctrines, exhibited a perfect character, to engage his country to embrace a religion which came recommended and enforced by so many evidences of its credibility and divine authority. But what converts had he made, what effects had the cause of God and truth, of liberty and immortality, produced? *This* was the painful reflection which *now* wounded his soul. He had come to his own, but his own had not received him! That nation, whose guardian angel he had probably ever been, and whom he had anxiously superintended in every period of time and change of government, had *now* rejected his person and his doctrines, and were going to imbrue their hands in his blood as an impostor. This disingenuity and ingratitude transfixed his soul, and a painful review of the insuperable prejudices, enormous corruptions, and determined impenitency of his country must necessarily oppress him, in this *hour of darkness*, with very deep distress, and contribute its weight of woes to produce that agony which he now endured.

Section II.

Another cause which conduced to occasion this extreme dejection and sorrow of our blessed Saviour, was the perception he had that he would immediately be abandoned by all his disciples and friends in these his last extremities. If my readers have ever known, by unhappy experience, the cruelty and infelicity of being deserted by a friend, at a time of impending adversity and distress, let them now recall to mind what they suffered on that occasion, and transfer their thoughts to our Saviour's sensibilities in the like circumstances. His disciples had been the companions of his labors. He had selected them from the world to be his attendants and friends. To them he had unbosomed his soul. *Having loved his own, he loved them unto the end*, says St. John. He maintained for them a most faithful and affectionate love, from the time he chose them to the last period of his life. They had relinquished their families, their occupations, and all their connections, to adhere to him and his cause. They had during the whole course of his ministry accompanied him from place to place, and mutually shared with him the reproach and odium of the world. But O dire reverse! O Adversity, how seldom art thou a witness to faithful friendship! The companions of his labors, from whose fidelity he might reasonably expect consolation, and whose firm adherence to his person and interests he might naturally hope would now give a sanction to the cause he and they had espoused, dishonorably desert him. When these last calamities invade him, lo, they fly,* and suffer persecution and death to overwhelm him, alone and unsupported. At a time when probably he should want the aids of true friendship most, to attest his innocence and assuage his sufferings, they have abandoned him, and appear ashamed of the cause in which they had all embarked.

But not only their unfaithfulness and disgraceful desertion of him, but the ingratitude and treachery of Judas, no doubt, in these moments he now spent in the garden of Gethsemane, must wound his generous mind with the most cruel anguish. We find that this baseness of Judas gave our Lord great distress. "When Jesus had thus said, he was *troubled in spirit,* and testified and said, Verily, verily, I say unto you, one of *you* shall *betray* me!" John xiii. 21. The reflection, that, in that small number whom he had selected to be his particular friends and companions, one should prove so ungrateful and perfidious as for a paltry sum to betray him to his enemies, and that in a very short time he should see this very person, whom he had admitted into his friendship, heading a mob to apprehend him, — the bitter reflection must rend a bosom so susceptible as our Saviour's appeareth to be. "Great minds have a delicacy in their perception. They feel ingratitude more than others, as they are less deserving

---

* "At simul intonuit, fugiunt, nec noscitur ulli,
Agminibus comitum qui modo cinctus erat."
Ovid. Trist.

of it. And indeed the best of men have met with this sort of ill usage. David, more than once, deplores the like, in language which shows how sensibly he was touched. 'Yea, my own familiar friend, in whom I trusted, who did eat of my bread, hath lift up his heel against me. For it was not an enemy that reproached me, then I could have borne it; but it was thou, a man mine equal, my guide, and mine acquaintance.' " *

Such was the situation of our Saviour. Rejected by the Jews; abandoned by his disciples. The review of life painful, the *immediate* prospect full of horror. Invaded with such complicated distress, can we wonder that he should so earnestly implore Almighty God to save him from this hour, and to let this cup pass from him that he might not drink it? It is the natural language of piety and virtue in distress: the first prayer which a dependent creature in afflictive circumstances addresses to Heaven.

Section III.

Another cause which may justly be assigned to account for this agony and the petition he preferred to God, was the strong perception of that insult, ignominy, and torture he was shortly to endure. The perception of these dreadful evils, we may reasonably suppose, greatly impressed his mind, and strongly affected his exquisitely tender and delicate sensibilities. His mind anticipated all that cruel and inhuman treatment he should very shortly experience, — the immediate arrest and seizure of his person, his illegal trial, his imprisonment as an impostor, his outrage from the Roman soldiers, who would treat him with the last indignities, scourge him, clothe him in robes of mock royalty, and insult him as the rival and enemy of Cæsar, — and, as the completion of all these evils, his condemnation to suffer the ignominious and excruciating death of crucifixion. Over these scenes his mind *now* brooded. He had the full idea of them impressed

* See Moore's Inquiry, p. 46.

on his soul. In the dire apprehension of these impending horrors, a mind possessed of such exquisite sensibilities must suffer great depression. The view of these approaching evils forced from him that petition, Father, save me from this hour! By which is manifestly meant the hour of death, as Grotius judiciously interprets it. It is to this the author of the Epistle to the Hebrews refers, when he says, that our Lord in the days of his flesh offered up prayers and supplications, with strong crying and tears, unto Him that was able to save from death. Heb. v. 7. I leave it to my reader's imagination to represent the situation of his Saviour in these moments. Let any person, endowed with the feelings of humanity, declare, whether in such circumstances the petition, *Let this cup pass from me*, be not natural language, and an exit big with barbarity, contumely, and horror is not to be deprecated. If the human mind shudders at the fancied representation of pain so exquisite and durable, and a death so excruciating and reproachful, who can with any consistency and honor censure our Saviour, in such a situation, for discovering a sense of it? We might as reasonably blame him for being a man, and for having the common affections, feelings, and sensations of human nature. Was our Saviour a frantic and extravagant Stoic, whose divine tranquillity pain and human evils could not solicit? Did he ever teach his followers that pain was no evil, or in his own person ever discover a total apathy and unconsciousness of the calamities and sufferings with which he encountered? Nothing less true. He assumed humanity, and had all the sensibilities of humanity. He had, says the Apostle, a feeling of our infirmities, being tempted in all points just as we are. Our Lord discovered great sensibility of soul. Jesus wept, — shed tears at the grave of his amiable deceased friend, Lazarus. Tears were also observed to stream from his eyes, when he looked down upon the city and uttered those pathetic expressions over it. O that thou, even thou, hadst known the things that belong to thy everlasting peace; but now they are hidden from thine eyes! He had an exquisite sense of human misery. In these unhappy exigencies he would offer up prayers and supplications with strong crying and tears. And could brutal insult, illegal condemnation, opprobrious mockery, disgraceful imprisonment, cruel buffeting and scourging, a mock investiture with royalty, public ignominy and crucifixion invade his heart, unaffected and unimpressed? Would not the certain immediate prospect of this train of evils make strong impressions on a mind so susceptible of strong impressions? Had he met and sustained the shock with unfeeling unconcernedness, and supported these his sufferings with an absolute insensibility of them, it would then have been asserted that he was not *really* invested with human nature, and that the assertions of his historians, that he was a man, were entirely hypothetical and imaginary. If he had endured these evils with a torpid composure, it would have been said that he never felt them, and that the human form he exhibited to the world was merely ideal and visionary. So that in this case strong objections would have been formed against the truth and reality of his person. Had he met his sufferings with a fearless intrepidity, and appeared in the midst of them with an idiot serenity, the world, I am persuaded, would have been *more* dissatisfied with his conduct, would have formed it into an argument against the truth of the Christian religion, and reviled its author as a frantic Stoic or an unfeeling enthusiast.

Do we admire some of the philosophers for their contempt of pain? Do we applaud their boasted tranquillity of mind, which no tortures could discompose, and secretly wish that our Lord had sustained his affliction with as great constancy and fortitude as some of them? But let me freely declare, that if we admire these old sages for their doctrines of insensibility of pain, and for their serenity of mind in the midst of the most racking disorders, we really admire them for philosophical madness, and a wild, extravagant, infatuated quixotism. Our passions are part of our nature. They can never be eradicated. We can by no arts and arguments annihilate our sensibilities. It is frenzy to attempt or to affect it. Our Saviour never taught, or practised upon, such an unnatural system. He had the same perception of human misery with ourselves, and suffered in the conflict, just as we do. Dr. Whitby delivers it as his opinion, that this extreme dejection and agony of our Saviour arose from the strongly impressed apprehension of those dreadful sufferings which would so speedily befall him, and further says, that it is extremely difficult to assign any other cause of this excess of sorrow and dispiritedness which *now* seized him. Some considerable time before, the thought of this violent exit seems greatly to have impressed our Saviour's mind. "I have a baptism to be baptized with, and how am I straitened until it be accomplished! Now is my soul troubled: but what shall I say? Father, save me from this hour!" Consider the wretchedness of such a death! The exquisite torture of having the hands and feet perforated with nails, being fastened to a cross, and for days and nights continuing, as many of these wretches did, in all this agonizing pain, till all the powers of life were exhausted in a lingering and most miserable manner. Think of this, and then censure our blessed Lord for being appalled at the prospect. Think of what he suffered, and you will see cause to justify the petition he preferred to Heaven amidst these pangs: "My God! my God! why hast thou forsaken me?" Impress your minds with an affecting sense of a person so illustrious, of innocence so distressed, of sufferings so intense and durable, of indignities and insults so dishonorable and injurious, of a death so excruciating and full of horror, and of such a spectacle displayed before angels and men, and then reflect whether his agony in the garden of Gethsemane may not be accounted for. Then consider, whether you cannot *rationally* account for *such* a supplication in *such* a situation: O my Father, let this cup pass from me! It was the near prospect and anticipation of such sufferings and such an exit as this, which made him, in the days of his flesh, offer up the most importunate requests and supplications, with strong cries and tears, to that Being who was able to extricate him from death, — and he was heard in that he feared.

Section IV.

It is highly probable that at this time our Lord had a strong perception of the various troubles and persecutions to which his disciples and followers would be subjected, in consequence of their attachment to him and his religion. This thought would greatly depress him, and deeply wound his tender spirit. And I make no doubt but the prescience and distinct view he had of that multiplicity of sorrows and sufferings which would invade his adherents after his death, greatly contributed to his present agony and extreme dejection. He knew they had to contend with innumerable difficulties in attempting to reform a superstitious and corrupt world. He evidently foresaw that the system of religion and morals he had delivered would everywhere be spoken against, would, on account of its genius and nature, prove a stumbling-block to the Jews, and to the Greeks foolishness. He knew that, for propagating his religion in the world, and for their inviolable adherence to his cause, they would endure the most miserable torments and deaths which the genius of men could devise, or the cruelty and odium of persecutors inflict. All these scenes of future persecution *now* crowded into his mind, and the painful anticipation overwhelmed him. It was his exquisite benevolent feelings which occasioned this extreme distress. The reflection that so many *innocent* persons should be involved in these calamities for embracing and spreading his doctrine, was too painful for him to support.* They were for several centuries to struggle under the incumbent weight of *established* error and superstition, — prince and magistrate, priest and people, would be confederated against them, — they were to wrestle, not only against flesh and blood, the common prejudices of mankind, but to contend with principalities and powers and spiritual rulers in high

---

* Τῶνδε γὰρ πλέον φέρω
Τὸ πένθος, ἢ καὶ τῆς ἐμῆς ψυχῆς πέρι.
Sophocles, Œd. Tyran., v. 93.

places; the secular sword would be everywhere unsheathed to extirpate the cause in which they had embarked; they would be driven from city to city, from country to country, Jews and Greeks differing in other things, but agreeing in this, to exterminate them and their religion from the world; they would be the objects of such implacable odium and detestation, that whoever should kill them would be esteemed as doing God eminent service; they were to endure poverty and indigence for their unshaken constancy to their principles, to wander about in deserts and mountains, and to seek refuge in dens and caves of the earth, being destitute, afflicted, tormented; they were to be precipitated into prisons and dungeons, to be exposed to the fury of wild beasts, to afford sport and diversion for a brutal rabble, and to be made a spectacle to the world, to angels and men; for the sake of Christ they were to be killed all the day long, to be accounted as sheep for the slaughter. These subsequent calamities our Lord perfectly knew. He saw the gathering storm which would soon break over their heads. He had met with every injury and indignity for his endeavors to reform a wicked nation, and from his own experience he knew that the same principles and conduct in them would produce the same consequences, and render them equally obnoxious to a depraved world. He knew they had every opposition to expect from those whose religious errors they condemned, and whose immoralities they freely censured; that superstitious and wicked persons, of all others, would most strenuously exert themselves to destroy a *kingdom* of truth and righteousness, by murdering those who attempted to erect and establish it. This reflection awakened all his tenderness, and his benevolence made him feel exquisite anguish for his faithful, suffering followers. Here his affections were powerfully excited, and his painful solicitude for the future fortunes of his disciples overpowered his soul. He loved them with the greatest warmth and delicacy of affection. Having loved his own who were in the world, he loved them to the end; and this love caused him to enter intimately into their future distresses, and affectionately to share them by a generous condolence. He antedated them, he represented them strongly to his mind, and by a painful anticipation, and exquisite sympathy, now felt all the severe force and weight of these evils. What mental anxiety and distress he felt on account of their future miseries and persecutions appears from that consolatory discourse, recorded by St. John, which was addressed to these his mournful and melancholy friends, who were in the last dejection at the thought of his departure from them. If the world hate you, you know that it hated me before it hated you. Remember the word that I said to you, The servant is not greater than his Lord. If they have persecuted me, they will also persecute you; if they have insidiously watched my words, they will insidiously watch yours also. Verily I say unto you, you shall weep and lament, but the world shall rejoice. With great reason, therefore, we may suppose that all these scenes of future woe *now* crowded into our Lord's mind at once. Love, pity, sympathy, benevolence, were the great emotions and passions which labored in his breast. The opposition his cause would meet with in the world, and the dreadful sufferings in which those would be involved who maintained it, wrung his heart with the acutest anguish, and overwhelmed it in the deepest sorrow. This painful reflection, conspiring with the other causes I have alleged; produced the deplorable situation here recorded, rendered him unequal to the shock, made the assistance of an angel necessary to support and strengthen him, and caused him to sweat, as it were,* great drops of blood falling to the ground.

---

* Observe, this is only a *simile* or comparison of the Evangelist to *illustrate the profuseness* of our Saviour's sweat. 'Εγένετο δὲ ὁ ἱδρὼς αὐτοῦ 'ΩΣΕΙ θρόμβοι αἵματος. Luke xxii. 44. Just as all the four Evangelists, intending to give their reader a just idea of the *rapid descent* of the Holy Spirit upon Christ, after his baptism, *compare* it to the *velocity* of a dove, 'ΩΣΕΙ περιστεράν, — not that the Holy Spirit assumed the *shape* of a dove, but descended and alighted upon our Lord with the *rapidity* with which a dove darts from the sky to the earth. *Probably* there was *now* the *same* appearance as at the day of Pentecost. The

SECTION V.

It appeareth to me, also, that the impending calamities and ruin of his country, in consequence of their enormities and of their ingratitude and wickedness in rejecting and crucifying him, may be reckoned as one of the principal causes which produced this agony. It is a very unjust and groundless objection which Lord Shaftesbury hath advanced against the Christian religion, that the author of it never recommended private friendship and the love of our country. Every one who is in the least acquainted with the life of Christ, cannot but know that our Lord was an example of both these. From his most intimate friends, the Apostles, he selected one, whose amiable temper and disposition appear to have been most similar to his own, and whom he honored with a peculiar delicacy and tenderness of affection. And how well he loved his *native country* appears from the whole of his life. He confined his instructions and labors solely to the lost sheep of the house of Israel, declaring that to them only he was sent. Never was there a philosopher or hero who loved his country with a more generous ardor of the truest and noblest benevolence than our blessed Saviour, if a constant study and active disposition to promote the welfare and happiness of the community in which one is born may be styled the love of one's country. Dear to us, says Tully, are our parents, our children, our relations, our friends; but our country compriseth and embraceth everything that is

---

word *θρόμβοι* is very beautiful and expressive. It does not occur in the New Testament but only in *this* passage. It signifies *large globules,* thick and clammy clots of gore or sweat, pitch, milk, &c. Hesychius explains *θρόμβος* by *αἷμα παχύ, πεπηγὸς ὡς βουνοί.* — *Ποταμὸς ἅμα τῷ ὕδατι θρόμβους ἀσφάλτου ἀναδιδοῖ πολλούς,* "Mixed with the water, the river sendeth up many large clots of bitumen." Herodotus, Clio, p. 386, Vol. I. Glasg. *Ὥστ' ἐν γάλακτι θρόμβον αἵματος σπάσαι.* Æschyli Choeph., vers. 531. *Θρόμβῳ δ' ἔμιξεν αἵματος φίλον γάλα.* Ibid. vers. 544. *Αἵματος θρόμβους μέλανας,* "Large black globules of blood." Hippocrates, Lib. III. § 19, edit. Linden.

dear and valuable to us. In conformity to this maxim our Saviour really acted. He broke every parental and fraternal connection, all the ties of consanguinity, and forsook all the endearments of private life to consult the welfare of his country. What can be more pathetic and expressive of the warmest benevolence, than that complaint and lamentation he uttered over his incorrigible and devoted country,—"O that thou, even thou, hadst known in this thy day the things that belong to thine everlasting peace!" The strong perception he had of their imminent calamities forced him in this plaintive and affectionate manner to deplore their wretched fate. One of the Evangelists informs us, that when he drew near the city he wept over it. Generous minds feel strongly for the unhappy. It was benevolence, pity, and love for his unfortunate country, which called forth his grief, and caused him to shed these tributary tears, at once the affecting memorials of his love, and the awful tokens of its approaching doom. As he had a perfect knowledge, so he had a painful sympathetic sense, of those dreadful calamities which would shortly overwhelm his country, for their enormities in disobeying and murdering the Lord of life. "Daughters of Jerusalem," said he to the women who were beating their breasts and deploring his unhappy fate, when he was led to Calvary, "weep not for me, but weep for yourselves and for your children: for behold the days are coming in which they shall say, Blessed are the barren, and the wombs that never bare, and the breasts that never gave suck. Then shall they begin to say to the mountains, Fall on us, and to the hills, Cover us; for if they do these things in a green tree, what shall be done in the dry?" Accordingly, in about *forty* years after his resurrection, the Romans invaded Judæa, spread desolation everywhere, at last invested the capital, enclosed an infinite number of people in it, who had then come from all parts to celebrate the Passover, drew lines of circumvallation round them, and thus devoted them to all the miseries of famine, pestilence, and war. After incredible numbers had perished by mutual assassinations and famine, the city was stormed and plundered, the temple burnt, the buildings demolished, the walls razed from the foundations, the greatest part of the Jews were put to the sword, the rest sold for slaves into foreign countries. These calamities, in severer than which never was any nation involved, had their completion in Adrian's time, who published an edict prohibiting every Jew, on pain of death, from setting a foot in Judæa.

All these scenes of national calamity and ruin our Lord perfectly knew; and the painful apprehension and view made him commiserate his falling country. What affection, pity, sympathy, and sorrow are mingled in that pathetic exclamation: "O Jerusalem! Jerusalem! thou that killest the prophets, and stonest those that are sent to thee! How often would I have gathered thy children, even as a hen gathereth her chickens under her wings, but you would not! Therefore is your house left unto you desolate." Now if our Saviour's mind, in the course of his ministry, was so much affected and depressed by the thought of his country's disobedience, and of their deplorable ruin, the certain effect of it, how much more may we justly suppose must he be dejected and distressed when he was *now* entering upon those sufferings which he knew would assuredly bring on his devoted country these dreadful inflictions. If he indulged and manifested such grief for only *one single person*, for the death of his dear friend Lazarus, how inexpressibly must he suffer for the destruction of a very *large collective body* of men, to whom he was connected by the common endearing bond of natural affection and country?

In this manner, I apprehend, the agony of our Lord, and his prayer to God that this cup might pass from him, may be rationally accounted for, without recurring to any impious and absurd hypothesis which derogates from the wisdom, rectitude, and goodness of the Deity, and disparages the innocence and merit of this illustrious sufferer, ascribing it, I mean, to the dereliction and wrath of God, the temptation and tyranny of Satan, into whose power he was during this scene totally delivered, or to the incumbent weight of all the sins of the whole world, whose ponderous and oppressive load, during these moments, he was permitted of God to feel and support. I humbly conceive that his unsuccessfulness in reclaiming and reforming the Jews; the desertion of his disciples; the perception of the insult and ill usage he was shortly to sustain, — the arrest and seizure of his person, the illegal process through which he was to pass, the injurious and contumelious treatment he would experience in the conduct of it, being buffeted, delivered up to the Romans, vested with mock royalty, scourged, imprisoned, crucified; the foresight of the calamities and persecutions of his followers for maintaining and spreading his religion; and the imminent destruction of his country; — these are causes adequate to such an effect. Especially if we add, that the great and unremitting labor in which he had been employed for the *five* days which preceded his *agony* must necessarily have contributed to render him low and weak at this time, and reduced him to a state of great debility and lassitude. This *combination* of painful ideas collecting, as in a focus, their whole accumulated energy and force, and pouring in a strong vehement stream upon an exquisitely sensible and tender spirit, so entirely penetrated and overwhelmed it, as to render the interposition of a heavenly messenger necessary to strengthen and support him. So violent was the commotion excited by these sad images obtruding all at once upon his mind, that he complained that his soul was exceeding sorrowful, even unto death.* And in such a situation, amidst the tumult of

* The expressions used by the sacred writers to represent the intenseness of his agony are the most strong and emphatical which could have been employed. Περίλυπος, *exceedingly sorrowful, excessively distressed.* Περίλυπός ἐστιν ἡ ψυχή μου ἕως θανάτου. Matt. xxvi. 38. 'Εκθαμβεῖσθαι, used by Mark, ch. xiv. 33, signifies to be *stunned and overwhelmed* with any passion, to be *fixed in astonishment,* to *be lost in wonder and amazement.* It is used to express the *extreme terror and consternation* of the women at the unexpected sight of an angel in our Lord's sepulchre. Mark xvi. 5, 6. And the *great amazement* of the multitude

so many painful reflections crowding in perpetual succession upon a delicate mind, and in the near prospect of such injurious treatment and such an excruciating death, is not the consternation and sensibility our Lord expressed *natural*, and the petition he preferred to heaven, in such a crisis, if it pleased God to let this cup pass from him, the very first dictate of the human heart, and the genuine, constant language of a dependent creature when involved in distress?

I shall conclude this Dissertation with the reflections of a very judicious author.* "In the first place," says this ingenious writer, "this befell our Lord just as he had finished his public ministry. Intenseness of thought, in a long course of

---

at beholding the miracle wrought on the lame man. Acts iii. 11. Ἀδημονεῖν is a strong expression, and signifies to be in *great dejection*, to suffer the *last anguish and distress of mind*. Κλεοπάτραν περιέμενε, καὶ βραδυνούσης ἀδημονῶν ἤλυε, "He [Antony] anxiously expected Cleopatra; and upon her delaying to come, he *sunk into the last dejection and distress*." Plutarch in Vita Antonii, p. 939, edit. Francof., 1620. Ἐφ' ᾧ δὴ ὁ ἕτερος αὐτῶν ἀδημονήσας, ἑαυτὸν ἔσφαξε, "On which account one of them was so *dejected*, that he laid violent hands on himself." Dio Cassius, Tom. II. p. 924, edit. Reimari, Hamburg, 1752. Κᾀν τούτῳ καὶ τῶν Ῥωμαίων τινὲς ἀδημονήσαντες, οἷα ἐν χρονίῳ πολιορκίᾳ, μετέστησαν, "In the mean time some of the Romans, being *extremely dejected*, as is usual in a tedious siege, revolted to the enemy." Dio Cassius, p. 1080, ejusdem editionis. Ἠδημονεῖ μὲν γὰρ ὁρῶν τὸ παράλογον τῆς γυναικὸς πρὸς αὐτὸν μῖσος οὐκ ἀποκεκρυμμένον, "He *suffered the last anguish and distress* at seeing his wife's abhorrence of him, which he did not expect, or she study to dissemble." Josephus, Tom. I. p. 760, edit. Havercamp. Ἠδημονοῦν δέ, μὴ φθάσας καταλῦσαι τὸ πᾶν ἔργον οὐκ ἐξαρκέσει πρὸς τέλος ἀγαγεῖν τὴν προαίρεσιν, "But they were *in the utmost distress*, lest the king, after demolishing the whole work, should not be able to execute his design." Josephus, p. 778, Haverc. Ἀδημονοῦντα δὲ τὸν βασιλέα ἐπὶ τῇ ἀπαγορεύσει, "The emperor being *greatly distressed* at this repulse." Sozomen, Hist. Eccles., Lib. I. p. 14, edit. Cantab. 1720. Ἀδημονοῦντας δὲ τοὺς ἰδίους στρατιώτας ὡς ἡττηθέντας ὁρῶν, "Seeing his soldiers *greatly dejected* on account of their being defeated." Socrates, Hist. Eccl., p. 137. See also p. 356, edit. Reading, Cantab. 1720.

* Moore on our Saviour's Agony, pp. 83 – 86.

exercise, is, ordinarily, productive of, or succeeded by, perceptions that are irksome and tedious. Such sort of business naturally ends with fatigue; and fatigue discovers itself through all the avenues of the senses, as well in the mind as in the body. And at such a season, it is notorious, the passions of grief and sorrow lie most open and exposed to objects which excite pain. Evils that are at other times tolerable, come now with double force, and make deep impression. The observation on this circumstance was the result of the first branch of our inquiry. It is repeated here because it serves to illustrate the reasons, or is itself one, why Jesus began to be sorrowful and very heavy.

"Again. This happened to him when he was entering upon a new scene of sufferings. At such a crisis we find things future begin to have an actual existence, and are, as it were, quickened into life. The passions, big with expectation, are ready to break forth to meet their objects. There is always something vivid and strong in the perception of bare novelty itself. But when the novelty has a group of painful objects, the perceptions are more interesting, and alarm the whole human frame. Let us suppose one's self to be about being reduced from a state of affluence to penury; or to be bereaved of one's friends; or to undergo the amputation of a leg or an arm; what kind of perceptions should we have? Would they not create a horror to the mind, agitate the animal spirits, or strike on the fine fibres of the heart and brain so as to make us shudder? If this be agreeable to common experience on such occasions, common experience is a clew that will help to unravel the causes of the sore amazement of our Lord at this juncture.

"Again. He was now on the spot where he was to prepare himself and meet his sufferings. There may be facts transacted, or a variety of events to which we are subject, which will make the bare sight of places raise a combination of ideas and disturb and perplex the mind. It is so natural to connect things with places, that very often we make the latter a sort of focus where the moment of the whole business is collected. Have we a cause to litigate, or are we called to defend our country? The entrance into the court of judicature, or first view of the field of battle, shall give a more warm and sensible turn to the affections and passions, than perhaps we shall feel through the whole trial, or meet with in the actual engagement. And if this was not exactly the case of our Lord, yet as he came hither on purpose to prepare and meet his sufferings, those sufferings must necessarily be represented and brought to the full view of his imagination. In order to suit ourselves to a condition, that condition must be surveyed and entered into by the mind. Wherefore we may suppose, that the first perception our Lord had, when he was at the place, was the kind and importance of the evils to which he was now to submit. This supposition is both pious and natural. Then we address the Supreme Being with propriety, when we have viewed the exigency of our affairs. We seldom need to court objects of pain. They are known to intrude themselves too often with a sort of eagerness. But in the present circumstance they are called for, and the attention of the mind to them is, as it were, demanded. Wherefore our Lord could not but be conscious of the perception he had of the evils before him. And that consciousness must increase in proportion to the number and weight they bore. It is agreeable to the natural order of things that it should be so. So that it is no wonder if a round of misery was the only perception he was for a time conscious of. Now here was he to be betrayed by one of his own disciples, seized and bound like a thief, abandoned by his friends, led away and treated with cruel and indignant usage. And the consequences hereof, replete with evils, found easy access, we may suppose, to a mind like his. The language of the best human heart on such an occasion would be, O what will become of my country, and of the men I love! What an agitation would a man feel in his animal spirits, and how acute and powerful the operation between his passions and their objects in such a state and crisis as this! It is evident the perception of misery, now, is right, and as it should be; and the commotion that ensues is natural, and what will be. With respect to the latter, reason is too sublime, or comes too slow to have anything presently to do in the case. The violence of the commotion must cease before the understanding can attend to the dictates of reason. After this manner, probably, was Jesus exercised at this juncture."

*"When Christ is compared to men who are said to have slept sound before a painful death, and to have discovered no sensibility in any period of it, the nature and use of his *example* is not considered; his natural weakness, if it may be so called, being better calculated to show the strength of his *faith*, and therefore affording more encouragement to us to follow his steps.

"But certainly our encouragement to follow Christ in suffering and dying is greatly lessened by the notion of his having had a power over his own sensations, so that in any situation he could feel more or less at pleasure, and even put an end to all sensation by a premature death, which is strictly prohibited to all his followers, and justly esteemed unbecoming the firmness that is expected of other men. Christians who entertain this idea of their Saviour cannot have reflected on the nature of the case.

"It may be said that, if Christ only felt as *a man* during his agony, we should find something similar to it in the accounts of some of the martyrs. But the probability is, that no history of any martyr was ever written with such perfect fidelity as that of Christ by the Evangelists. It has been too much the object of the writers, and from the best views, namely, the encouragement of others, to exhibit the fortitude and heroism of the sufferers in the strongest light.

"It must also be considered, that what a person suffers in his own mind, in the expectation of pain and death, is gen-

---

* From the Theological Repository, Vol. VI. pp. 314–319.—G. R. N.

erally known only to himself; and that the affections of the bodily frame are seldom so great, when he is in company, as to be visible to others. What our Saviour himself felt would not have been known, if he had not, for the best reasons, chosen that some of his disciples should be witnesses of it. For anything that appears, his agony might not last half an hour, and presently after it he was perfectly composed; and his behavior the day following was such as could have given no person the least suspicion of what he had felt the preceding night.

"But though nothing is related of any particular martyr that approaches to the case of our Saviour, yet, besides what we may judge from our own experience in the expectation of less evils, of what *must* have sometimes been felt in the expectation of greater ones, some circumstances are occasionally mentioned by martyrologists, which sufficiently illustrate the account of the Evangelists. There are numberless cases in which martyrs are represented as peculiarly intrepid during their trial, and also immediately before, and even during the time of extreme torture, compared with what they had felt on the more distant view of it, though the manner in which they were affected by that more distant view is not distinctly noted.

"Many letters are preserved of martyrs, written in the interval between their apprehension and their deaths. But, besides that historians would seldom choose to publish any letters except such as, in their opinion, would do them credit, and serve the cause for which they suffered, that is, show their fortitude, a man who is capable of writing must be tolerably composed, and would not in general be himself inclined to dwell upon circumstances which would give himself and his friends pain.

"From the account of one of the English martyrs, however, namely, Richard Woodman, it may easily be collected, that his sufferings during his conflict with himself, when, as he says (Fox's Book of Martyrs, Vol. III. p. 673), while he was 'loth to forego his wife and children and goods,' were extreme. 'This battle,' he says, 'lasted not a quarter of an hour; but it was sharper than death itself for the time, I dare say.' After this he appears to have been perfectly calm, and he suffered with great fortitude.

"Having now, I presume, some idea of the extreme distress and agony of mind under which our Lord labored, greater perhaps than any other man had ever felt before him, and also of the *causes* which produced it, let us consider his strength of mind in supporting the prospect of them. That he should wish to avoid going through the dreadful scene, we cannot think extraordinary. He would not have been a *man* if he had not, and that this wish should be expressed in the form of a prayer to that great Being at whose sovereign disposal he and all mankind always are, was quite natural. In a truly devout mind, which respects the hand of God in everything, an earnest *wish* and a *prayer* are the same thing. Our Saviour, in this agony, did pray that, *if it was possible, the bitter cup might pass from him.* But by *possible* must, no doubt, be meant *consistently with the designs of divine government.* He therefore only expressed his desire that his painful death and sufferings might be dispensed with, if the same great and good ends could have been attained without them. For there can be no doubt but that *with God all things are* naturally *possible.* Our Lord's wish or prayer was therefore only *conditional*, and not *absolute.* He did not wish to be excused from suffering, whatever might be the consequence. Even in this most painful state of apprehension, he did not look to himself only, but to God, and the great ends of his government.

"We may think it extraordinary that our Lord should for a moment suppose that what he wished or prayed for was, in any sense of the word, *possible*, knowing, as he himself observes, that *for that end he came unto that hour;* his dying, with a view to a future resurrection, being a necessary part of that plan which he was to be the principal instrument in executing. But, besides that, in a highly agitated state of mind, the thing might for a moment appear in a different light, our Lord well knew that the appointments of God, even when expressed in the most absolute terms, are not always so intended. We have more instances than one of similar orders and appointments, by which nothing was meant but the trial of a person's faith.

"This was the case when Abraham was ordered to offer up his beloved son Isaac. Till the moment that his hand was actually raised to slay his son, that patriarch had no reason whatever to think that the death of his son, and that by his own hand, was not intended by the Divine Being. The order for the destruction of Nineveh in forty days was also delivered in absolute terms, though it was intended to be conditional, and in the event did not take place. Notwithstanding, therefore, all that had passed in the communications which Jesus had with God, he could not tell but that *possibly* his death might not be necessary, and that the same end might be gained without it. In these circumstances, considering the natural love of life, and the dread of pain and death, the merest possibility, or the supposition of a possibility, would certainly justify our Lord's prayer, especially when it is considered that, in the same breath with which he uttered it, he added, *Nevertheless, not as I will, but as thou wilt.* Notwithstanding the dread and horror of mind with which he viewed his approaching sufferings, he had no objection to them, if it was the determined will of God that he should bear them. This was a degree of resignation and fortitude which far exceeds anything that we read of in history. In all other instances in which persons have sweated through the fear of death, they would have given, or have done, anything to have avoided it. To them it appeared the greatest of all evils.

"The courage which any man may show while his nerves are firm, is not to be compared with that of our Saviour's, when his were, in a manner, broken and subdued. It was not only while he was calm, and had a perfect command of himself, but when his perturbation and distress of mind was so great as to throw him into a profuse sweat, that he said,

Not as I will, but as thou wilt. No man in any cool moment can form to himself an adequate idea of the heroism of this act. Because no man, in a cool moment, and under no terror of mind himself, can tell what his own wishes and prayers would be in a state of such dreadful agony as that of our Saviour. It will therefore be greater than he can conceive it to be. It is probable that nothing but the consciousness of his peculiarly near relation to God, and his full assurance of such a state of future glory as no other man would ever arrive at, could have supported him, and have preserved his resignation and fortitude, in a state of mind so peculiarly unfavorable to them."

OF OUR LORD'S FORTITUDE.

By WILLIAM NEWCOME,

ARCHBISHOP OF ARMAGH, AND PRIMATE OF IRELAND.*

Our Lord exhorted his apostles not to fear their persecutors, who killed the body and could not kill the soul; but rather to fear Him who was able to destroy both body and soul in hell.† This was an exhortation to fortitude in professing and propagating the true religion. His example taught this duty in its whole extent.

He showed a noble contempt of worldly greatness by appearing in a low condition of life. During his public ministry he had not where to lay his head,‡ some of his pious attendants ministered to him of their substance,§ and he paid the tribute-money by miracle.‖ He suffered hunger, thirst, and weariness; he was ever contending with the dulness of his disciples, the incredulity of his kinsfolk, and the reproaches and injuries of the Jews. And he "pleased not himself"¶; but submitted to many and great evils, that he might please God and benefit mankind.

Let us observe in particular instances what "contradiction of sinners"** he endured, and what greatness of mind he displayed.

---

* From his "Observations on our Lord's Conduct as a Divine Instructor," &c.

† Matt. x. 26, 28. ‡ Matt. viii. 20. § Luke viii. 3.
‖ Matt. xvii. 27. ¶ Rom. xv. 3. ** Heb. xii. 3.

When he had pronounced forgiveness of sins to a paralytic, some of the Scribes and Pharisees charged him with blasphemy for invading God's prerogative. But they made the accusation in the reasonings of their hearts; and did not avow it openly. Notwithstanding this, Jesus, unawed by their authority, firmly but calmly expostulated with them for their evil thought;* and argued that the discernment of a man's moral state might justly be allowed to him whom God had vested with the power of working miracles.

Having healed a man on the Sabbath, who had labored under an infirmity for thirty and eight years, the Jews persecuted him and sought to kill him. Jesus answered, "My Father worketh hitherto, and I work":† My Father preserves, governs, and benefits the world without distinction of days; and therefore I also extend good to men on the Sabbath. This mode of expressing himself furnished the Jews with an additional reason for seeking his life. Observe now, throughout the whole of the discourse immediately following, with what magnanimity our Lord perseveres in the same language. "The Son can do nothing of himself, but what he seeth the *Father* do."‡ "The *Father* loveth the Son, and showeth him all things which he himself doeth."§ "The *Father* judgeth no man, but hath committed all judgment unto the Son: that all men should honor the Son, even as they honor the *Father*."‖

Probably on the Sabbath after he had restored the lame man at the pool of Bethesda, our Lord intrepidly vindicated his disciples against the Pharisees, who had censured them for plucking and eating ears of corn on that day.¶ And, thinking it expedient to wean the Jews from their excessive veneration for the law which he was about to abolish, on the Sabbath which next succeeded, though the Scribes and Pharisees watched him, he healed a man with a withered hand

---

* Mark ii. 6 – 11. † John v. 17. ‡ Ver. 19. § Ver. 20.
‖ Ver. 22, 23. So ver. 21, 26, 30, 36, 37, 43, 45.
¶ Luke vi. 1 – 4.

publicly in the synagogue.* This filled them with madness; and they took counsel how they might destroy him.

Afterwards, as he was teaching in one of the synagogues on the Sabbath, he restored a woman who had been bowed together eighteen years, confuted the ruler of the synagogue who with indignation restrained the people from coming to be healed on the Sabbath, reproved his hypocrisy, as he concealed many vices under this semblance of piety, and made all his adversaries ashamed. †

Again: as he was eating bread with a ruler of the Pharisees on the Sabbath, and those of that powerful sect insidiously observed his conduct, a man with a dropsy stood before them. Jesus said to the teachers of the Law and the Pharisees, Is it lawful to heal on the Sabbath day? Knowing how invincibly he reasoned on this point, they kept silence. But Jesus "took him, and healed him, and sent him away." ‡ Conscious of his rectitude, he was fearless of their power.

Once more: at the Feast of Tabernacles, though it was the Sabbath, Jesus made clay and opened the eyes of one blind from his birth: § and he wrought this miracle immediately after the Jews had taken up stones to cast at him, and had sent officers to apprehend him. ||

I do not find in the history of the Apostles that they had the disengagement from prejudice, and the courage, to imitate this part of our Lord's conduct.

There are other instances which show that Jesus paid no deference to the wrong notions of the leading Jews. The Scribes and Pharisees murmured because he ate with publicans and sinners in the house of Matthew the publican. ¶ This censure did not deter him from saying to Zaccheus, a chief of the publicans, at a time when multitudes surrounded him, This day I must abide in thine house.**

When the Scribes and Pharisees from Jerusalem asked

---

* Luke vi. 6 – 11.
† Luke xiii. 10 – 17.
‡ Luke xiv. 1 – 6.
§ John ix. 14.
|| See ch. vii., viii., ix.
¶ Luke v. 30.
** Luke xix. 2 – 7.

him why "his disciples walked not according to the tradition of the elders, but ate bread with unwashen hands"; he expostulated with them for their hypocrisy, proved to them that they made void the commandment of God by their tradition, characterized them as blind leaders of the blind, and thus introduced his explanation of moral defilement: "He called unto him all the multitude, and said unto them, Hearken unto me, all of you, and understand." *

Another proof of our Lord's fortitude was, that, although his first preaching at Nazareth had exposed his life to danger,† the unbelief, the ingratitude, the outrage and violence of his countrymen, could not divert him from attempting their conversion a second time. ‡

We have seen how undauntingly he reproved his enemies on just occasions; and these were often the Jewish rulers who had his life in their power.

He met death for the wisest and best ends, the glory of God and the salvation of mankind. He astonished his timid disciples by the readiness with which he went before them in the way to Jerusalem, on the approach of the Passover at which he suffered; § when they all knew that his enemies were conspiring against his life, and he himself knew that he should suffer a most painful and ignominious death: he entered the city in a kind of public triumph: in the hearing of the multitude he reproved the vices of the Scribes and Pharisees to their face, ‖ with unequalled energy, and with words "quick and powerful, and sharper than a two-edged sword": ¶ when Judas rose from the paschal supper to betray him, he said to his disciples, with wonderful composure, "Now is the Son of Man glorified, and God is glorified through him": ** he witnessed before the high-priest, and before Pontius Pilate, a good confession; and showed that he voluntarily submitted to death, because he had mirac-

---

* Mark vii. 1 – 15. † Luke iv. 29. ‡ Mark vi. 1 – 6.
§ Mark x. 32; Luke xix. 28. ‖ Matt. xxiii. 1.
¶ Heb. iv. 12. ** John xiii. 31.

ulously preserved his life at the preceding feasts of Tabernacles and Dedication.*

It is natural to object, that our Lord's agony was inconsistent with the fortitude which some good men have actually displayed. I shall give this objection its full force; † and shall consider it with the attention which it demands.

We read that our Lord often foretold his sufferings, and many particulars of them; that he most sharply rebuked Peter for wishing them far from him; ‡ and that when Moses and Elias appeared to him at his transfiguration, they spake of his departure which he was about to accomplish at Jerusalem. § He likewise knew that, according to the ancient prophecies, the Messiah ought to suffer what the Jews inflicted, ‖ and to enter into his glory: ¶ and accordingly he predicted his resurrection on the third day,** his ascension into heaven,†† and his elevation to his glorious throne. ‡‡ It must be added, that his pre-existing and divine state gave him a large and perfect view of this and every other plan of God's moral government.

On the other hand, we must consider that our Lord was perfect man, and left men an example that they should follow his steps. §§ He partook of flesh and blood, ‖‖ like the children given him by the common Father of all. "In all things it behooved him to be made like unto his brethren; that he might be a merciful and faithful high-priest." He said to his apostles, "Ye are they who have continued with me in my *temptations*." ¶¶ "He was in all points *tempted* like as we

---

* John viii. 59; x. 39.

† Celsus thus states it, Orig. l. 2, § 24. Τί οὖν ποτνιᾶται καὶ ὀδύρεται, καὶ τὸν τοῦ ὀλέθρου φόβον εὔχεται παραδραμεῖν, λέγων ὧδε πως· Ὦ πάτερ, κ. τ. λ.

‡ Matt. xvi. 22, 23.

§ Luke ix. 31.

‖ Mark ix. 12; John iii. 14; Luke xviii. 31; xxii. 37; John xiii. 1, 3; xix. 28.

¶ John xvii. 24; Matt. xix. 28; xxv. 31.

** Matt. xx. 19.

†† John vi. 62.

‡‡ See the texts quoted at ¶.

§§ 1 Pet. ii. 21.

‖‖ Heb. ii. 13, 14, 17.

¶¶ Luke xxii. 28.

are, yet without sin";* that he might be touched with the feeling of our infirmities. He himself was "compassed with infirmity";† that he might pardon the ignorant and erroneous, and be moderately and not rigorously affected towards them.

We must also carefully remark of him, that he possessed the most exquisite feelings of human nature in the highest degree.‡ He was susceptible of joy, which instantly burst forth in devout thanksgiving.§ He was prone to compassion, and repeatedly melted into tears. The innocence of children engaged his affection; his heart was open to the impressions of friendship; and when he saw any degree of virtue, he loved it.‖ He was grieved at unbelief, and had a generous indignation against vice: and we find him touched with the quickest sense of his own wrongs: "Are ye come out as against a thief, with swords and staves, to take me?"¶

Sometimes he spake of his sufferings with the greatest sensibility. "I have a baptism to be baptized with: and how am I straitened till it be accomplished!"** "Now is my soul troubled: and what shall I say? Father, save me from this hour! But for this cause came I unto this hour."††

It is true that he frequently foretold his death with much composure; and that he sternly reprehended Peter, when, from worldly views, that apostle began to rebuke him for uttering one of these predictions.‡‡

The horror of the sharpest sufferings which can be undergone will sometimes be greater, and sometimes less, in the firmest and best minds;§§ as the evil is considered in its own nature, or under the idea of duty and resignation to God. The contest between reason and religion, and the natural dread of the greatest evils, must subsist when the most per-

---

* Heb. iv. 15. † Heb. v. 2.

‡ See Barrow, Vol. I. Serm. XXXII. p. 475, ed. fol. 1683.

§ Matt. xi. 25. Luke x. 21. ‖ Mark x. 21. ¶ Matt. xxvi. 55.

** Luke xii. 50. †† John xii. 27. ‡‡ Mark viii. 32.

§§ Ignominiæ cruciatuum et mortis horrorem in Christi carne modo majorem modo minorem fuisse apparet. Grot. in Matt. xvi. 23.

fect virtue is called on to suffer them. and where it ends in a becoming resolution, and a pious submission to the wise and great Disposer of all events, the character is a consummate one in a moral and religious view.*

Let us now turn our eyes to our Lord's conduct on the night before his crucifixion. Nothing can exceed the sedateness, the wisdom, and benevolence, which appear throughout the whole of it at the celebration of the paschal supper. He first gently censured the contention for superiority which had arisen among the Apostles.† He then illustrated his doctrine of humility by an example of it, in washing their feet. He proceeded to declare with much emotion his knowledge of Judas's ungrateful and perfidious intention;‡ he mentioned the aggravations and the dreadful consequences of his guilt; but described the traitor covertly, and addressed him obscurely, till compelled by Judas's own question to point him out publicly. He exhorted his disciples to mutual love with a paternal affection.§ In consequence of Peter's declared self-confidence, he foretold his fall; but when Peter vehemently repeated his asseveration, our Lord did not repeat his prediction.|| He instituted a most simple, expressive, and useful rite in commemoration of his death; instructed, advised, and comforted his disciples with the most unbounded affection; and closed with a solemn act of piety as striking a scene as imagination can conceive of lowliness and benignity, of prudence and wisdom, of decorum and majesty, of composure and resignation.¶

He then resorted to his accustomed place of retirement,

---

* Aristotle thus describes the man of fortitude: *δεῖ φοβεῖσθαι μέν, ὑπομένειν δέ*, "Evils must be feared by him, and yet undergone." Magna Mor., p. 160, ed. Du Val. So Eth. Nicom., III. vii. 1: *φοβήσεται μὲν οὖν καὶ τὰ τοιαῦτα· ὡς δὲ δεῖ, καὶ ὡς λόγος, ὑπομενεῖ, τοῦ καλοῦ ἕνεκα*, "The man of fortitude will fear human evils; but will undergo them as he ought, and as reason prescribes, for the sake of what is becoming and right."

† Luke xxii. 25, &c. ‡ John xiii. 21. § John xiii. 34.

|| Matt. xxvi. 35. ¶ John xvii.

and where he knew that Judas would execute his treason: for he knew all things which should befall him.*

I shall now inquire what were the causes of that agony † and deadly sorrow, ‡ of that sore amazement and heavy anguish, § which seized him on the approach of his sufferings; and which drew from him such intense and persevering supplications that God would avert them.

I cannot suppose that he was penetrated with a sense of God's indignation at this time. That is the portion of those

---

* John xviii. 4.

† The word ἀγωνία, Luke xxii. 44, has not so strong a sense as the corresponding one in our language. It properly signifies the fear which men have when they are about to contend with an antagonist; and in this sense is opposed to great fear. When Hector was on the point of engaging with Ajax, the Trojans feared greatly; but Hector only ἠγωνία. See Dionysius Hal. in Clarke's note on Il. VII. 216. Aristotle describes it to be fear at the beginning of an undertaking: φόβος τις πρὸς ἀρχὴν ἔργου. Probl. II. 31, p. 691, ed. Du Val. The Stoics defined it to be the fear of an uncertain event: φόβος ἀδήλου πράγματος. Diog. Laert. Zeno, VII. Sect. 113, p. 435, ed. Amst. 4to. It is twice used by Diodorus Siculus for the anxiety of the Egyptians while the Nile was rising, ed. Wess., p. 44. And an apposite passage is quoted by Lardner on the Logos, p. 7, from Nic. Damascen. apud Vales. excerpt. p. 841, where all are said to be ἀγωνιῶντες, and Julius Cæsar to be μεστὸς ἀγωνίας, while Octavius's life was in danger from illness. "Per catachresin ponitur pro quovis timore," says H. Stephens in voc. and accordingly in Syr. ἀγωνία is rendered by *fear*, from דחל, timuit. See Wetstein in loc.

‡ H. Stephens translates the word ἐκθαμβέομαι, "Stupore attonito percellor, Pavore attonito perterreor." He derives it from θήπω, stupeo. It denotes wonder; see Mark x. 32; Luke iv. 36; v. 9; Acts iii. 10, 11; ix. 6. It also denotes that fear which often accompanies wonder. Compare Mark xvi. 5, 6, with Luke xxiv. 5, Matt. xxviii. 5. The word θάμβησεν, Il. I. 199, is explained by Didymus, ἐφοβήθη, ἐξεπλάγη. See Pearson on the Creed, Article *Suffered*.

§ 'Αδήμων, whence ἀδημονέω, is derived from ἀδέω tædio afficior, proprie præ defatigatione. Ἄδος signifies satietas; defatigatio, quæ est laboris velut satietas. And Eustathius defines ἀδημών, "one who fails," (animo concidit,) as it were from a satiety of sorrow. Ὁ ἐκ.λύπης, ὡς οἷα καί τινος κόρου, (ὃς ἄδος λέγεται,) ἀναπεπτωκώς. See H. Stephens: Reimar's Dion Cassius, p. 924, note, § 215. Wetstein in loc. Phil. ii. 26.

only who do evil. A voice from heaven repeatedly pronounced our Lord the beloved Son of God, in whom he was well pleased. And he was now about to evidence his obedience and love to his Father in a most illustrious manner.* He was also about to sanctify himself † for the sake of his disciples, and of all mankind. And what are his own words? "Therefore doth my Father *love* me, because I lay down my life that I may take it again." ‡

Nor was Christ at this time under the immediate power of Satan. In the concluding scenes of his life, the evil one might be said to "bruise his heel," § because he afflicted him by his instruments. After the temptation, the Devil is said to depart from him "for a season." ‖ If the phrase implies that he returned during our Lord's agony and sufferings, what his emissaries and imitators did may be attributed to his agency. When our Lord said to his apostles, at the paschal supper, "the prince of this world cometh"; ¶ the meaning is, that he was coming by those unjust and violent men who resembled him. And again, when Jesus said to the Jewish rulers, "this is your hour, and the power of darkness"; ** he meant the power of wickedness, of men who hated the light, and came not to it lest their deeds should be reproved. But that the mind of Christ was now disquieted and harassed by Satan himself is a horrid idea, the dictate of gloomy minds, and wholly inconsistent with God's goodness to the Son of his love.††

Nor was he oppressed and overcome by the sense that he was to bear the sins of mankind in his own body on the tree; ‡‡ and to redeem us from the curse of the law, being made a curse for us. §§ A foresight of conferring unspeakable benefits on the human race would tend to alleviate, and not to embitter, the sufferings of the benevolent Jesus: unless

* John xiv. 31.
† John xvii. 19; Matt. xx. 28; xxvi. 28; 2 Cor. v. 14.
‡ John x. 17.
§ Gen. iii. 15.
‖ Luke iv. 13.
¶ John xiv. 30.
** Luke xxii. 53.
†† Col. i. 13.
‡‡ 1 Pet. ii. 24.
§§ Gal. iii. 13.

18

at this time he was [judicially] stricken, smitten of God, and afflicted;* an idea which the prophet excludes, and which his own sinless rectitude and God's perfect goodness exclude. Though God had wise reasons for not restraining those who afflicted our Lord, yet he was so far from heightening his afflictions above their natural course, that he sent an angel from heaven to strengthen him.† Jesus suffered by the wickedness of men; but he was not punished by the hand of God. Nor should his death, and the bitter circumstances preceding it, be considered as a full compensation to strict justice; but as God's merciful and gracious method of reconciling man to himself.

Those divines entertain the most just and rational notions who do not think that our Lord's broken and dejected spirit was a trial supernaturally induced; but assign natural causes for the feelings which shook his inmost frame. He felt for the wickedness and madness of those who persecuted him in so unrelenting a manner, notwithstanding his beneficent conduct, his laborious and admirable instructions, and the convincing evidences of his divine mission; for the irresolution, timidity, and despondency of his friends, and for the ingratitude, perfidy, and guilt of the wretched and devoted Judas. He foresaw the unjust offence which his death on the cross would give both to Jews and Gentiles; the exemplary destruction of his country; the spirit of hatred and persecution which would arise against his Church, and even among those who were called by his name; and the unbelief and sins of mankind, which exposed them to such a weight of punishment here and hereafter. And these and such like painful sensations and gloomy prospects made the deepest impression at a

---

* Isa. liii. 4.

† Luke xxii. 43. That some omitted this part of the history, see Lardner's Cred., Part II. Vol. III. p. 132; Hist. of Heretics, 252; and Grotius's note in loc., who says: "Illaudabilis fuit et superstitio et temeritas illorum qui hanc particulam et sequentem de sudore delevere. — Christus destitutus divinitatis in se habitantis virtute, humanæque naturæ relictus, — opus habuit angelorum solatio."

time when he had a lively view of the immediate indignities and insults, of the disgrace, and horrid pains of death, which awaited him during the long and sharp trial of his wisdom and goodness.*

When he came to the place where a follower and friend was to betray him, and where the Jews were ignominiously to seize and bind him as a malefactor, the scene excited a perturbation of mind, and he was depressed by sorrow and anguish proportioned to his exquisite sensibility, the consciousness of his wrongs, and his extensive foresight.

And how did our Lord act under the extreme sorrow which overwhelmed him? He offered up the following prayer to his Father: † "My Father, all things which are fit and right are possible with thee: if it be possible, if the wise plan of thy moral government admit of it, let this bitter and deadly cup pass from me: nevertheless, not as I will, but as thou wilt. If this cup of pain and torture cannot pass from me, but that I drink it, thy will be done." ‡ He thrice addressed himself to his Father in words of the same import. And being in an agony, having the prospect of an excruciating death immediately before him, he prayed the more intensely: and his body was so affected by the state of his mind, that drops exuded from him, the copiousness of which bore resemblance to drops of blood. § The author of the Epistle to the

---

* See most of these causes well enlarged on in Dr. Harwood's Dissertation on our Saviour's Agony.

† Jortin says, after Grotius on Matt. xxvi. 39: "We must observe that our Lord was made like unto us in all things, sin excepted; and that, upon this and other occasions, he experienced in himself what we also frequently find within us, two contrary wills, or, to speak more accurately, a strife between inclination and reason; in which cases, though reason gets the better of inclination, we may be said to do a thing willingly, yet with an unwilling mind." Vol. IV. Serm. III. p. 42. The whole discourse should be attended to by those who study this subject. I likewise recommend a careful perusal of Lardner's Sermons on our Lord's sufferings.

‡ Matt. xxvi. 39, &c., and parallel places.

§ *Τοὺς παχεῖς ἐκείνους, καὶ παραπλησίους αἵματος θρόμβοις, ἱδρῶτας ἐξίδρωσε.* Photii ep. 138, p. 194, ed. Lond. 1651.

Hebrews observes that he "offered up prayers and supplications to him who was able to save him from death, with a strong cry and with tears; and was heard" from the filial reverence with which he prayed.* God administered to him extraordinary consolation.† But thus far only his supplications availed. For the cup of death was not removed from him.

Of this scene our Lord intended to make three of his apostles witnesses: for he advanced only a small distance from them, and the moon was full. But they slept through sorrow; contrary to their Master's commands, ever given for the gravest reasons, and which should have been particularly obeyed in such circumstances. At the close of it he said, The design for which I separated you from my other disciples being ended, "sleep on now, and take your rest."‡ On uttering these words, he heard the approach of those who came to apprehend him, and immediately added: "It is enough: the hour is come: behold, the Son of Man is betrayed into the hands of sinners. Rise, let us advance: behold, he who betrayeth me is at hand."§

Here some observations are necessary.

The Captain of our salvation, who was made perfect through sufferings,‖ set a most useful example to his followers who were doomed to undergo the same fiery trial. He gave them no lesson of a proud and stoical insensibility. The natural evils of life he treated as evils;¶ and a violent death by lingering torture, as the greatest natural evil.

---

* Heb. v. 7. † Luke xxii. 43. ‡ Matt. xxvi. 45.

§ Mark xiv. 41, 42. The word ἀπέχει, which Hesychius explains by ἀπόχρη, ἐξαρκεῖ, seems a retracting of what he had just allowed. "But enough of sleep." He is represented as speaking *to the instant.*

‖ Heb. ii. 10.

¶ With a view to the evils which are thick sown in life, or, perhaps, to the persecutions of his followers, he observed, that sufficient unto the day was the *evil* thereof. (Matt. vi. 34.) He spoke the language of nature, when he called the temporal advantages of riches *good* things; and Lazarus's pain and poverty, *evil* things. (Luke xvi. 25.) And, again, when he thus foretold Peter's crucifixion, that another should gird him, and carry him whither *he would not.* (John xxi. 18.)

He foresaw that some of his disciples would madly court persecution.* But he gave no sanction to such enthusiasm by his own conduct. He had before taught them to use prudence in avoiding persecution; † and he now taught them to pray against it with perseverance and earnestness, but at the same time with the most entire resignation. And this is true constancy in a Christian martyr, if he first fervently prays against sufferings which every man must abhor, and then firmly undergoes them, if it is God's will not to avert them from him. It was fit that our Lord's example in this respect should be openly proposed to the world; and I believe that every sober and pious Christian, of the greatest constitutional fortitude, has publicly or secretly followed it, from the irresistible bent of human nature. ‡

Our Lord also taught Christians in all ages, what the depravity of the world made it necessary for many to bear in mind, that a state of the sharpest sufferings was consistent with the favor of God; and that the most perfect innocence, and the brightest prospect of future glory, could not overcome the natural horror of them. To prevent despair in any, he made himself a pattern to the *weakest* and *tenderest* of mankind.§ "He sanctified the passion of fear, and hallowed natural sadnesses, that we might not think the infelicities of our nature and the calamities of our temporal condition to become criminal, so long as they make us not to omit a duty. He that fears death, and trembles at the approximation of it, and yet had rather die again than sin once, hath not sinned in his fear: Christ hath hallowed it, and the necessitous condition of his nature is his excuse." ‖

I have supposed that our Lord prayed against his death, and not against his dejection of mind; agreeably to his words in another place, where his crucifixion *must* be meant:

* Lardner's Testimonies, II. 174, 358; III. 349, 351. On Heretics, p. 238.

† Matt. x. 23.

‡ See Luke xviii. 7.

§ Archbishop Tillotson, Serm. CXXXVI. p. 236, fol.

‖ Bishop Taylor's Life of Christ, p. 488.

"Shall I not drink of the cup which my Father hath given me?" * I do not else see how the Apostle's words have due force; where he observes that our Lord prayed to him who was *able to save him from death.*† I cannot else understand St. Matthew's words, "O my Father, if this cup may not pass from me, unless I drink it, thy will be done": ‡ which must refer to a future cup of suffering, and not to one which he had already drunk. Nor do the strong expressions used by our Lord admit of the other supposition. He could not doubt whether it were *possible* § that God could remove from him his discomposure and dismay.

I say then that our Lord prayed against his *death:* "My Father, if it be possible, let this cup pass from me." ‖ "Father, all things are possible with thee: remove this cup from me." ¶ "Father, if thou be willing to remove from me this cup, *well.*" ** However, he immediately added words to this effect: "Nevertheless, not my will, but thine, be done." But how could he pray against an event which he himself and so many prophets had foretold? Lardner has answered, that, notwithstanding predictions, good and evil will influence the mind; and we should perform our duty suitably to our circumstances. Our Lord, says he, foretold the fall of Peter, the treachery of Judas, and the destruction of Jerusalem; and yet used the natural means to prevent them. †† What this judicious writer has suggested may be strengthened by observing that many of God's commands and predictions, though expressed absolutely, appear in the history of his providence to have been conditional and revocable. Abraham was commanded to sacrifice his son; and God recalled the command, when he had proved his faith and obedience. ‡‡ David besought God for his child with fasting and tears, after Nathan had foretold his death: for he said, "Who can tell whether God will be gracious unto me, that the child may

* John xviii. 11. † Heb. v. 7. ‡ Ch. xxvi. 42.
§ Matt. xxvi. 39, 42; Mark xiv. 35, 36. ‖ Matt. xxvi. 39.
¶ Mark xiv. 36. ** Luke xxii. 42.
†† Sermons, Vol. II. p. 70. ‡‡ Gen. xxii.

live?" * Jonah was sent to prophesy against the inhabitants of Nineveh, that their city should be overthrown in forty days; and yet God spared them on their humiliation and repentance. † God said to Ahab by the Prophet Elijah, "Behold, I will bring evil upon thee": ‡ and yet the sentence was remitted in part; for God afterwards declared that, because Ahab humbled himself, he would not bring the evil in his days; but in his son's days would he bring the evil on his house. And though, in Hezekiah's sickness, God said to him by Isaiah, "Give charge concerning thy family; for thou shalt die, and not live"; § yet, in consequence of his fervent supplication, God healed him on the third day, and added to his life fifteen years.

But why were not the prayers offered up by our Lord effectual; since he said to Peter very soon afterwards, "Thinkest thou that I cannot now pray to my Father, and he shall give me at hand more than twelve legions of angels?" ‖ I answer, because our Lord prayed with resignation to his Father's will, and not absolutely. "None took his life from him, but he laid it down of himself. He had power to lay it down, and he had power to take it again." ¶ He submitted to death from a conviction of its fitness. When his anguish of mind was allayed, and his commotion natural to man subsided, his language was, "Shall I not drink the cup which my Father hath given me?" ** "How [else] shall the Scripture be fulfilled, that thus it must be?" as if this particular reason for his death had been recollected by him, or had been recalled to his mind †† by the angel who appeared to him. ‡‡

But it may be urged that he, who had a glory with the

---

* 2 Sam. xii. † Jon. iii. ‡ 1 Kings xxi. 21, 29.

§ 2 Kings xx. Here see 1 Sam. xxiii. 12; Jer. xviii. 7, 8; xxxviii. 17.

‖ Matt. xxvi. 53.

¶ John x. 18. ** Matt. xxvi. 54; Mark xiv. 49.

†† See Mark ix. 12; Luke xviii. 31; Matt. xxvi. 24.

‡‡ Luke xxii. 43.

Father before the world was,* must have known the necessity of that event against which he prayed.

I answer, that to assert the strict and absolute necessity of Christ's death becomes not us who know so little of God's unsearchable ways; † that we do not understand the manner in which the divine and human natures were united in Christ, and therefore may doubt whether the superior nature did not sometimes forsake the inferior, ‡ and withhold its communications from it; and that the wise providence of God might so order events as they would most benefit the world in a moral view, and therefore might exhibit our Lord in such circumstances as furnished most instruction and consolation to his persecuted followers.

I now proceed to show our Lord's composure of mind, after he had thus strongly expressed the perturbation which had been raised in him by his foreknowledge of the many dark events which awaited him, and particularly by his abhorrence of a violent and excruciating death.

He went forth to meet the traitor, and the officers sent to apprehend him; § he discovered himself to them; ‖ and when God had struck them with such a miraculous awe that

---

* John xvii. 5.

† See Ben Mordecai, Letter VI. 85, p. 748, &c., 8vo.

‡ See Ben Mordecai, VI. 89. "As to the objection that the weakness of the flesh was absorbed in the divinity, it may just as safely be asserted that the power of the divinity was absorbed in the flesh: for as to the consequence of the conjunction of the angel of the covenant with the flesh in which he was incarnate; or in what degree the temptations of Christ might affect him; that is, how easy or how difficult it might be for Christ to resist them; I presume we are entirely ignorant: and have no right to argue from our ignorance against the fact itself." And Grotius and Tillotson say that the Divine Wisdom communicated itself to Christ's human soul according to his pleasure, and as circumstances required. Grot. on Mark xiii. 32. Tillotson, Vol. IX. p. 273. Beza also says, "Imo et ipsa θεότητος plenitudo sese, prout et quatenus ipsi libuit, humanitati assumptæ insinuavit." On Luke ii. 52. These three last authorities are quoted by Mr. Farmer on the Temptation, p. 130. See Mark iii. 9; Luke ix. 52; Mark xi. 13; xiii. 32; Matt. xxiv. 20.

§ John xviii. 4. ‖ John xviii. 5.

they fell on the ground,* and had thus demonstrated Jesus's power of restraining their violence, our Lord made them this wise and benevolent request, "If ye seek me, let these [my attendants] depart." † He mildly addressed the perfidious Judas: ‡ he was so collected as instantly to perceive the necessity of working a miracle to prevent the ill consequences of Peter's affectionate but rash violence; § and he forewarned that apostle, and all mankind, that drawing the sword in the cause of his religion would involve the good and bad, the persecuted and persecutor, in undistinguished destruction: ‖ he declared his readiness to fulfil the Scriptures by his death: ¶ he meekly expostulated with the people for their violent and disgraceful manner of apprehending him: ** while he stood before Caiaphas, he showed a composed attention to Peter's irresolution and timidity,†† and penetrated him with a sense of them by the majesty of his eye: at the same time, he replied with the most exemplary self-command to the officer who struck him for answering the high-priest, in a manner full of reason and dignity: ‡‡ before Caiaphas, and the whole council of the chief priests, elders, and scribes, he entered into no vindication of himself, no explanation of his perverted expressions, against the false witnesses suborned to accuse him: §§ but when adjured by the living God to say whether he was the Christ, the Son of the blessed God, he answered, I am; though he knew that they would impute it to him as blasphemy, a crime which by the law of Moses was punishable with death. ‖‖

Fortitude under actual sufferings, is patience; and submission to them because they are the will of God, is resignation.

How did Jesus act, when those who beheld him spat in his

---

* John xviii. 6.
† John xviii. 8.
‡ Matt. xxvi. 50; Luke xxii. 48.
§ Luke xxii. 51.
‖ Matt. xxvi. 52.
¶ Matt. xxvi. 54.
** Matt. xxvi. 55.
†† Luke xxii. 61.
‡‡ John xviii. 23.
§§ Matt. xxvi. 62.
‖‖ Lev. xxiv. 16.

face;* when they blindfolded him, and smote him on the face with the palms of their hands, or struck him with their staves; when they derided his prophetic spirit and Messiahship in this taunting language, Prophesy who is he that smote thee? Under all these circumstances of indignity, "he opened not his mouth, like a lamb led to the slaughter." †

When he stood before Pilate, he astonished him by not seeking to avert death in the usual way of defending himself against the accusations of his enemies: ‡ and as before the Jewish high-priest and council he acknowledged himself to be the Christ, the Son of God, which had the appearance of blasphemy; so before the Roman governor he confessed that he was a king, which had the appearance of sedition. §

Before Herod he conducted himself with the same majesty, the same patient endurance of wrongs, and the same resolution to decline the means of self-preservation which became his peculiar circumstances. ‖ He refused to gratify the idle curiosity of the tetrarch by working a miracle, and to give that account of his life and ministry which might have been credited on the authority of others: for which Herod and his soldiers treated him with contempt and scorn, and sent him back to Pilate arrayed in a gorgeous robe, in derision of his claim as a king.

When our Lord was again brought before Pilate, a robber and a murderer ¶ was preferred to him by that very multitude

* Matt. xxvi. 67, 68, and parallel places. What a very strong mark of contempt spitting on a person is accounted in the East, see in Bishop Lowth on Isaiah l. 6. Demosthenes closes the aggravating circumstances of a striker in this manner, *ὅταν κονδύλοις, ὅταν ἐπὶ κόῤῥης*, *when with the hand, when on the cheek:* he adds, *these circumstances κινεῖ καὶ ἐξίστησι, move and transport with rage;* and in the same oration he observes, *οὐκ ἐστὶ τῶν πάντων οὐδὲν ὕβρεως ἀφορητότερον*, *of all things there is nothing more intolerable than petulant and insolent injury.* In Midian. So Quinct. Lib. VI. c. 1: "Plurimum affert atrocitatis modus, si *contumeliosè:* ut Demosthenes ex parte percussi corporis invidiam Midiæ quærit."

† Isa. liii. 7.

‡ Matt. xxvii. 13, 14.

§ John xviii. 37.

‖ Luke xxiii. 8 – 11.

¶ Matt. xxvii. 20, and parallel places.

who had heard his divine instructions, and seen, or perhaps experienced, his beneficial power: * nor did even this vile indignity extort from the meek Jesus a word of expostulation.

Then Pilate commanded that Jesus should be scourged; † after which severe and ignominious punishment the whole band of the Roman soldiers made him their sport, crowned him with thorns, clothed him in purple, delivered him a mock-sceptre, paid him mock-adoration, addressed him with mock-titles of royalty, spat on him, and smote him on the head.

The sight of Jesus, thus derided and afflicted, did not satiate the fury of his enemies; but after they had afforded him a further opportunity of displaying his dignity, and resolution to meet death, by giving no answer to Pilate's question, "Whence art thou?" ‡ they extorted the condemnation of him from his worldly-minded judge by their loud and artful solicitations. §

Then was Jesus led away to be crucified: his cross, or part of it, was laid on him, as the manner was; and he bare it till his exhausted strength sunk under it: "and two others also, *who were* malefactors, were led with him to be put to death." ‖ On the way, a great multitude of women bewailed and lamented him: but he turned about to them, and, with a heart full of commiseration, bade them deplore their own impending sufferings, and not his; declaring at the same time, but in figurative and covert language, that, if the innocent suffered

---

* Josephus, speaking of the Pharisees, says, *τοσαύτην δὲ ἔχουσι τὴν ἰσχὺν παρὰ τῷ πλήθει, ὡς καὶ κατὰ βασιλέως τι λέγοντες, καὶ κατὰ ἀρχιερέως, εὐθὺς πιστεύεσθαι.* Ant. 13. 10. 5, quoted by Harwood on John ii. 24. "They have so much power with the people, that, even if they allege anything against the king or high-priest, they are immediately believed."

† John xix. 1 – 3, and parallel places. ‡ John xix. 9.

§ We may account for Pilate's conduct from his knowledge of Tiberius's extreme jealousy and cruelty.

‖ So Luke xxiii. 32 should be translated and pointed. "Sed oblitus sum Lucæ xxiii. 32 in *κακοῦργοι* utrinque hypostigmen notare," says H. Stephens, in his curious preface to his Greek Testament, 12mo, 1576.

such calamities, much greater would befall those whose crimes made them ripe for destruction: "If they do these things in the green tree, what shall be done in the dry." *

When he came to the place of crucifixion, he was offered wine mingled with myrrh, which was designed to blunt the sense of pain by inducing a state of stupefaction: but he received it not: he declined this office of humanity, that he might show himself unappalled by the horrors of instant crucifixion; and that he might fully possess his reason, and thus display the virtues suitable to his high character in the season of so severe a trial.

A title, deriding his royal descent and dignity, was placed on the cross to which he was fixed. He was crucified between two malefactors; and, probably while the nails were piercing his hands and feet, when the sense and feeling of his ignominious sufferings were strongest, he thus prayed and pleaded for his murderers: "Father, forgive them; for they know not what they do." †

In this situation, which might have excited the pity of the most unfeeling spectator, and of the bitterest enemy, ‡ our Lord was reviled and mocked, his power was questioned, his prophecies perverted, and his dignity blasphemed, by the Jewish people, by the Roman soldiers, and by the chief priests, scribes, and elders; the rulers mixing themselves with the throng, to feast their eyes with his sufferings, and to insult him under them.

But such conduct served only to display the greatness of the sufferer. The patience of Jesus remained unmoved. Here, as when he stood before his judges, he left his life and doctrine, his prophecies and miracles, the supernatural knowledge displayed by him, and the voices from heaven which bare him

---

* Luke xxiii. 27 – 31.

† Luke xxiii. 34.

‡ Θέαμα δ' ἦν
Τοιοῦτον οἷον καὶ στυγοῦντ' ἐποικτίσαι.
Œd. Tyr. 1319.

"Such a sight
Might raise compassion in an enemy."

witness, to speak for him a stronger language than words could convey. As Origen observes,* his silence, under all the indignities and reproaches which he met with, showed more fortitude and patience than anything said by the Greeks under their sufferings.

And again, when one of the malefactors reproached him, he answered him not: but when the other said, "Lord, remember me when thou comest into thy kingdom," † he thus acknowledged himself to be a king, and one who had the keys of heaven and hell: ‡ "Verily I say unto thee, to-day shalt thou be with me in paradise"; in the state of those who are separated, as in a garden of delight, for God's acceptance.

It is a remarkable instance of our Lord's composure, that, in the midst of his exquisite pains, he recommended his mother to that most benevolent Apostle, St. John.

The next circumstance in the order of events is, that about the ninth hour our Lord cried with a loud voice, "My God! my God! why hast thou forsaken me?" § As the words in the original Psalm ‖ do not import a dereliction of the Deity, they cannot be thus understood when used by our Lord. In this strong language the Psalmist described imminent distress and danger ¶ from the sword ** of scornful †† and mighty enemies. ‡‡ He did not mean that he was totally forsaken by Jehovah, whom he afterwards entreated not to be far from him, §§ whom he called his strength, ‖‖ whom he characterized as not hiding his face from the afflicted, ¶¶ and to whom he promised praise and thanksgiving in return for the mercies which he implored.*** In the same terms our Lord expressed the greatness of his anguish; when, in the prophetic words of the Psalm, which is sometimes applicable to David and sometimes to the Messiah, "he was poured out like water, his bones were separated from each other, his heart was like

* Lib. VII. § 54–56, pp. 368, 369. Lardner's Test. II. 317.
† Luke xxiii. 42. ‡ Rev. i. 18. § Matt. xxvii. 46.
‖ Psalm xxii. ¶ Ibid., 11. ** Ibid., 20.
†† Ibid., 7, 8. ‡‡ Ibid., 12, 13, 21. §§ Ibid., 11, 19.
‖‖ Ibid., 19. ¶¶ Ibid., 24. *** Ibid., 25.

wax, it was melted within him." * Our Lord's language, I say, was dictated by extreme suffering, and not by distrust. In the style of the Hebrew Scriptures,† when God permitted individuals or nations to be oppressed and afflicted, he was said to hide his face from them, to forget, reject, or forsake them. Our Lord could not suppose that God had cast him off, because immediately before and after these words he reposed an entire confidence in him. During his crucifixion he twice called God his Father, ‡ he declared his assurance that he should enter into a state of happiness, § and accordingly he resigned his departing spirit into his Father's hands. ‖ He likewise saw, during the space of three hours before he expired, that God miraculously interposed in his behalf, by diminishing the light of the sun and shedding a comparative darkness over the whole land, or, at least, that part of it which was adjacent to Jerusalem. When Jesus had thus poured forth his sorrows, in the words of a sacred hymn which foretold many circumstances of his death, God, who had, as it were, hidden his face from him for a moment, had mercy on him with everlasting kindness, ¶ and speedily closed the scene of his sufferings. For, immediately after this, "Jesus, knowing that all things were now accomplished, that the Scripture might be fulfilled, saith, I thirst." ** This thirst was the natural consequence of his pains, and of that effusion of blood which was occasioned by piercing his hands and his feet. But, unless it had remained that the prophecy †† of the Psalmist should receive its full completion, ‡‡ it was a circumstance on which he would have observed a majestic silence: such was his command over himself, and so attentive was he

---

* Psalm xxii. 14.

† See Job xx. 19; Psalm xxxvii. 25; xxxviii. 10, 21, 22; xlii. 9; xliii. 2; lxxi. 11, 12, 18; Isa. xlix. 14; liv. 7, 8.

‡ Luke xxiii. 34, 46. § Ibid., 43. ‖ Ibid., 46.

¶ Isa. liv. 7, 8. ** John xix. 28.

†† See Lardner's Test., II. 303, § 24, where Origen objects that Jesus was unable patiently to endure thirst.

‡‡ See Psalm lxix. 21; Matt. xxvii. 34.

that not one jot or tittle of the prophets should pass away. "Now there was set a vessel full of vinegar,"* the mean drink of the Roman soldiers; and one of the by-standers filled a sponge with vinegar, and placed it upon a bunch of hyssop, and by means of a reed advanced it to his mouth. "When Jesus therefore had received the vinegar, he said, It is finished": † the prophecies concerning me, antecedently to my death, have had their accomplishment: I have finished my laborious and painful course: I have thus far performed thy will, O God. Immediately after this, he expired with words expressive of a perfect reliance on God, and a firm persuasion of his acceptance: "Father, into thy hands I commend my spirit." ‡

Thus did our Lord appear as great in his sufferings as in his actions, in his death as in his life; and thus did he exhibit a wonderful example of forgiveness and composure, of magnanimity and conscious dignity, of filial love and pious resignation, in the midst of the most horrid tortures that human nature is capable of sustaining.

---

* John xix. 29, and parallel places.

† John xix. 30.

‡ Luke xxiii. 46.

THE DOCTRINE OF THE ATONEMENT.

By BENJAMIN JOWETT, M. A.,

REGIUS PROFESSOR OF GREEK IN THE UNIVERSITY OF OXFORD.*

THE doctrine of the Atonement stands in the same relation to the doctrine of righteousness by faith, as the object in the language of philosophy to the subject. Either is incomplete without the other, yet they admit also of being considered separately. When we pierce the veil of flesh, and ask the meaning of the bleeding form on Mount Calvary, a voice answers, "The atonement once made for the sins of men." It seems like the form of any other dying man, but a mystery is contained in it. We penetrate deeper into the meaning of the word "atonement," and new relations disclose themselves between God and man. There is more than we see in that outward fact, more than we can understand in that mysterious word, "The Lamb of God, that taketh away the sins of the world." "God in Christ reconciling the world to himself, and not imputing their trespasses unto them."

Yet how can this be, consistently with the truth and holiness of God? Can he see us other than we really are? Can he impute to us what we never did? Would he have punished us for what was not our own fault? It is not the pride of human reason which suggests these questions, but the

---

* From his Commentary on St. Paul's Epistles, &c.

moral sense which he himself has implanted in the breast of each one of us. Here is a lesson of comfort and also of perplexity; Jesus Christ is a corner-stone and a stumbling-block at once. We can hardly receive the consolation without seeking to remove the perplexity. Our faith would shake if taken off the foundations of truth and right. The feeble brain of man reaches but a little way into the counsels of the Most High: — "My thoughts are not as your thoughts, neither are your ways my ways," saith the Lord. But no difference between God and man can be a reason for regarding God as less just or less true than the being whom he has made. He is only incomprehensible to us because he is infinitely more so.

It might seem at first sight no hard matter to prove that God was just and true. It might seem as if the suggestion of the opposite needed no other answer than the exclamation of the Apostle, "God forbid! for how shall God judge the world?" But the perplexities of the doctrine of the Atonement are the growth of above a thousand years; rooted in language, disguised in figures of speech, fortified by logic, they seem almost to have become a part of the human mind itself. Those who first spoke of satisfaction were unconscious of its inconsistency with the Divine attributes, just as many good men are in our own day; they do not think of it, or they keep their minds off it. And one cannot but fear whether it be still possible so to teach Christ as not to cast a shadow on the holiness and truth of God; whether the wheat and the tares have not grown so long together, that their husbandman, in pulling up the one, may be plucking up the other also. Erroneous as are many modes of expression used on this subject, there are minds to whom they have become inseparable from the truth itself.

The doctrine of the Atonement, as commonly understood, is the doctrine of the sacrifice or satisfaction of Christ for the sins of men. There are two kinds of language in which it is stated: the first figurative, derived from the Old Testament; the second logical, and based chiefly on distinctions of the schoolmen. According to the first mode of expression, the atonement of Christ is regarded as a sacrifice, which stands in the same relation to the world in general as the Jewish sacrifices did to the individuals who offered them. Mankind were under a curse, and he redeemed them, just as the blood of bulls or of goats redeemed the first-born devoted to God. That was the true sacrifice once offered on Mount Calvary for the sins of men; of which all other sacrifices, since the beginning of the world, are types and shadows, and can never take away sin. Wherever the words blood, or sprinkling, or atonement, or offering, occur in the Old Testament, these truly refer to Christ; wherever uncleanness, or impurity, or ceremonial defilement are spoken of, these truly refer to the sins of men. And, as nearly all these things are purged with blood, so the sins of mankind are purged, and covered, and veiled in the blood of Christ.

To state this view of the doctrine at length, is but to translate the New Testament into the language of the Old. Where the mind is predisposed to receive it, there is scarcely a law, or custom, or rite of purification, or offering, in the Old Testament, which may not be transferred to the Gospel. Christ is not only the sacrificial lamb, but the paschal "lamb without spot," the seal of whose blood makes the wrath of God to pass over the people; he is Isaac on the altar, and also the ram caught in the thicket, upon whom is laid the iniquity of man. Neither need we confine ourselves to this circle of images. Mankind are slaves, and Christ ransoms them: he is the new Lord, who has condescended to buy them, who pays the price for them, which price is his blood. He is devoted and accursed for them; he pays the penalty for their sins; he washes them in his blood; he hides them from the sight of God. All that they are, he is; all that he is, they become.

Upon this figurative or typical statement of the doctrine of the Atonement is raised a further logical one. A new framework is furnished by philosophy, as the types of the Old Testament fade and become distant; figures of speech acquire a sort of coherence when built up into logical statements;

they at length cease to be figurative, and are repeated as simple facts. Rhetoric becomes logic, as the age becomes logical rather than rhetorical; and arguments and reasonings take the place of sermons and apologies.

The logical view of the doctrine of the Atonement commences with the idea of a satisfaction to be made for the sins of men. God is alienated from man; man in like manner is alienated from God. The fault of a single man involves his whole posterity. God is holy, and they are sinful; there is no middle term by which they can be connected. Mankind are miserable sinners, the best of whose thoughts are but evil continually; who have a corrupt nature which can never lead to good. They are not only sinners, but guilty before God, and in due course, in the order of Providence, to suffer punishment for their sins. Their present life is one continued sin; their future life is one awful punishment. They were free to choose at first, and they chose death, and God does but leave them to the natural consequences.

Were we to stop here, every honest and good heart would break in upon these sophistries, and dash in pieces the pretended freedom and the imputed sin of mankind, as well as the pretended justification of the Divine attributes, in the statement that man necessarily or naturally brought everlasting punishment on himself. No slave's mind was ever reduced so low as to justify the most disproportionate severity inflicted on himself; neither has God so made his creatures that they will lie down and die, even beneath the hand of him who gave them life. But although God, it is said, might in justice have stopped here, there is another side of this doctrine which must be viewed as inseparable from it, and was known from the beginning; namely, that God intended to send his only begotten Son for the redemption of mankind. God was always willing that mankind should be saved. But it was just that they should suffer the penalty. He could not save them, if he would. He felt like a judge who pitied the criminal, but could not "in foro conscientiæ" acquit him. Man was fearful of his doom, and God willing to save; but the least particle of the Divine justice must not be impeached; the sentence must be exacted to the uttermost farthing.

At this point is introduced the sacrifice of Christ. The Son takes human nature upon him, and dies once for all. The Father, before angry, and alienated, and averse to man, is reconciled to him through the Son. His justice is satisfied in Christ; his mercy is also shown in Christ. The impossibility has become possible; the necessity, in the nature of things, for the condemnation of man, has been done away. Nor can it be urged that the offences are the sins of many; the satisfaction is only of one. For the satisfaction is of itself infinite, sufficient not for this world only, but for many more; yea, if it please God so to extend it, for the universe itself, and all things that are, have been, or shall be in it.

And this scheme, as already remarked, must not be considered in part only, but as a whole. When God created man, "sufficient to have stood, though free to fall," he foresaw also his fall, redemption, and sanctification in a single indivisible instant. Therefore we should thankfully accept the whole scheme, and not stop to reason on a part. He who condemned us is the same as he who redeemed us through Christ. There was one way of death leading onward to eternal punishment; there was another way of life leading to salvation, which God, to our infinite gain and his own loss, was pleased to take. Neither can we doubt, if we may say so reverently, that God himself was under a sort of constraint to take this way, and no other, for the salvation of mankind. Had it been otherwise, he would have surely spared his only Son. The chasm in the moral government of the world could only be filled up by the satisfaction of Christ for the sins of all mankind.

Thus far the parts of the logical structure are "fitly joined together"; but the main question is yet untouched: "In what did this satisfaction consist?" Was it that God was angry, and needed to be propitiated like some heathen deity of old? Such a thought refutes itself by the very indignation which it calls up in the human bosom. Or that, as "he looked upon the face of his Christ," pity gradually took the place of wrath, and, like some conqueror, he was willing to include in the reversal of the sentence, not only the hero, but all those who were named after his name? Human feelings again revolt at the idea of attributing to the God in whom we live and move and have our being, the momentary clemency of a tyrant. Or was it that there was a debt due to him, which must be paid ere its consequences could be done away? But even "a man's" debt may be freely forgiven, nor could the after payment change our sense of the offender's wrong: we are arguing about what is moral and spiritual from what is legal, or, more strictly, from a shadow and figment of law. Or that there were some "impossibilities in the nature of things," which prevented God from doing other than he did? Thus we introduce a moral principle superior to God, just as in the Grecian mythology fate and necessity are superior to Jupiter. But we have not so learned the Divine nature, believing that God, if he transcend our ideas of morality, can yet never be in any degree contrary to them.

Or, again, if we take a different line of explanation, it may be urged that the atonement is not a satisfaction of Divine justice, but only a "quasi satisfaction," or rather an exhibition of Divine justice in the eyes of mankind and of the angels. Something of this kind may be supported (according to one interpretation of the passage) by the words of the third chapter of Romans, "To show forth, I say, at this time his righteousness on account of the non-observance of sins that are past"; where the reason given for the manifestation of Christ seems to be the justification of the ways of God to men. According to this view, it is regarded as shocking, that God himself should have needed any atonement or satisfaction. But yet it would seem as if God's horror of sin were not sufficiently marked, — that man, to use a homely phrase, was let off too easily, — unless there were some great and open manifestation that God was really on the side of truth and of right. To demonstrate this was the object of the death of Christ. It was a reality in one sense, that is, so far as the sufferings were real; an appearance in another, as its true import related to mankind and the world, and not to God.

If this scheme avoids the difficulty of offering an unworthy satisfaction to God, and so doing violence to his attributes, we can scarcely free it from the equal difficulty of interposing a painful fiction between God and man. Was the spectacle real which was presented before God and the angels on Mount Calvary? If we say no, then we can neither trust our eyes or ears, nor the promises of God, nor the words of Scripture. If the greatest fact of the whole is an illusion, why not all else? That the chief figure in the scene is the Son of God, only makes the illusion the more impossible. Or if we say that it was all real, and yet that its great object was an exhibition to men and angels, to what a wonderful straitness do we reduce Divine power, which can only show forth its justice by allowing men to commit in itself the greatest of human crimes, that redeems the sin of Adam by the murder of Christ! This second theory has no advantage over the preceding, except that which the more shadowy statement must ever have, in rendering difficulties themselves more shadowy. It avoids the physical illusion of the old heretics, and introduces a moral illusion of a worse kind.

For if we substitute for "satisfaction" "demonstration or exhibition of Divine justice," we are not better off than in the previous attempt to explain "satisfaction." How could the sufferings of a good or Divine man exhibit the righteousness of God? Rather they would seem to indicate his indifference to those sufferings in permitting them; in not giving his Son "ten legions of angels" to overcome his enemies. Is it to the Roman soldiers, or to the Jews, or to the disciples, that this exhibition is supposed to have a meaning; or to the world afterwards, who, in the sufferings of Christ, are expected to see for all time the indignation of God against sin? When the doctrine is stated, it betrays itself. For how could there be an exhibition of Divine justice which was known to be a fiction; which, if it were true and real, would be horrible and revolting; which not only exhibits the sins of the guilty laid upon the innocent, but alleviates human feelings by assuring us that they are laid upon that innocent Being, not as the payment of a penalty or satisfaction of the Divine nature, but as the demonstration of Divine justice? The doctrine thus stated is the surface or shadow of the preceding, with the substance or foundation cut away. It removes one difficulty, and, in removing, it raises up a number of others.

Whether, then, we employ the term "sacrifice," or "satisfaction or exhibition of Divine justice," the moment we pierce beneath the meaning of the words, theological criticism seems to detect something which is irreconcilable with the truth and holiness of God. Gladly, if it were possible, we would rest in the thing signified, and know only "Jesus Christ, and him crucified." But, in the present day, we can no longer receive the kingdom of God as little children. The speculations of theologians have insensibly taken possession of the world; the abstractions of a thousand years since have become the household words of our own age; and before we can build up, we have also to clear away.

We are trespassing on holy ground. There will be many who say, It is good to adore in silence a mystery that we can never understand. But there are "idols of the temple," as well as idols of the market-place. These idols consist in human reasonings and definitions which are erected into articles of faith. We are willing to adore in silence, but not the inventions of man. The controversialist naturally thinks, that, in assailing the doctrine of satisfaction as inconsistent with truth and morality, we are fighting not with himself, but with God. True reverence proceeds by a different path; it is careful to separate the human from the Divine; figures of speech from realities; the history of a doctrine from its truth; the formulas of schoolmen and theologians from the hope of the believer in life and death: it is fearful, above all other things, lest it cast the faintest shadow of a cloud on that which is the central light of all religion, the justice and truth of God.

In all ages of the world, and in every country where Christianity is preached, the Old Testament has ever been taking the place of the New, the Law of the Gospel, the outward and temporal of the spiritual and eternal. Even where there has been no sensible image to which mankind might bow, they have filled up the desire of their eyes by imagining an outward form (of doctrine it may be) instead of resting in higher and unseen objects of faith. Ideas must be given through something; those of a new religion ever clothe themselves in the old. The mind itself readily falls back on the "weak and beggarly elements" of sense and imagination. To be told that Christ performed the greatest act that was ever done in this world, does not seem so much as to be told that he was the sacrifice for the sins of men. All history combines to strengthen the illusion; the institution of sacrifice is regarded as part of a Divine design in the education of the world. We cease any more to inquire how far the blood of bulls or of goats can be a real or adequate representation of the relation in which Christ stood to his Father and mankind. We delight to think of the religions of all nations bearing witness "to him that was to come."

It must be remembered that the Apostles were Jews; they were so before their conversion; they remained so afterwards in their thoughts and language; they could not lay aside their first nature, or divest themselves at once of Jewish modes of expression. Sacrifice and atonement were leading ideas of the Jewish dispensation; without shedding of blood, there was no remission. In thinking of the death of Christ and the fulfilment of which he spoke, it was natural to them to think of him as a "sacrifice" and "atonement" for sin. To him bear all the prophets witness, as well as the types of the law and the history of the Jewish people. All their life long they had been sacrificing and living in the commandments of the Law blameless. What a striking view must it have been to their minds, that their rites and ceremonies were not in vain, but only done in ignorance of their true design and import; not that they were nothing, but that there was more in them than the chief priests and Pharisees could even conceive! And the very deadness of them as practised by the Jews in general, and the entire passing away of their original meaning, would greatly assist their new application. There was something in the sacrifices that they could not comprehend, as they truly felt that there was in the death of Christ also far more than they could understand, and they interpreted the one by the other. And when once the thought was suggested to men's minds, at every opening of the book of the Old Testament a new light fell upon the page: the history of Abraham, the settlement in the promised land, the least details of the Temple and the Tabernacle, were written for their instruction.

It is in the Epistle to the Hebrews that the reflection of the New Testament in the Old is most distinctly brought before us. There the temple, the priest, the sacrifices, the altar, the persons, of Jewish history are the figures of Christ and the Church. In the Epistles of St. Paul it is the rarity rather than the frequency of such images which is striking. It is the opposition and not the identification of the Law and the Gospel which is the leading thought of his mind. But in the Epistle to the Hebrews they are fused in one; the New Testament is hidden in the Old, the Old revealed in the New. And from this source, and not from the Epistles of St. Paul, the language of which we are speaking has passed into the theology of modern times. While few persons, comparatively speaking, have ever understood the relation of the Law and faith in the Epistles to the Romans and Galatians, the language of the Epistle to the Hebrews is familiar to all.

We cannot avoid asking ourselves the question, how far these notions of sacrifice or atonement can have the same meaning for us that they had for the first believers. We may use the words correctly; every one may imagine themselves to understand them; but are we not mistaking our familiarity with the sound for a realization of the thing signified? The Apostles lived amid the temple sacrifices; the smoke of their offerings, even in the city of Jerusalem under its Roman governor, as of old in the wilderness, still went up before the Lord; the carcasses of dead animals strewed the courts of the temple. It would be a sight scarcely tolerable to us; neither, if at the present moment we could witness it in remote parts of the world, could we bear to think of what we saw as typical of the Gospel. Nor, indeed, do we think of what we are saying when we speak of Christ offered for the sins of men; the image is softened by distance, and has lost its original associations. We repeat it as a sacred word, hallowed by the usage of Scripture, and ennobled by its metaphorical application. The death of Christ is not a sacrifice in the Levitical sense; but what we mean by the word *sacrifice*, is the death of Christ.

The notion of sacrifice gained a new foundation in the after history of the Church and the world. More and more, as the Christian Church became a kingdom and a hierarchy, did it see the likeness of itself in the history of the Jewish people. The temple which had been pulled down was again built up; the spirit of the old dispensation revived in the new; there was a priest as well as a sacrifice; a Church without which there was no salvation, as much separated from the world as the Jews from the heathen of old. What was a shadow to St. Paul was becoming a reality to the Nicene, and had actually become one to the Mediæval, Church. The body and blood of Christ was not only received spiritually in the celebration of the Lord's Supper, but literally offered again and again in the sacrifice of the Mass, as formerly by the Jewish, so now by the Christian priest. A priesthood and a sacrifice naturally implied each other. As Christ in a figure bore the person of the high-priest entering once into the holy place, so the priest in turn bore the person of Christ. And after the notion of the priesthood passed away in the Reformed Churches, that of the atonement and sacrifice, which during so many centuries had been supported by it, was still retained, because it seemed to rest on a Scriptural foundation. The "antithesis" of the Reformation was not between the Gospel as without sacrifices, and Romanism as retaining sacrifices, or between the law as having a mediator, and the promise as a more "open way"; but between the Gospel as having one mediator, and a sacrifice once offered, and the Roman Church with many priests, and the ever-recurring sacrifice of the Mass.

An additional support for the doctrine of a sacrifice or satisfaction is found in the heathen sacrifices, which, like the Jewish, are viewed only by the light of their Christian fulfilment. All the religions of the world, it has been said, agree in enjoining sacrifices. They seem to conspire together in bearing witness to Him that was to come. Can we account for this common witness, except upon the supposition of a primeval revelation? Certainly, it may be argued that we cannot affirm the Divine origin and the typical meaning of the Jewish sacrifices, without admitting the same with respect to heathen sacrifices also. That could hardly be a sign Divinely appointed for the Jewish people, which, in almost every nation under heaven, the light of human reason discovered for itself. Was it, then, a Divine revelation to both or neither? If we say, to both, we are compelled to admit, in reference to the heathen world, that the farther we trace backward the indications of old language or of mythology, the slighter are the vestiges of a promised revelation. We cannot, therefore, assume one in the particular instance of the institution of sacrifices. If we say, to neither, we seem to reduce the Jewish dispensation to the level of the heathen; it is "the first of the Ethnic religions," as Goethe said, "but still Ethnic." We may escape from this alternative by pointing out the superior morality of the Old Testament; its revelation of the true God; its anticipation of truths utterly unknown to other nations in the age of the world in which the Law was given: still we cannot help admitting a connection of some kind between the heathen and Jewish custom of sacrifices.

But not to pursue the alternative here suggested, we may go on to ask the further question, "What was the inward meaning among the heathen of that outward rite which they termed sacrifice?" Did they, as a modern writer has expressed it, intend to imply, by this act of sacrificing an animal, that they acknowledged the claim of a superior power over their own life? Did they mean to say, "As I now devote to thee this victim, O Apollo, Juno, Jupiter, so do I acknowledge myself justly devoted to thee"? They meant (1.) that the gods, who were like men, should feast like men; this is the prevailing character of the sacrifices in Homer. They meant (2.) in the East something unintelligible to us, but closely connected with the deification of animal life; from the blood of the animal a power seemed to flow forth upon the earth, which by a sort of magic communicated itself to the offerer. They meant (3.) to supply a want, and, in later times, to perform an ancient rite, which still subsisted, though the meaning of it had long passed away; if, indeed, it could have been said to express anything except the vague and undefined awe of the first sons of men towards the mysterious beings by whom they were surrounded. They meant (4.) the abolition of ceremonial pollution, the purification of guilt like that of the Alcmæonidæ in a panic-stricken nation. They meant to do an act, which varied with the character of the people or the state of religion, cheerful or sad, of obligation or free will; differing in Greece and the East, and to the Greek in the age of Pericles and in that of Homer, which might be nothing more than Fetichism, which might comprehend also the devotion of the Decii. They meant, however, nothing which throws any light on the mystery of the death of Christ. Human sacrifices, which are in outward act the nearest, are in spirit the farthest removed from it.

Heathen and Jewish sacrifices rather show us what the sacrifice was not, than what it was. They are the dim, vague, rude, (may we not say?) almost barbarous expression of that want in human nature which has received satisfaction in Him only. Men are afraid of something; they wish to give away something; they feel themselves bound by something; the fear is done away, the gift offered, the obligation fulfilled, in Christ. Such fears and desires can no more occupy their souls; they are free to lead a better life; they are at the end of the old world, and at the beginning of a new one.

Nature and Scripture and the still small voice of Christian feeling give a simpler and a truer explanation of the doctrine of the atonement than theories of satisfaction or the history of sacrifice, — an explanation that does not shift with the metaphysical schools of the age, which is for the heart rather the head. Nature bids us look at the misery of the whole creation groaning and travailing together until now; Christian feeling requires only that we should cast all upon Christ, whose work the Scripture sets forth under many different figures, lest we should rest in one only. This variety is an indication of the simplicity with which we are to learn Christ. The Jewish sacrifices had many meanings and associations. Nor are these the only types under which the Mediator of the new covenant is set forth to us in Scripture. He is the sin-offering, and the paschal lamb, and the priest, and the temple, all in one. Out of all these, why are we to select one to be the foundation of our theological edifice? As figures, we may still use them. But the writings of the Apostle supply another kind of language which is not figurative, and which underlies them all; which is far more really present and lively to us than the conception of a sacrifice, and which remains within the limits of our spiritual consciousness, instead of passing beyond them. That is the spirit of which the other is the letter; the substance of which it is the form and shadow.

I. Everywhere St. Paul speaks of the Christian as one with Christ. This union with him is a union, not in his death merely, but in all the stages of his existence; living with him, suffering with him, dying with him, crucified with him, buried with him, rising again with him, renewed in his image, glorified together with him, — these are the expressions by which this union is denoted. There is enough here for faith to feed on, without sullying the mirror of God's justice or overclouding his truth: peace and consolation enough without raising a suspicion which secretly destroys peace. It is a great thing to set Christ always before us as an example; and he who does so is not far from the kingdom of heaven. But that of which the Apostle speaks is not merely the example of Christ, but communion with him; the indwelling of Christ in our hearts, the conscious recognition that he is the will and the power within us to do rightly.

II. But we need also to pass out of ourselves, and find an assurance which is independent of the liveliness or intensity of our own consciousness. We wish to know that when we close our eyes the light is there; that when the grave covers us, there is a God to whom we still live. That assurance is given us by the life and death of Christ. That perfect harmony of nature, that absolute self-renunciation, that pure love, that entire resignation, continued through life and ending in death, are facts, independent of our feelings, which remain as they were, whether we acknowledge them or not. Not the sacrifice, nor the satisfaction, nor the ransom, but the greatest moral act ever done in this world, — the act, too, of one in our likeness, — is the assurance to us that God in Christ is reconciled to the world.

III. It is a true and Christian feeling, that, after we have done all, we are unprofitable servants. Even the best of us well know that the less we think of our own lives the better. Our actions will not bear taking to pieces, — the garment of self is a ragged and tattered patchwork. If an eminent servant of God could rise from the grave and read the narrative of his own life, written by another, he would feel pain at the recital of his virtues. "Not unto us, O Lord! not unto us, but unto thy name be the praise." And yet this most true sense of man's unprofitableness is accompanied also by an unshaken confidence in the mercy of God. No account can be given of this confidence, which is quite unlike the confidence we feel in the honesty, or good faith, or character of one of our fellow-men. There are rules for judging of this too; but they are different in kind from those by which we judge, or ought to judge, of ourselves in relation to God. He who has this confidence finds the reasons of it desert him the moment he begins to consider them. He is two persons in one, hoping against hope, if so be that God will be merciful; and all the time not the less assured of his mercy. Philosophy, rather than faith, going beyond this double consciousness, seeks by a theory of satisfaction to harmonize the discordant elements. "God is alienated in himself, but reconciled in Christ; man is evil in himself, but holy in Christ." Such statements are neither philosophy nor faith; they do but afford a transient resting-place to the mind, which is satisfied with an answer to its peculiar difficulty, however narrowing it may be to its view of "the ways of God to man."

IV. There is more in the life and death of Christ than we pretend to fathom. Definite statements respecting the relation of Christ either to God or man are but human figures transferred to a subject which is beyond speech and thought. There may seem to be a kind of feebleness in falling back on mystery, when the traditional language of ages is so clear and explicit. But mystery is the nearest approach that we can make to the truth: only by indefiniteness can we avoid putting words in the place of things. We know nothing of the objective act on God's part, by which he reconciled the world to himself, the very description of it as an act being only a figure of speech; and we seem to know that we never can know anything. While clinging to the ground of fact, we feel also that there is more in that fact than we see or understand. This is not a ground of fear, but of hope, — not of uncertainty, but of peace. There is hope and peace in what we see: yet more as we believe in possibilities of which we are ignorant.

We can live and die in the language of St. Paul and St. John, without fear for ourselves or dishonor to the name of Christ. We need not change a word that they use, or add on a single consequence to their statement of the truth. There is nothing there repugnant to our moral sense. There are others to whom tradition and devotional use may have made another kind of language familiar, who employ it by a sort of happy inconsistency, without perceiving the contradiction which it involves to the attributes of God. Neither let them condemn us, neither let us condemn them. There is enough in what has been said, and in the very nature of the subject itself, to make us tolerant of each other. It is a natural, though hardly excusable weakness, to clothe with peculiar awe and sacredness that which is really of human invention; to be zealous in defence of those points which we instinctively know to be least capable of standing the test of theological criticism.

ON RIGHTEOUSNESS BY FAITH.

By BENJAMIN JOWETT.

No doctrine in later times has been looked at so exclusively through the glass of controversy as that of justification. From being the simplest it has become the most difficult; the language of the heart has lost itself in a logical tangle. Differences have been drawn out as far as possible, and then taken back and reconciled. The extreme of one view has produced a reaction in favor of the other. Many senses have been attributed to the same words, and simple statements carried out on both sides into endless conclusions. New formulas of conciliation have been put in the place of old-established phrases, and have soon died away, because they had no root in language or in the common sense or feeling of mankind. The difficulty of the subject has been increased by the different degrees of importance attached to it: while to some it is an *articulus stantis aut cadentis ecclesiæ*, others have never been able to see in it more than a verbal dispute.

The abstract as well as controversial form of the doctrine of righteousness by faith has arisen out of the circumstances of the age in which it seemed to revive. Men felt at the Reformation the need of a spiritual religion, and could no longer endure the yoke which had been put upon their fathers. The heart turned inwards upon itself to commune alone with God. But when the need was supplied, and those who had felt it could no longer remain in the stillness of the closet, but formed themselves into a Church and an army, going forth to war against principalities and powers and the wisdom of this world, they found no natural expression of their belief; they had to borrow the weapons of their enemies before they could take up a position and fortify their camp.

In other words, the Scholastic Logic had been for six centuries previous the great instrument of training the human mind; it had grown up with it, and become a part of it. Neither would it have been more possible for the Reformers to have laid it aside than to have laid aside the use of language itself. Around theology it lingers still, seeming reluctant to quit a territory which is peculiarly its own. No science has hitherto fallen so completely under its power; no other is equally unwilling to ask the meaning of terms; none has been so fertile in reasonings and consequences. The change of which Lord Bacon was the herald, has hardly yet reached it; much less could the Reformation have anticipated the New Philosophy.

The whole mental structure of that time rendered it necessary that the Reformers, no less than their opponents, should resort to the scholastic methods of argument. The difference between the two parties did not lie here. Perhaps it may be said with truth that the Reformers were even more schoolmen than their opponents, because they dealt more with abstract ideas, and were more concentrated on a single topic. The whole of Luther's teaching was summed up in a single article, "Justification by Faith." That was to him the Scriptural expression of a Spiritual religion. But this, according ta the manner of that time, could not be left in the simple language of St. Paul, but needed to be guarded by the strictest definitions first, and was then liable to be drawn out into endless conclusions.

And yet, why was this? Why not repeat, with a slight alteration of the words rather than the meaning of the Apostle, Neither justification by faith nor justification by works, but "a new creature"? Was there not yet "a more excellent way" to oppose things to words, — the life, and spirit, and freedom of the Gospel, to the deadness, and powerlessness, and slavery of the Roman Church? So it seems natural to us to reason, looking back after an interval of three centuries on the weary struggle; so absorbing to those who took part in it once, so distant now either to us or them. But so it could not be. The temper of the times, and the education of the Reformers themselves, made it necessary that one dogmatic system should be met by another. The scholastic divinity had become a charmed circle, and no man could venture out of it, though he might oppose or respond within it.

And thus justification by faith, and justification by works, became the watchwords of two parties. We may imagine ourselves at that point in the controversy when the Pelagian dispute had been long since hushed, and that respecting Predestination had not yet begun; when men were not differing about original sin, and had not begun to differ about the Divine decrees. What Luther sought for was to find a formula which expressed most fully the entire, unreserved, immediate dependence of the believer on Christ. What the Catholic sought for was so to modify this formula as not to throw dishonor on the Church by making religion a merely personal or individual matter; or on the lives of holy men of old, who had wrought out their salvation by asceticism; or endanger morality by appearing to undervalue good works. It was agreed by all, that men are saved through Christ; — not of themselves, but of the grace of God, was equally agreed since the condemnation of Pelagius; — that faith and works imply each other, was not disputed by either. A narrow space is left for the combat, which has to be carried on within the outworks of an earlier creed, in which, nevertheless, the greatest subtlety of human thought and the greatest differences of human character admit of being displayed.

On this narrow ground the first question that naturally arises is, how faith is to be defined. Is it to include love and holiness, or to be separated from them? If the former, it seems to lose its apprehensive, dependent nature, and to be scarcely distinguishable from works; if the latter, there is a logical subtlety in the statement, which, although made by Luther, could scarcely be retained even by his immediate followers, much less by the common sense of mankind. Again, is it an act or a state? are we to figure it as a point, or as a line? Is the whole of our spiritual life anticipated in the beginning, or may faith no less than works, justification equally with sanctification, be conceived of as going on to perfection? Is justification in God or man an objective act of Divine mercy, or a subjective state of which the believer is conscious in himself? Is the righteousness imparted by it imputed or inherent, an attribute of the merits of Christ, or a renewal of the human heart itself? What is the test of a true faith? And is it possible for those who are possessed of it to fall away? How can we exclude the doctrine of human merit consistently with Divine justice? How do we account for the fact that some have this faith, while others are destitute of it, and this apparently independent of their moral state? If faith comes by grace, is it imparted to few or to all? And in what relation does the whole doctrine stand to Predestinarianism on the one hand, and to the Catholic or Sacramental theory on the other?

Such are a few of the most obvious questions to which this controversy has given birth. To which some obsolete differences of an earlier date might be added; such as the theory of congruity and condignity, in which an attempt was made to transfer the analogy of Christianity to heathenism, and to look upon the doer of good works before justification as a shadow of the perfected believer. Neither must we omit to observe that, as the doctrine of justification by faith had a close connection with the Pelagian controversy, carrying the decision of the Church a step farther, in not only making Divine Grace the source of human action, but in requiring the consciousness of it as well in the believer himself: so also it put forth its roots in another direction, attaching itself to Anselm as well as Augustine, and comprehending the idea of satisfaction ; not now, as formerly, of Christ offered in the sacrifice of the mass, but of one sacrifice, once offered for the sins of men, whether considered as an expiation by suffering, or implying only a reconciliation between God and man, or a mere manifestation of the righteousness of God.

Such is the whole question, striking deep, and spreading far and wide with its offshoots. It is not our intention to enter on the investigation of all these subjects, many of which belong to the history of the Church, but have no real bearing on the interpretation of St. Paul's Epistles, and a comparatively slight one on our own life and practice. Our inquiry will embrace two heads: (1.) What did St. Paul mean by the expression "righteousness of faith," in that age ere controversies about his meaning arose; and (2.) What do we mean by it, now that such controversies have died away, and the interest in them is retained only by the theological student, and the Church and the world are changed, and there is no more question of Jew or Gentile, circumcision or uncircumcision, and we do not become Christians, but are so from our birth. Many volumes are not required to explain the meaning of the Apostle; nor can the words of eternal life be other than few and simple to ourselves.

There is one interpretation of the Epistles of St. Paul which is necessarily in some degree false; that is, the interpretation put upon them by later controversy. It seems to be legitimately derived from the text; and it is really introduced into it. Our minds are filled with a particular circle of ideas, and we catch at any stray verse and make it the centre of our previous ideas. The Scripture is never looked upon as a whole, but broken into fragments, and each fragment made the corner of a new spiritual edifice. Words seem to be the same, but the things signified by them are different. Luther and St. Paul use the same term, "justified by faith"; and the strength of the Reformer's words is the authority of St. Paul. Yet, observe how far this agreement is one of words: how far of things. For Luther is speaking solely of individuals, St. Paul also of nations; Luther of faith absolutely, St. Paul of faith as relative to the law. With St. Paul faith is the symbol of the universality of the Gospel. Luther entirely excludes this or any analogous point of view. In St. Paul there is no opposition of faith and love; nor does he further determine righteousness by faith as meaning a faith in the blood or even in the death of Christ; nor does he suppose consciousness or assurance in the person justified. But all these are prominent features of the Lutheran doctrine. Once more; the faith of St. Paul has reference to the evil of the world of sight; which was soon to vanish away, that the world in which faith walks might be revealed; but no such allusion is implied in the language of the Reformer. Lastly; the change in the use of the substantive "righteousness" to "justification" is of itself the indication of a wide difference between St. Paul and Luther; and not without significance, as showing the direction which this difference has taken.

These contrasts make us feel that St. Paul can only be interpreted by himself, and not from the writings even of one who had so much in common with him as Luther, much less from the treatises of theologians of a later date. It is the spirit of St. Paul which Luther represents, not the meaning of his words; nor is there wanting a link of human feeling which makes them kin. Without bringing down one to the level of the other, we can imagine St. Paul returning that singular affection, almost like an attachment, to a living friend, which the great Reformer felt towards the Apostle. But this degree of personal attachment or resemblance in no way lessens the necessary difference between the preaching of Luther and of St. Paul, which lay partly in their individual character, but chiefly in the different circumstances and modes of thought of their respective ages. At the Reformation we are at another stage of the human mind, in which system and logic and the abstractions of Aristotle seem to have a kind of necessary force, when words have so completely taken the place of things, that the minutest distinctions appear to have an intrinsic value.

It has been said (and the remark admits of a peculiar

application to theology) that few persons know sufficient of things to be able to say whether disputes are merely verbal or not. Yet, on the other hand, it must be admitted that, whatever accidental advantage theology may derive from system and definition, mere accurate statements can never form the substance of our belief. No one doubts that Christianity could be in the fullest sense taught to a child or a savage, without any mention of justification or satisfaction or predestination. Why should we not receive the Gospel as little children? Why adopt abstractions which are so subtle in their meaning as to be in the greatest danger in their translation from one language to another? which are always running into consequences inconsistent with our moral nature, and the knowledge of God derived from it? which are not the prevailing usage of Scripture, but technical terms which we have gathered from one or two passages, and made the key-notes of our scale? The words satisfaction and predestination nowhere occur in Scripture; the word regeneration only twice, and but once in a sense at all similar to that which it bears among ourselves; the word justification twice only, and nowhere as a purely abstract term.

But although language and logic have so transfigured the meaning of Scripture, we cannot venture to say that all theological controversies are questions of words. If from their winding mazes we seek to retrace our steps, we still find differences which have a deep foundation in the opposite tendencies of the human mind, and the corresponding division of the world itself. That men of one temper of mind adopt one expression rather than another, may be partly an accident; but the adoption of an expression by persons of marked character makes the difference of words a reality also. That can scarcely be thought a matter of words which cut in sunder the Church, which overthrew princes, which made the line of demarcation between Jewish and Gentile Christians in the Apostolic age, and is so, in another sense, between Protestant and Catholic at the present day. And in a deeper way of reflection than this, if we turn from the Church to the individual, we seem to see around us opposite natures and characters, whose lives really exhibit a difference corresponding to that of which we are speaking. The one incline to morality, the other to religion; the one to the sacramental, the other to the spiritual; the one to multiplicity in outward ordinances, the other to simplicity; the one consider chiefly the means, the other the end; the one desire to dwell upon doctrinal statements, the other need only the name of Christ; the one turn to ascetic practices, to lead a good life, and to do good to others, the other to faith, humility, and dependence on God. We may sometimes find the opposite attributes combine with each other (there have ever been cross divisions on this article of belief in the Christian world; the great body of the Reformed Churches, and a small minority of Roman Catholics before the Reformation, being on the one side; and the whole Roman Catholic Church since the Reformation and a section of the Protestant Episcopalians, and some lesser communions, on the other); still, in general, the first of these characters answers to that doctrine which the Roman Church sums up in the formula of justification by works; the latter is that temper of mind which finds its natural dogmatic expression in the words "We are justified by faith."

These latter words have been carried out of their former circle of ideas into a new one by the doctrines of the Reformation. They have become hardened, stiffened, sharpened, by the exigencies of controversy, and torn from what may be termed their context in the Apostolical age. To that age we must return ere we can think in the Apostle's language. His conception of faith, although simpler than our own, has nevertheless a peculiar relation to his own day; it is at once wider, and also narrower, than the use of the word among ourselves, — wider in that it is the symbol of the admission of the Gentiles into the Church, but narrower also in that it is the negative of the law. Faith is the proper technical term which excludes the law; being what the law is not, as the law is what faith is not. No middle term connects the two, or at least none which the Apostle admits, until he has first widened the breach between them to the uttermost. He does not say, "Was not Abraham our father justified by works (as well as by faith), when he had offered up Isaac his son on the altar?" but only, "What saith the Scripture? Abraham believed God, and it was counted to him for righteousness."

The Jewish conception of righteousness was the fulfilment of the Commandments. He who walked in all the precepts of the Law blameless, like Daniel in the Old Testament, or Joseph and Nathanael in the New, was righteous before God. "What shall I do to inherit eternal life? Thou knowest the Commandments. Do not commit adultery, do not steal, do not bear false witness. All these have I kept from my youth up." Such is a picture of Jewish righteousness as it presents itself in its most favorable light. But it was a righteousness which comprehended the observance of ceremonial details as well as moral duties; it might be nothing more than an obedience to the Law as such, losing itself on the surface of religion, in distinctions about meats and drinks, or forms of oaths, or purifications, without any attempt to make clean that which is within. It might also pierce inward to the dividing asunder of the soul. Then was heard the voice of conscience crying, "All these things cannot make the doers thereof perfect." When every external obligation was fulfilled, the internal began. Actions must include thoughts and intentions, — the Seventh Commandment extend to the adultery of the heart; in one word, the Law must become a spirit.

But to the mind of St. Paul the spirit presented itself, not so much as a higher fulfilment of the Law, but as antagonistic to it. From this point of view, it appeared, not that man could never fulfil the law perfectly, but that he could never fulfil it at all. What God required was something different in kind from legal obedience. What man needed was a return to God and nature. He was burdened, straitened, shut out from the presence of his Father, — a servant, not a son; to whom, in a spiritual sense, the heaven was become as iron, and the earth brass. The new righteousness must raise him above the burden of ordinances, and bring him into a living communion with God. It must be within, and not without him, — written, not on tables of stone, but on fleshly tables of the heart. But inward righteousness was no peculiar privilege of the Israelites; it belonged to all mankind. And the revelation of it, as it satisfied the need of the individual soul, vindicated also the ways of God to man; it showed God to be equal in justice and mercy to all mankind.

As the symbol of this inward righteousness, St. Paul found an expression already in use among the Jews, — righteousness by faith, — derived from those passages in the Old Testament which spoke of Abraham being justified by faith. The very idea of faith carried men into the unseen world, — out of the reach of ordinances, — beyond the evil of this present life; it revealed to them that world which was now hidden, but was soon to appear. The Jewish nation were too far out of the way to be saved as a nation: the Lord was at hand. As at the last hour, when we have to teach men rather how to die than how to live, the Apostle could only say to those who would receive it, "Believe; all things are possible to him that believes."

Such are some of the peculiar aspects of the Apostle's doctrine of righteousness by faith. To our own minds it has become a later stage or a particular form of the more general doctrine of salvation through Christ, of the grace of God to man, or of the still more general truth of spiritual religion. It is the connecting link by which we appropriate these to ourselves, — the hand which we put out to apprehend the mercy of God. It was not so to the Apostle. To him grace and faith and the Spirit are not parts of a doctrinal system, but different expressions of the same truth. "Beginning in the Spirit" is another way of saying "Being justified by faith." He uses them indiscriminately, and therefore we cannot suppose that he could have laid any stress on distinctions between them. Even the apparently precise antithesis of the prepositions ἐν διὰ varies in different passages. Only in reference to the law, faith, rather than grace, is the more correct and natural expression. It was Christ, or not Christ; the Spirit, or not the Spirit; faith and the law, that were the dividing principles; not Christ through faith as opposed to Christ through works; or the Spirit as communicated through grace, to the Spirit as independent of grace.

Illusive as are the distinctions of later controversies as guides to the interpretation of Scripture, there is another help, of which we can hardly avail ourselves too much, — the interpretation of fact. To read the mind of the Apostle we must read also the state of the world and the Church by which he was surrounded. Now, there are two great facts which correspond to the doctrine of righteousness by faith, which is also the doctrine of the universality of the Gospel: first, the vision which the Apostle saw on the way to Damascus; secondly, the actual conversion of the Gentiles by the preaching of the Apostle. Righteousness by faith, admission of the Gentiles, even the rejection and restoration of the Jews, are — himself under so many different points of view. The way by which God had led him was the way also by which he was leading other men. When he preached righteousness by faith, his conscience also bore him witness that this was the manner in which he had himself passed from darkness to light, from the burden of ordinances to the power of an endless life. In proclaiming the salvation of the Gentiles, he was interpreting the world as it was; their admission into the Church had already taken place before the eyes of all mankind; it was a purpose of God that was actually fulfilled, not waiting for some future revelation. Just as when doubts are raised respecting his Apostleship, he cut them short by the fact that he was an Apostle, and did the work of an Apostle; so, in adjusting the relations of Jew and Gentile, and justifying the ways of God, the facts, read aright, are the basis of the doctrine which he teaches. All that he further shows is, that these facts were in accordance with the Old Testament, with the words of the prophets, and the dealings of God with the Jewish people. And the Apostles at Jerusalem, equally with himself, admitted the success of his mission as an evidence of its truth.

But the faith which St. Paul preached was not merely the evidence of things not seen, in which the Gentiles also had part, nor only the reflection of "the violenee" of the world around him, which was taking the kingdom of heaven by force. The true source, the hidden life, to which justification attaches, is Christ. It is true that we nowhere find in the Epistles the expression "justification by Christ" exactly in the sense of modern theology. But, on the other hand, we are described as dead with Christ, we live with him, we are members of his body, we follow him in all the stages of his being. All this is another way of expressing "We are justified by faith." That which takes us out of ourselves and links us with Christ, which anticipates in an instant the rest of life, which is the door of every heavenly and spiritual relation, presenting us through a glass with the image of Christ crucified, is faith. The difference between our own mode of thought and that of the Apostle is only this, that to him Christ is set forth more as in a picture, and less through the medium of ideas or figures of speech; and that while we conceive the Saviour more naturally as an object of faith, to St. Paul he is rather the indwelling power of life which is fashioned in him, the marks of whose body he bears, the measure of whose sufferings he fills up.

When in the Gospel it is said, "Believe on the Lord Jesus Christ, and thou shalt be saved," this is substantially the same truth as "We are justified by faith." Yet we may note two points of difference, as well as two of resemblance, in the manner in which the doctrine is set forth in the Gospel as compared with the manner of the Epistles of St. Paul. First, in the omission of any connection between the doctrine of faith in Christ and the admission of the Gentiles. The Saviour is within the borders of Israel; and accordingly little is said of the "sheep not of this fold," or the other husbandmen who shall take possession of the vineyard. Secondly, there is in the words of Christ no antagonism or opposition to the Law, except so far as the Law itself represented an imperfect or defective morality, or the perversions of the Law had become inconsistent with every moral principle. Two points of resemblance have also to be remarked between the faith of the Gospels and of the Epistles. In the first place, both are accompanied by forgiveness of sins. As our Saviour to the disciple who affirms his belief says, " Thy sins be forgiven thee " ; so St. Paul, when seeking to describe, in the language of the Old Testament, the state of justification by faith, cites the words of David, " Blessed is the man to whom the Lord will not impute sin." Secondly, they have both a kind of absoluteness which raises them above earthly things. There is a sort of omnipotence attributed to faith, of which the believer is made a partaker. " Whoso hath faith as a grain of mustard-seed, and should say unto this mountain, Be thou removed and be thou cast into the sea, it shall be done unto him," is the language of our Lord. " I can do all things through Christ that strengtheneth me," are the words of St. Paul.

Faith, in the language of the Apostle, is almost synonymous with freedom. That quality in us which in reference to God and Christ is faith, in reference to ourselves and our fellow-men is Christian liberty. " With this freedom Christ has made us free " ; " where the spirit of the Lord is, there is liberty." It is the image also of the communion of the world to come. " The Jerusalem that is above is free," and " the creature is waiting to be delivered into the glorious liberty of the children of God." It applies to the Church as now no longer confined in the prison-house of the Jewish dispensation ; to the grace of God, which is given irrespectively to all ; to the individual, the power of whose will is now loosed ; to the Gospel, as freedom from the Law, setting the conscience at rest about questions of meats and drinks, and new moons and Sabbaths ; and, above all, to the freedom from the sense of sin. The law of the spirit of life is also the law of freedom.

In modern language assurance has been deemed necessary to the definition of a true faith. There is a sense also in which final assurance entered into the conception of the faith of the Epistles. Looking at men from without, it was possible for them to fall away finally; it was possible also to fall without falling away; as St. John says, there is a sin unto death, and there is a sin not unto death. But looking inwards into their hearts and consciences, their salvation was not a matter of probability; they knew whom they had believed, and were confident that He who had begun the good work in them would continue it unto the end. All calculations respecting the future were to them lost in the fact that they were already saved, — *οἱ σωζόμενοι* and *οἱ σωθησόμενοι* indifferently. To use a homely expression, they had no time to inquire whether the state to which they are called was permanent and final. The same intense faith which separated them from the world, and all things in it, had already given them a part in the world to come. They had not to win the crown, — it was already won: this life, when they thought of themselves in relation to Christ, was the next; as their union with him seemed far more true and real than the mere accidents of their temporal existence.

A few words will briefly recapitulate the doctrine of righteousness by faith as gathered from the Epistles of St. Paul.

Faith, then, according to the Apostle, is the spiritual principle whereby we go out of ourselves to hold communion with God and Christ; not like the faith of the Epistle to the Hebrews, clothing itself in the shadows of the Law; but opposed to the Law, and of a nature purely moral and spiritual. It frees man from the flesh, the Law, the world, and from himself also; that is, from his sinful nature, which is the meeting of these three elements in his spiritual consciousness. And to be "justified" is to pass into a new state; such as that of the Christian world when compared with the Jewish or Pagan; such as that which St. Paul had himself felt at the moment of his conversion; such as that which he reminds the Galatian converts they had experienced, "before whose eyes Jesus Christ was evidently set forth crucified"; an inward or subjective state, to which the outward or objective act of calling, on God's part, through the preaching of the Apostle, corresponded; which, considered on a wider scale, was the acceptance of the Gentiles and of every one who feared God; corresponding in like manner to the eternal purpose of God; indicated in the case of the individual by his own inward assurance; in the case of the world at large, testified by the fact; accompanied in the first by the sense of peace and forgiveness, and implying to mankind generally the last final principle of the Divine government, — "God concluded all under sin that he might have mercy upon all."

We acknowledge that there is a difference between the meaning of justification by faith to St. Paul and to ourselves. Eighteen hundred years cannot have passed away, leaving the world and the mind of man, or the use of language, the same as it was. But while acknowledging this difference, our object is not to base some new doctrine upon our natural instincts, or to rear some fabric of philosophical speculation, framed in the same terms, yet different in meaning and spirit. Christianity is not a philosophy, but a life; and religious ideas, unless designed to destroy the simplicity of religion, must be simple and practical. The true use of philosophy in reference to religion is to restore its simplicity, by freeing it from those perplexities which the love of system or past philosophies, or the imperfection of language, or the mere lapse of ages, may have introduced into it. To understand St. Paul we found it necessary to get rid of the scholastic definitions and deductions, which might be described as a sort of mazy undergrowth of some noble forest, which must be cleared away ere we can wander in its ranges. Neither is it less necessary for ourselves to return to the plain letter of Scripture, and seek a truth to live and die in; not to be the subject of verbal disputes, which entangle the religious sense in scholastic perplexities. Whatever logical necessity there may be supposed to be in drawing out Christianity as a system, whether as food for the intellect, or as a defence against heresy, the words of eternal life will ever be few and simple, "Believe on the Lord Jesus Christ, and thou shalt be saved."

Once more, then, we return to Scripture; not to explain it away, but to translate it into the language of our own hearts, and to separate its accidents from its essence. Looking at it as a rule of life and faith for ourselves, no less than for the early Church, we must not leave out of sight the great differences by which we are distinguished from those for whom it was first written. The greatest difference of all is, that the words of life and inspiration as they were to them are to us words of fixed and conventional meaning; they no longer express feelings of the heart, but ideas of the head. Nor is the difference less between the state of the world then and now, not only of the outward world in which we live, but of that inner world in which we ourselves are. The Law is indeed dead to us, and we to the Law, and yet the whole language of St. Paul is relative to what has not only passed away, but has left no trace of itself in the thoughts of men. The perpetual variations and transitions of meaning in the use of the word Law, which have been enlarged upon elsewhere, tend also to a corresponding variation in the meaning of faith. We are not looking for the immediate coming of Christ, and do not anticipate, therefore, in a single generation, the whole course of the world, or the history of a life, in the moment of baptism or conversion. To us this life and the next have each their fixed boundary, — time and eternity, as we call them, — which it would appear mysticism to do away. Last of all, we are partakers of this world, and not wholly living in the world to come; which makes it difficult for us to imagine the intensity of meaning in such expressions as "dead with Christ," "if ye then be risen with Christ."

The neglect of these essential differences between ourselves and the first disciples has sometimes led to a distortion of doctrine and a perversion of life, in the attempt to reproduce exactly the scriptural image; where words have had nothing to correspond to them, views of human nature have been invented to suit the language of St. Paul; thus, for example, the notion of legal righteousness is indeed a fiction as applied to our own times. Nor, in truth, is the pride of human nature, or the tendency to rebel against the will of God, or to attach an undue value to good works, better founded. Men are evil in all sorts of ways: they deceive themselves and others; they walk by the opinion of others, and not by faith; they give way to their passions; they are imperious and oppressive to one another. But if we look closely, we perceive that most of their sins are not consciously against God; the pride of rank, or wealth, or power, or intellect, may show itself towards their brethren, but no man is proud towards God. No man does wrong for the sake of rebelling against God. The evil is not, that men are bound under a curse by the ever-present consciousness of sin, but that sins pass unheeded by; not that they wantonly offend God, but that they know him not. So, again, there may be a false sense of security towards God, as is sometimes observed on a death-bed, when mere physical weakness seems to incline the mind to patience and resignation; yet this more often manifests itself in a mistaken faith, than in a reliance on good works. Or, to take another instance, we are often surprised at the extent to which men who are not professors of religion seem to practise Christian virtues; yet their state, however we may regard it, has nothing in common with legal or self-righteousness.

Leaving, then, the scholastic definitions, as well as the peculiar and relative aspect of the Pauline doctrine, we have again to ask ourselves the meaning of justification by faith. We may divide the subject, first, as it may be considered in the abstract; and, secondly, as consciously appropriated to ourselves.

I. Our justification may be regarded as an act on God's part. It may be said that this act is continuous, and commensurate with our whole lives; that although "known unto God are all his works from the beginning," yet that, speaking as men, and translating what we term the acts of God into human language, we are ever being more and more justified, as in theological writers we are admitted to be more and more sanctified. At first sight it seems that to deny this involves us in a fiction and absurdity; that is, it is a kind of fiction to say that we are justified at once, but sanctified all our life long. Yet consider it practically, and is it not so? If we look at the truth objectively, must we not admit that it is his unchangeable will that all mankind should be saved? The consciousness of justification in the mind of the believer is but the knowledge of this fact, which always was. It is not made more a fact by our knowing it for many years or our whole life. And this is what is witnessed to by actual experience; for he who is justified by faith does not go about doubting in himself or his future destiny, but trusting in God. From the first moment that he turns earnestly to God he is sure that he is saved; not from any confidence in himself, but from an overpowering sense of the love of God and Christ.

II. It is an old problem in philosophy, What is the beginning of our moral being? What is that prior principle which makes good actions produce good habits? Which of those acts raises us above the world of sight? Plato would have answered, The contemplation of the idea of good. Some of ourselves would answer by the substitution of a conception of moral growth for the mechanical theory of habits. Leaving out of sight our relation to God, we can only say, that we are fearfully and wonderfully made, with powers which we are unable to analyze. It is a parallel difficulty in religion which is met by the doctrine of justification by faith. We grow up spiritually, we cannot tell how; not by outward acts, nor always by energetic effort, but stilly and silently, by the grace of God descending upon us, as the dew falls upon the earth. If we imagine a person anxious and fearful about his future state, straining every nerve lest he should fall short of the requirements of God, overpowered with the memory of his past sins, — that is not the temper of mind in which he can truly serve God, or work out his own salvation. Without peace it is impossible for him to act. At once and immediately the Gospel tells him that he is justified by faith, that his pardon is simultaneous with the very moment of his belief, that he may go on his way rejoicing to fulfil the duties of life; for, in human language, God is no longer angry with him.

III. Thus far, in the consideration of righteousness by faith, we have obtained two aspects of the doctrine, in which, even when regarded in the abstract, it has still a meaning; first, as expressing the unchangeableness of the mercy of God; and, secondly, the mysteriousness of human action. As we approach nearer, we are unavoidably led to regard the gift of righteousness rather in reference to the subject than to the object, in relation to man rather than God. What quality, feeling, temper, habit in ourselves answers to it? It may be more or less conscious to us, more of a state and less of a feeling, showing itself rather in our lives than our lips. But for these differences we can make allowance. It is the same faith still, though showing itself in divers ways and under various circumstances. We must suppose it conscious for us to be able to describe it.

IV. The expression "righteousness by faith" indicates, first, the personal character of salvation; not what we do, but what we are, is the source of our acceptance with God. Who can bear to think of his own actions as they are seen by the eye of the Almighty? Looking at their defective performance, or analyzing them into the secondary motives out of which they have sprung, do we seem to have any ground on which we can stand with God? is there anything which satisfies ourselves? That which makes us acceptable to God is something besides all this, which frees us from the burden of our good works, which raises us above the tangle of human life. The love of a parent to a child is not measured out in proportion to the child's good qualities. And although the measure of God's love to man is perfect justice, yet the relation in which we can most adequately conceive of God is, that of a person to persons, who condescends to draw us towards him, who allows us to attach ourselves to him. The symbol and mean of this personal relation of man to God is faith; and the righteousness which consists not in what we do, but in what we are, is the righteousness of faith.

V. Faith may be spoken of in the language of the Epistle to the Hebrews, as the substance of things unseen. But what are the things unseen? Not merely an invisible world ready to flash through the thraldom of the material at the appearance of Christ; not angels, or powers of darkness, or even God himself seated, as the Old Testament described, on the circle of the heavens; but the kingdom of truth and justice, the things that are within, of which God is the centre, and with which men everywhere by faith hold communion. Faith is the belief in the existence of this kingdom; that is, in the truth and justice and mercy of God, who disposes all things, — not perhaps in our judgment for the greatest happiness of his creatures, but absolutely in accordance with our moral notions. And that this is not seen to be the case here, makes it a matter of faith and not of sight, that it will be so in some future world, or is so in some ways that we are unable to comprehend. He that believes on God believes, first, that he is; and, secondly, that he is the rewarder of them that seek him.

VI. Now, if we go on to ask what is it that gives us this absolute and present assurance of the truth and justice of God, the answer is, the life and death of Christ, who is the image of God and man alike, the Son of God; the First-born of the redeemed. We know what he himself has told us of God, and we cannot conceive perfect goodness separate from perfect truth; nay, this goodness itself is the only and the highest conception we can form of God, if we confess and comprehend what the mere immensity of the material world tends to suggest, that God is a Being different in kind from any physical power; a Being of whom the reason of man, however feeble, forms a far truer (though most inadequate) conception than imagination in its highest flights. Admit the statements of the Gospel respecting Christ; it is not so much a matter to be proved by dubious inference from texts, as manifest on the surface that he is Divine in all that truly constitutes divinity except this outward garb of flesh.

That is the only image of God which we are capable of conceiving; an image not of physical, nor even of spiritual power, seen in the sufferings rather than in the miracles of Christ our Saviour; the image of perfect goodness and peace and truth and love.

We are on the edge of a theological difficulty; for who can deny, that the image of that goodness may fade from the mind's eye after so many centuries, or that there are those who recognize the idea and may be unable to admit the fact? Can we say that this error of the head is also an error of the heart? The lives of such unbelievers in the facts of Christianity would sometimes refute our explanation. And yet it is true that Providence has made our spiritual life dependent on the belief in certain truths, and those truths run up into matters of fact, with the belief in which they have ever been associated; it is true also, that the most important moral consequences flow from unbelief. We grant the difficulty: no complete answer can be given to it on this side the grave. Doubtless God has provided a way that the sceptic no less than the believer shall receive his due; he does not need our timid counsels for the protection of the truth. If among those who have rejected the facts of the Gospel history some have been rash, hypercritical, inflated with the pride of intellect, or secretly alienated by sensuality from the faith of Christ, — there have been others, also, upon whom we may believe to rest a portion of that blessing which comes to such as "have not seen and yet have believed."

VII. In the Epistles of St. Paul, and yet more in the Epistle to the Hebrews, the relation of Christ to mankind is expressed under figures of speech taken from the Mosaic dispensation: he is the Sacrifice for the sins of men, "the Lamb of God that taketh away the sins of the world"; the Antitype of all the types, the impersonation of the Jewish Law. There are two ways in which we may treat such expressions; we may regard them as figures of speech, which from their variety and incongruity with each other, we seem justified in doing (compare "Essay on the Doctrine of the Atonement"), or as realities, true so far as we are capable of conceiving, about which we may as surely reason as about any other statements of fact: thus, for example, we may speak of the infinite sacrifice of Christ; of nothing less being capable of satisfying the wrath of God; of God seeing man in Christ other than he really is. But such expressions, whatever comfort they may have given those who think of God under human figures, seem inevitably to dissolve when we rise to the contemplation of him as the God of truth, without parts or passions, who knows all things, and cannot be angry with any, or see them other than they truly are. What is indicated by them, to us who are dead to the Law, is, that God has manifested himself in Christ as the God of mercy; who is more ready to hear than we to pray; who has forgiven us almost before we ask him; who has given us his only Son, and how will he not with him also give us all things? They intimate, on God's part, that he is not extreme to mark what is done amiss; in human language, "he is touched with the feeling of our infirmities": on our part, that we say to God, "Not of ourselves, but of thy grace and mercy, O Lord." Not in the fulness of life and health, nor in the midst of business, nor in the schools of theology; but in the sick chamber, where are no more earthly interests, and in the hour of death, we have before us the living image of the truth of justification by faith, when man acknowledges, on the confines of another world, the unprofitableness of his own good deeds, and the goodness of God even in afflicting him, and his absolute reliance, not on works of righteousness that he has done, but on the Divine mercy.

VIII. A true faith has been sometimes defined to be, not a faith in the unseen merely, or in God or Christ, but a personal assurance of salvation. Such a feeling may be only the veil of sensualism; it may be also the noble confidence of St. Paul. "I am persuaded that neither death, nor life, nor angels, nor principalities, nor powers, nor things present, nor things to come, nor height, nor depth, nor any other creature, shall be able to separate us from the love of God which is in Christ Jesus our Lord." It may be like the anticipation of any other fact; or an emotion, resting on no other ground except that we believe; or, thirdly, a conviction deeply rooted in our life and character. The whole spirit of Scripture, as well as our own knowledge of human nature, seems to require that we should have this personal confidence in our own salvation: and yet to assume that we are at the end of the race may make us lag in our course. Whatever danger there is in the doctrine of the Divine decrees, the danger is nearer home, and more liable to influence practice, when our belief takes the form of personal assurance. How, then, are we to escape from the dilemma, and have a rational confidence in the mercy of God?

IX. This confidence must rest, first, on a practical sense of the truth and justice of God, rising far above perplexities of fact in the world around us, or the tangle of metaphysical or theological difficulties. But although such a sense of the truth or justice of God is the beginning of our final assurance respecting ourselves, yet a link of connection is wanting before we can venture to appropriate that which we acknowledge in the abstract. The justice of God may lead to our condemnation as well as to our justification. Are we, then, in the language of the ancient tragedy, to say that no one can be counted happy before he dies, or that salvation is only imparted in a certain qualified sense before the end of our course is seen? Not so: the Gospel encourages us to regard ourselves, beyond all doubt or scruple, as already saved; for the work of Christ is already done, and we have already participated in it and appropriated it by faith. But this appropriation of it means nothing short of the utter, entire renunciation of self and its interests, the absolute will and intention to conform to the service of God. He who feels this in himself feels also the absolute certainty of salvation. Only while we are halting between right and wrong, between this world and the next, can we have any doubt of our future destiny.

Thus then we seem to find a rational ground for final assurance, beginning in a clear insight into the perfect justice and mercy of God, and ending in an entire appropriation of it to ourselves, dependent only on the unreservedness of our devotion to his service. The same difficulty may seem to spring up again with the question, how we are to define an unreserved devotion to the service of God; or, in other words, what is such a true faith as is sufficient to justify a final assurance? To which it may be answered, first, that we know it by such test as we know the truth and sincerity of any other disposition of mind or heart, that is, by the effects; and, secondly, that unless our faith be real in a sense far above the ordinary conventional belief even of good men, none can be justified in making it the ground of final assurance.

"And now abideth faith, hope, and love, these three; but the greatest of these is love." There seems to be a sort of contradiction in love being placed first, and yet faith the sole instrument of justification. Love, according to some, is preferred to faith, because when faith and hope are swallowed up in sight, love abides still. Love, according to others, is one principle of justification, faith another. The true reason seems to be, because love describes a closer and more intimate union with God and our fellow-men than faith. It is a kind of pre-eminence that love enjoys over faith, that it has never yet passed into the technical language of theology. But there is a reflection that these words of St. Paul naturally suggest in reference to our present subject. It is this: Christian truth has many phases, and will be received by one temper of mind in one way, by another in another. There is diversity of doctrine, but the same spirit: love is the more natural expression to St. John, faith to St. Paul. Human minds are different, and the same mind varies at different times; and even the best of men have but a feeble sense of the unseen world. We cannot venture further to dim that consciousness by confining it to one expression of belief; and therefore, while speaking of faith as the instrument of justification, because faith best indicates the apprehensive, dependent character of our Christian life, we are bound also to deny that the truth of Christ is contained in any one statement, or the Christian life linked to any one quality. We must acknowledge the imperfection of language and thought, seeking rather to describe than to define the work of the Spirit, which has as many forms as the qualities, tempers, faculties, circumstances, and accidents of our nature.

ON THE IMPUTATION OF THE SIN OF ADAM.

By BENJAMIN JOWETT.

THAT so many opposite systems of theology seek their authority in Scripture, is a fair proof that Scripture is different from them all. That is to say, Scripture often contains in germ, what is capable of being drawn to either side; it is indistinct, where they are distinct; it presents two lights, where they present only one; it speaks inwardly, while they clothe themselves in the forms of human knowledge. That indistinct, intermediate, inward point of view at which the truth exists but in germ, they have on both sides tended to extinguish and suppress. Passing allusions, figures of speech, rhetorical oppositions, have been made the foundation of doctrinal statements, which are like a part of the human mind itself, and seem as if they could never be uprooted, without uprooting the very sentiment of religion. Systems of this kind exercise a constraining power, which makes it difficult for us to see anything in Scripture but themselves.

For example, how slender is the foundation in the New Testament for the doctrine of Adam's sin being imputed to his posterity, — two passages in St. Paul at most, and these of uncertain interpretation. The little cloud, no bigger than a man's hand, has covered the heavens. To reduce such subjects to their proper proportions, we should consider: First, what space they occupy in Scripture; Secondly, how far the language used respecting them is literal or figurative;

Thirdly, whether they agree with the more general truths of Scripture and our moral sense, or are not "rather repugnant thereto"; Fourthly, whether their origin may not be prior to Christianity, or traceable in the after history of the Church; Fifthly, how far to ourselves they are anything more than words.

The two passages alluded to are Rom. v. 12, 21, 1 Cor. xv. 21, 22, 45 – 49, in both of which parallels are drawn between Adam and Christ. In both the sin of Adam is spoken of, or seems to be spoken of, as the source of death to man. "As by one man's transgression sin entered into the world, and death by sin," and "As in Adam all die." Such words appear plain at first sight; that is to say, we find in them what we bring to them: let us see what considerations modify their meaning. If we accept the Pelagian view of the passage, which refers the death of each man to actual sin, there is an end of the controversy. But it does not equally follow that, if what is termed the received interpretation is given to the words, the doctrine which it has been attempted to ground upon them would have any real foundation.

We will suppose, then, that no reference is contained in either passage to "actual sin." In some other sense than this mankind are identified with Adam's transgression. But the question still remains, whether Adam's sin and death are merely the type of the sin and death of his posterity, or more than this the cause. The first explanation quite satisfies the meaning of the words "As in Adam all die"; the second seems to be required by the parallel passage in the Romans, "As by one man sin came into the world," and "As by one man many were made sinners," if taken literally.

The question involves the more general one, whether the use of language in St. Paul makes it necessary that we should take his words literally in this passage. Is he speaking of Adam's sin being the cause of sin and death to his posterity, in any other sense than he spoke of Abraham being a father of circumcision to the uncircumcised? (Chap. iv.) Yet no one would think of basing a doctrine on these words.

Or is he speaking of all men dying in Adam, in any other sense than he says in 2 Cor. v. 15, that if one died for all, then all died. Yet in this latter passage, while Christ died literally, it was only in a figure that all died. May he be arguing in the same way as when he infers from the word "seed" being used in the singular, that "thy seed is Christ"? Or, if we confine ourselves to the passage under consideration: Is the righteousness of Christ there imputed to believers, independently of their own inward holiness? and if so, should the sin of Adam be imputed independently of the actual sins of men?

I. A very slight difference in the mode of expression would make it impossible for us to attribute to St. Paul the doctrine of the imputation of the sin of Adam. But we have seen before how varied, and how different from our own, are his modes of thought and language. Compare i. 4, iv. 25. To him, it was but a slight transition, from the identification of Adam with the sins of all mankind, to the representation of the sin of Adam as the cause of those sins. To us there is the greatest difference between the two statements. To him it was one among many figures of the same kind, to oppose the first and second Adam, as elsewhere he opposes the old and new man. With us this figure has been singled out to be made the foundation of a most exact statement of doctrine. We do not remark that there is not even the appearance of attributing Adam's sin to his posterity, in any part of the Apostle's writings in which he is not drawing a parallel between Adam and Christ.

II. The Apostle is not speaking of Adam as fallen from a state of innocence. He could scarcely have said, "The first man is of the earth, earthy," if he had had in his mind that Adam had previously existed in a pure and perfect state. He is only drawing a parallel between Adam and Christ. The moment we leave this parallel, all is uncertain and undetermined. The logical consequences which are appended to his words are far out of his sight. He would hardly have found language to describe the nature of Adam's act, whether occurring by his own free will or not, or the way in which the supposed effect was communicated to his posterity.

III. There are other elements of St. Paul's teaching, which are either inconsistent with the imputation of Adam's sin to his posterity, or at any rate are so prominent as to make such a doctrine, if held by him, comparatively unimportant. According to St. Paul, it is not the act of Adam, but the law, that

"Brought sin into the world and all our woe."

And the law is almost equivalent to "the knowledge of sin." But original sin is, or may be, wholly unconscious; born with our birth, and growing with our growth. Not so the sin of which St. Paul speaks, which is inseparable from consciousness, as he says himself: "I was alive without the law once," which would be dead, if we were unconscious of it.

IV. It will be admitted that we ought to feel still greater reluctance to press the statement of the Apostle to its strict logical consequences, if we find that the language which he here uses is that of his age and country. From the circumstance of our first reading the doctrine of the imputation of Adam's sin to his posterity in the Epistles of St. Paul, we can hardly persuade ourselves that this is not its original source. The incidental manner in which it is alluded to, might indeed lead us to suppose that it would scarcely have been intelligible, had it not been also an opinion of his time. But if this inference should seem doubtful, there is direct evidence to show that the Jews connected sin and death, and the sins and death of mankind, with the sin of Adam, in the same way as the Apostle. The earliest trace of such a doctrine is found in the apocryphal Book of Wisdom, ii. 24. It was a further refinement of some of their teachers, that when Adam sinned the whole world sinned; because at that time Adam was the whole world, or because the soul of Adam comprehended the souls of all, so that Adam's sin conveyed an hereditary taint to his posterity. It was a confusion of a half physical, half logical or metaphysical notion, arising in the minds of men who had not yet learnt the lesson of our Saviour: "That which is from without defileth not a man." That human nature or philosophy sometimes rose up against such inventions is certainly true; but it seems to be on the whole admitted, that the doctrine of Augustine is in substance generally agreed to by the Rabbis, and that there is no trace of their having derived it from the writings of St. Paul.

But not only is the connection of sin and death with each other, and with the sin of Adam, found in the Rabbinical writings; the type and antitype of the first and second Adam are also contained in them. In reading the first chapters of Genesis, the Jews made a distinction between the higher Adam, who was the light of the world, and had control over all things, who was mystically referred to where it is said, they two shall be one flesh; and the inferior Adam who was Lord only of the creation; who had "the breath of life," but not "the living soul." Schœttgen, I. 512 – 514, 670 – 673. By some, indeed, the latter seems to have been identified with the Messiah. By Philo, on the other hand, the λόγος is identified with the πρῶτος 'Αδάμ, who is without sex, while the ἄνθρωπος χοϊκος is created afterwards by the help of the angels. It is not the object of this statement to reconcile these variations, but merely to indicate, first, that the idea of the first and second Adam was familiar to the Jews in the time of St. Paul, and that one or other of them was regarded by them as the Word and the Messiah.

V. A slighter, though not less real, foundation of the doctrine has been what may be termed the logical symmetry of the imputation of the righteousness of Christ and of the sin of Adam. The latter half is the correlative of the former; they mutually support each other. We place the first and second Adam in juxtaposition, and seem to see a fitness or reason in the one standing in the same relation to the fallen as the other to the saved.

VI. It is hardly necessary to ask the further question, what meaning we can attach to the imputation of sin and guilt which are not our own, and of which we are unconscious. God can never see us other than we really are, or judge us without reference to all our circumstances and antecedents. If we can hardly suppose that he would allow a fiction of mercy to be interposed between ourselves and him, still less can we imagine that he would interpose a fiction of vengeance. If he requires holiness before he will save, much more, may we say in the Apostle's form of speech, will he require sin before he dooms us to perdition. Nor can anything be in spirit more contrary to the living consciousness of sin of which the Apostle everywhere speaks, than the conception of sin as dead unconscious evil, originating in the act of an individual man, in the world before the flood.

On the whole, then, we are led to infer, that, in the Augustinian interpretation of this passage, even if it agree with the letter of the text, too little regard has been paid to the extent to which St. Paul uses figurative language, and to the manner of his age in interpretations of the Old Testament. The difficulty of supposing him to be allegorizing the narrative of Genesis is slight, in comparison with the difficulty of supposing him to countenance a doctrine at variance with our first notions of the moral nature of God.

But when the figure is dropped, and allowance is made for the manner of the age, the question once more returns upon us, "What is the Apostle's meaning?" He is arguing, we see, *κατ' ἄνθρωπον*, and taking his stand on the received opinions of his time. Do we imagine that his object is no other than to set the seal of his authority on these traditional beliefs? The whole analogy, not merely of the writings of St. Paul, but of the entire New Testament, would lead us to suppose that his object was, not to reassert them, but to teach, through them, a new and nobler lesson. The Jewish Rabbis would have spoken of the first and second Adam; but which of them would have made the application of the figure to all mankind? A figure of speech it remains still, an allegory after the manner of that age and country, but yet with no uncertain or ambiguous interpretation. It means that "God hath made of one blood all the nations of the earth"; that "he hath concluded all under sin, that he may have mercy upon all"; that life answers to death, the times before to the times after the revelation of Jesus Christ. It means that we are one in a common sinful nature which, even if it be not derived from the sin of Adam, exists as really as if it were. It means that we shall be made one in Christ by the grace of God, in a measure here, more fully and perfectly in another world. More than this it also means, and more than language can express, but not the weak and beggarly elements of Rabbinical tradition. We may not encumber St. Paul with the things which he "destroyed." What it means further is not to be attained by theological distinctions, but by putting off the old man and putting on the New Man.

ON CONVERSION AND CHANGES OF CHARACTER.

By BENJAMIN JOWETT.

Thus have we the image of the life-long struggle gathered up in a single instant.* In describing it we pass beyond the consciousness of the individual into a world of abstractions; we loosen the thread by which the spiritual faculties are held together, and view as objects what can, strictly speaking, have no existence, except in relation to the subject. The divided members of the soul are ideal, the conflict between them is ideal, so also is the victory. What is real that corresponds to this, is not a momentary, but a continuous conflict, which we feel rather than know, — which has its different aspects of hope and fear, triumph and despair, the action and reaction of the Spirit of God in the depths of the human soul, awakening the sense of sin and conveying the assurance of forgiveness.

The language in which we describe this conflict is very different from that of the Apostle. Our circumstances are so changed that we are hardly able to view it in its simplest elements. Christianity is now the established religion of the civilized portion of mankind. In our own country it has become part of the law of the land; it speaks with authority, it is embodied in a Church, it is supported by almost universal opinion, and fortified by wealth and prescription. Those who know least of its spiritual life, do not deny its greatness

---

* Viz., in Rom. vii. 7 – 25.

as a power in the world. Analogous to this relation in which it stands to our history and social state, is the relation in which it stands also to the minds of individuals. We are brought up in it, and unconsciously receive it as the habit of our thoughts and the condition of our life. It is without us, and we are within its circle; we do not become Christians, we are so from our birth. Even in those who suppose themselves to have passed through some sudden and violent change, and to have tasted once for all of the heavenly gift, the change is hardly ever in the form or substance of their belief, but in its quickening power; they feel, not a new creed, but a new spirit within them. So that we might truly say of Christianity, that it is "the daughter of time"; it hangs to the past, not only because the first century is the era of its birth, but because each successive century strengthens its form and adds to its external force, and entwines it with more numerous links in our social state. Not only may we say, that it is part and parcel of the law of the land, but part and parcel of the character of each one, which even the worst of men cannot wholly shake off.

But if with ourselves the influence of Christianity is almost always gradual and imperceptible, with the first believers it was almost always sudden. There was no interval which separated the preaching of Peter on the day of Pentecost, from the baptism of the three thousand. The eunuch of Candace paused for a brief space on a journey, and was then baptized into the name of Christ, which a few hours previously he had not so much as heard. There was no period of probation like that which, a century or two later, was appropriated to the instruction of the Catechumens. It was an impulse, an inspiration passing from the lips of one to a chosen few, and communicated by them to the ear and soul of listening multitudes. As the wind bloweth where it listeth, and we hear the sounds thereof; as the lightning shineth from the one end of the heaven to the other; so suddenly, fitfully, simultaneously, new thoughts come into their minds, not to one only, but to many, to whole cities almost at once. They were pricked with the sense of sin; they were melted with the love of Christ; their spiritual nature "came again like the flesh of a little child." And some, like St. Paul, became the very opposite of their former selves; from scoffers, believers; from persecutors, preachers; the thing that they were, was so strange to them, that they could no longer look calmly on the earthly scene which they hardly seemed to touch, which was already lighted up with the wrath and mercy of God. There were those among them who "saw visions and dreamed dreams," who were "caught up," like St. Paul, "into the third heaven," or like the twelve, "spake with other tongues, as the Spirit gave them utterance." And sometimes, as in the Thessalonian Church, the ecstasy of conversion led to strange and wild opinions, such as the daily expectation of Christ's coming. The "round world" itself began to reel before them, as they thought of the things that were shortly to come to pass.

But however sudden were the conversions of the earliest believers, however wonderful the circumstances which attended them, they were not for that reason the less lasting or sincere. Though many preached "Christ of contention," though "Demas forsook the Apostle," there were few who, having once taken up the cross, turned back from "the love of this present world." They might waver between Paul and Peter, between the circumcision and the uncircumcision; they might give ear to the strange and bewitching heresies of the East; but there is no trace that many returned to "those that were no gods," or put off Christ; the impression of the truth that they had received was everlasting on their minds. Even sins of fornication and uncleanness, which from the Apostle's frequent warnings against them we must suppose to have lingered, as a sort of remnant of heathenism in the early Church, did not wholly destroy their inward relation to God and Christ. Though "their last state might be worse than the first," they could never return again to live the life of all men after having tasted "the heavenly gift and the powers of the world to come."

Such was the nature of conversion among the early Christians, the new birth of which by spiritual descent we are ourselves the offspring. Is there anything in history like it? anything in our own lives which may help us to understand it? That which the Scripture describes from within, we are for a while going to look at from a different point of view, not with reference to the power of God, but to those secondary causes through which he works, — the laws which experience shows that he himself imposes on the operations of his spirit. Such an inquiry is not a mere idle speculation; it is not far from the practical question, "How we are to become better." Imperfect as any attempt to analyze our spiritual life must ever be, the changes which we ourselves experience or observe in others, compared with those greater and more sudden changes which took place in the age of the Apostle, will throw light upon each other.

In the sudden conversions of the early Christians we observe three things which either tend to discredit, or do not accompany, the working of a similar power among ourselves. First, that conversion was marked by ecstatic and unusual phenomena; secondly, that it fell upon whole multitudes at once; thirdly, that, though sudden, it was permanent.

When we consider what is implied in such expressions as "not many wise, not many learned," were called to the knowledge of the truth, we can scarcely avoid feeling that there must have been much in the early Church which would have been distasteful to us as men of education; much that must have worn the appearance of excitement and enthusiasm. Is the mean conventicle, looking almost like a private house, more like that first assembly of Christians in the large upper room, or the Catholic church arrayed in all the glories of Christian art? Neither of them is altogether like in spirit perhaps, but in externals the first. Is the dignified hierarchy that occupy the seats around the altar, more like the multitude of first believers, or the lowly crowd that kneel upon the pavement? If we try to embody in the mind's eye the forms of the first teachers, and still more of their followers, we cannot help reading the true lesson, however great may be the illusions of poetry or of art. Not St. Paul standing on Mars' Hill in the fulness of manly strength, as we have him in the cartoon of Raphael, is the true image; but such a one as he himself would glory in, whose bodily presence was weak and speech feeble, who had an infirmity in his flesh, and bore in his body the marks of the Lord Jesus.

And when we look at this picture "full in the face," however we might by nature be inclined to turn aside from it, or veil its details in general language, we cannot deny that many things that accompany the religion of the uneducated now, must then also have accompanied the Gospel preached to the poor. There must have been, humanly speaking, spiritual delusions where men lived so exclusively in the spritual world; there were scenes which we know took place such as St. Paul says would make the unbeliever think that they were mad. The best and holiest persons among the poor and ignorant are not entirely free from superstition, according to the notions of the educated; at best they are apt to speak of religion in a manner not quite suited to our taste; they sing with a loud and excited voice; they imagine themselves to receive Divine oracles, even about the humblest cares of life. Is not this, in externals at least, very like the appearance which the first disciples must have presented, who obeyed the Apostle's injunction, "Is any sad? let him pray; is any merry? let him sing psalms." Could our nerves have borne to witness "the speaking with tongues," or "the administration of baptism," or the love-feasts as they probably existed in the early Church?

This difference between the feelings and habits of the first Christians and ourselves, must be borne in mind in relation to the subject of conversion. For as sudden changes are more likely to be met with amongst the poor and uneducated in the present day, it certainly throws light on the subject of the first conversions, that to the poor and uneducated the Gospel was first preached. And yet these sudden changes were as real, nay, more real than any gradual changes which take place among ourselves. The Stoic or Epicurean philosopher who had come into an assembly of believers speaking with tongues, would have remarked, that among the vulgar religious extravagances were usually short-lived. But it was not so. There was more there than he had eyes to see, or than was dreamed of in a philosophy like his. Not only was there the superficial appearance of poverty and meanness and enthusiasm, from a nearer view of which we are apt to shrink, but underneath this, brighter from its very obscurity, purer from the meanness of the raiment in which it was apparelled, was the life hidden with Christ and God. There, and there only, was the power which made a man humble instead of proud, self-denying instead of self-seeking, spiritual instead of carnal, a Christian instead of a Jew; which made him embrace, not only the brethren, but the whole human race, in the arms of his love.

But it is a further difference between the power of the Gospel now and in the first ages, that it no longer converts whole multitudes at once. Perhaps this very individuality in its mode of working, may not be without an advantage in awakening us to its higher truths and more entire spiritual freedom. Whether this be so or not, which is not our present question, we seem to see a diminution of its collective force on the hearts of men. In our own days the preacher sees the seed, sown gradually, spring up; first one, then another, begins to lead a better life; then a change comes over the state of society, often from causes over which he has no control; he makes some steps forwards and a few backwards, and trusts far more, if he is wise, to the silent influence of religious education than to the power of preaching; and, perhaps, the result of a long life of ministerial labor is far less than that of a single discourse from the lips of the Apostles or their followers. Even in missions to the heathen the vital energies of Christianity cease to operate to any great extent, at least on the effete civilization of India and China; the limits of the kingdoms of light and darkness are nearly the same as heretofore. At any rate it cannot be said that Christianity has wrought any sudden amelioration of mankind by the immediate preaching of the word, since the conversion of the barbarians. Even within the Christian world there is a parallel retardation. The ebb and flow of reformation and counter-reformation have hardly changed the permanent landmarks. The age of spiritual crises is past. The growth of Christianity in modern times may be compared to the change of the body, when it has already arrived at its full stature. In one half-century so vast a progress was made, in a few centuries more the world itself seemed to "have gone after Him," and now for near a thousand years the voice of experience is repeating to us, "Hitherto shalt thou go, but no further."

Looking at this remarkable phenomenon of the conversion of whole multitudes at once, not from its Divine but from its human aspect, that is, with reference to that provision that God himself has made in human nature for the execution of his will, the first cause to which we are naturally led to attribute it, is the power of sympathy. Why it is that men ever act together is a mystery of which our individual self-consciousness gives no account, any more than why we speak a common language, or form nations or societies, or merely in our physical nature are capable of taking diseases from one another. Nature and the God of nature have made us thus dependent on each other both in body and soul. Whoever has seen human beings collected together in masses, and watched the movements that pass over them, like "the trees of the forest moving in the wind," will have no difficulty in imagining, if not in understanding, how the same voice might have found its way at the same instant to a thousand hearts, without our being able to say where the fire was first kindled, or by whom the inspiration was first caught. Such historical events as the Reformation, or the Crusades, or the French Revolution, are a sufficient evidence that a whole people, or almost, we may say, half a world, may be "drunk into one spirit," springing up, as it might seem, spontaneously in the breast of each, yet common to all. A parallel yet nearer is furnished by the history of the Jewish people, in whose sudden rebellion, and restoration to God's favor, we recognize literally the momentary workings of, what is to ourselves a figure of speech, a national conscience.

In ordinary cases we should truly say that there must have been some predisposing cause of a great political or religious revolution; some latent elements acting alike upon all, which, though long smouldering beneath, burst forth at last into a flame. Such a cause might be the misery of mankind, or the intense corruption of human society, which could not be quickened except it die, or the long-suppressed yearnings of the soul after something higher than it had hitherto known upon earth, or the reflected light of one religion or one movement of the human mind upon another. Such causes were actually at work, preparing the way for the diffusion of Christianity. The law itself was beginning to pass away in an altered world, the state of society was hollow, the chosen people were hopelessly under the Roman yoke. Good men refrained from the wild attempt of the Galilean Judas; yet the spirit which animated such attempts was slumbering in their bosoms. Looking back at their own past history, they could not but remember, even in an altered world, that there was one who ruled among the kingdoms of men, "beside whom there was no God." Were they to suppose that his arm was straitened to save? that he had forgotten his tender mercies to the house of David? that the aspirations of the prophets were vain? that the blood of the Maccabean heroes had sunk like water into the earth? This was a hard saying; who could bear it? It was long ere the nation, like the individual, put off the old man, that is, the temporal dispensation, and put on the new man, that is, the spiritual Israel. The very misery of the people seemed to forbid them to acquiesce in their present state. And with the miserable condition of the nation sprang up also the feeling, not only in individuals, but in the race, that for their sins they were chastened, the feeling which their whole history seemed to deepen and increase. At last the scales fell from their eyes: the veil that was on the face of Moses, was first transfigured before them, then removed; the thoughts of many hearts turned simultaneously to the hope of Israel, "Him whom the law and the prophets foretold." As they listened to the preaching of the Apostles, they seemed to hear a truth both new and old; what many had thought, but none had uttered; which in its comfort and joyousness seemed to them new, and yet, from its familiarity and suitableness to their condition, not the less old.

Spiritual life, no less than natural life, is often the very opposite of the elements which seem to give birth to it. The preparation for the way of the Lord, which John the Baptist preached, did not consist in a direct reference to the Saviour. The words "He shall baptize you with the Holy Ghost and with fire," and "He shall burn up the chaff with fire unquenchable," could have given the Jews no exact conception of Him who "did not break the bruised reed, nor quench the smoking flax." It was in another way that John prepared for Christ, by quickening the moral sense of the people, and sounding in their ears the voice, "Repent, for the kingdom of heaven is at hand." Beyond this useful lesson, there was a kind of vacancy in the preaching of John. He himself, as "he was finishing his course," testified that his work was incomplete, and that he was not the Christ. The Jewish people were prepared by his preaching for the coming of Christ, just as an individual might be prepared to receive him by the conviction of sin, and the conscious need of forgiveness.

Except from the Gospel history and the writings of Josephus and Philo, we know but little of the tendencies of the Jewish mind in the time of our Lord. Yet we cannot doubt that the entrance of Christianity into the world was not sudden and abrupt; that is an illusion which arises in the mind from our slender acquaintance with contemporary opinions. Better and higher and holier as it was, it was not absolutely distinct from the teaching of the doctors of the law either in form or substance; it was not unconnected with, but gave life and truth to, the mystic fancies of Alexandrian philosophy. Even in the counsels of perfection of the Sermon on the Mount, there is probably nothing which might not be found, either in letter or spirit, in Philo or some other Jewish or Eastern writer. The peculiarity of the Gospel is, not that it teaches what is wholly new, but that it draws out of the treasure-house of the human heart things new and old, gathering together in one the dispersed fragments of the truth. The common people would not have "heard him gladly," but for the truth of what He said. The heart was its own witness to it. The better nature of man, though but for a moment, responded to it, spoken as it was with authority, and not as the Scribes; with simplicity, and not as the great teachers of the law; and sanctified by the life and actions of Him from whose lips it came, and "who spake as never man spake."

And yet, after reviewing the circumstances of the first preaching of the Gospel, there remains something which cannot be resolved into causes or antecedents; which eludes criticism, and can no more be explained in the world than the sudden changes of character in the individual. There are processes of life and organization about which we know nothing, and we seem to know that we shall never know anything. "That which thou sowest is not quickened, except it die"; but the mechanism of this new life is too complex, and yet too simple for us to untwist its fibres. The figure which St. Paul applies to the resurrection of the body, is true also of the renewal of the soul, especially in the first ages, of which we know so little, and in which the Gospel seems to have acted with such far greater power than among ourselves.

Leaving further inquiry into the conversion of the first Christians at the point at which it hides itself from us in mystery, we have now to turn to a question hardly less mysterious, though seemingly more familiar to us, which may be regarded as a question either of moral philosophy or of theology, — the nature of conversion and changes of character among ourselves. What traces are there of a spiritual power still acting upon the human heart? What is the inward nature, and what are the outward conditions of changes in human conduct? Is our life a gradual and insensible progress from infancy to age, from birth to death, governed by fixed laws; or is it a miracle and mystery of thirty, or fifty, or seventy years' standing, consisting of so many isolated actions or portions knit together by no common principle?

Were we to consider mankind only from without, there could be no doubt of the answer which we should give to the last of these questions. The order of the world would scarcely even *seem* to be infringed by the free-will of man. In morals, no less than in physics, everything would appear to proceed by regular law. Individuals have certain capacities, which grow with their growth and strengthen with their strength; and no one by taking thought can add one cubit to his stature. As the old proverb says, "The boy is father to the man." The lives of the great majority have a sort of continuity: as we know them by the same look, walk, manner; so when we come to converse with them, we recognize the same character as formerly. They may be changed; but the change in general is such as we expect to find in them from youth to maturity, or from maturity to decay. There is something which they do not change, by which we perceive them to be the same. If they were weak, they remain so still; if they were sensitive, they remain so still; if they were selfish or passionate, such faults are seldom cured by increasing age or infirmities. And often the same nature puts on many veils and disguises, different indeed on the surface, but within unchanged.

The appearance of this sameness in human nature has led many to suppose that no real change ever takes place. Does a man from a drunkard become sober? from a knight errant become a devotee? from a sensualist a believer in Christ? or a woman from a life of pleasure pass to a romantic and devoted religion? It has been maintained that they are the same still; and that deeper similarities remain than the differences which have sprung up on the surface. Those who make the remark would say, that such persons exhibit the same vanity, the same irritability, the same ambition;

that sensualism still lurks under the disguise of refinement, or earthly and human passion transfuses itself into devotion.

This "practical fatalism," which says that human beings can be what they are and nothing else, has a certain degree of truth, or rather, of plausibility, from the circumstance that men seldom change wholly, and that the part of their nature which changes least is the weakness and infirmity that shows itself on the surface. Few, comparatively, ever change their outward manner, except from the mere result of altered circumstances; and hence, to a superficial observer, they appear to change less than is really the fact. Probably, St. Paul never lost that trembling and feebleness which was one of the trials of his life. Nor, in so far as states of the mind are connected with the body, can we pretend to be wholly free agents. The mind does indeed rule the body, but in a subtle and mysterious way, as it were by predisposing it to a particular course of action. The body may enslave the mind: it is the image of freedom, not of slavery, which expresses the relation of the mind to the body.

If from this external aspect of human things we turn inward, there seems to be no limit to the changes which we deem possible. At any moment we can form the resolution to lead a new life; in idea at least no time is required for the change. One instant we may be proud, the next humble; one instant sinning, at the next repenting; one instant, like St. Paul, ready to persecute, at another, to preach the Gospel; full of malice and hatred one hour, melting into tenderness the next. As we hear the words of the preacher, there is a voice within telling us, that "now, even now, is the day of salvation"; and if certain clogs and hinderances of earth could only be removed, we seem ready to pass immediately into another state. But besides such feelings as these, which we know to be partly true, partly illusive, every one's experience of himself appears to teach him, that he has gone through many changes and had many special providences in life; he says to himself that he has been led in a mysterious and peculiar way, not like the way of other men, and had feelings not common to others; he compares different times and places, and contrasts his own conduct here and there, now and then. In other men he remarks similarity of character; in himself he sees chiefly diversity. Other men seem to move by regular rule and order, while his own actions are instinct with will and life. Is he then the only exception, or do other men appear to themselves to be exceptions too?

Common sense, of course, replies, that what our inward experience assures us of, every other person of the same reflection and sensibility is assured of too. And yet it does not follow, that this inward fact is to be set aside as the result of egotism and self-consciousness. It may be not merely the dreamy reflection of our life and actions in the mirror of self, but the subtle and delicate spring of the whole machine. To purify the feelings or to move the will, the first sense may be as necessary to us as the second is to regulate and sustain them. Even to the formula of the fatalist, that "freedom is the consciousness of necessity," it may be replied, that that very consciousness, as he terms it, is as essential as any other link in the chain in which "he binds fast the world." Without touching further on the metaphysical question of the freedom of the will, we will proceed to consider some practical aspects of this supposed regularity or irregularity in human conduct.

For the doctrine of conversion, the moralist substitutes the theory of habits. Good actions, he says, produce good habits; and the repetition of good actions makes them easier to perform, and "fortifies us indefinitely against temptation." There are bodily and mental habits, — habits of reflection, and habits of action. Practice gives skill or sleight of hand; constant attention, the faculty of abstraction; so the practice of virtue makes us virtuous, that of vice, vicious. The more meat we eat, to use the illustration of Aristotle, in whom we find a cruder form of the same theory, the more we are able to eat meat; the more we wrestle, the more able we are to wrestle; and so forth. If a person has some duty to perform, say of common and trivial sort, to rise at a particular hour in the morning, to be at a particular place at such an hour, to conform to some rule about abstinence, we tell him that he will find the first occasion difficult, the second easy, and the difficulty is supposed to vanish by degrees until it wholly disappears. If a man has to march into a battle, or to perform a surgical operation, or to do anything else from which human nature shrinks, his nerves, we say, are gradually strengthened; his head, as was said of a famous soldier, clears up at the sound of the cannon; like the gravedigger in Hamlet, he has soon no "feeling of his occupation."

From a consideration of such instances as these the rule has been laid down, that "as the passive impression weakens, the active habit strengthens." But is not this saying of a great man founded on a narrow and partial contemplation of human nature? For, in the first place, it leaves altogether out of sight the motives of human action; it is equally suited to the most rigid formalist, and to a moral and spiritual being. Secondly, it takes no account of the limitation of the power of habits, which, neither in mind nor body, can be extended beyond a certain point; nor of the original capacity or peculiar character of individuals; nor of the different kinds of habits, nor of the degrees of strength and weakness in different minds; nor of the enormous difference between youth and age, childhood and manhood, in the capacity for acquiring habits. Old age does not move with accumulated force, either upwards or downwards; they are the lesser habits, not the great springs of life, that show themselves in it with increased power. Nor can the man who has neglected to form habits in youth, acquire them in mature life; like the body, the mind ceases to be capable of receiving a particular form. Lastly, such a description of human nature agrees with no man's account of himself; whatever moralists may say, he knows himself to be a spiritual being. "The wind bloweth where it listeth," and he cannot "tell whence it cometh, or whither it goeth."

All that is true in the theory of habits seems to be implied in the notion of order or regularity. Even this is inadequate to give a conception of the structure of human beings. Order is the beginning, but freedom is the perfection, of our moral nature. Men do not live at random, or act one instant without reference to their actions just before. And in youth especially, the very sameness of our occupations is a sort of stay and support to us, as in age it may be described as a kind of rest. But no one will say that the mere repetition of actions until they constitute a habit, gives any explanation of the higher and nobler forms of human virtue, or the finer moulds of character. Life cannot be explained as the working of a mere machine, still less can moral or spiritual life be reduced to merely mechanical laws.

But if, while acknowledging that a great proportion of mankind are the creatures of habit, and that a great part of our actions are nothing more than the result of habit, we go on to ask ourselves about the changes of our life, and fix our minds on the critical points, we are led to view human nature, not only in a wider and more liberal spirit, but also in a way more accordant with the language of Scripture. We no longer measure ourselves by days or by weeks; we are conscious that at particular times we have undergone great revolutions or emotions; and then, again, have intervened periods lasting perhaps for years, in which we have pursued the even current of our way. Our progress towards good may have been in idea an imperceptible and regular advance; in fact, we know it to have been otherwise. We have taken plunges in life; there are many eras noted in our existence. The greatest changes are those of which we are the least able to give an account, and which we feel the most disposed to refer to a superior power. That they were simply mysterious, like some utterly unknown natural phenomena, is our first thought about them. But although unable to fathom their true nature, we are capable of analyzing many of the circumstances which accompany them, and of observing the impulses out of which they arise.

Every man has the power of forming a resolution, or,

without previous resolution, in any particular instance, acting as he will. As thoughts come into the mind one cannot tell how, so too motives spring up, without our being able to trace their origin. Why we suddenly see a thing in a new light, is often hard to explain; why we feel an action to be right or wrong which has previously seemed indifferent, is not less inexplicable. We fix the passing dream or sentiment in action; the thought is nothing, the deed may be everything. That day after day, to use a familiar instance, the drunkard will find abstinence easier, is probably untrue; but that from once abstaining he will gain a fresh experience, and receive a new strength and inward satisfaction, which may result in endless consequences, is what every one is aware of. It is not the sameness of what we do, but its novelty, which seems to have such a peculiar power over us; not the repetition of many blind actions, but the performance of a single conscious one, that is the birth to a new life. Indeed, the very sameness of actions is often accompanied with a sort of weariness, which makes men desirous of change.

Nor is it less true, that by the commission, not of many, but a single act of vice or crime, an inroad is made into our whole moral constitution, which is not proportionably increased by its repetition. The first act of theft, falsehood, or other immorality, is an event in the life of the perpetrator which he never forgets. It may often happen that no account can be given of it; that there is nothing in the education, nor in the antecedents of the person, that would lead us, or even himself, to suspect it. In the weaker sort of persons especially, suggestions of evil spring up we cannot tell how. Human beings are the creatures of habit; but they are the creatures of impulse too; and from the greater variableness of the outward circumstances of life, and especially of particular periods of life, and the greater freedom of individuals, it may, perhaps, be found that human actions, though less liable to wide-spread or sudden changes, have also become more capricious, and less reducible to simple causes, than formerly.

Changes in character come more often in the form of feeling than of reason, from some new affection or attachment, or alienation of our former self, rather than from the slow growth of experience, or a deliberate sense of right and duty. The meeting with some particular person, the remembrance of some particular scene, the last words of a parent or friend, the reading of a sentence in a book, may call forth a world within us of the very existence of which we were previously unconscious. New interests arise such as we never before knew, and we can no longer lie grovelling in the mire, but must be up and doing; new affections seem to be drawn out, such as warm our inmost soul and make action and exertion a delight to us. Mere human love at first sight, as we say, has been known to change the whole character and produce an earthly effect, analogous to that heavenly love of Christ and the brethren, of which the New Testament speaks. Have we not seen the passionate become calm, the licentious pure, the weak strong, the scoffer devout? We may not venture to say with St. Paul, "This is a great mystery, but I speak concerning Christ and the Church." But such instances serve, at least, to quicken our sense of the depth and subtlety of human nature.

Of many of these changes no other reason can be given than that nature and the God of nature have made men capable of them. There are others, again, which we seem to trace, not only to particular times, but to definite actions, from which they flow in the same manner that other effects follow from their causes. Among such causes none are more powerful than acts of self-sacrifice and devotion. A single deed of heroism makes a man a hero; it becomes a part of him, and, strengthened by the approbation and sympathy of his fellow-men, a sort of power which he gains over himself and them. Something like this is true of the lesser occasions of life no less than of the greatest; provided in either case they are not of such a kind that the performance of them is a mere violence to our nature. Many a one has stretched himself on the rack of asceticism, without on the whole raising his nature; often he has seemed to have gained in self-control only what he has lost in the kindlier affections, and by his very isolation to have wasted the opportunities which nature offered him of self-improvement. But no one with a heart open to human feelings, loving not man the less, but God more, sensitive to the happiness of this world, yet aiming at a higher, — no man of such a nature ever made a great sacrifice, or performed a great act of self-denial, without impressing a change on his character, which lasted to his latest breath. No man ever took his besetting sin, it may be lust, or pride, or love of rank and position, and, as it were, cut it out by voluntarily placing himself where to gratify it was impossible, without sensibly receiving a new strength of character. In one day, almost in an hour, he may become an altered man; he may stand, as it were, on a different stage of moral and religious life; he may feel himself in new relations to an altered world.

Nor, in considering the effects of action, must the influence of impressions be lost sight of. Good resolutions are apt to have a bad name; they have come to be almost synonymous with the absence of good actions. As they get older, men deem it a kind of weakness to be guilty of making them; so often do they end in raising "pictures of virtue, or going over the theory of virtue in our minds." Yet this contrast between passive impression and active habit, is hardly justified by our experience of ourselves or others. Valueless as they are in themselves, good resolutions are suggestive of great good; they are seldom wholly without influence on our conduct; in the weakest of men they are still the embryo of action. They may meet with a concurrence of circumstances in which they seem to grow spontaneously, coinciding with some change of place, or of pursuits, or of companions, or of natural constitution, in which they acquire a double power. They are the opportunities of virtue, if not virtue itself. At the worst they make us think; they give us an experience of ourselves; they prevent our passing our lives in total unconsciousness. A man may go on all his life making and not keeping them; miserable as such a state appears, he is perhaps not the worse, but something the better, for them. The voice of the preacher is not lost, even if he succeed but for a few instants in awakening them.

A further cause of sudden changes in the moral constitution is the determination of the will by reason and knowledge. Suppose the case of a person living in a narrow circle of ideas, within the limits of his early education, perplexed by innumerable difficulties, yet never venturing beyond the wall of prejudices in which he has been brought up. A new view of his relation to the world, and to God, is suddenly presented to him; such, for example, as in St. Paul's day was the grand acknowledgment that God was not the God of the Jews only, but also of the Gentiles; such as in our own age would be the clear perception of the moral nature of God, and of his infinite truth and justice. He is convinced, not only of the supernatural character, but of the reasonableness, of religion, and it becomes to him at once a self-imposed law. No longer does the human heart seem to rebel; no longer has he "to pose his understanding" with that odd resolution of Tertullian, "certum quia impossibile." He perceives that the perplexities of religion have been made, not by the appointment of God, but by the ingenuity of man.

Lastly. Among those influences, by the help of which the will of man seems to disengage itself from the power of habit, must not be omitted the influence of circumstances. If men are creatures of habit, much more are they creatures of circumstances. These two, nature without us, and "the second nature" that is within, are the counterbalancing forces of our being. Between them (so we may figure to ourselves the working of the mind) the human will inserts itself, making the force of one a lever against the other, and seeming to rule both. We fall under the power of habit, and feel ourselves weak and powerless to shake off the almost physical influence which it exerts upon us. The enfeebled frame cannot rid itself of the malady; the palsied springs of action cannot be strengthened for good, nor fortified against evil. Transplanted into another soil, and in a different air, we renew our strength. In youth especially, the character seems to respond kindly to the influence of the external world. Nature and the God of nature have given us many aids in the battle with self, the greatest of which, humanly speaking, is change of circumstances.

We have wandered far from the subject of conversion in the early Church, into another sphere in which the words "grace, faith, the spirit," have disappeared, and notions of moral philosophy have taken their place. It is better, perhaps, that the attempt to analyze our spiritual nature should assume this abstract form. We feel that words cannot express the life hidden with Christ in God; we are afraid of declaring on the housetop, what may only be spoken in the closet. If the rites and ceremonies of the elder dispensation, which have so little in them of a spiritual character, were a figure of the true, much more may the moral world be regarded as a figure of the spiritual world of which religion speaks to us.

There is a view of the changes of the characters of men which begins where this ends, which reads human nature by a different light, and speaks of it as the seat of a great struggle between the powers of good and evil. It would be untrue to identify this view with that which has preceded, and scarcely less untrue to attempt to interweave the two in a system of "moral theology." No addition of theological terms will transfigure Aristotle's Ethics into a "Summa Theologiæ." When St. Paul says, "O wretched man that I am, who shall deliver me from the body of this death?" "I thank God through Jesus Christ our Lord"; he is not speaking the language of moral philosophy, but of religious feeling. He expresses what few have truly felt concentrated in a single instant, what many have deluded themselves into the belief of, what some have experienced accompanying them through life, what a great portion even of the better sort of mankind are wholly unconscious of. It seems as if Providence allowed us to regard the truths of religion and morality in many ways which are not wholly unconnected with each other, yet parallel rather than intersecting; providing for the varieties of human character, and not leaving those altogether without law, who are incapable in a world of sight of entering within the veil.

As we return to that "hidden life" of which the Scripture speaks, our analysis of human nature seems to become more imperfect, less reducible to rule or measure, less capable of being described in a language which all men understand. What the believer recognizes as the record of his experience is apt to seem mystical to the rest of the world. We do not seek to thread the mazes of the human soul, or to draw forth to the light its hidden communion with its Maker, but only to present in general outline the power of religion among other causes of human action.

Directly, religious influences may be summed up under three heads: The power of God; the love of Christ; the efficacy of prayer.

(1.) So far as the influence of the first of these is capable of analysis, it consists in the practical sense that we are dependent beings, and that our souls are in the hands of God, who is acting through us, and ever present with us in the trials of life and in the work of life. The believer is a minister who executes this work, hardly the partner in it; it is not his own, but God's. He does it with the greatest care, as unto the Lord and not to men, yet is indifferent as to the result, knowing that all things, even through his imperfect agency, are working together for good. The attitude of his soul towards God is such as to produce the strongest effects on his power of action. It leaves his faculties clear and unimpassioned; it raises him into communion with nature and God; it places him above accidents; it perfects strength in weakness. It gives the assurance of a real and present possession of all things, as St. Paul says: "All things are ours, whether life or death, or things present or things to come." It is the source of power and freedom. It affords the perfect peace of a soul stayed on God.

In merely human things, the aid and sympathy of others increase our power to act: it is also the fact, we can work more effectually and think more truly, where the issue is not staked on the result of our thought and work. The confidence of success would be more than half the secret of success, did it not also lead to the relaxation of our efforts. But in the life of the believer, the sympathy, if such a figure of speech may be allowed, is not human, but Divine; the confidence is not a confidence in ourselves, but in the power of God, which at once takes us out of ourselves and increases our obligation to exertion. The instances just mentioned have an analogy, though but a faint one, with that which we are considering. They are shadows of the support we receive from the Infinite and Everlasting. As the philosopher said that his theory of fatalism was absolutely required to insure the repose necessary for moral action, it may be said, in a far higher sense, that the consciousness of a Divine Providence is necessary to enable a rational being to meet the present trials of life, and to look without fear on his future destiny.

(2.) But yet more strongly is it felt that the love of Christ has this constraining power over souls, that here, if anywhere, we are unlocking the twisted chain of sympathy, and reaching the inmost mystery of human nature. The light, once for all, of Christ crucified, recalling the thought of what, more than eighteen hundred years ago, he suffered for us, has ravished the heart and melted the affections, and made the world seem new, and covered the earth itself with a fair vision, that is, a heavenly one. The strength of this feeling arises from its being directed towards a person, a real being, an individual like ourselves, who has actually endured all this for our sakes, who was so much above us, and yet became one of us and felt as we did, and was, like ourselves, a true man. The love which he felt towards us, we seek to return to him; the unity which he has with God, he communicates to us. By looking upon him we become like him, and at length we see him as he is. Mere human love rests on instincts, the working of which we cannot explain, but which nevertheless touch the inmost springs of our being. So too we have spiritual instincts, acting towards higher objects, still more suddenly and wonderfully capturing our souls in an instant, and making us indifferent to all things else. Such instincts show themselves in the weak no less than in the strong; they seem to be not so much an original part of our nature, as to fulfil our nature, and add to it, and draw it out, until they make us different beings to ourselves and others. It was the quaint fancy of a sentimentalist to ask whether any one who remembers the first sight of a beloved person, could doubt the existence of magic. Much more truly we may ask, Can any one who has ever once known the love of Christ doubt the existence of a spiritual power?

(3.) Another power or instrument by the help of which we become servants of God, which is of a peculiar nature, and seems to be intermediate between feeling and action, and to partake of both, is prayer. Prayer is the concentration of faith in a definite act, which is at once inward and outward, the influence of which on the character, like that of any other act, is proportioned to its intensity. The imagination of doing rightly adds little to our strength; even the wish to do so is not necessarily accompanied by a change of heart and conduct. But in prayer we imagine, and wish, and perform all in one. Our imperfect resolutions are brought into the presence of God; our weakness becomes strength, our words deeds. No other action is so mysterious; there is none in which we seem, in the same manner, to renounce ourselves that we may be one with God.

Of what nature that prayer is which is effectual to the obtaining of these results, is a question of the same kind as what constitutes a true faith. That prayer, we should answer, which is itself most of an act, which is most immediately followed by action, which is most truthful, manly, self-controlled, which seems to lead and direct, rather than to follow, our natural emotions. Prayer is the very reverse of the assertion of ourselves before God; yet in kneeling before him, while we remember that he is God, he bids us remember also that we are men, whom, even when humbled before him, he would not have fall below the reason that he has given us.

In prayer, as in all religion, there is something that it is impossible to describe, and that seems to be untrue the moment it is expressed in words. In the communion of man with God, it is vain to attempt to separate what belongs to the finite and what to the infinite. We can feel, but we cannot analyze it. We can lay down practical rules for it, but can give no adequate account of it. It is a mystery which we do not seek to fathom. In all religion there is an element of which we are conscious; there is that beyond which we feel rather than know.

This indistinctness in the very subject of religion, even independent of mysticism or superstition, may become to intellectual minds a ground for doubting the truth of that which will not be subjected to the ordinary tests of human knowledge, which seems to elude our grasp, and retire into the recesses of the soul the moment we ask for the demonstration of its existence. Against this natural suspicion let us set the fact, that, judged by its effects, the power of religion is of all powers the greatest. Knowledge itself is a weak instrument to stir the soul compared with religion; morality has no way to the heart of man; but the Gospel reaches the feelings and the intellect at once. In nations as well as individuals, in barbarous times as well as civilized, in the great crises of history especially, even in the latest ages, when the minds of men seem to wax cold, and all things remain the same as at the beginning, it has shown itself to be a reality without which human nature would cease to be what it is. Almost every one has had the witness of it in himself. No one, says Plato, ever passed from youth to age in unbelief of the gods, in heathen times. Hardly any educated person in a Christian land has passed from youth to age without some aspiration after a better life, some thought of the country to which he is going.

As a fact it would be admitted by most, that at some period of their lives the thought of the world to come and of future judgment, the beauty and loveliness of the truths of the Gospel, the sense of the shortness of our days here, have wrought a more quickening and powerful effect than any moral truths or prudential maxims. Many a one would acknowledge that he has been carried whither he knew not; and had nobler thoughts, and felt higher aspirations, than the course of his ordinary life seemed to allow. These were the most important moments of his life for good or for evil; the critical points which have made him what he is, either as he used or neglected them. They came he knew not how, sometimes with some outward and apparent cause, at other times without, — the result of affliction or sickness, or "the wind blowing where it listeth."

And if such changes and such critical points should be found to occur in youth more often than in age, in the poor and ignorant rather than in the educated, in women more often than in men, — if reason and reflection seem to weaken as they regulate the springs of human action, this very fact may lead us to consider that reason, and reflection, and education, and the experience of age, and the force of manly sense, are not the links which bind us to the communion of the body of Christ; that it is rather to those qualities which we have, or may have, in common with our fellow-men, that the Gospel is promised; and that it is with the weak, the poor, the babes in Christ, not with the strong-minded, the resolute, the consistent, that we shall sit down in the kingdom of heaven.

CASUISTRY.

BY BENJAMIN JOWETT.

RELIGION and morality seem often to become entangled in circumstances. The truth which came, not "to bring peace upon earth, but a sword," could not but give rise to many new and conflicting obligations. The kingdom of God had to adjust itself with the kingdoms of this world; though "the children were free," they could not escape the fulfilment of duties to their Jewish or Roman governors; in the bosom of a family there were duties too; in society there were many points of contact with the heathen. A new element of complexity had been introduced in all the relations between man and man, giving rise to many new questions, which might be termed, in the phraseology of modern times, "cases of conscience."

Of these the one which most frequently recurs in the Epistles of St. Paul, is the question respecting meats and drinks, which appears to have agitated both the Roman and Corinthian Churches, as well as those of Jerusalem and Antioch, and probably, in a greater or less degree, every other Christian community in the days of the Apostle. The scruple which gave birth to it was not confined to Christianity: it was Eastern rather than Christian, and originated in a feeling into which entered, not only Oriental notions of physical purity and impurity, but also those of caste and of race. With other Eastern influences it spread towards the West, in the flux of all religions, exercising a peculiar power on the susceptible temper of mankind.

The same tendency exhibited itself in various forms. In one form it was the scruple of those who ate herbs, while others "had faith" to eat anything. The Essenes and Therapeutæ among the Jews, and the Pythagoreans in the heathen world, had a similar feeling respecting the use of animal food. It was a natural association which led to such an abstinence. In the East, ever ready to connect, or rather incapable of separating, ideas of moral and physical impurity, — where the heat of the climate rendered animal food unnecessary, if not positively unhealthful; where corruption so soon infected the remains of animals; where, lastly, ancient tradition and ceremonies told of the sacredness of animals and the mysteriousness of animal life, — nature and religion alike seemed to teach the same lesson, it was safer to abstain. It was the manner of such a scruple to propagate itself. He who revolted at animal food could not quietly sit by and see his neighbor partake of it. The ceremonialism of the age was the tradition of thousands of years, and passed by a sort of contagion from one race to another, from Paganism or Judaism to Christianity. How to deal with this "second nature" was a practical difficulty among the first Christians. They were not an Essene sect; and the Church could not exclude those who held the scruple, could not be narrowed to them, could not pass judgment on them at all. Hence the force of the Apostle's words: "Him that is weak in the faith receive, but not to the decision of doubts."

There was another point in reference to which the same spirit of ceremonialism propagated itself; namely, meats offered to idols. Even if meat in general were innocent and a creature of God, it could hardly be a matter of indifference to partake of that which had been "sacrificed to devils"; least of all, to sit at meat in the idol's temple. True, the idol was "nothing in the world," — a block of stone, to which the words good or evil were only misapplied; but it was impossible that the first believers could so regard it.

When they saw the worshippers of the idol revelling in impurity, they could not but believe that a spirit of some kind was there. Their warfare, as the Apostle himself had told them, was not against flesh and blood, but against principalities, against powers, against the rulers of the darkness of this world. And if they had been completely free from superstition, and could have regarded the heathen religions which they saw enthroned over the world simply with contempt, still the question would have arisen, What connection were they to have with them and with their worshippers? a question not easy to be answered in the bustle of Rome and Corinth, where every circumstance of daily life, every amusement, every political and legal right, was in some way bound up with the heathen religions. Were they to go out of the world? if not, what was to be their relation to those without? It was a branch of this more general question, the beginning of the difficulty so strongly felt and so vehemently disputed about in the days of Tertullian, which St. Paul discusses in reference to meats offered to idols. Where was the line to be drawn? Were they to visit the idol's temple, to sacrifice like other men to Diana or Jupiter? That could hardly be consistent with their Christian profession. But granting this, where were they to stop? Was it lawful to eat meats offered to idols? But if not, then how careful should they be to discover what was offered to idols! How easily might they fall into sin unawares! The scruple once indulged would soon gather strength, until the very provision of their daily food would become difficult by their disuse of the markets of the heathen.

A third instance of the same ceremonialism so natural to that age, and to ourselves so strange and unmeaning, is illustrated by the words of the Jerusalem Christians to the Apostle, "Thou wentest in unto men uncircumcised, and didst eat with them"; a scruple so strong that, probably, St. Peter himself was never entirely free from it, and at any rate yielded to the fear of it in others when withstood by St. Paul at Antioch. This scruple may be said in one sense not to be capable of an explanation, and in another not to need one. For, probably, nothing can give our minds any conception of the nature of the feeling, the intense hold which it exercised, the concentration which it was of every national and religious prejudice, the constraint which was required to get rid of it as a sort of "horror naturalis" in the minds of Jews; while, on the other hand, feelings at the present day not very dissimilar exist, not only in Eastern countries, but among ourselves. There is nothing strange in human nature being liable to them, or in their long lingering and often returning, even when reason and charity alike condemn them. We ourselves are not insensible to differences of race and color, and may therefore be able partially to comprehend (allowing for the difference of East and West) what was the feeling of Jews and Jewish Christians towards men uncircumcised.

On the last point St. Paul maintains but one language: "In Christ Jesus there is neither circumcision nor uncircumcision." No compromise could be allowed here, without destroying the Gospel that he preached. But the other question of meats and drinks, when separated from that of circumcision, admitted of various answers and points of view. Accordingly, there is an appearance of inconsistency in the modes in which the Apostle resolves it. All these modes have a use and interest for ourselves. Though our difficulties are not the same as those of the early Christians, the words speak to us, so long as prudence, and faith, and charity are the guides of Christian life. It is characteristic of the Apostle that his answers run into one another, as though each of them to different individuals, and all in their turn, might present the solution of the difficulty.

Separating them under different heads, we may begin with 1 Cor. x. 25, which may be termed the rule of Christian prudence: "Whatsoever is sold in the shambles, that eat, asking no question for conscience' sake." That is to say: "Buy food as other men do. Perhaps what you purchase has come from the idol's temple, perhaps not. Do not encourage your conscience in raising scruples: life will become impossible if you do. One question involves another and another and another without end. The manly and the Christian way is to cut them short; both as tending to weaken the character, and as inconsistent with the very nature of spiritual religion."

So we may venture to amplify the Apostle's precept, which breathes the same spirit of moderation as his decisions respecting celibacy and marriage. Among ourselves the remark is often made that "extremes are practically untrue." This is another way of putting the same lesson: If I may not sit in the idol's temple, it may be plausibly argued, neither may I eat meats offered to idols; and if I may not eat meats offered to idols, then it logically follows that I ought not to go into the market where idols' meat is sold. The Apostle snaps the chain of this misapplied logic: there must be a limit somewhere; we must not push consistency where it is practically impossible. A trifling scruple is raised to the level of a religious duty, and another and another, until religion is made up of scruples, and the light of life fades, and the ways of life narrow themselves.

It is not hard to translate the Apostle's precept into the language of our time. Instances occur in politics, in theology, in our ordinary occupations, in which beyond a certain point consistency is impossible. Take for example the following: A person feels that he would be wrong in carrying on his business, or going to public amusements, on a Sunday. He says: If it be wrong for me to work, it is wrong to make the servants in my house work; or if it be wrong to go to public amusements, it is wrong to enjoy the recreation of walking on a Sunday. So it may be argued that, because slavery is wrong, therefore it is not right to purchase the produce of slavery, or that of which the produce of slavery is a part; and so on without end, until we are forced out of the world from a remote fear of contagion with evil. Or I am engaged in an employment which may be in some degree deleterious to the health or injurious to the morals of those who are employed in it, or I let a house to another who is so engaged. Numberless questions of the same kind relating to the profession of an advocate, a soldier, or a clergyman, have been pursued into endless consequences. In all these cases there is a point at which necessity comes in and compels us to adopt the rule of the Apostle, which may be paraphrased, "Do as other men do in a Christian country." Conscience may say, "He who is guilty of the least, is guilty of all." In the Apostle's language it then becomes "the strength of sin," encouraging us to despair of all; because in that mixed condition of life in which God has placed us, we cannot fulfil all.

In accordance with the spirit of the same principle of doing as other men do, the Apostle further implies that believers are to accept the hospitality of the heathen. (1 Cor. x. 27.) But here a modification comes in, which may be termed the law of Christian charity or courtesy: Avoid giving offence, or, as we might say, "Do not defy opinion." Eat what is set before you; but if a person sitting at meat pointedly says to you, "This was offered to idols," do not eat. All things are lawful, but all things are not expedient, and this is one of the not expedient class. There appears to be a sort of inconsistency in this advice, as there must always be inconsistency in the rules of practical life which are relative to circumstances. It might be said: "We cannot do one thing at one time, and another thing at another; now be guided by another man's conscience, now by our own." It might be retorted: "Is not this the dissimulation which you blame in St. Peter?" To which it may be answered in turn: "But a man may do one thing at one time, another thing at another time, 'becoming to the Jews a Jew,' if he do it in such a manner as to avoid the risk of misconstruction." And this again admits of the retort: "Is it possible to avoid misconstruction? Is it not better to dare to be ourselves, to act like ourselves, to speak like ourselves, to think like ourselves?" We seem to have lighted unawares on two varieties of human disposition: the one harmonizing and adapting itself to the perplexities of life, the other rebelling against them, and seeking to disentangle itself from them. Which side of this argument shall we take; neither, or both? The Apostle appears to take both sides; for in the abrupt transition that follows, he immediately adds, "Why is my liberty to be judged of another man's conscience? what right has another man to attack me for what I do in the innocence of my heart?" It is good advice to say, "Regard the opinions of others"; and equally good advice to say, "Do not regard the opinions of others." We must balance between two; and over all, adjusting the scales, is the law of Christian love.

Both in 1 Cor. viii. and Rom. xiv. the Apostle adds another principle, which may be termed the law of individual conscience, which we must listen to in ourselves and regard in others. "He that doubteth is damned; whatsoever is not of faith is sin." All things are lawful to him who feels them to be lawful, but the conscience may be polluted by the most indifferent things. When we eat, we should remember that the consequence of following our example may be serious to others. For not only may our brother be offended at us, but also by our example be drawn into sin; that is, to do what, though indifferent in itself, is sin to him. And so the weak brother, for whom Christ died, may perish through our fault; that is, he may lose his peace and harmony of soul and conscience void of offence, and all through our heedlessness in doing some unnecessary thing, which were far better left undone.

Cases may be readily imagined, in which, like the preceding, the rule of conduct here laid down by the Apostle would involve dissimulation. So many thousand scruples and opinions as there are in the world, we should have to go out of the world to fulfil it honestly. All reserve, it may be argued, tends to break up the confidence between man and man; and there are times in which concealment of our opinions, even respecting things indifferent, would be treacherous and mischievous; there are times, too, in which things cease to be indifferent, and it is our duty to speak out respecting the false importance which they have acquired. But, after all qualifications of this kind have been made, the secondary duty yet remains, of consideration for others, which should form an element in our conduct. If truth is the first principle of our speech and action, the good of others should, at any rate, be the second. "If any man (not see thee who hast knowledge sitting in the idol's temple, but) hear thee discoursing rashly of the Scriptures and the doctrines of the Church, shall not the faith of thy younger brother become confused? and his conscience being weak shall cease to discern between good and evil. And so thy weak brother shall perish for whom Christ died."

The Apostle adds a fourth principle, which may be termed the law of Christian freedom, as the last solution of the difficulty: "Therefore, whether ye eat or drink, do all to the glory of God." From the perplexities of casuistry, and the conflicting rights of a man's own conscience and that of another, he falls back on the simple rule, "Whatever you do, sanctify the act." It cannot be said that all contradictory obligations vanish the moment we try to act with simplicity and truth; we cannot change the current of life and its circumstances by a wish or an intention; we cannot dispel that which is without, though we may clear that which is within. But we have taken the first step, and are in the way to solve the riddle. The insane scruple, the fixed idea, the ever-increasing doubt begins to pass away; the spirit of the child returns to us; the mind is again free, and the road of life open. "Whether ye eat or drink, do all to the glory of God"; that is, determine to seek only the will of God, and you may have a larger measure of Christian liberty allowed to you; things, perhaps, wrong in others may be right for you.

The law, then, of Christian prudence, using that moderation which we show in things pertaining to this life; or the law of Christian charity, resolving and, as it were, absorbing our scruples in the love of other men; or the law of the individual conscience, making that right to a man, in matters in themselves indifferent, which seems to be so; or the law of freedom, giving us a spirit, instead of a letter, and enlarging the first principles of the doctrine of Christ; or all together, shall furnish the doubting believer with a sufficient rule of faith and conduct. Even the law of Christian charity is a rule of freedom rather than of restraint, in proportion as it places men above questions of meats and drinks, and enables them to regard such disputes only by the light of love to God and man. For there is a tyranny which even freedom may exercise, when it makes us intolerant of other men's difficulties. "Where the Spirit of the Lord is, there is liberty"; but there is also a liberty without the Spirit of the Lord. To eat with unwashen hands defileth not a man; but to denounce those who do, or do not do so, may, in St. Paul's language, cause, not only the weak brother, but him that fancieth he standeth, to fall; and so, in a false endeavor to preach the Gospel of Christ, men "may perish for whom Christ died."

The general rule of the Apostle is, "Neither circumcision availeth anything, nor uncircumcision"; "neither if we eat not are we the better, neither if we eat are we the worse." But then "all things are lawful, but all things are not expedient," even in reference to ourselves, and still more as we are members one of another. There is a further counsel of prudence: "Receive such an one, but not to the determination of his doubts." And lastly, as the guide to the spirit of our actions, remember the words: "I will eat no meat as long as the world standeth, lest I make my brother to offend."

Questions of meats and drinks, of eating with washen or unwashen hands, have passed from the stage of religious ordinances, to that of proprieties and decencies of life. Neither the purifications of the law of Moses, nor the seven precepts of Noah, are any longer binding upon Christians. Nature herself teaches all things necessary for health and comfort. But the spirit of casuistry in every age finds fresh materials to employ itself upon, laying hold of some question of a new moon or a Sabbath, some fragment of antiquity, some inconsistency of custom, some subtlety of thought, some nicety of morality, analyzing and dividing the actions of daily life; separating the letter from the spirit, and words from things; winding its toils around the infirmities of the weak, and linking itself to the sensibility of the intellect. Out of this labyrinth of the soul the believer finds his way, by keeping his eye fixed on that landmark which the Apostle himself has set up: "In Christ Jesus neither circumcision availeth anything, nor uncircumcision, but a new creature."

There is no one probably, of any religious experience, who has not at times felt the power of a scrupulous conscience. In speaking of a scrupulous conscience, the sense of remorse for greater offences is not intended to be included. These may press more or less heavily on the soul; and the remembrance of them may ingrain themselves, with different degrees of depth, on different temperaments; but whether deep or shallow, the sorrow for them cannot be brought under the head of scruples of conscience. There are "many things in which we offend all," about which there can be no mistake, the impression of which on our minds it would be fatal to weaken or do away. But quite independently of real sorrows for sin, most religious persons in the course of their lives have felt unreal scruples or difficulties, or exaggerated real but slight ones; they have abridged their Christian freedom, and thereby their means of doing good; they have cherished imaginary obligations, and artificially hedged themselves in a particular course of action. Honor or truth seems to be at stake about trifles light as air, or conscience has become a burden too heavy for them to bear in some doubtful matter of conduct. Scruples of this kind are ever liable to increase: as one vanishes, another appears; the circumstances of the world and of the Church, and even the complication of modern society, have a tendency to create them. The very form in which they come is of itself sufficient to put us on our guard against them; for we can give no account of them to ourselves; they are seldom affected by the opinion of others; they are more often put down by the exercise of authority than by reasoning or judgment. They gain hold on the weaker sort of men, or on those not naturally weak, in moments of weakness. They often run counter to our wish or interest, and for this very reason acquire a kind of tenacity. They seem innocent mistakes, at worst on the safe side, characteristic of the ingenuousness of youth, or indicative of a heart uncorrupted by the world. But this is not so. Creatures as we are of circumstances, we cannot safely afford to give up things indifferent, means of usefulness, instruments of happiness to ourselves, which may affect our lives and those of our children to the latest posterity. There are few greater dangers in religion than the indulgence of such scruples, the consequences of which can never be seen until too late, and which affect the moral character of a man at least as much as his temporal interests.

Strange as it may appear, it is nevertheless true, that scruples about lesser matters almost always involve some dereliction of duty in greater and more obvious ones. A tender conscience is a conscience unequal to the struggles of life. At first sight it seems as if, when lesser duties were cared for, the greater would take care of themselves. But this is not the lesson which experience teaches. In our moral, as in our physical nature, we are finite beings, capable only of a certain degree of tension, ever liable to suffer disorder and derangement, to be over-exercised in one part and weakened in another. No one can fix his mind intently on a trifling scruple, or become absorbed in an eccentric fancy, without finding the great principles of truth and justice insensibly depart from him. He has been looking through a microscope at life, and cannot take in its general scope. The moral proportions of things are lost to him; the question of a new moon or a Sabbath has taken the place of diligence or of honesty. There is no limit to the illusions which he may practise on himself. There are those, all whose interests and prejudices at once take the form of duties and scruples, partly from dishonesty, but also from weakness, and because that is the form in which they can with the best grace maintain them against other men, and conceal their true nature from themselves.

Scruples are dangerous in another way, as they tend to drive men into a corner in which the performance of our duty becomes so difficult as to be almost impossible. A virtuous and religious life does not consist merely in abstaining from evil, but in doing what is good. It has to find opportunities and occasions for itself, without which it languishes. A man has a scruple about the choice of a profession; as a Christian, he believes war to be unlawful; in familiar language, he has doubts respecting orders, difficulties about the law. Even the ordinary ways of conducting trade appear deficient to his nicer sense of honesty; or perhaps he has already entered on one of these lines of life, and finds it necessary to quit it. At last, there comes the difficulty of "how he is to live." There cannot be a greater mistake than to suppose that a good resolution is sufficient in such a case to carry a man through a long life.

But even if we suppose the case of one who is endowed with every earthly good and instrument of prosperity, who can afford, as is sometimes said, to trifle with the opportunities of life, still the mental consequences will be hardly less injurious to him. For he who feels scruples about the ordinary enjoyments and occupations of his fellows, does so far cut himself off from his common nature. He is an isolated being, incapable of acting with his fellow-men. There are plants which, though the sun shine upon them, and the dews water them, peak and pine from some internal disorder, and appear to have no sympathy with the influences around them. So is the mind corroded by scruples of conscience. It cannot expand to sun or shower; it belongs not to the world of light; it has no intelligence of, or harmony with, mankind around. It is insensible to the great truth, that though we may not do evil that good may come, yet that good and evil, truth and falsehood, are bound together on earth, and that we cannot separate ourselves from them.

It is one of the peculiar dangers of scruples of conscience, that the consequence of giving way to them is never felt at the time that they press upon us. When the mind is worried by a thought secretly working in it, and its trial becomes greater than it can bear, it is eager to take the plunge in life that may put it out of its misery; to throw aside a profession it may be, or to enter a new religious communion. We shall not be wrong in promising ourselves a few weeks of peace and placid enjoyment. The years that are to follow we are incapable of realizing: whether the weary spirit will require some fresh posture, will invent for itself some new doubt; whether its change is a return to nature or not, it is impossible for us to anticipate. Whether it has in itself that hidden strength which, under every change of circumstances, is capable of bearing up, is a question which we are the least able to determine for ourselves. In general we may observe, that the weakest minds and those least capable of enduring such consequences, are the most likely to indulge the scruples. We know beforehand the passionate character, the active yet half-reasoning intellect, which falls under the power of such illusions.

In the Apostolic Church "cases of conscience" arose out of religious traditions, and what may be termed the ceremonial cast of the age; in modern times the most frequent source of them may be said to be the desire of logical or practical consistency, such as is irreconcilable with the mixed state of human affairs and the feebleness of the human intellect. There is no lever like the argument from consistency, with which to bring men over to our opinions. A particular system or view, Calvinism perhaps, or Catholicism, has taken possession of the mind. Shall we stop short of pushing its premises to their conclusions? Shall we stand in the midway, where we are liable to be over-ridden by the combatants on either side in the struggle? Shall we place ourselves between our reason and our affections; between our practical duties and our intellectual convictions? Logic would have us go forward, and take our stand at the most advanced point, — we are there already, it is urged, if we were true to ourselves, — but feeling, and habit, and common sense bid us stay where we are, unable to give an account of ourselves, yet convinced that we are right. We may listen to the one voice, we may listen also to the other. The true way of guiding either is to acknowledge both; to use them for a time against each other, until experience of life and of ourselves has taught us to harmonize them in a single principle.

So, again, in daily life cases often occur, in which we must do as other men do, and act upon a general understanding, even though unable to reconcile a particular practice to the letter of truthfulness or even to our individual conscience. It is hard in such cases to lay down a definite rule. But in general we should be suspicious of any conscientious scruples in which other good men do not share. We shall do right to make a large allowance for the perplexities and entanglements of human things; we shall observe that men of strong minds brush away our scruples; we shall consider that not he who has most, but he who has fewest scruples, approaches most nearly the true Christian. For, as the Apostle says, "Whatsoever is not of faith is sin"; and "Blessed is he who condemneth not himself in that which he alloweth."

So far we seem to arrive at a general conclusion like St. Paul's: "Whether ye eat or drink, do all to the glory of God"; "Have the spirit of truth, and the truth shall make you free"; and the entanglements of words and the perplexities of action shall disappear. But there is another way in which such difficulties have been resolved, which meets them in detail; namely, the practice of confession, and the rules of casuistry which are the guides of the confessor. When the spirit is disordered within us, it may be urged that we ought to go out of ourselves and confess our sins one to another. But he who leads, and he who is led, alike require some rules for the examination of conscience, to quicken or moderate the sense of sin, to assist experience, to show men to themselves as they really are, neither better nor worse. Hence the necessity for casuistry.

It is remarkable, that what is in idea so excellent that it may be almost described in St. Paul's language as "holy, just, and good," should have become a by-word among mankind for hypocrisy and dishonesty. In popular estimation, no one is supposed to resort to casuistry but with the view of evading a duty. The moral instincts of the world have risen up and condemned it; *corruptio optimi pessima.* Bad as it is, it has a good side, which is the chief source of its influence. It will be proper for us to consider it from both sides,—in its origin, and in its perversion. Why it existed, and why it has failed, furnish a lesson in the history of the human mind of importance and instruction.

The unseen power by which the systems of the casuists were brought into being was the necessity of the Roman Catholic Church. Like the allegorical interpretation of Scripture, they formed a link between the present and the past. At the time of the Reformation the doctrines of the ancient, no less than of the Reformed faith awakened into life. But they required to be put in a new form, to reconcile them to the moral sense of mankind. Luther ended the work of self-examination by casting all his sins on Christ. But the casuists could not thus meet the awakening of men's consciences and the fearful looking for judgment. They had to deal with an altered world, in which the spectres of the past, purgatory, penance, mortal sin, were again rising up. Hallowed as they were by authority and antiquity, they could not cast them aside, they could but explain them away. If they had placed distinctly before men's eyes, that for some one act of immorality or dishonesty they were in a state of mortal sin, the heart true to itself would have recoiled from such a doctrine, and the connection between the Church and the world would have been for ever severed. And yet the doctrine was a part of ecclesiastical tradition; it could not be held, it could not be given up. The Jesuits escaped the dilemma by holding and evading it.

So far it would not be untrue to say, that casuistry had originated in an effort to reconcile the Roman Catholic faith with nature and experience. The Roman system was, if strictly carried out, horrible and impossible; a doctrine not, as it has been sometimes described, of salvation made easy, but of universal condemnation. From these fearful conclusions of logic the subtlety of the human intellect was now to save it. The analogy of law, as worked out by jurists and canonists, supplied the means. What was repugnant to human justice could not be agreeable to Divine. The scholastic philosophy, which had begun to die out and fade away before the light of classical learning, was to revive in a new form, no longer hovering between heaven and earth, out of the reach of experience, yet below the region of spiritual truth, but, as it seemed, firmly based in the life and actions of mankind. It was the same sort of wisdom which defined the numbers and order of the celestial hierarchy, which was now to be adapted to the infinite modifications of which the actions of men are capable.

It is obvious that there are endless points of view in which the simplest duties may be regarded. Common sense says, "A man is to be judged by his acts," "There can be no mistake about a lie," and so on. The casuists proceed by a different road. Fixing the mind, not on the simplicity, but on the intricacy of human action, in the hope of gaining simplicity they study every point of view, and introduce every conceivable distinction. A first most obvious distinction is that of the intention and the act; ought the one to be separated from the other? The law itself seems to teach that this may hardly be; rather the intention is held to be that which gives form and color to the act. Then the act by itself is nothing, and the intention by itself almost innocent. As we play between the two different points of view, the act and the intention together evanesce. But, secondly, as we consider the intention, must we not also consider the circumstances of the agent? For, plainly, a being deprived of free-will cannot be responsible for his actions. Place him in thought under the conditions of a necessary agent, and his actions are innocent. Or suppose a man ignorant, or half ignorant, of what is the teaching of the Church, or the law of the land, here another abstract point of view arises, leading us out of the region of common sense to difficult and equitable considerations, which may be determined fairly, but which we have the greatest motive to decide in favor of ourselves. Or again, try to conceive an act without reference to its consequences, or in reference to some single consequence, without regarding it as a violation of morality or of nature, or in reference solely to the individual conscience. Or imagine the will half consenting to, half withdrawing from its act; or acting by another, or in obedience to another, or with some good object, or under the influence of some imperfect obligation, or of opposite obligations. Even conscience itself may be at last played off against the plainest truths.

By the aid of such distinctions the simplest principles of morality multiply to infinity. An instrument has been introduced of such subtlety and elasticity that it can accommodate the canons of the Church to any consciences, to any state of the world. Sin need no longer be confined to the dreadful distinction of mortal and venial sin; it has lost its infinite and mysterious character; it has become a thing of degrees, to be aggravated or mitigated in idea, according to the expediency of the case or the pliability of the confessor. It becomes difficult to perpetrate a perfect sin. No man need die of despair; in some page of the writings of the casuists will be found a distinction suited to his case. And this without in any degree interfering with a single doctrine of the Church, or withdrawing one of its anathemas against heresy.

The system of casuistry, destined to work such great results, in reconciling the Church to the world, and to human nature, like a torn web, needing to be knit together, may be regarded as a science or profession. It is a classification of human actions, made in one sense without any reference to practice. For nothing was further from the mind of the casuist than to inquire whether a particular distinction would have a good or bad effect, was liable to perversion or not. His object was only to make such distinctions as the human mind was capable of perceiving and acknowledging. As to the physiologist objects in themselves loathsome and disgusting may be of the deepest interest, so to the casuist the foulest and most loathsome vices of mankind are not matters of abhorrence, but of science, to be arranged and classified, just like any other varieties of human action. It is true that the study of the teacher was not supposed to be also open to the penitent. But it inevitably followed that the spirit of the teacher communicated itself to the taught. He could impart no high or exalted idea of morality or religion, who was measuring it out, as it were, by inches, not deepening men's idea of sin, but attenuating it, and doing away its awful and mysterious nature.

The science was further complicated by the "doctrine of probability," which consisted in making anything approved or approvable that was confirmed by authority; even as was said by some of a single casuist. That could not be very wrong which a wise and good man had once thought to be right, — a better than ourselves perhaps, surveying the circumstances calmly and impartially. Who would wish that the rule of his daily life should go beyond that of a saint and doctor of the Church? Who would require such a rule to be observed by another? Who would refuse another such an escape out of the labyrinth of human difficulties and perplexities? As in all the Jesuit distinctions, there was a kind of reasonableness in the theory of this; it did but go on the principle of cutting short scruples by the rule of common sense.

And yet what a door was here opened for the dishonesty of mankind! The science itself had dissected moral action until nothing of life or meaning remained in it. It had thrown aside, at the same time, the natural restraint which the moral sense itself exercises in determining such questions. And now for the application of this system, so difficult and complicated in itself, so incapable of receiving any check from the opinions of mankind, the authority, not of the Church, but of individuals, was to be added as a new lever to overthrow the last remains of natural religion and morality.

The marvels of this science are not yet ended. For the same changes admit of being rung upon speech as well as upon action, until truth and falsehood become alike impossible. Language itself dissolves before the decomposing power; oaths, like actions, vanish into air when separated from the intention of the speaker; the shield of custom protects falsehood. It would be a curious though needless task to follow the subject into further details. He who has read one page of the casuists has read all. There is nothing that is not right in some particular point of view, — nothing that is not true under some previous supposition.

Such a system might be left to refute itself. Those who have strayed so far away from truth and virtue are self-condemned. Yet it is not without interest to trace by what false lights of philosophy or religion good men, revolting themselves at the commission of evil, were led, step by step, to the unnatural result. We should expect to find that such a result had originated, not in any settled purpose to corrupt the morals of mankind, but in an intellectual error; and we could hardly avoid reflecting how fearfully and wonderfully our moral nature was composed, when an intellectual error had the power to produce such consequences. Such we find to be the fact. The conception of moral action on which the system depends, is as erroneous and imperfect as that of the scholastic philosophy respecting the nature of ideas.

1. It ignores the difference between thought and action. Actions are necessarily external. The spoken word constitutes the lie; the outward performance, the crime. The highest wisdom, it is true, has identified the two. "He that looketh on a woman to lust after her hath already committed adultery with her in his heart." But this is not the rule by which we are to judge our past actions, but to guard our future ones. He who has thoughts of lust or passion is not innocent in the sight of God, and is liable to be carried on to perform the act on which he suffers himself to dwell. And, in looking forward, he will do well to remember this caution of Christ; but in looking backward, in thinking of others, in endeavoring to estimate the actual amount of guilt or trespass, if he begins by placing thought on the level of action,

he will end by placing action on the level of thought. It would be a monstrous state of mind in which we regarded mere imagination of evil as the same with action; hatred as the same with murder; thoughts of impurity as the same with adultery. It is not so that we must learn Christ. Actions are one thing, and thoughts another, in the eye of conscience, no less than of the law of the land; of God as well as man. Morality ventures a little way into the spiritual world; it would be apt to lose its nature if it went further. However important it may be to us to remember that the all-seeing eye of God tries the reins, it is no less important to remember also that morality consists in definite acts, capable of being seen and judged of by our fellow-creatures, impossible to escape ourselves.

2. It is quite true that actions the same in name, are, in the scale of right and wrong, as different as can be imagined; varying with the age, temperament, education, circumstances of each individual. The casuist is not in fault for maintaining this difference, but for supposing that he can classify or distinguish them so as to give any conception of their innumerable shades and gradations. All his folios are but the weary effort to abstract or make a brief of the individuality of man. The very actions which he classifies change their nature as he writes them down. Know ourselves we sometimes truly may, but we cannot know others, and no other can know us. No other can know or understand us in the same wonderful or mysterious way; no other can be conscious of the spirit in which we have lived. No other can see that which is within. God has placed a veil of flesh between ourselves and other men, to screen the nakedness of our soul. Into the secret chamber he does not require that we should admit any other judge or counsellor but himself. Two eyes only are upon us, — the eye of our own soul, the eye of God, — and the one is assisted by the other. The knowledge which they give us of our own nature is different in kind from that which the confessor extracts from the books of the casuists.

3. There are many cases in which our first thoughts, or, to speak more correctly, our instinctive perceptions, are true and right; in which it is not too much to say, that he who deliberates is lost. The very act of turning to a book, or referring to another, enfeebles our power of action. In the arts we produce an effect, we know not how, by some simultaneous movement of hand and thought, which seem to lend to each other force and meaning. So in moral action, the true view does not separate the intention from the act, or the act from the circumstances which surround it, but regards them as one and absolutely indivisible. In the performance of the act and in the judgment of it, the will and the execution, the hand and the thought, are to be considered as one. Those who act most energetically, who in difficult circumstances judge the most truly, do not separately pass in review the rules, and principles, and counter-principles of action, but grasp them at once, in a single instant. Those who act most truthfully, honestly, firmly, manfully, consistently, take least time to deliberate. Such should be the attitude of our minds in all questions of right and wrong, truth and falsehood: we may not inquire, but act.

4. Casuistry not only renders us independent of our own convictions, it renders us independent also of the opinion of mankind in general. It puts the confessor in the place of ourselves, and in the place of the world. By making the actions of men matters of science, it cuts away the supports and safeguards which public opinion gives to morality. The confessor, in the silence of the closet, easily introduces principles from which the common sense or conscience of mankind would have shrunk back. Especially in matters of truth and falsehood, in the nice sense of honor shown in the unwillingness to get others within our power, his standard will probably fall short of that of the world at large. Public opinion, it is true, drives men's vices inwards; it teaches them to conceal their faults from others, and if possible from themselves, and this very concealment may sink them in despair, or cover them with self-deceit. Yet the good of this is, on the whole, greater

than the evil. Not only is the outward aspect of society more decorous, and the confidence between man and man less liable to be impaired, but the mere fact of men's sins being known to themselves and God only, and the support afforded even by the undeserved opinion of their fellows, are of themselves great helps to a moral and religious life. Many a one by being thought better than he was has become better; by being thought as bad or worse, has become worse. To communicate our sins to those who have no right to know them is of itself a diminution of our moral strength.

To conclude, the errors and evils of casuistry may be summed up as follows: It makes that abstract which is concrete, scientific which is contingent, artificial which is natural, positive which is moral, theoretical which is intuitive and immediate. It puts the parts in the place of the whole, exceptions in the place of rules, system in the place of experience, dependence in the place of responsibility, reflection in the place of conscience. It lowers the heavenly to the earthly, the principles of men to their practice, the tone of the preacher to the standard of ordinary life. It sends us to another for that which can only be found in ourselves. It leaves the highway of public opinion, to wander in the labyrinths of an imaginary science; the light of the world, for the darkness of the closet. It is to human nature what anatomy is to our bodily frame; instead of a moral and spiritual being, preserving only "a body of death."

ON THE CONNECTION OF IMMORALITY AND IDOLATRY.

By BENJAMIN JOWETT.

"An idol is nothing in the world," says the Apostle; "yet he that commits fornication sins against his own body." It is foolishness to bow to an idol; but immorality and licentiousness are real and essential evil. No mere outward act can make a man different from what he was before, while no inward act can leave him the same after as before its performance. A belief about Jupiter or Hades is not necessarily inconsistent with truth and purity of life. The evils, whether of a heathen or of a Christian country, are not always associated with the corruptions of religion. Whence, then, the connection often spoken of by theologians, and not unfelt by the heathen themselves, between immorality and idolatry?

It is first to be sought for in their origin. As the Christian religion may be regarded as the great pillar and rock of morality, so the heathen religions sprang up in an age prior to morality. We see men, in the dawn of the world's history, just raised above the worship of stocks and stones, "making themselves gods to go before them." These gods represent partly the maxims and opinions of uncivilized races, partly the actions and passions of mankind in general, partly the irregularity of the course of the world itself, the fearful law of which is the wayward fancy of heaven. Must not such an enthronement of injustice above tend to confuse and stunt the natural ideas of morality? The God who had possession of the heart of man was a half physical, half demoniacal, and in part also human, being, who represented the vices of mankind on an ideal stage in aggravated proportions, yet not without a certain affinity to man himself. The worst side of humanity, the false notion of the order of the world, the capricious passions of individuals, the enmities of nations, were deified and perpetuated in him. Human nature grew and human beings spread over the earth; but they carried with them, wherever they went, the weary load of superstition, the chains of servitude to their former beliefs, with which their separate existence as a nation seemed to be bound up. Far otherwise would it have been if the good of states, or the dictates of natural feeling and affection, had been made the standard to which religion was to conform. And accordingly it has everywhere happened, that, as reflection has gained ground, or civilization spread, mankind have risen up against the barbarities of early mythology, either openly disowning them or secretly explaining them away; and thus in either case bearing witness that idolatry is not on a level with man's reason, but below it. In the case of the Greeks, especially, many of the grosser forms of religion disappeared from the light of day into the seclusion of the mysteries.

But the connection between idolatry and immorality does not arise merely out of the degradation of the nature of God, or the consecration of the vices of one age, as examples for another. Idolatry is a sort of religious passion, almost on a level with a physical want, which from time to time bursts forth and gives rein to every other passion. In the presence of the gods themselves in the idol's temple, as the festive pomp passes, or the mystic hymn sounds, there is a place for sensuality. It is not repugnant, but acceptable to them, and a part of their service. Impure religious rites are not the invention of magicians or priests, but deeply rooted in human nature itself. Like every other impulse of man, sensual love seeks to find expression, and perceives likenesses and resemblances of itself in the world around. It is one of the elements of nature-worship, consecrated by antiquity, and in later times graced and half concealed by art. The deification of it belongs to the earliest, simplest, grossest forms of human belief. The introduction of the Bacchanalia at a comparatively late period in the history of Greece, and the attempted introduction of them at Rome, is an indication of the partial reawakening of the same religious passions when older modes of faith failed to satisfy them. Yet more monstrous forms of evil arose when in things not to be named men seemed to see a likeness to the operations and powers of nature. The civilized Greek and Roman knew well that there were frenzies of religious licentiousness unworthy of a rational being, improper and dangerous for a government to allow. As East and West met and mingled, the more did these strange rites spread themselves, passing from Egypt and Phœnicia to Greece, from the mountains of Phrygia to the streets and temples of Rome.

But, besides this direct connection between idolatry and every form of moral evil, there is also an indirect and general influence which it exercised, even in its better form, adverse to morality. Not from religion, but from philosophy, come the higher aspirations of the human soul in Greece and Rome. Idolatry detains men in the world of sight; it offers an outward form to the eye and imagery to the fancy; it draws the many-colored veil of art over the corruption of human nature. It heals the strife of man with himself superficially. It takes away the conscious want of the higher life, but leaves the real need. But morality has to do with an unseen world: it has no form nor comeliness, when separated from the hope which the Gospel holds out; it is severe and stoical in its demands. It tells men to look within; it deepens the battle with self. It presents duty almost as an abstraction which in the face of death they must pursue, though there be no reward here, though their name perish for evermore. The spirit of all idolatry is the very opposite of this; it bids men rest in this world, it pacifies them about another. The nature of God, who is the ideal and perfection of all morality, it lowers to the level of man; the virtue which is above, the truth which is beyond us, it embodies in the likeness of the human form, or the wayward and grotesque fancies of the human mind. It bids us seek without for what can only be found within.

There remains yet a further parallel to be drawn between immorality and idolatry in the age in which St. Paul himself lived, when the ancient religions had already begun to be discredited and explained away. At this time they had become customs rather than beliefs, — maxims of state, rather than opinions. It is, indeed, impossible to determine how far in any minds they commanded respect, or how much of the reverence that was refused to established modes of worship was accorded to the claims of newly-imported deities. They were in harmony with the outer world of the Roman Empire, — that is, with its laws, institutions, traditions, buildings; but strangely out of harmony with its inner life. No one turned to the mythology of Greece and Rome to find a rule of life. Perhaps no one had ever done so, but now least of all. Their hold was going or gone; there was a space in the mind of man which they could not longer fill up, in which Stoic and Epicurean philosophers were free to walk; the chill darkness of which might receive a ray of light and warmth from the Alexandrian mystic; where, too, true voices of philosophy and experience might faintly make themselves heard, and the heart ask itself and find its own solution of the problem, "What is truth?" In all this latter period the relation of morality to religion might be said to be one of separation and antagonism. And, upon the whole, this very freedom was favorable to right and truth. It is difficult to determine how far the spectacle of a religion which has outlived its time may corrupt the moral sense, how far the necessary disbelief of an existing superstition tends to weaken and undermine the intellectual faculties of mankind; but there can be little doubt that it does so less than if it were still believed, and still ministered to the sensuality or ignorance of the world.

THE OLD TESTAMENT.

BY BENJAMIN JOWETT.

Ηνίκα δ' ἂν ἐπιστρέψῃ πρὸς κύριον, περιαιρεῖται τὸ κάλυμμα. — 2 Cor. iii. 16.

THUS we have reached another stage in the development of the great theme. The new commandment has become old; faith is taught in the Book of the Law. "Abraham had faith in God, and it was counted to him for righteousness." David spoke of the forgiveness of sins in the very spirit of the Gospel. The Old Testament is not dead, but alive again. It refers not to the past, but to the present. There are the truths that we feel most deeply written for our instruction. There are the consciousness of sin, and the sense of acceptance. There is the veiled remembrance of a former world, which is also the veiled image of a future one.

To us the Old and New Testaments are two books, or two parts of the same book, which fit into one another, and can never be separated or torn asunder. They double one against the other, and the New Testament is the revelation of the Old. To the first believers it was otherwise: as yet there was no New Testament; nor is there any trace that the authors of the New Testament ever expected their own writings to be placed on a level with the Old. We can scarcely imagine what would have been the feeling of St. Paul, could he have foreseen that later ages would look, not to the faith of Abraham in the Law, but to the Epistle to the Romans, as the highest authority on the doctrine of justification by faith; or that they would have regarded the allegory of Hagar and Sarah, in the Galatians, as a difficulty to be resolved by the inspiration of the Apostle. Neither he who wrote, nor those to whom he wrote, could ever have thought, that words which were meant for a particular church were to give life also to all mankind; and that the Epistles in which they occurred were one day to be placed on a level with the Books of Moses themselves.

But if the writings of the New Testament were regarded by the contemporaries of the Apostle in a manner different from that of later ages, there was a difference which it is far more difficult for us to appreciate, in their manner of reading the Old Testament. To them it was not half, but the whole, needing nothing to be added to it or to counteract it, but containing everything in itself. It seemed to come home to them; to be meant specially for their age; to be understood by them as its words had never been understood before. "Did not their hearts burn within them?" as the Apostles expounded to them the Psalms and Prophets. The manner of this exposition was that of the age in which they lived. They brought to the understanding of it, not a knowledge of the volume of the New Testament, but the mind of Christ. Sometimes they found the lesson which they sought in the plain language of Scripture; at other times, coming round to the same lesson by the paths of allegory, or seeming even in the sound of a word to catch an echo of the Redeemer's name. Various as are the writings of the Old Testament, composed by such numerous authors, at so many different times, so diverse in style and subject, in them all they read only — the truth of Christ. They read without distinctions of moral and ceremonial, type and antitype, history or prophecy, without critical inquiries into the original meaning of passages, without theories of the relation of the Old and New Testaments. Whatever contrast existed was of another kind, not of the parts of a book, but of the law and faith; of the earlier and later dispensations. The words of the book were all equally for their instruction; the whole volume lighted up with new meaning.

They read the Old Testament after the manner of their age, and found every verse suggestive of the circumstances of the Church, and of the life and death of Christ. Are we doing more than following their example, if we read the Scriptures by the light of those principles, whether of criticism or of morality, which, in our own age, we cannot but feel and know, and of which it is as impossible for us to divest ourselves, as it would have been for them to fail of seeing Christ in the lives of the Patriarchs?

ON THE QUOTATIONS FROM THE OLD TESTAMENT IN THE NEW.

By BENJAMIN JOWETT.

The New Testament is ever old, and the Old is ever entwined with the New. Not only are the types of the Old Testament shadows of good things to come; not only are the narratives of events and lives of persons in Jewish history "written for our instruction"; not only is there a deep-rooted identity of the Old and New Testament in the revelation of one God of perfect justice and truth; not only is "the law fulfilled in Christ to all them that believe"; not only are the spiritual Israel the true people of God: a still nearer, though more superficial connection is formed by the volume of the Old Testament itself, which, like some closely-fitting vesture, enfolds the new as well as the old dispensation in its language and imagery, the words themselves, as well as the thoughts contained in them, becoming instinct with a new life, and seeming to interpenetrate with the Gospel.

This verbal connection of new and old is not peculiar to Christianity. All nations who have ancient writings have endeavored to read in them the riddle of the past. The Brahmin, repeating his Vedic hymns, sees them pervaded by a thousand meanings, which have been handed down by tradition: the one of which he is ignorant is that which we perceive to be the true one. Without more reason, and almost with an equal disregard or neglect of its natural import, the Jewish Alexandrian and Rabbinical writers analyzed the Old Testament; in a similar spirit Gnostics and Neo-platonists cited lines of Homer or Pindar. Not unlike is the way in which the Fathers cite both the Old and New Testament; and the manner in which the writers of the New Testament quote from the Old has more in common with this last than with modern critical interpretations of either. That is to say, the quotations are made almost always without reference to the connection in which they originally occur, and in a different sense from that in which the Prophet or Psalmist intended them. They are fragments culled out and brought into some new combination; jewels, and precious stones, and corner-stones disposed after a new pattern, to be the ornaments of another temple. It is their place in that new temple, not their relation to the old, which gives them their effect and meaning.

Such "tessellated work" was after the manner of the age: it was no new invention or introduction of the sacred writers. Closely as it is wrought into the New Testament, it belongs to its externals rather than to its true life. There are few, if any, traces of it in the discourses of our Lord himself, though it frequently recurs in the comments of the Evangelists. The fact that all religions which are possessed of sacred books, and many even without them, have passed through a like secondary stage, however different may have been their relation to the earlier forms of the same religions from that in which the Gospel stands to the Old Testament, leads us to regard this verbal connection as a phenomenon of the mind which may receive light from heathen parallels. There seem to be times in which human nature yearns toward the past, though it has lost the power of interpreting it. Overlooking the chasm of a thousand years, it seeks to extract from ancient writings food for daily life. The mystery of a former world lies heavy upon it, hardly less than of the future, and it lightens this burden by attributing to "them of old time" the thoughts and feelings of contemporaries. It feels the unity of God and man in all ages, and it attempts to prove this unity by reading the same thoughts in every word which has been uttered from the beginning. Even the words themselves it will sometimes alter in conformity with the new spirit which appears to pervade them.

The Gnostic and Alexandrian writings are a meeting-point between the past and the future, in which the present is lost sight of, and ideas supersede facts. But something analogous is observable in the New Testament itself; which may be described also as the meeting-point of past and future on the ground of the present, taking its origin, not from ideas, but facts. The mode of thought of the age by which the old is ever new, and the new ever entwined with the old, is common to both; and language, equally with thought, seems to relax its bonds, and lose those harder lines of demarcation and definition which make it incapable of spiritual life. Gradually and naturally, as it were a soul entering into a body that had been prepared for it, the new takes the form of the old. Yet the very truth and power of the Gospel prevent this new creation from resembling the fantastic process of Eastern heresy. The writers of the New Testament adopt the modes of speech and citation of their age, but they also ennoble and enlighten them. That traces of their age should appear in them is the necessary condition of their speaking to the men of their age. To mankind then, as to individuals now, God would have us speak in a language that they can understand.

Still, however striking may be the superficial similarity, essential differences lie beneath. There are three points which may be said to distinguish the manner in which the Old Testament is quoted in the New, from the manner in which early poets are quoted by heathen writers, or the Old Testament itself by Alexandrian or Christian authors. First, the Old Testament looks forward to the New, as the New Testament looks backward on the Old. Reading the Psalmists or Prophets, even with the veil on our eyes, which was also on theirs, we cannot but feel that they were pilgrims and strangers, looking for more than was on the earth, whose sadness was not yet turned into joy. There are passages in which the Old Testament goes beyond itself, in which it almost seems to renounce itself; even solitary expressions, of which it might be said, either in Christian or heathen language, "that it speaks not of itself"; or, that "its voice reaches to a thousand years." It is otherwise with heathen literature. There is no future to which Homer or Hesiod looked forward; no higher moral truth beyond themselves which they dimly see. The life of the world was not to awaken in their song. They were poetry only, out of which came statues of gods and heroes. Secondly, if the connection between the Old and New Testament be on the surface arbitrary, or, more properly speaking, after the manner of the age, that deeper connection which lies below is founded on reason and conscience. The language of the greater part of the Old Testament is the natural, may we not say the most true and inward, expression of Christian feeling. In the hour of sorrow, or joy, or repentance, or triumph, we seem to turn to the Old Testament even more readily than to the New. Thirdly and lastly, not to speak of the great difference in degree, a difference in kind is observable between the way in which quotations are made use of by the Alexandrian writers and in the New Testament. In the one they are the form of thought; in the other, the mode of expression. That is to say, while in the one they exercise an influence on the thought; in the other, they are controlled by it, and are but a sort of incrustation on it, or ornament of it; in some cases the illustration or allegory through which it is conveyed. The writings of St. Paul are not the less one in feeling and spirit because the language in which he continually clothes his thoughts is either avowedly or unconsciously taken from the Old Testament.

Even in our own use of quotations we may observe a sort of necessary inconsistency which illustrates the mode of citation in the New Testament. We resort to quotation not only as an ingenious device for expressing our meaning; it is also an appeal to an authority. And yet its point or force frequently consists in a slight, or even a great, deviation from the sense in which a quotation was uttered by its author. Its aptness lies in its being at once old and new; often in bringing into juxtaposition things so remote, that we should not have imagined they were connected; sometimes in a word rather than in a sentence, even in the substitution of a word, or in a logical inference not wholly warranted.

Something analogous to this we find in the quotations of the New Testament. They unite a kind of authority with a new interpretation of the passage quoted. Sometimes the application of them is a sort of argument from their exact rhetorical or even grammatical form. Their connection often hangs upon a word, and there are passages in which the word on which the connection turns is itself inserted. There are citations too, which are a composition of more than one passage, in which the spirit is taken from one and the words from another. There are other citations in which a similarity of spirit, rather than of language, is caught up and made use of by the Apostle. There are passages which are altered to suit the meaning given to them; or in which the spirit of the New Testament is substituted for that of the Old; or the spirit of the Old Testament expands into that of the New. Lastly, there are passages, though but few of them occur in the writings of St. Paul, which have one sense in the Old Testament, and have an entirely different or opposite one in the New. Almost all gradations occur between exact verbal correspondence with the Greek of the LXX.; and discrepancy in which resemblance is all but lost: between the greatest similarity and difference, almost opposition, of spirit in the original passage and its application. In no passage in the Epistles of St. Paul is there any certain evidence that the first connection was present to the Apostle's mind.

The quotations in the writings of St. Paul may be classified under the following heads:—

I. Passages in which (α.) the meaning, and (β.) the words of the Old Testament are altered, or (γ.) both: the alterations, sometimes arising from no assignable cause, sometimes from a composition of passages.

II. Passages in which (α.) the spirit or (β.) the language of the Old Testament is exactly retained, or with no greater variation of words than may be supposed to arise out of difference of texts, and no greater diversity of spirit than necessarily arises from the transfer of any passage in the Old Testament into another connection in the New.

III. Allegorical passages.

I. (1.) An instance in which the meaning of the quotation has been altered, and also in which the new meaning given to it is derived from another passage, occurs in Rom. ii. 24: *τὸ γὰρ ὄνομα τοῦ θεοῦ δι' ὑμᾶς βλασφημεῖται ἐν τοῖς ἔθνεσιν·* where the Apostle is speaking of the scandal caused by the violence and hypocrisy of the Jews. The words are taken from Isa. lii. 5: *δι' ὑμᾶς διαπαντὸς τὸ ὄνομά μου βλασφημεῖται ἐν τοῖς ἔθνεσι·* where, however, they refer, not to the sins of the house of Israel, but to their sufferings at the hand of their enemies. The turn which the Apostle has given the passage is gathered from Ezek. xxxvi. 21–23: *καὶ ἐφεισάμην αὐτῶν διὰ τὸ ὄνομά μου τὸ ἅγιον ὃ ἐβεβήλωσαν οἶκος Ἰσραὴλ ἐν τοῖς ἔθνεσιν οὗ εἰσήλθοσαν ἐκεῖ, κ. τ. λ.*

A composition of passages occurs also in Rom. xi. 8, which appears to be a union of Isa. vi. 9, 10 and xxix. 10. The play upon the word *ἔθνη* (nations = Gentiles) is repeated in Rom. iv. 17 (Gen. xvii. 5), Gal. iii. 8 (Gen. xii. 3).

(2.) A similar instance in which the general tone of a quotation is taken from one passage, and a few words added from another, is to be found in Rom. ix. 33: *ἰδοὺ τίθημι ἐν Σιὼν λίθον προσκόμματος καὶ πέτραν σκανδάλου καὶ ὁ πιστεύων ἐπ' αὐτῷ οὐ καταισχυνθήσεται.* The greater part of this passage occurs in Isa. xxviii. 16: *ἰδοὺ ἐγὼ ἐμβάλλω εἰς τὰ θεμέλια Σιὼν λίθον πολυτελῆ, ἔκλεκτον, ἀκρογωνιαῖον, ἔντιμον, εἰς τὰ θεμέλια αὐτῆς, καὶ ὁ πιστεύων οὐ μὴ καταισχύνθῃ.* But the words *λίθον προσκόμματος* are introduced from Isa. viii. 14. And the remainder of the passage (*καὶ . . . . καταισχυνθήσεται*) is really inconsistent with these words, though both parts are harmonized in Him who is in one sense a stumbling-stone and rock of offence; in another, a foundation-stone and chief corner-stone.

(3.) A slighter example of alteration occurs in 1 Cor. iii. 19, where the Apostle quotes from Ps. xciv. 11: κύριος γινώσκει τοὺς διαλογισμοὺς τῶν σόφων ὅτι εἰσὶ μάταιοι. Here the words τῶν σόφων are substituted for τῶν ἀνθρώπων in the LXX., which in this passage agrees with the Hebrew. They are required to connect the quotation in the Epistle with the previous verses. A similar instance of the introduction of a word (πᾶς) on which the point of an argument turns, occurs in Rom. x. 11: λέγει γὰρ ἡ γραφή· πᾶς ὁ πιστεύων ἐπ' αὐτῷ οὐ καταισχυνθήσεται· where the addition is the more remarkable, as the Apostle had quoted the words without πᾶς a few verses previously.

(4.) Another instance of addition, rather than alteration, is furnished by 1 Cor. xiv. 21: ἐν τῷ νόμῳ γέγραπται· ὅτι ἐν ἑτερογλώσσοις καὶ ἐν χείλεσιν ἑτέρων λαλήσω τῷ λαῷ τούτῳ, καὶ οὐδ' οὕτως εἰσακούσονταί μου, λέγει κύριος. This quotation, which is said to be "written in the law" (comp. John x. 34, xii. 34, xv. 25), is from Isa. xxviii. 11, 12, where the words in the LXX. are διὰ φαυλισμὸν χειλέων, διὰ γλώσσης ἑτέρας, ὅτι λαλήσουσι τῷ λαῷ τούτῳ, and in the English translation, "with stammering lips and another tongue will he speak unto this people." But the last words, οὐδ' οὕτως εἰσακούσονται, are taken from the following verse, where a clause nearly similar occurs in a different connection: λέγοντες αὐτοῖς, τοῦτο τὸ ἀνάπαυμα τῷ πεινῶντι, καὶ τοῦτο τὸ σύντριμμα, καὶ οὐκ ἠθέλησαν ἀκούειν, v. 12. The whole is referred by the Apostle to the gift of tongues, which he infers from this passage "to be a sign to unbelievers."

(5.) An adaptation, which has led to an alteration of words, occurs in Rom. x. 6–9: ἡ δὲ ἐκ πίστεως δικαιοσύνη οὕτω λέγει· μὴ εἴπῃς ἐν τῇ καρδίᾳ σου· τίς ἀναβήσεται εἰς τὸν οὐρανόν; τοῦτ' ἔστι χριστὸν καταγαγεῖν· ἢ τίς καταβήσεται εἰς τὴν ἄβυσσον; τοῦτ' ἔστι χριστὸν ἐκ νεκρῶν ἀναγαγεῖν. ἀλλὰ τί λέγει; ἐγγύς σου τὸ ῥῆμά ἐστιν, ἐν τῷ στόματί σου καὶ ἐν τῇ καρδίᾳ σου· τοῦτ' ἔστι τὸ ῥῆμα τῆς πίστεως, ὃ κηρύσσομεν· ὅτι ἐὰν ὁμολογήσῃς ἐν τῷ στόματί σου κύριον Ἰησοῦν, καὶ πιστεύσῃς ἐν τῇ καρδίᾳ σου ὅτι ὁ θεὸς αὐτὸν ἤγειρεν ἐκ νεκρῶν, σωθήσῃ. The substance of this passage is taken from Deut. xxx. 11 – 14: *ὅτι ἡ ἐντολὴ αὕτη ἣν ἐγὼ ἐντέλλομαί σοι σήμερον οὐχ ὑπέρογκός ἐστιν, οὐδὲ μακρὰν ἀπὸ σοῦ ἐστιν· οὐκ ἐν τῷ οὐρανῷ ἄνω ἐστὶ, λέγων· τίς ἀναβήσεται ἡμῖν εἰς τὸν οὐρανὸν, καὶ λήψεται ἡμῖν αὐτὴν, καὶ ἀκούσαντες αὐτὴν ποιήσομεν; οὐδὲ πέραν τῆς θαλάσσης ἐστὶ, λέγων· τίς διαπεράσει ἡμῖν εἰς τὸ πέραν τῆς θαλάσσης, καὶ λάβῃ ἡμῖν αὐτὴν, καὶ ἀκουστὴν ἡμῖν ποιήσῃ αὐτὴν, καὶ ποιήσομεν; ἐγγύς σού ἐστι τὸ ῥῆμα σφόδρα, ἐν τῷ στόματί σου καὶ ἐν τῇ καρδίᾳ σοῦ καὶ ἐν ταῖς χερσί σου, ποιεῖν αὐτό.* To these verses the Apostle has added what may be termed a running commentary, applying them to Christ. To make the words *πέραν τῆς θαλάσσης* thus applicable, the Apostle has altered them to *εἰς τὴν ἄβυσσον*, a change which we should hesitate to attribute to him, but for the other examples which have been already quoted of similar changes. (Compare also Rom. xi. 8; xii. 19; Eph. v. 14. The latter passage, in which the name of Christ is introduced as here, being probably an adaptation of Isa. lx. 1.) Considering the frequency of such changes, it would be contrary to the rules of sound criticism to attribute the introduction of the words to a difference of text in the Old Testament.

(6.) The words of 1 Cor. xv. 45, *οὕτως καὶ γέγραπται· Ἐγένετο ὁ πρῶτος Ἀδὰμ εἰς ψυχὴν ζῶσαν· ὁ ἔσχατος Ἀδὰμ εἰς πνεῦμα ζωοποιοῦν*, afford a remarkable instance of discrepancy, both in words and meaning, from Gen. ii. 7: *ἐνεφύσησεν εἰς τὸ πρόσωπον αὐτοῦ πνοὴν ζωῆς· καὶ ἐγένετο ὁ ἄνθρωπος εἰς ψυχὴν ζῶσαν·* to the two clauses of which the Apostle appears to have applied a distinction analogous to that which Philo draws (De Legum Alleg., I. 12; De' Creat. Mun., 24, 46) between the earthly and the heavenly man (Gen. ii. 7 and i. 27).

II. A good example of the second class of quotations is the passage from Hab. ii. 4, quoted in Rom. i. 17: *ὁ δὲ δίκαιος ἐκ πίστεως ζήσεται·* which occurs also in two other places, Heb. x. 38, Gal. iii. 11, which the LXX. read, *ὁ δὲ δίκαιος ἐκ πίστεώς μου ζήσεται*, and the English version translates from the Hebrew, "but the just shall live by *his* faith." It is remarkable, that in Rom. i. 17, Gal. iii. 11, it should be quoted in the same manner, and that slightly different either from the LXX. or the Hebrew; in Heb. x. 38 it agrees precisely with the LXX. Like the other great text of the Apostle, "Abraham believed God, and it was counted to him for righteousness," it is an instance of the way in which the language of the Old Testament was enlarged and universalized in the New; the particular faith of Abraham or of the Israelite becoming the type of faith generally for all mankind in all ages.

Other examples of the second class of quotations are to be found in such passages as the following: "Blessed is the man whose iniquity is forgiven, and whose sin is pardoned; blessed is the man to whom the Lord doth not impute sin," Rom. iv. 7, from Ps. xxxii. 1, 2. "The reproaches of them that reproached thee fell on me," Rom. xv. 3, from Ps. lxix. 9. "Who hath believed our report?" Rom. x. 16, from Isa. liii. 1; in which the instinct of the Apostle has caught the common spirit of the Old and New Testament, though the texts quoted contain no word which is a symbol of his doctrine.

Passages which might be placed under either head are Rom. x. 13, "Jacob have I loved, and Esau have I hated," the words of which exactly agree with the LXX., although their original meaning in Mal. i. 2, 3, whence they are taken, has to do, not with the individuals Jacob and Esau, but with the natives of Edom and Israel: the cento of quotations in Rom. iii. descriptive of the wickedness of the Psalmist's enemies, or of those who were the subjects of the prophetical denunciations, which are transferred by the Apostle to the world in general, Rom. xii. 20, "Therefore if thine enemy hunger, feed him; if he thirst, give him drink; for in so doing thou shalt heap coals of fire on his head," the words of which are exactly quoted from the LXX. (Prov. xxv. 21, 22), though the meaning given to them is ironical; for which reason the succeeding clause, "But the Lord shall reward thee," which would have destroyed the irony, is omitted.

III. Once more. In a few passages only the Apostle, after

the manner of his time, has recourse to allegory. These are: 1. The allegory of the woman who had lost her husband, in Rom. vii.; 2. Of the children of Israel in the wilderness, in 1 Cor. x.; 3. Of Hagar and Sarah, in Gal. iii.; 4. Of the veil on the face of Moses, in 2 Cor. iii.; 5. Abraham himself, who is a kind of centre of allegory, the actions of whose life, as well as the promises of God to him, are symbols of the coming dispensation; 6. The history of the patriarchs, and cutting short of the house of Israel, in Rom. ix., x. Of these examples, the first, third, and fourth are what we should term illustrations; while the second, fifth, and sixth have not merely an analogous or metaphorical meaning, but a real inward connection with the life and state of the first believers.

A few general results of an examination of the quotations from the Old Testament in St. Paul's Epistles, may be summed as follows: —

1. The whole number of quotations is about eighty-seven, of which about fifty-three are found in the Romans, fifteen in 1 Corinthians, six in 2 Corinthians, ten in Galatians, two in the Ephesians, one in 1 Timothy. Of these nearly half show a precise verbal agreement with the LXX.; while, of the remaining passages, at least two thirds exhibit a degree of verbal similarity which can only be accounted for by an acquaintance with the LXX.

2. None of these passages offer any certain proof that the Apostle was acquainted with the Hebrew original. That he must have been acquainted with it can hardly be doubted yet it seems improbable that he could have familiarly known it without straying into parallelisms with the Hebrew text, in those passages in which it varies from the LXX. His acquaintance with it was probably of such a kind as we might acquire of a version of the Scriptures not in the vernacular. No Englishman incidentally quoting the English version from memory would adapt it to the Greek, though he might very probably adapt the Greek to the English. On the other hand, the Apostle must have possessed a minute knowledge of the LXX., as is found by the fragmentary character of the quotations, no less than their verbal agreement.

3. Several of these quotations are what may be termed latent quotations, as, for example, Rom. iii. 4; x. 18; 1 Cor. vi. 2; ix. 7; xv. 25, 27; while a few others, as, for example, Rom. xii. 19; 1 Cor. xv. 45, are hardly, if at all, discernible in the text of the Old Testament. The very familiarity with the Old Testament which has led to the first of these two phenomena, may be in part also the cause of the second. As the words suggest themselves unconsciously, so the spirit without the words occasionally comes into the Apostle's mind; or the language and spirit of different passages blend in one.

4. There is no evidence that the Apostle remembered the verbal connection in which any of the passages quoted by him originally occurred. He isolates them wholly from their context; he reasons from them as he might from statements of his own, "going off upon a word," as it has been called, in one instance almost upon a letter (Gal. iii. 16), drawing inferences which in strict logic can hardly be allowed, extending the meaning of words beyond their first and natural sense. But all this only implies that he uses quotations from the Old Testament after the manner of his age; clinging more than his contemporaries to the spirit and less to the letter, his very inaccuracy about the letter arising partly from his feeling for the spirit.

5. It seems strange that the Apostle should use the law to establish the law, and at the same time condemn the law by itself. What made him apply one text to the law, "The man that doeth these things shall live in them," and another to the Gospel, "The word is very nigh unto thee, even in thy mouth and in thy heart?" No answer can be given to this question. To separate the Old Testament into two parts, to throw away one half, and make the other the means of conveying the Gospel to the minds of his hearers, to bring forth from his treasury things new and old, and to harmonize all in one spirit, is a part of his appointed mission.

FRAGMENT ON THE CHARACTER OF ST. PAUL.

By BENJAMIN JOWETT.

Οἴδατε δὲ ὅτι δι' ἀσθένειαν τῆς σαρκὸς εὐηγγελισάμην ὑμῖν τὸ πρότερον, καὶ τὸν πειρασμὸν ὑμῶν ἐν τῇ σαρκί μου· οὐκ ἐξουθενήσατε οὐδὲ ἐξεπτύσατε, ἀλλὰ ὡς ἄγγελον θεοῦ ἐδέξασθέ με, ὡς Χριστὸν Ἰησοῦν. — Gal. iv. 13, 14.

THE narrative of the Gospel gives no full or perfect likeness of the character of the Apostles. Human beings do not admit of being constructed out of a single feature; nor is imagination able to supply details which are really wanting. St. Peter and St. John, the two Apostles whose names are most prominent in the Gospels and early portion of the Acts, both seem to unite two extremes in the same person; the character of St. John combining gentleness with vehemence, almost with fierceness; while in St. Peter we seem to trace rashness and timidity at once, the spirit of freedom at one period of his life, and of narrowness and exclusiveness at another. He is the first to confess, and the first to deny Christ. Himself the captain of the Apostles, and yet wanting in the very qualities necessary to constitute a leader. Such extremes may easily meet in the same person; but we do not possess sufficient knowledge to say how they were really reconciled. Each of the Apostles grew up to the fulness of the stature of the perfect man. Even those, who to us are little more than names, had individual features as lively as our own contemporaries. But the mention of their sayings or acts on four or five occasions while they followed the footsteps of the Lord on earth, and then on two or three occasions soon after he was taken from them, then once again after an interval of twelve or fourteen years, is not sufficient to enable us to judge of their whole character. We may distinguish Peter from John, or James from either; but we cannot set them up as a study to be compared with each other.

More features appear of the character of St. Paul, yet not sufficient to give a perfect picture. We should lose the individuality which we have, by seeking to idealize and generalize from some more common type of Christian life. It has not been unusual to describe St. Paul as a man of resolute will, of commanding energy, of high-souled eloquence, of classic taste. Not of such a one would the Apostle himself "have gloried." It was not the wisdom of this world which he spoke, but "the hidden wisdom of God in a mystery." All his life long he felt himself to be one "whose strength was perfected in weakness"; he was aware of the impression of feebleness which his own appearance and discourse made upon his converts; who was sometimes in weakness and fear and trembling before them, "having the sentence of death in himself," and at other times "in power and the Holy Ghost and in much assurance"; and so far from having one unchanging purpose or insight, that though determined to know one thing only, "Jesus Christ and him crucified," yet in his manner of teaching he wavers between opposite views or precepts in successive verses. He is ever feeling, if haply he may find them, after the hearts of men. He is carried away by sympathy, at times even for his opponents. He is struggling to express what is in process of revelation to him. Such are some of the individual traits which he has left in his writings; they are traits far more interesting and more like himself than any general image of heroism or goodness. Whatever other impression he might have made upon us, could we have seen him face to face, there can be little doubt that he would have left the impression of what was remarkable and uncommon.

There are questions which it is interesting to suggest, even when they can never receive a perfect and satisfactory answer. One of these questions may be asked respecting St. Paul: "What was the relation in which his former life stood to the great fact of his conversion?" He himself, in looking back upon the times in which he persecuted the Church of God, thought of them chiefly as an increasing evidence of the mercy of God, which was afterwards extended to him. It seemed so strange to have been what he had been, and to be what he was. Nor does our own conception of him, in relation to his former self, commonly reach beyond this contrast of the old and new man; the persecutor and the preacher of the Gospel; the young man at whose feet the witnesses against Stephen laid down their clothes, and the same Paul disputing against the Grecians, full of visions and revelations of the Lord, on whom in later life came daily the care of all the churches.

Yet we cannot but admit also the possibility, or rather the probable truth, of another point of view. If there were any among the contemporaries of St. Paul who had known him in youth and in age, they would have seen similarities such as escape us in the character of the Apostle at different periods of his life. The zealot against the Gospel might have seemed to them transfigured into the opponent of the law; they would have found something in common in the Pharisee of the Pharisees, brought up at the feet of Gamaliel, and the man who had a vow on his last journey to Jerusalem. And when they heard the narrative of his conversion from his own lips, they might have remarked that to one of his temperament only could such an event have happened, and would have noted many superficial resemblances which showed him to be the same man, while the great inward change which had overflowed upon the world was hid from their eyes.

The gifts of God to man have ever some reference to natural disposition. He who becomes the servant of God does not thereby cease to be himself. Often the transition is greater in appearance than in reality, from its very suddenness. There is a kind of rebellion against self and nature and God, which, through the mercy of God to the soul, seems almost necessarily to lead to reaction. Persons have been worse than their fellow-men in outward appearance, and yet there was within them the spirit of a child waiting to return home to their father's house. A change passes upon them which we may figure to ourselves, not only as the new man taking the place of the old, but as the inner man taking the place of the outer. So fearfully and wonderfully are we made, that the very contrast to what we are has often an inexpressible power over us. It seems sometimes as if the same religious education had tended to contrary results; in one case to a devout life, in another to a reaction against it; sometimes to one form of faith, at other times to another. Many parents have wept to see the early religious training of their children draw them, by a kind of repulsion, to a communion which is the extreme opposite of that in which they have been brought up. Such facts as these have but a remote bearing on the character of St. Paul; but they serve to make us think, that all spiritual influences, however antagonistic they may appear, have more in common with each other than they have with the temper of the world; and that it is easier to pass from one form of faith to another, than from leading the life of all men to either. There is more in common between those who anathematize each other, than between either and the spirit of toleration which characterizes the ordinary dealings of man and man, or much more the Spirit of Christ, for whom they are alike contending.

Perhaps we shall not be far wrong in concluding, that those who have undergone great religious changes, have been of a fervid, imaginative cast of mind; looking for more in this world than it was capable of yielding; easily touched by the remembrance of the past, or inspired by some ideal of the future. When with this has been combined a zeal for the good of their fellow-men, they have become the heralds and champions of the religious movements of the world. The change has begun within, but has overflowed without them. "When thou art converted, strengthen thy brethren," is the order of nature and of grace. In secret they brood over their own state; weary and profitless their soul fainteth within them. The religion they profess is a religion not of life to them, but of death; they lose their interest in the world, and are cut off from the communion of their fellow-men. While they are musing, the fire kindles, and at the last "they speak with their tongue." Then pours forth irrepressibly the pent-up stream "unto all and upon all" their fellow-men; the intense flame of inward enthusiasm warms and lights up the world. First, they are the evidence to others; then, again, others are the evidence to them. All religious leaders cannot be reduced to a single type of character; yet in all, perhaps, two characteristics may be observed; the first, great self-reflection; the second, intense sympathy with other men. They are not the creatures of habit or of circumstance, leading a blind life, unconscious of what they are; their whole effort is to realize their inward nature, and to make it palpable and visible to their fellows. Unlike other men who are confined to the circle of themselves or of their family, their affections are never straitened; they embrace with their love all men who are like-minded with them; almost all men too, who are unlike them, in the hope that they may become like.

Such men have generally appeared at favorable conjunctures of circumstances, when the old was about to vanish away, and the new to appear. The world has yearned towards them, and they towards the world. They have uttered what all men were feeling; they have interpreted the age to itself. But for the concurrence of circumstances, they might have been stranded on the solitary shore, they might have died without a follower or convert. But when the world has needed them and God has intended them for the world, they are endued with power from on high; they use all other men as their instruments, uniting them to themselves.

Often such men have been brought up in the faith which they afterwards oppose, and a part of their power has consisted in their acquaintance with the enemy. They see other men, like themselves formerly, wandering out of the way in the idol's temple, amid a burdensome ceremonial, with prayers and sacrifices unable to free the soul. They lead them by the way themselves came to the home of Christ. Sometimes they represent the new as the truth of the old; at other times as contrasted with it, as life and death, as good and evil, as Christ and anti-Christ. They relax the force of habit, they melt the pride and fanaticism of the soul. They suggest to others their own doubts, they inspire them with their own hopes, they supply their own motives, they draw men to them with cords of sympathy and bonds of love; they themselves seem a sufficient stay to support the world. Such was Luther at the Reformation; such, in a far higher sense, was the Apostle St. Paul.

There have been heroes in the world, and there have been prophets in the world. The first may be divided into two classes; either they have been men of strong will and character, or of great power and range of intellect; in a few instances, combining both. They have been the natural leaders of mankind, compelling others by their acknowledged superiority as rulers and generals; or in the paths of science and philosophy, drawing the world after them by a yet more inevitable necessity. The prophet belongs to another order of beings: he does not master his thoughts; they carry him away. He does not see clearly into the laws of this world or the affairs of this world, but has a light beyond, which reveals them partially in their relation to another. Often he seems to be at once both the weakest and the strongest of men; the first to yield to his own impulses, the mightiest to arouse them in others. Calmness, or reason, or philosophy are not the words which describe the appeals which he makes to the hearts of men. He sways them to and fro rather than governs or controls them. He is a poet, and more than a poet, the inspired teacher of mankind; but the intellectual gifts which he possesses are independent of knowledge, or learning, or capacity; what they are much more akin to is the fire and subtlety of genius. He too, for a time, has ruled kingdoms and even led armies; "an Apostle, not of man, nor by men"; acting, not by authority or commission of any prince, but by an immediate inspiration from on high communicating itself to the hearts of men.

Saul of Tarsus is called an Apostle rather than a prophet, because Hebrew prophecy belongs to an age of the world before Christianity. Now that in the Gospel that which is perfect is come, that which is in part is done away. Yet, in a secondary sense, the Apostle St. Paul is also "among the prophets." He, too, has "visions and revelations of the Lord," though he has not written them down "for our instruction," in which he would fain glory because they are not his own. Even to the outward eye he has the signs of a prophet. There is in him the same emotion, the same sympathy, the same "strength made perfect in weakness," the same absence of human knowledge, the same subtilty in the use of language, the same singleness in the delivery of his message. He speaks more as a man, and less immediately under the impulse of the Spirit of God; more to individuals, and less to the nation at large; he is less of a poet, and more of a teacher or preacher. But these differences do not interfere with the general resemblance. Like Isaiah, he bids us look to "the man of sorrows"; like Ezekiel, he arouses men to a truer sense of the ways of God in his dealings with them; like Jeremiah, he mourns over his countrymen; like all the prophets who have ever been, he is lifted above this world, and is "in the Spirit at the day of the Lord." (Rev. i. 10.)

Reflections of this kind are suggested by the absence of materials such as throw any light on the early life of St. Paul. All that we know of him before his conversion is summed up in two facts, "that the witnesses laid down their clothes with a young man whose name was Saul," and that he was brought up at the feet of Gamaliel, one of the few Rabbinical teachers of Greek learning in the city of Jerusalem. We cannot venture to assign him either to the "choleric" or the "melancholic" temperament. [Tholuck.] We are unable to determine what were his natural gifts or capacities; or how far, as we often observe to be the case, the gifts which he had were called out by the mission on which he was sent, or the theatre on which he felt himself placed "a spectacle to the world, to angels, and to men." Far more interesting is it to trace the simple feelings with which he himself regarded his former life. "Last of all he was seen of me also, who am the least of the Apostles, that am not worthy to be called an Apostle, because I persecuted the Church of God." Yet there was a sense also that he was excusable, and that this was the reason why the mercy of God extended itself to him. "Yet I obtained mercy, because I did it ignorantly in unbelief." And in one passage he dwells on the fact, not only that he had been an Israelite, but more, that after the strictest sect of the Jews' religion he lived a Pharisee, as though that were an evidence to himself, and should be so to others, that no human power could have changed him; that he was no half Jew, who had never properly known what the law was, but one who had both known and strictly practised it.

We are apt to judge extraordinary men by our own standard; that is to say, we often suppose them to possess, in an extraordinary degree, those qualities which we are conscious of in ourselves or others. This is the easiest way of conceiving their characters, but not the truest. They differ in kind rather than in degree. Even to understand them truly seems to require a power analogous to their own. Their natures are more subtile, and yet more simple, than we readily imagine. No one can read the ninth chapter of the First, or the eleventh and twelfth chapters of the Second Epistle to the Corinthians, without feeling how different the Apostle St. Paul must have been from good men among ourselves. We marvel how such various traits of character come together in the same individual. He who was "full of visions and revelations of the Lord," who spake with tongues more than they all, was not "mad, but uttered the words of truth and soberness." He who was the most enthusiastic of all men, was also the most prudent; the Apostle of freedom, and yet the most moderate. He who was the strongest and most enlightened of all men, was also (would he have himself refrained from saying?) at times the weakest; on whom there came the care of all the churches, yet seeming also to lose the power of acting in the absence of human sympathy.

Qualities so like and unlike are hard to reconcile; perhaps they have never been united in the same degree in any other human being. The contradiction in part arises, not only from the Apostle being an extraordinary man, but from his being a man like ourselves in an extraordinary state. Creation was not to him that fixed order of things which it is to us; rather it was an atmosphere of evil just broken by the light beyond. To us the repose of the scene around contrasts with the turmoil of man's own spirit; to the Apostle peace was to be sought only from within, half hidden even from the inner man. There was a veil upon the heart itself which had to be removed. He himself seemed to fall asunder at times into two parts, the flesh and the spirit; and the world to be divided into two hemispheres, the one of the rulers of darkness, the other bright with that inward presenee which should one day be revealed. In this twilight he lived. What to us is far off both in time and place, if such an éxpression may be allowed, to him was near and present, separated by a thin film from the world we see, ever ready to break forth and gather into itself the frame of nature. That sense of the invisible which to most men it is so difficult to impart, was like a second nature to St. Paul. He walked by faith, and not by sight; what was strange to him was the life he now led; which in his own often repeated language was death rather than life, the place of shadows, and not of realities. The Greek philosophers spoke of a world of phenomena, of true being, of knowledge, and opinion; and we know that what they meant by these distinctions is something different from the tenets of any philosophical school of the present day. But not less different is what St. Paul meant by the life hidden with Christ in God, the communion of the spirit, the possession of the mind of Christ; only that this was not a mere difference of speculation, but of practice also. Could any one say now,—"the life," not that I live, but that "Christ liveth in me"? Such language with St. Paul is no mere phraseology, such as is repeated from habit in prayers, but the original consciousness of the Apostle respecting his own state. Self is banished from him, and has no more place in him, as he goes on his way to fulfil the work of Christ. No figure is too strong to express his humiliation in himself, or his exaltation in Christ.

Could we expect this to be otherwise when we look back at the manner of his conversion? Could he have looked upon the world with the same eyes that we do, or heard its many voices with the same ears, who had been caught up into the seventh heaven, whether in the body, or out of the body, he could not tell? Must not his whole life have seemed to him like a gradual revelation, an inspiration, an ecstasy? Once he had looked upon the face of Christ, and heard Him speak from heaven. All that followed in the Apostle's history was continuous with that event, a stream of light flowing from it, "planting eyes" in his soul, transfiguring him "from glory to glory," clothing him with the elect "in the exceeding glory."

Yet this glory was not that of the princes of this world, "who come to naught": it is another image which he gives us of himself;—not the figure on Mars' hill, in the cartoons of Raphael, nor the orator with noble mien and eloquent gesture before Festus and Agrippa; but the image of one lowly and cast down, whose bodily presence was weak, and speech contemptible; of one who must have appeared to the rest of mankind like a visionary, pierced by the thorn in the flesh, waiting for the redemption of the body. The saints of the Middle Ages are in many respects unlike St. Paul, and yet many of them bear a far closer resemblance to him than is to be found in Luther and the Reformers. The points of resemblance which we seem to see in them are the same withdrawal from the things of earth, the same ecstasy, the same consciousness of the person of Christ. Who would describe Luther by the words "crucified with Christ"? It is in another manner that the Reformer was called upon to war,—with weapons earthly as well as spiritual, with a strong right hand and a mighty arm.

There have been those who, although deformed by nature, have worn the expression of a calm and heavenly beauty; in whom the flashing eye has attested the presence of thought in the poor, withered, and palsied frame. There have been others again, who have passed the greater part of their lives in intense bodily suffering, who have, nevertheless, directed states or led armies, the keenness of whose intellect has not been dulled, nor their natural force of mind abated. There have been those also, on whose faces men have gazed "as upon the face of an angel," while they pierced or stoned them. Of such an one, perhaps, the Apostle himself might have gloried; not of those whom men term great or noble. He who felt the whole creation groaning and travailing together until now, was not like the Greek drinking in the life of nature at every pore. He who through Christ was crucified to the world, and the world to him, was not in harmony with nature, nor nature with him. The manly form, the erect step, the fulness of life and beauty, could not have gone along with such a consciousness as this; any more than the taste for literature and art could have consisted with the thought, "not many wise, not many learned, not many mighty." Instead of these, we have the visage marred more than the sons of men, the cross of Christ to the Greeks foolishness, the thorn in the flesh, the marks in his body of the Lord Jesus.

Often the Apostle St. Paul has been described as a person the furthest removed from enthusiasm; incapable of spiritual illusion; by his natural temperament averse to credulity or superstition. By such considerations as these a celebrated author confesses himself to have been converted to the belief in Christianity. And yet, if it is intended to reduce St. Paul to the type of what is termed "good sense" in the present day, it must be admitted that the view which thus describes him is but partially true. Far nearer the truth is that other quaint notion of a modern writer, "that St. Paul was the finest gentleman that ever lived"; for no man had nobler forms of courtesy, or a deeper regard for the feelings of others. But "good sense" is a term not well adapted to express either the individual, or the age and country in which he lived. He who wrought miracles, who had handkerchiefs carried to him from the sick, who spake with tongues more than they all, who lived amid visions and revelations of the Lord, who did not appeal to the Gospel as a thing long settled, but, himself, saw the process of revelation actually going on before his eyes, and communicated it to his fellow-men, could never have been such an one as ourselves. Nor can we pretend to estimate whether, in the modern sense of the term, he was capable of weighing evidence; or how far he would have attempted to sever between the workings of his own mind and the Spirit which was imparted to him.

What has given rise to this conception of the Apostle's character has been the circumstance, that with what the world terms mysticism and enthusiasm are united a singular prudence and moderation, and a perfect humanity, searching the feelings and knowing the hearts of all men. "I became all things to all men, that I might win some"; not only, we may believe, as a sort of accommodation, but as the expression of the natural compassion and love which he felt for them. There is no reason to suppose that the Apostle took any interest in the daily life of men, in the great events which were befalling the Roman Empire, or in the temporal fortunes of the Jewish people. But when they came before him as sinners, lying in darkness and the shadow of God's wrath, ignorant of the mystery that was being revealed before their eyes, then his love was quickened for them, then they seemed to him as his kindred and brethren; there was no sacrifice too great for him to make; he was willing to die with Christ, yea, even to be accursed from Him, that he might "save some of them."

Mysticism, or enthusiasm, or intense benevolence and philanthropy, seem to us, as they commonly are, at variance with worldly prudence and moderation. But in the Apostle these different and contrasted qualities are mingled and harmonized.

The mother watching over the life of her child has all her faculties aroused and stimulated; she knows almost by instinct how to say or do the right thing at the right time; she regards his faults with mingled love and sorrow. So, in the Apostle, we seem to trace a sort of refinement or nicety of feeling, when he is dealing with the souls of men. All his knowledge of mankind shows itself for their sakes; and yet not that knowledge of mankind which comes from without, revealing itself by experience of men and manners, by taking a part in events, by the insensible course of years making us learn from what we have seen and suffered. There is another experience that comes from within, which begins with the knowledge of self, with the consciousness of our own weakness and infirmities; which is continued in love to others, and in works of good to them; which grows by singleness and simplicity of heart. Love becomes the interpreter of how men think, and feel, and act, and supplies the place of, or passes into, a worldly prudence wiser than the prudence of this world. Such is the worldly prudence of St. Paul.

Once more: there is in the Apostle, not only prudence and knowledge of the world, but a kind of subtilty of moderation, which considers every conceivable case, and balances one with another; in the last resort giving no rule, but allowing all to be superseded by a more general principle. An instance of this subtile moderation is his determination, or rather omission, to determine the question of meats and drinks, which he first regards as indifferent, secondly, as depending on men's own conscience, and this again as limited by the consciences of others, and lastly resolves all these finer precepts into the general principle, "Whatever ye do, do all to the glory of God." The same qualification of one principle by another recurs again in his rules respecting marriage. First, "do not marry unbelievers," and "let not the wife depart from her husband." But if you are married, and the unbeliever is willing to remain, then the spirit of the second precept must prevail over the first. Only in an extreme case, where both parties are willing to dissolve the tie, the first principle in turn may again supersede the second. It may be said in the one case, "Your children are holy"; in the other, "What knowest thou, O wife, if thou shalt save thy husband?" In a similar spirit he withdraws his censure on the incestuous person, lest such an one, criminal as he was, should be swallowed up with overmuch sorrow. There is a religious aspect of either course of conduct, and either may be right under given circumstances. So the kingdoms of this world admit of being regarded almost as the kingdom of God, in reference to our duties towards their rulers; and yet touching the going to law before unbelievers, we are to think rather of that other kingdom in which we shall judge angels.

The Gospel, it has been often remarked, lays down principles rather than rules. The passages in the Epistles of St. Paul which seem to be exceptions to this statement, are exceptions in appearance rather than reality. They are relative to the circumstances of those whom he is addressing. He who became "all things to all men," would have been the last to insist on temporary regulations for his converts being made the rule of Christian life in all ages. His manner of church government was the very reverse of an immutable and unbending law. In all his instructions to the churches, the Apostle is ever with them, and seems to follow in his mind's eye their working and effect; whither his Epistles go, he goes in thought; absent, in his own language, in the body, but present in spirit. What he says to the churches, he seems to make them say; what he directs them to do, they are to do in that common spirit in which they are united with him; if they live, he lives; time and distance never snap the cord of sympathy. His government of them is a sort of communion with them; a receiving of their feelings and a pouring forth of his own, hardly ever bare command; a spirit which he seeks to infuse into them, not a law by which he rules them.

Great men are sometimes said to possess the power of command, but not the power of entering into the feelings of others. They have no fear of their fellows, but neither are they always capable of immediately impressing them, or of perceiving the impression which their words or actions make upon them. Often they live in a kind of solitude, on which other men do not venture to intrude; putting forth their strength on particular occasions, careless or abstracted about the daily concerns of life. Such was not the greatness of the Apostle St. Paul; not only in the sense in which he says that "he could do all things through Christ," but in a more earthly and human one, was it true that his strength was his weakness, and his weakness his strength. His dependence on others was in part also the source of his influence over them. His natural character was the type of that communion of the Spirit which he preached; the meanness of appearance which he attributes to himself, the image of that contrast which the Gospel presents to human greatness. Glorying and humiliation, life and death, a vision of angels strengthening him, the "thorn in the flesh" rebuking him, the greatest tenderness not without sternness, sorrows above measure, consolations above measure, are some of the contradictions which were reconciled in the same man. The centre in which things so strange met and moved was the cross of Christ, "whose marks in his body he bore"; what was "behind of whose afflictions" he rejoiced to fill up. Let us look once more, a little closer, at that "visage marred" in his Master's service. A poor decrepit being, afflicted perhaps with palsy, certainly with some bodily defect, — led out of prison between Roman soldiers, probably at times faltering in his speech, the creature, as he seemed to spectators, of nervous sensibility, — yearning, almost with a sort of fondness, to save the souls of those whom he saw around him, — spoke a few eloquent words in the cause of Christian truth, at which kings were awed, telling the tale of his own conversion with such simple pathos, that after ages have hardly heard the like.

Such is the image, not which Christian art has delighted to consecrate, but which the Apostle has left in his own writings of himself; an image of true wisdom, and nobleness, and affection, but of a wisdom unlike the wisdom of this world; of a nobleness which must not be transformed into that of the heroes of the world; an affection which seemed to be as strong and as individual towards all mankind, as other men are capable of feeling towards a single person.

ST. PAUL AND THE TWELVE.

By BENJAMIN JOWETT.

The narrative of the second chapter of the Epistle to the Galatians suggests an inquiry, which lies at the foundation of all inquiries into the history of the early Church: "In what relation did St. Paul stand to the Apostles at Jerusalem?" To which inquiry three answers may be given: (1.) the answer which identifies the preaching of St. Paul and the Twelve; or, (2.) which opposes them; or, (3.) which, without absolutely either identifying or opposing them, allows for important differences arising from variety of external circumstances and of individual character. The first answer is that which would be gathered from the Acts of the Apostles, which presents only the picture of an unbroken unity; a view to which the Church in after ages naturally inclined, and which may be said to be caricatured in the explanation of Chrysostom and Jerome, that the dispute between the Apostles at Antioch was only a concerted fiction. Secondly, the answer which would be supplied by the Clementine homilies, in which St. Paul sustains the character of Simon Magus, and St. Peter is the Apostle of the Gentiles; such an answer as would probably have been given also in the writings (had they been preserved to us) of Marcion, by whom St. Paul in turn was magnified to the exclusion of the Twelve. The third answer is that which we believe would be drawn from a careful examination of the Epistles of St. Paul himself, the only contemporary documents: "Separation not opposition, antagonism of the followers rather than of the leaders, personal antipathy of the Judaizers to St. Paul rather than of St. Paul to the Twelve."

The inquiry to which these three answers have been given, unavoidably runs up into the more general question of the relation of the Gospel of the circumcision and the uncircumcision, and of the Jew to the Gentile. If in the second century these distinctions yet survived, if animosities against St. Paul were burning still, if a party without the Church ranged itself under his name, if later controversies have anything in common with that first difference of circumcision and uncircumcision, if in the earliest ecclesiastical history we find a silence respecting the person and an absence of the spirit of St. Paul, it is impossible to separate these facts from the record of the Apostle himself, that on a great occasion the other Apostles "added nothing to him"; and that at Antioch, which was more peculiarly his own sphere, he withstood Peter to the face. We recognize in the personal narrative of the Epistle to the Galatians, the germ of what reappears afterwards as the history of the Church. And had no record of either kind survived, had there been no hint anywhere dropped of divisions between St. Paul and the Twelve, no memorial extant of Judaizing heresies, we should feel that some account was still needed of the manner in which circumcision became uncircumcision, and the Jew was lost in the Gentile. Probably we might conjecture not in all places with equal readiness, nor equally after and before the destruction of Jerusalem or the revolt under Adrian, nor without imparting many elements of the Law to the Gospel, nor, in accordance with the general laws of human nature, without some violence of party and opinion.

Events of the greatest importance in the history of mankind are not always seen to be important, until the time for preserving them is past. They have vanished into outline, and the details are filled up by the imagination or by the feelings of a later generation. This is especially the case with such events as stand in no relation to the public life of the time. Events of this kind, the most fruitful in results, may disappear themselves as though they had never been; they may also be magnified by present interests into false and exaggerated proportions. Who can tell what went on in a "large upper room" about the year 40? which may, nevertheless, have had vital consequences for the history of the world and the Church. Allusions in contemporary writings will be often insufficient to retain the true meaning of institutions or events, or to dispel the errors that may distort or cover them. And the events which of all others are least likely to preserve their real aspect, — most subject to be forgotten on the one hand, or to be exaggerated on the other, — the most liable to be perverted, the least possible to read aright even in contemporary writings, — are the differences of the first teachers of a religion, when they leave no permanent impress on its after history.

These are the reasons why, on such a subject as the one we are considering, so much is left for speculation and for conjecture; why the result of so many books is so small; why there is so much criticism, and so little history. Not only are the materials slender, but the light by which they are seen is feeble; and hence the new combinations and constructions of them are necessarily uncertain. They cannot be left to lie flat upon the page of Scripture; least of all can they be put together on the pattern of ecclesiastical tradition. Church history, like other history, may be made by the workings of the human mind to acquire a deceitful unity; it may gather to itself form and feature; it may convey a harmonious impression, which, from its mere internal consistency, it is difficult to resist. The philosophy of history readily weaves the tangle, developing the growth of ideas and connecting together causes and effects; but the unity which it creates is only artificial. Some other combination may be equally possible. Tradition, on the other hand, has a natural unity; but it is the unity of idea, which a later age gives to the past. It tells not what a former generation was, but what an after one thought it should have been. Many things came to light in the second century, which were unknown in the first. Still more in the third, that were unknown in the second. We turn from " this idol of the temple " to our earliest materials, the least hint in which, slender as they are, will be often of more value than all later traditions put together.

Many causes combine to produce a singular illusion in reference to the Church of the Apostolic age. There is the universal temptation to look back to a time when human nature was better than it is, when virtue and brotherly love were not an ideal only, but had an actual habitation on the earth among men. The times of the Apostles are the golden age of the Church, in which, without spot, or wrinkle, or any such thing, it seems to come from the hands of its Divine Author, — the New Jerusalem descending from heaven, arrayed in a portion of that glory with which the faith of the Apostles clothed it. Such is the idea which we instinctively form of the primitive Church, prior to any examination of the New Testament; an idea which is with difficulty laid aside in the face of the plainest facts. The misconception is further increased by the circumstance, that in modern times even more than in ancient, we have made the first century the battle-field of our controversies; instead of asking what was right, or true, or probable, what was the spirit or mind of Christ, we have constantly repeated the question, " What was the belief, constitution, practice, of the primitive Church? " — a question which we had, in reality, the smallest materials for answering, and which we had, therefore, the greatest temptation to answer according to our previous conception. The vacant space was in some way to be filled up. Could anything be more natural than that it should be filled up with the features of the third century? If we analyze closely what is the origin of many familiar conceptions respecting the Apostolic Church, we shall find that they consist of a sort of ideal, clothed in some of the externals of Tertullian or of Augustine, and conforming, as far as possible, to the use and practice of our own time.

The slightest knowledge of human nature is sufficient to assure us, that in the primitive Church there must have existed all the varieties of practice, belief, speculation, doctrine, which the different circumstances of the converts, and the different natures of men acting on those circumstances, would be likely to produce. The least examination of the Epistles is sufficient to show, not only what must have been, but what was. Even the Apostles and their immediate followers did not work together in the spirit of an order; but like men of strongly marked individual character, going by different roads to what did not always prove to be a common end. Not to anticipate the great division of which we are about to speak, Paul, and Barnabas, and Apollos, and even Priscilla and Aquila, seem to have their separate spheres of labor and ways of acting; and a similar difference, though slightly marked, is observable in the relation of St. Peter to St. James. When the Apostles were withdrawn, the differences which had commenced during their lifetime were not likely to disappear; in all that conflict of opinions, philosophies, religions, races, they must, for a time at least, have found food, and gathered strength.

Leaving such general speculations, we will now go back to the subject out of which they arose, — the difference of St. Paul and the Twelve, " the little cloud no bigger than a man's hand," the sign of that greater difference which spread itself over the face of the Church and the world.

The narrative of this difference is contained in the second chapter of the Epistle to the Galatians. The Apostle begins by asserting his Divine commission and independence of human authority, with an emphasis which implies that this could not have been acknowledged by the Judaizing Christians. After a few sharp words of remonstrance, he touches on such points in his personal history as tended to show that he had no connection with the Twelve. It was not by their ministry that he was converted; and after his conversion, he had seen them only twice; once for so short a time that he was unknown by face to the churches of Judæa; on the latter of the two occasions, they had "added nothing to him" in a conference about circumcision. Afterwards, at Antioch, when Peter showed a disposition partially to retrace his steps, at the instigation of certain who came from James, he withstood him to the face, and rebuked his inconsistency, even though his helper, Barnabas, and all the other Jews, were against him. The reason for narrating all this is to show, not how nearly the Apostle agreed with the Twelve, but how entirely he maintained his ground, meeting them on terms of freedom and equality.

There are features in this narrative which indicate a hostile, as there are other features which also indicate a friendly, bearing in the two parties who are here spoken of. Among the first may be classed the mention of false brethren, "who came in to spy out our liberty in Christ Jesus." Were they Jews or Christians? and how came they to be present if the Apostles at Jerusalem could have prevented them? The number of them seems to indicate that there was no strong line of demarcation between the Jews and Christians at Jerusalem; and from the tone of the narrative we can hardly avoid drawing the conclusion, that the other Apostles scarcely resisted them, but left the battle to be fought by St. Paul. The second point which leads to the unfavorable inference is the manner in which the Apostles of Jerusalem are spoken of, — "those who seemed to be somewhat, whatsoever they were, it maketh no matter to me"; *οἱ δοκοῦντες εἶναί τι*, v. 6, who are shown by the form of the sentence to be the same as *οἱ δοκοῦντες στῦλοι εἶναι*, in v. 9. Thirdly, the distinction of the Gospels of the circumcision and uncircumcision, which was not merely one of places, but in some degree of doctrine also. Fourthly, the use of the words (*ὑπόκρισις*) "hypocrisy," and (*κατεγνωσμένος*) "condemned," in reference to Peter's conduct; and, lastly, in v. 12, the mention of certain who came from James, under whose influence the Apostle supposed Peter to have acted; which raises the suspicion of a regular opposition to St. Paul, acting in concert with the heads of the Church at Jerusalem. In the end, the other

Apostles were determined by the fact, that a Church had grown up external to them, which was its own witness.

Yet in this very passage there are also kindlier features, which restore us more nearly to our previous conception of the Apostolic Church. In the first place, there is no indication here, any more than elsewhere in the Epistles, of an open schism between St. Paul and the Twelve, which, had it existed, could not have failed to appear. Secondly, the differences are not of such a nature as to preclude the Church of Jerusalem from receiving, or the Apostle from giving, the alms of the Gentiles. Lastly, the expression, *οἱ δοκοῦντες εἶναί τι*, "who seemed to be somewhat," although ironical, is softened by what follows, *οἱ δοκοῦντες εἶναι στῦλοι*, "who seemed to be pillars," in which the Apostle expresses the real greatness and high authority of the Twelve in their separate field of labor. Singular as the juxtaposition is of the false brethren, the Apostles "who added nothing to him," "the persons who came from James," the tone of the passage, as well as of every passage in which they are named, shows that on St. Paul's part there could have been no personal antagonism to the Twelve.

But not to anticipate the conclusion, we must here enter on a further stage of the same inquiry, the evidence supplied by the Epistles of St. Paul, and other portions of the New Testament, on the subject which we are considering. Is it a mere passing incidental circumstance, happening for once in their lives, that the Apostles of Jerusalem and St. Paul met and had a partial difference? or is the difference alluded to, in a manner so unlike the violence of later controversy, merely an indication of a greater and more radical difference in the Church itself, faintly discernible in the persons of its leaders? We might be disposed to answer "yes" to the first alternative, were the first two chapters of the Galatians all that remained to us; we are compelled to say "yes" to the second, when we extend our view to other parts of Scripture.

Everywhere in the Epistles of St. Paul and in the Acts of

the Apostles, we find traces of an opposition between the Jew and Gentile, the circumcision and the uncircumcision. It is found, not only in the Epistle to the Galatians, but in a scarcely less aggravated form in the two Epistles to the Corinthians, softened, indeed, in the Epistle to the Romans, and yet distinctly traceable in the Epistle to the Philippians; the party of the circumcision appearing to triumph in Asia, at the very close of the Apostle's life, in the second Epistle to Timothy. In all these Epistles we have proofs of a reaction to Judaism, but, though they are addressed to churches chiefly of Gentile origin, never of a reaction to heathenism. Could this have been the case, unless within the Church itself there had been a Jewish party urging upon the members of the Church the performance of a rite repulsive in itself, if not as necessary to salvation, at any rate as a counsel of perfection, seeking to make them, in Jewish language, not merely proselytes of the gate, but proselytes of righteousness? What, if not this, is the reverse side of the Epistles of St. Paul? that is to say, the motives, object, or basis of teaching of his opponents, who came with "epistles of commendation" to the church of Corinth, 2 Cor. iii. 1; who profess themselves "to be Christ's" in a special sense, 2 Cor. x. 7; who say they are of Apollos, or Cephas, or Christ, 1 Cor. i. 12; or James, Gal. ii. 12; who preach Christ of contention, Phil. i. 15, 17; who deny St. Paul's authority, 1 Cor. ix. 1, Gal. iv. 16; who slander his life, 1 Cor. ix. 3, 7. We meet these persons at every turn. Are they the same, or different? Are they mere chance opponents? or do they represent to us one spirit, one mission, one determination to root out the Apostle and his doctrine from the Christian Church?

Nothing but the fragmentary character of St. Paul's writings would conceal from us the fact, that here was a concerted and continuous opposition. The same features recur, the same spirit breathes, the same accusations are repeated against the Apostle. Of going back to dumb idols there is never a word; it is not that sort of return which Paul fears, but the enforcement of circumcision, the observance of days and weeks, the loss of the freedom of the Gospel. It hardly needs to be proved, that St. Paul everywhere and at all times met with opposition; it is equally evident on the surface of the Epistles, that this opposition chiefly proceeded from Judaizing Christians. Still the question recurs, In what relation did its leaders stand to the Apostles at Jerusalem? Before attempting to answer this question finally, we must pause a moment to collect in one the evidence supplied by the Acts of the Apostles.

That from the beginning the elements of a division existed in the Christian Church is clear from the murmuring of the Grecians against the Hebrews for the neglect of their widows in the daily ministration, which led to the appointment of the seven deacons. Indeed, they may be said to have pre-existed in the Jewish and Gentile world; many "schoolmasters" were bringing men to Christ, and the past history of man, then as now, seemed occasionally to reawaken in the feelings of individuals. A first epoch in the history of the division is marked by the death of Stephen, which scattered a portion of the Church, whom the very circumstance of their persecution, as well as their dispersion in foreign countries, would tend to alienate from the observance of the Jewish law. A second epoch is distinguished by the preaching of St. Paul at Antioch; immediately after which we are informed that the disciples were first called Christians. Then follows the Council, the more exact account of which is supplied by the Epistle to the Galatians, to which, however, one point is added in the narrative of the Acts, — the mention of certain who came from Jerusalem to Antioch, saying, "Except ye be circumcised, ye cannot be saved." Passing onwards a little, we arrive at the address of St. Paul to the elders of the church of Ephesus (Acts xx. 29, 30), which seems to allude to the same alienation from himself which had actually taken place in the Second Epistle to Timothy (2 Tim. i. 15). At length we come to St. Paul's last journey to Jerusalem, and his interview with James, which was the occasion on which, by the advice of James, he took a vow upon him, in hope of calming the apprehensions of the multitude of "the many thousand Jews who believed and were all zealous for the law," in which passage express reference is made to the decree of the Council. These leading facts are interspersed with slighter allusions, which must not be passed over as unimportant. Such are the words, "Of the rest durst no man join himself to them," indicating the way of life of the Apostles; "A great company of the priests were obedient unto the faith," vi. 7; "They that were scattered abroad upon the persecution of Stephen, preached the word to Jews only," viii. 4; the priority attributed to James in Acts xii. 17, "Go show these things to James and the brethren"; the mention of the alms brought by Barnabas and Saul to Jerusalem in the days of Claudius Cæsar, xi. 29. Such in the latter half of the Acts (xxiii. 6) is the declaration of St. Paul that he is a Pharisee. Nor is it without significance, that, in the discussion of this question of the admission of the Gentiles, no reference is made to the command of the Gospels, "Go and baptize all nations," nor to the intercourse of Peter with Cornelius; and that nowhere are the other Apostles described as at variance with the Jewish Christians; nor in the whole later history of the Acts as suffering persecution from the Jews, or as taking any share in the persecution of St. Paul.

Now, with all the circumstances of the case before us, what shall we say in reply to the question from which we digressed? What was the relation of the Judaizing Christians to the Apostles at Jerusalem? Did those who remained behind in the Church regard the death of the martyr Stephen with the same feelings as those who were scattered abroad? Were the Apostles at Jerusalem one in heart with the brethren at Antioch? Were the teachers who came from Jerusalem to Antioch, saying, "Except ye be circumcised, ye cannot be saved," commissioned by the Twelve? Were the Twelve absolutely at one among themselves? Are the commendatory epistles spoken of in the Epistle to the Corinthians, to be ascribed to the Apostles at Jerusalem? Can "the grievous wolves," whose entrance into the Church of

Ephesus the Apostle foresaw, be other than the Judaizing teachers? Lastly, Were the multitude of believing Jews, zealous for the law, and quickened in their zeal for it by the very sight of St. Paul, engaged in the tumult which follows? These are different ways of stating the same question, or subordinate questions connected with it, which of themselves assist in supplying an answer.

If we conceive of the Apostles as exercising a strict and definite authority over the multitude of their converts, living heads of the Church as they might be termed, Peter or James of the circumcision, and Paul of the uncircumcision, it would be hard to avoid connecting them with the acts of their followers. One would think that, in accordance with the spirit of the concordat, they should have "delivered over to Satan" the opponents of St. Paul, rather than have lived in communion and company with them. To hold out the right hand of fellowship to Paul and Barnabas, and yet secretly to support or not to discountenance those who opposed them, would be little short of treachery to their common Master, especially when we observe how strongly the Judaizers are characterized by St. Paul as the false brethren who came in unawares, the false Apostles transforming themselves into Apostles of Christ, "grievous wolves entering in," &c. Nothing can be more striking than the contrast between the vehemence with which St. Paul treats his Judaizing antagonists, and the gentleness or silence which he never fails to preserve towards the Apostles at Jerusalem.

Yet it may be questioned whether the whole difficulty does not arise from a false conception of the authority of the Apostles in the early Church. Although the first teachers of the word of Christ, they were not the acknowledged rulers of the Catholic Church; they were its prophets, not its bishops. The influence which they exercised was personal rather than official, derived doubtless from their having seen the Lord, and the fact of their appointment by himself, yet confined also to a comparatively narrow sphere; it was exercised in places in which they were, but hardly extended to places where they were not. The Gospel grew up around them, they could not tell how; and the spirit which their preaching awakened soon passed out of their control. They seemed no longer to be the prime movers, but rather the spectators of the work of God which went on before their eyes. The thousands of Jews that believed and were zealous for the law, would not lay aside the garb of Judaism at the bidding of James or Peter; the false teachers of Corinth or of Ephesus would not have been less likely to gain followers, had they been excommunicated by them. The movement which, in twenty years from the death of Christ, had spread so widely over the earth, they no more sought to reduce to rule and compass. It was out of their power, beyond their reach, extending to churches which had no connection with themselves, of the circumstances of which they were hardly informed, and in which, therefore, it was not natural that they should interfere between St. Paul and his opponents.

The moment we think of the Church, not as an ecclesiastical or political institution, but as it was in the first age, a spiritual body, that is to say, a body partly moved by the Spirit of God, but dependent also on the tempers and sympathies of men, and swayed to and fro by religious emotion, the narrative of Scripture seems perfectly truthful and natural. When the waves are high, we see but a little way over the ocean; the very intensity of religious feeling is inconsistent with a uniform level of church government. It is not a regular hierarchy, but "some apostles, some prophets, some evangelists, others pastors and teachers," who grew together "into the body of Christ." The image of the earlier Church that is everywhere presented to us in the Epistles implies great freedom of individual action. Apollos and Barnabas were not under the guidance of Paul; those "who were distinguished among the Apostles before him" could hardly have owned his authority. Nor is any attempt made to bring the different churches under a common system. We cannot imagine any bond by which they could have been linked together, without an order of clergy or form of church government common to them all; and of this there is no trace in the Epistles of St. Paul. It was hard to keep the church at Corinth at unity with itself; how much harder to have brought other churches into union with it!

Of this fluctuating state of the Church, which was not yet addicted to any one rule, we find an indication of a different kind in the freedom, almost levity, with which professing Christians embraced "traditions of men." Nothing was less like the attitude of the church of Corinth towards the Apostle, than the implicit belief in a faith "once delivered to the saints." We know not whether Apollos was or was not a teacher of Alexandrian learning among its members, or what was the exact nature of "the party of Christ," 1 Cor. i. 12. That heathen as well as Jewish elements had found their way into the Church is indicated by the false "wisdom," the denial of the resurrection, and the resort to the idol's temple. In the church at Colossæ, again, something was suspected by the Apostle, which is dimly seen by us, and seems to have held an intermediate position between Judaism and heathenism; or rather to have partaken of the nature of both. It was wisdom the Greek sought after, the want of which in the Gospel was his great stumbling-block, which he was most likely, therefore, to intrude upon its teaching. The tendency of the Jew was at once to humanize and mysticize it; he could never have enough of wonders (1 Cor. i. 22), yet was unable to understand its true wonder, "the cross of Christ."

Amid such fluctuation and variety of opinions we can imagine Paul and Apollos, or Paul and Peter, preaching side by side in the church of Corinth or of Antioch, like Wesley and Whitefield in the last century, or Luther and Calvin at the Reformation, with a sincere reverence for each other, not abstaining from commenting on or condemning each other's doctrine or practice, and yet also forgetting their differences in their common zeal to save the souls of men. Personal regard is quite consistent with differences of religious belief; some of which, with good men, are a kind of form, belonging only to their outer nature, most of which, as we hope, exist only on this side the grave. We can imagine the followers of such men as we have been describing incapable of acting in their noble spirit, with a feebler sense of their high calling, and a stronger one of their points of disagreement; losing the great principle for which they were alike contending in "oppositions of knowledge," in prejudice and personality. And lastly, we may conceive the disciples of Wesley or of Whitefield (for of the Apostles themselves we forbear to move the question) reacting upon their masters, and drawing them into the vicious circle of controversy, disuniting them in their lives, though at the last hour incapable of making a separation between them.

Of such a nature we believe the differences to have been which separated St. Paul and the Twelve, arising in some degree from differences of individual character, but much more from their followers, and the circumstances of their lives. They were differences which seldom brought them into contact, and once or twice only into collision; they did not with logical exactness divide the world. It may have been, "I unto the heathen, and they unto the circumcision"; and yet St. Paul may have felt a deep respect for those "that seemed to be pillars," and they may have acknowledged thankfully the success of his labors. It is not even necessary to suppose that the agreement of the Council, the terms of which are differently described in Galatians ii. and Acts xv., was minutely observed for a long period of years. The freedom which made it possible that the differences between Jew and Gentile should coexist, made it impossible that the Twelve should always be able to control their followers, and unlikely that they themselves should wholly abstain from showing their sympathy towards those who seemed to be joined to them by the ties of nationality. A party in the church of Corinth sought to call itself by their name, in opposition to that of St. Paul: it was they, probably, who gave "the epistles of commendation" to those who taught at Corinth: they, or at least one of their number, sent messengers from Jerusalem to Antioch, at a critical moment, in the dispute about circumcision.

Admitting even the darkest color that can be put upon these latter facts, still the absence of all hostile allusion to the Twelve in the writings of St. Paul, the circumstance of the Jerusalem church being supported by the contributions of the Gentiles, the other circumstance of teachers of the circumcision being among the companions of St. Paul in his imprisonment (Col. iv. 10, 11), the appeal to the witness and example of the other Apostles (1 Cor. xv. 5, ix. 5), are sufficient to justify the view which we took at the outset of the relation of St. Paul to the Twelve: "Separation, not opposition, antagonism of the followers rather than of the leaders, personal antipathy of the Judaizers to St. Paul, more than of St. Paul to the Judaizers." Many things must have been done by the fanaticism of professing adherents, of which it was impossible for the Twelve to approve, — which, when separated by distance, it was equally impossible for them to repress. Even at Jerusalem, under the eye of the Apostles, though it may be uncertain whether "the multitude zealous for the law" were the same or partly the same with that which was engaged in the tumult against St. Paul, it is plain that James speaks of them as incapable of being swayed by his authority. It was the impossibility of exercising this authority that justified the Twelve, and made it possible, in spite of their adherents, that they should remain in the love of their common Lord towards St. Paul.

Regarding, then, the whole number of believers in Judæa, in Greece, in Italy, in Egypt, in Asia, as a sort of fluctuating mass, of whom there were not many wise, not many learned, not all governed by the maxims of common prudence, needing many times to have the way of God expounded to them more perfectly, and, from their imperfect knowledge, arrayed against one another, subject to spiritual impulses, and often mingling with the truth Jewish and sometimes heathen notions; we seem to see the Twelve placed on an eminence above them, and, as it were, apart from them, acting upon them rather than governing them, retired from the scene of St. Paul's labors, and therefore hardly coming into conflict with him, either by word or by letter. They led a life such as St. James is described as leading by Hegesippus, "going up into the temple at the hour of prayer," reverenced by a multitude of followers zealous for the law, themselves, like Peter, half conscious of a higher truth, and yet by their very position debarred from being its ministers. Though bearing the common name of Christ, it was not by accident, but by agreement, that they were led to labor in different spheres. The world, as we might say, was wide enough for them both. The Apostle St. Paul's rule is not to intrude upon another man's labors, but he does not aim at confining any province or district to himself or to his followers. He makes no claim to be the visible head of any section of the Church, but only the servant of Christ. Even the hold he retains over his own converts is precarious and uncertain. The idea of a Catholic Church one and indivisible throughout the earth had not as yet come into existence, though the way for it was preparing, and the elements out of which it arose were already working.

The inquiry into the relation in which St. Paul stood to the Twelve runs up into a further question respecting the Gospel which they preached. "What was that different form or aspect of Christian truth which was called the Gospel of the circumcision, as compared with that of the uncircumcision?" Was it a difference of doctrine or of practice, of belief or of spirit? Viewed as a matter of doctrine, we are almost surprised to find into how small a compass the difference reduces itself. So St. Paul himself seems to have felt, even amid his strongest denunciations of the Judaizing teachers. All were baptized in the name of Christ, with whom the Twelve had walked while he was upon earth; whom St. Paul, equally with them, had seen with the spiritual eye, as "one born out of due time." It was the same Christ whom they preached (there was no dispute about this), though the manner of preaching may have differed with difference of natural character or education, or the different manner of his revelation to them. "Other foundation could no man lay," as the Apostle says to the church at Corinth, though he might build many superstructures. It was not "another Gospel," as he indignantly declares to the church in Galatia, for there was not and could not be another. Or, according to another manner of speaking (2 Cor. xi. 4), it was still Jesus, though another Jesus; and the spirit, though another spirit. In the church of Rome, as the Apostle writes to the Philippians, there were those who preached Christ of contention, in which the Apostle nevertheless rejoiced, as an honor to the name of Christ. That in the Judaizing teachers, as well as the Apostles themselves, St. Paul saw at any time true though mistaken preachers of the Word, is a fact of great significance in reference to our present purpose. The cross of Christ was peculiarly the symbol of St. Paul, yet all probably, or almost all, looked with common feelings of affection to Him who died for them.

But not only did St. Paul and the Twelve regard the name of Christ with the same feelings (a statement which might be made almost equally of nearly all the earliest heretical sects), but they agreed also in considering the Old Testament, rightly understood, as the source of the New. The mystery of past ages was latent there. Through so many centuries, it had been misunderstood or unknown: it had now come to light. The same God who at sundry times and in divers manners spake in times past to the fathers by the prophets, had in these last days spoken to men by his Son. There was no opposition between the Old Testament and the New; it was the law, with its burden on the conscience, and its questions respecting meats and drinks, and new moons and Sabbaths, which contrasted with the Gospel.

Once more: besides the name of Christ, and the connection of the Old and New Testament, another point common to St. Paul and the Twelve was their expectation of the day of the Lord. Nowhere does the Apostle appear so much "a Hebrew of the Hebrews," as in speaking of the invisible world. He opposes this world and the next, as the times before and after the coming of the Messiah were divided by the Jews themselves; he sees them peopled with a celestial hierarchy of good and evil angels. He is waiting for the revelation of Antichrist, and the manifestation of the sons of God. The same signs follow the reception of the Gospel in the churches founded by the Twelve and by St. Paul; "The Holy Ghost fell upon them as upon us at the beginning," might have been the description of the church of Corinth, no less than of the church at Jerusalem. And, as St. Paul says, in the Epistle to the Romans, in reference to the admission of the Gentiles, "God is no respecter of persons," Peter commences his address to Cornelius with the words, "Of a truth I perceive God is no respecter of persons."

Even setting aside the last passage, as hard to reconcile with the subsequent conduct of Peter, still enough remains to show that the Gospel preached by St. Paul and the Twelve was in substance the same. To preach to the Gentiles, it must be remembered, was a command of Christ himself. If, with the exception of the Epistle of St. James, we have no epistles extant which bear the impress of Jewish Christianity, still we can hardly doubt that the three first Gospels represent in the main the model on which was based the teaching of the Twelve; that is to say, the difference between St. Paul's Epistles and the Gospel of St. Matthew is a fair measure of the utmost limits of the distance which separated the Apostle of the Gentiles from the Apostles of the Circumcision.

Admitting such points of agreement, the differences lie within narrow limits; they could not have originated in anything that we should consider fundamental articles of the Christian faith. They may have arisen out of a sympathy for, or antipathy towards, the Alexandrian learning. The mere difference of language may have made the same kind of difference between the church at Jerusalem and those founded by St. Paul, as divides the Old Testament from the later Apocryphal books. Much also, humanly speaking, may have arisen from the difference in their way of life. Those who went up to the temple at the hour of prayer, who lived amid the smoke of the daily sacrifices, could hardly have felt and thought and spoken as the Apostle of the Gentiles, wandering through Greece and Asia, from city to city, in barbarous as well as civilized countries; they at least could not have been expected to say, "Let no man judge you of a new moon or a Sabbath day." Like our Lord remaining within the confines of Judæa, there were many truths which they were not called upon to utter in the same emphatic way as St. Paul.

Such are a few conjectures respecting the nature of the difference which separated St. Paul from the Twelve. The point that is independent of conjecture is, that it related to the obligation on the Gentiles to keep the Mosaic law. It is characteristic of the earliest times of the Church, that the dispute referred rather to a matter of practice than of doctrine. Long ere the Gospel was drawn out in a system of doctrine, the difference between Judaism and Christianity was instinctively felt. There were times and places in which, even in the mind of the Christian, Jewish prejudices seemed too strong for the freedom wherewith Christ had made him free. There was no difficulty in allowing that all nations were to be baptized in the name of Christ, and that there was to be one fold and one Shepherd. This had been determined by an authority from which there could be no appeal. The difficulty was to go in "to men uncircumcised, and eat with them," amid the derision or persecution of Jews, or Jewish Christians. Our Lord had decided that Gentiles were to be admitted to the Church; but on what conditions they were to be so admitted, was left to be inferred from the spirit of his teaching. There was no putting an end to the controversy; and the timidity of St. Peter, and the conciliatory temper of St. Paul, indicate a disposition to maintain these scruples, or an unwillingness to disturb them.

The adoption of a theory, which, however innocently, we fail to carry out in practice, almost necessarily involves inconsistency. Suppose a person maintaining liberty of conscience, yet refusing to avail himself of that liberty, or to act as though he maintained it, is it not nearly certain that, when surrounded by particular influences, he would cease to maintain it? Few, comparatively, have sufficient strength of character to carry a single speculative principle through life. Experience shows that inconsistency, so far from being rare, is the commonest of all failings. Narrowness of intellect, and feebleness of perception, are quite as common causes of it as weakness of character. The mind, under the pressure of new circumstances, and in a strange place, ceases to perceive that old principles are still applicable. Its sympathies draw it one way, its sense of right another. The habits of youth, or the instincts of childhood, reassert themselves in mature life. He who is the first, and even the ablest, to speak, may be often deficient in firmness of will or grasp of mind. Such reflections on human nature are sufficient to explain the conduct of Peter, and they are confirmed by what we know of him.

Adding to our former indications of the relations in which the Apostle of the Gentiles stood to the Twelve such further evidences as we are able to glean from the teaching and character of St. Peter and St. Paul, we have to carry our inquiry into a third stage, as it reappears once more in what may be termed the twilight of ecclesiastical history, — that century after the Neronian persecution, of which we know so little, and desire to know so much; the aching void of which we are tempted to fill up with the image of the century which succeeds it. To collect together all the scattered rays which might illustrate our subject, would carry us too far into the general history of the Church, and lead to discussions respecting the genuineness of Patristic writings, and the truth of events narrated in them. The "romance of heresy" would be the mist of fiction, through which we should endeavor to penetrate to the light. The origin of episcopal government, which seems to stand in a sort of antagonism to heresy, would be one of the elements of our uncertainty. We should have to begin by forming a criterion of the credibility of Irenæus, Clement, Tertullian, Origen, and Eusebius. But a subject so wide is matter not for an essay, but for a book; it is the history of the Church of the first two centuries. We must therefore narrow our field of vision as much as possible, and confine ourselves to the consideration of this third stage of our subject, so far as it throws a remote light back on the differences of the Apostles, drawing conclusions only which rest on facts that are generally admitted.

Two general facts meet us at the outset, which it is necessary to bear in mind in the attempt to balance the more particular statements that follow. First, the utter ignorance of the third century respecting the first, and earlier half of the second. We cannot err in supposing that those who could add nothing to what is recorded in the New Testament of the life of Christ and his Apostles, had no real knowledge of lesser matters, as, for example, the origin of episcopacy. They could not appreciate; they had no means of preserving the memory of a state of the Church which was unlike their own. Irenæus, who lived within a century of St. Paul, has not added a single circumstance to what we gather from the New Testament. Eusebius, with the writings of Papias and Hegesippus, and all ecclesiastical antiquity before him, has preserved nothing which relates to the difference of St. Paul and the Twelve, or which throws the smallest light on any other difficulty in the New Testament. The image of the primitive Church which they seemed to see, when it was not mere vacancy, was the image of themselves.

The second general fact is the unconsciousness of this ignorance, and the readiness with which the vacant space is filled up, and the Church of the second century assimilated to that of the third and fourth. Human nature tends to conceal that which is discordant to its preconceived notions; silently dropping some facts, exaggerating others, adding, where needed, new tone and coloring, until the disguise of history can no longer be detected. By some such process has the circumstance we are inquiring into been forgotten and reproduced. Not only what may be termed the "animus" of concealment is traceable in the strange account of the dispute between the Apostles, given by Jerome and Chrysostom, but in earlier writings, in which the two Apostles appear side by side as cofounders, not only of the Roman, but also of the

Corinthian church; as pleading their cause together before Tiberius; dying on the same day; buried, according to some, in the same grave. The motive, or, more strictly speaking, the unconscious instinct, which gave birth to this acknowledged fiction was, probably, the desire to throw a veil over that occasion on which they withstood one another to the face. And the truth indistinctly shines through this legend of the latter part of the second century, when it is further recorded that St. Paul was the head of the Gentile Church, Peter of the circumcision.

Bearing in mind these two general facts, the tendency of which is to throw a degree of doubt on the early ecclesiastical tradition, and so to lead us to seek for indications out of the regular course of history, we have to consider, in reference to our present subject, the following statements: —

1. That Justin, and probably Hegesippus and Papias, living at a time when the Epistles of St. Paul must have been widely spread, were unacquainted with them or their author.

2. That Marcion, who was their contemporary, appealed exclusively to the authority of St. Paul in opposition to the Twelve.

3. That in the account of James the Just, given by Josephus and Hegesippus, he is represented as a Jew among Jews; living, according to Hegesippus, the life of a Nazarite; praying in the temple until his knees became hard as a camel's, and so entirely a Jew as to be unknown to the people for a Christian; a picture which, though its features may be exaggerated, yet has the trace of a true resemblance to the part which we find him acting in the Epistle to the Galatians.

4. That in the Clementine Homilies, A. D. 160, though a work otherwise orthodox, St. Paul is covertly introduced under the name of Simon Magus, as the enemy who had pretended visions and revelations, and who withstood and blamed Peter. No writer doubts the allusion in these passages to the Epistle to the Galatians. Assuming their connection, we cannot but ask, as bearing on our present inquiry, What was the state of mind which could have led an orthodox Christian,

who lived probably at Rome, about the middle of the second century, to affix such a character to St. Paul? and what was the motive which induced him to veil his meaning? What, too, could have been the state of the Church in which such a romance could have grown up? and how could the next generation have read it without perceiving its true aim? Doubtful as may be the precise answer to these questions, we cannot attribute this remarkable work to the wayward fancy of an individual; it is an indication of a real tendency of the first and second century, at a time when the flame was almost extinguished, but still slumbered in the mind of the writer of the Clementine Homilies.

5. Lastly, that in later writings we find no trace of the mind of St. Paul. His influence, for a season, seems to vanish from the world. On such a basis as "where the Spirit of the Lord is, there is liberty," it might have been impossible to rear the fabric of a hierarchy. But the tide of ecclesiastical feeling set in an opposite direction. It was not merely that after-writers fell short of St. Paul, or imperfectly interpreted him, but that they formed themselves on a different model. It was not merely that the external constitution of the Church had received a definite form and shape, but that the inward perception of the nature of the Gospel was different. No writer of the latter half of the second century would have spoken as St. Paul has done of the Law, of the Sabbath, of justification by faith only, of the Spirit, of grace. An echo of a part of his teaching is heard in Augustine; with this exception, the voice of him who withstood Peter to the face at Antioch was silent in the Church until the Reformation.

Gathering around us, then, once more, the grounds on which our judgment must be formed from the Epistles of St. Paul, the Acts of the Apostles, and the earliest ecclesiastical tradition, we arrive once more at the thrice-repeated conclusion, that the relation of St. Paul and the Twelve was separation, not opposition; antagonism of the followers, rather than of the leaders; enmity of the Judaizers to St. Paul, not of

St. Paul to the Judaizers. Naturally, the principle of the Apostle was triumphant; commencing like the struggle of Athanasius against the world, it ended as the struggle of the world must end against the half-extinct remnant of the Jewish race. But the good fight which the Apostle fought, was not immediately crowned by the final victory. In the dawn of ecclesiastical history, as the Twelve were one by one withdrawn from the scene, the battle was still going on, dimly seen by us within and without the Church; its last shadows seeming to retire from view in the Easter controversy of the second century. Two events especially exercised a great influence on it. First, the destruction of Jerusalem, and the flight to Pella of the Christian community; secondly, the revolt under Barchocab; both tending to separate, more and more, both in fact and the opinion of mankind, the Christian from the Jew. At length, the succession of Jewish Christian episcopacy ceased; the first Bishop of Ælia Capitolina being a Gentile.

That that intermediate century of which we know so little was not a period in which the Church had reason to glory, is witnessed to by the very absence of memorials respecting it. There was a want of great teachers after the Apostles were withdrawn; then, according to the idea of a later generation, when there were no more living heads, heresy sprang up. There was something in that century which those who followed it were either unwilling to recall, or unable to comprehend. The Church was in process of organization, fencing itself with creeds and liturgies, taking possession of the earth with its hierarchy. The principle of St. Paul triumphs, and yet it seems to have lost the spirit and power of St. Paul. There is no more question of Jew and Gentile; but neither is there any trace of the freedom of the Apostle. The lesson which that age silently learned, was that of ecclesiastical order and government. It built up the body of Christ from without, as St. Paul had built it up from within. And there would have been the same inconsistency in supposing that the doctrine of the Apostle could have been fully received in the second century, as in supposing that he himself would have preached it in Palestine in the first.

It would be vain to carry our inquiry further, with a view to glean a few doubtful results respecting the first half of the second century. Remote probabilities and isolated facts are hardly worth balancing. By some course of events with which we are imperfectly acquainted, the providence of God leading the way, and the thoughts of man following, the Jewish Passover became the Christian Easter; the Jewish Sabbath the Christian Sunday; circumcision passed into uncircumcision; the law was done away in Christ, while the Old Testament retained its authority over Gentile as well as Jewish Christians; and the party which would have excommunicated St. Paul, before the end of the second century had itself left the Church. The relation of St. Paul to the Twelve may be regarded as the type and symbol, and, in some degree, the cause of that final adjustment of the differences between Jew and Gentile, without which it would not have been possible, humanly speaking, that the Gospel could have become an universal religion.

EVILS IN THE CHURCH OF THE APOSTOLICAL AGE.

By BENJAMIN JOWETT.

Were we, with the view of forming a judgment of the moral state of the early Church, to examine the subjects of rebuke most frequently referred to by the Apostles, these would be found to range themselves under four heads: first, licentiousness; secondly, disorder; thirdly, scruples of conscience; fourthly, strifes about doctrine and teachers. The consideration of these four subjects, the two former falling in with the argument of the Epistle to the Thessalonians, the two latter more closely connected with the Romans and the Galatians, will give what may be termed the darker side of the primitive Church.

1. Licentiousness was the besetting sin of the Roman world. Except by a miracle, it was impossible that the new converts could be at once and wholly freed from it. It lingered in the flesh when the spirit had cast it off. It had interwoven itself in the pagan religions; and, if we may believe the writings of adversaries, was ever reappearing on the confines of the Church in the earliest heresies. Even within the pale of the Church, it might assume the form of a mystic Christianity. The very ecstasy of conversion would often lead to a reaction. Nothing is more natural than that in a licentious city, like Corinth or Ephesus, those who were impressed by St. Paul's teaching should have gone their way, and returned to their former life. In this case it would

seldom happen that they apostatized into the ranks of the heathen: the same impulse which led them to the Gospel would lead them also to bridge the gulf which separated them from its purer morality. Many may have sinned and repented again and again, unable to stand themselves in the general corruption, yet unable to cast aside utterly the image of innocence and goodness which the Apostle had set before them. There were those, again, who consciously sought to lead the double life, and imagined themselves to have found in licentiousness the true freedom of the Gospel.

The tone which the Apostle adopts respecting sins of the flesh differs in many ways from the manner of speaking of them among moralists of modern times. He says nothing of the poison which they infuse into society, or the consequences to the individual himself. It is not in this way that moral evils are presented to us in Scripture. Neither does he appeal to public opinion as condemning them, or dwell on the ruin involved in them to one half of the human race. True and forcible as these aspects of such sins are, they are the result of modern reflection, not the first instincts of reason and conscience. They strengthen the moral principles of mankind, but are not of a kind to touch the individual soul. They are a good defence for the existing order of society; but they will not purify the nature of man, or extinguish the flames of lust.

Moral evils in the New Testament are always spoken of as spiritual. They corrupt the soul; they defile the temple of the Holy Ghost; they cut men off from the body of Christ. Of morality, as distinct from religion, there is hardly a trace in the Epistles of St. Paul. What he seeks to penetrate is the inward nature of sin, not its outward effects. Even its consequences in another state of being are but slightly touched upon, in comparison with that living death which itself is. It is not merely a vice or crime, or even an offence against the law of God, to be punished here or hereafter. It is more than this. It is what men feel within, not what they observe without them, — not what shall be, but what is, — a terrible consciousness, a mystery of iniquity, a communion with unseen powers of evil.

All sin is spoken of in the Epistles of St. Paul as rooted in human nature, and quickened by the consciousness of law; but especially is this the case with the sin which is more than any other the type of sin in general, — fornication. It is, in a peculiar sense, the sin of the flesh, with which the very idea of the corruption of the flesh is closely connected, just as, in 1 Thess. iv. 3, the idea of holiness is regarded as almost equivalent to abstinence from the commission of it. It is a sin against a man's own body, distinguished from all other sins by its personal and individual nature. No other is at the same time so gross and so insidious; no other partakes so much of the slavery of sin. As marriage is the type of the communion of Christ and his Church, as the body is the member of Christ, so the sin of fornication is a strange and mysterious union with evil.

But although such is the tone of the Apostle, there is no violence to human nature in his commands respecting it. He knew how easily extremes meet, how hard it is for asceticism to make clean that which is within, how quickly it might itself pass into its opposite. Nothing can be more different from the spirit of early ecclesiastical history on this subject, than the moderation of St. Paul. The remedy for sin is not celibacy, but marriage. Even second marriages are, for the prevention of sin, to be encouraged. In the same spirit is his treatment of the incestuous person. He had committed a sin not even named among the Gentiles, for which he was to be delivered unto Satan, for which all the Church should humble themselves; yet upon his true repentance, no ban is to separate him from the rest of the brethren, no doom of endless penance is recorded against him. Whatever might have been the enormity of his offence, he was to be forgiven, as in heaven, so on earth.

The manner in which the Corinthian church are described as regarding this offence, before the Apostle's rebuke to them, no less than the lenient sentence of the Apostle himself afterwards, as well as his constant admonitions on the same subject in all his Epistles, must be regarded as indications of the state of morality among the first converts. Above all other things, the Apostle insisted on purity as the first note of the Christian character; and yet the very earnestness and frequency of his warnings show that he is speaking, not of a sin hardly named among saints, but of one the victory over which was the greatest and most difficult triumph of the cross of Christ.

2. It is hard to resist the impression which naturally arises in our minds, that the early Church was without spot, or wrinkle, or any such thing; as it were, a bride adorned for her husband, the type of Christian purity, the model of Apostolical order. The real image is marred with human frailty; its evils, perhaps, arising more from this cause than any other, that in its commencement it was a kingdom not of this world; in other words, it had no political existence or legal support; hence there is no evil more frequently referred to in the Epistles than disorder.

This spirit of disorder was manifested in various ways. In the church of Corinth the communion of the Lord's Supper was administered so as to be a scandal; "one was hungry, and another was drunken." There was as yet no rite or custom to which all conformed. In the same church the spiritual gifts were manifested without rule or order. It seemed as if God was not the author of peace, but of confusion. All spoke together, men and women, apparently without distinction, singing, praying, teaching, uttering words unintelligible to the rest, with no regular succession or subordination (1 Cor. xiv.). The scene in their assemblies was such, that if an unbeliever had come in, he would have said they were mad.

Evils of this kind in a great measure arose from the absence of church authority. Even the Apostle himself persuades more often than commands, and often uses language which implies a sort of hesitation whether his rule would be acknowledged or not. The diverse offices, the figure of the members and the body, do not refer to what was, but to what ought to be, to an ideal of harmonious life and action, which the Apostle holds up before them, which in practice was far from being realized. The Church was not organized, but was in process of organization. Its only punishment was excommunication, which, as in modern so in primitive times, could not be enforced against the wishes of the majority. In two cases only are members of the Church "delivered unto Satan" (1 Cor. v. 5; 1 Tim. i. 20). It was a moral and spiritual, not a legal control, that was exercised. Hence the frequent admonitions given, doubtless because they were needed: "Obey them that have the rule over you."

A second kind of disorder arose from unsettlement of mind. Of such unsettlement we find traces in the levity and vanity of the Corinthians; in the fickleness with which the Galatians left St. Paul for the false teachers; almost (may we not say?) in the very passion with which the Apostle addresses them; above all, in the case of the Thessalonians. How few among all the converts were there capable of truly discerning their relation to the world around! or of supporting themselves alone when the fervor of conversion had passed away, and the Apostle was no longer present with them! They had entered into a state so different from that of their fellow-men, that it might well be termed supernatural. The ordinary experience of men was no longer their guide. They left their daily employments. The great change which they felt within seemed to extend itself without, and involve the world in its shadow. So "palpable to sense" was the vision of Christ's coming again, that their only fear or doubt was how the departed would have a share in it. No religious belief could be more unsettling than this: that to-day, or to-morrow, or the third day, before the sun set or the dawn arose, the sign of the Son of Man might appear in the clouds of heaven. It was not possible to take thought for the morrow, to study to be quiet and get their own living, when men hardly expected the morrow. Death comes to individuals now, as nature prepares them for it; but the immediate expectation of Christ's coming is out of the course of nature. Young and old alike look for it. It is a resurrection of the world itself, and implies a corresponding revolution in the thoughts, feelings, and purposes of men.

A third kind of disorder may have arisen from the same causes, but seems to have assumed another character. As among the Jews, so among the first Christians, there were those who needed to be perpetually reminded, that the powers that be were ordained of God. The heathen converts could not at once lay aside the licentiousness of manners amid which they had been brought up; no more could the Jewish converts give up their aspirations, that at this time "the kingdom was to be restored to Israel," which had perhaps been in some cases their first attraction to the Gospel. A community springing up in Palestine under the dominion of the Romans, could not be expected exactly to draw the line between the things that were Cæsar's and the things that were God's, or to understand in what sense "the children were free," in what sense it was nevertheless their duty to pay tribute. The frequent exhortations to obey magistrates, are a proof at once of the tendency to rebellion, and of the energy with which the Apostles set themselves against it.

3. The third head of our inquiry related to scruples of conscience, which were chiefly of two kinds; regarding either the observance of days, or the eating with the unclean or unbelievers. Were they, or were they not, to observe the Jewish Sabbath, or new moon, or passover? Such questions as these are not to be considered the fancies or opinions of individuals; but, as mankind are quick enough to discover, involve general principles, and are but the outward signs of some deep and radical difference. In the question of the observance of Jewish feasts, and still more in the question of going in unto men uncircumcised and eating with them, was implied the whole question of the relation of the disciple of Christ to the Jew, just as the question of sitting at meat in the idol's temple was the question of the relation of the disciple of Christ

to the Gentile. Was the Christian to preserve his caste, and remain within the pale of Judaism? Was he in his daily life to carry his religious scruples so far as to exclude himself from the social life of the heathen world? How much prudence and liberty and charity was necessary for the solution of such difficulties?

Freedom is the key-note of the Gospel, as preached by St. Paul. "All things are lawful." "There is no distinction of Jew or Greek, barbarian or Scythian, bond or free." "Let no man judge you of a new moon or a Sabbath." "Where the spirit of the Lord is, there is liberty." And yet, if we go back to its origin, the Christian Church was born into the world marked and diversified with the features of the religions that had preceded it, bound within the curtains of the tabernacle, colored with Oriental opinions that refused to be washed out of the minds of men. The scruples of individuals are but indications of the elements out of which the Church was composed. There were narrow paths in which men walked, customs which clung to them long after the reason of them had ceased, observances which they were unable to give up, though conscience and reason alike disowned them, which were based on the traditions of half the world, and could not be relinquished, however alien to the spirit of the Gospel. Slowly and gradually, as Christianity itself became more spread, these remnants of Judaism or Orientalism disappeared, and the spirit which had been taught from the beginning, made itself felt in the hearts of men and in the institutions of the Church.

4. The heresies of the Apostolical age are a subject too wide for illustration in a note. We shall attempt no more than to bring together the names and heads of opinion which occur in Scripture, with the view of completing the preceding sketch.

There was the party of Peter and of Paul, of the circumcision and of the uncircumcision. There were those who knew Christ according to the flesh; those who, like St. Paul, knew him only as revealed within. There were others who, after casting aside circumcision, were still struggling between the old dispensation and the new. There were those who never went beyond the baptism of John; others, again, to whom the Gospel of Christ clothed itself in Alexandrian language. There were prophets, speakers with tongues, discerners of spirits, interpreters of tongues. There were those who looked daily for the coming of Christ; others who said that the Resurrection was passed already. There were seekers after knowledge, falsely so called; worshippers of angels, intruders into things they had not seen. There were those who maintained an Oriental asceticism in their lives, "forbidding to marry, commanding to abstain from meats." There was the doctrine of the Nicolaitans, the synagogue of Satan, who "said that they were Jews and are not," "the woman Jezebel, which calleth herself a prophetess." There were wild heretics, "many Antichrists," "grievous wolves, entering into the fold," apostasy of whole churches at once. There were mingled anarchy and licentiousness, "filthy dreamers, despising dominion, speaking evil of dignities," of whom no language is too strong for St. Paul or St. John to use, though they seem to have been separated by no definite line from the Church itself. There were fainter contrasts, too, of those who agreed in the unity of the same spirit, aspects and points of view, as we term them, of faith and works, of the Epistle to the Romans and the Epistle to the Hebrews.

How this outline is to be filled up must for ever remain, in a great degree, matter of speculation. Yet there is not a single trait here mentioned, which does not reappear in the second century, either within the Church or without it, more or less prominent as favored by circumstances or the reverse. The beginning of Ebionitism, Sabaism, Gnosticism, Montanism, Alexandrianism, Orientalism, and of the wild licentiousness which marked the course of several of them, are all discernible in the Apostolical age. They would be more correctly regarded, not as offshoots of Christianity, but as the soil in which it arose. Some of them seem to acquire a temporary principle of life, and to grow up parallel with the

Church itself. As opinions and tendencies of the human mind, many linger among us to the present day. Only after the destruction of Jerusalem, with the spread of the Gospel over the world, as the spirit of the East moves towards the West, Judaism fades and dies away, to rise again, as some hold, in the glorified form of a mediæval Church.

Such is the reverse side of the picture of the Apostolical age; what proportions we should give to each feature it is impossible to determine. We need not infer that all churches were in the same disorder as Corinth and Galatia; nor can we say how far the more flagrant evils were tamely submitted to by the Church itself. There was much of good that we can never know; much also of evil. And perhaps the general lesson which we gather from the preceding considerations is, not that the state of the primitive Church was better or worse than our first thoughts would have suggested, but that its state was one in which good and evil exercised a more vital power, were more subtly intermingled with, and more easily passed into, each other. All things were coming to the birth, some in one way, some in another. The supports of custom, of opinion, of tradition, had given way; human nature was, as it were, thrown upon itself and the guidance of the spirit of God. There were as many diversities of human character in the world then as now; more strange influences of religion and race than have ever since met in one; a far greater yearning of the human intellect to solve the problems of existence. There was no settled principle of morality independent of and above religious convictions. All these causes are sufficient to account for the diversities of opinion or practice, as well as for the extremes which met in the bosom of the primitive Church.

ON THE BELIEF IN THE COMING OF CHRIST IN THE APOSTOLICAL AGE.

By BENJAMIN JOWETT.

The belief in the near approach of the coming of Christ is spoken of, or implied, in almost every book of the New Testament, in the discourses of our Lord himself as well as in the Acts of the Apostles, in the Epistles of St. Paul no less than in the Book of the Revelation. The remains of such a belief are discernible in the Montanism of the second century, which is separated by a scarcely definable line from the Church itself. Nor is there wanting in our own day a dim and meagre shadow of the same primitive faith, though the world appears dead to it, and all things remain the same as at the beginning. There are still those who argue from the very lapse of time, that "now is their salvation nearer than when they believed." All religious men have at times blended in their thoughts earth and heaven, while there are some who have raised their passing feelings into doctrinal truth, and have seemed to see in the temporary state of the first converts the type of Christian life in all ages.

The great influence which this belief exercised on the beginnings of the Church, and the degree of influence which it still retains, render the consideration of it necessary for the right understanding of St. Paul's Epistles. Yet it is a subject from which the interpreter of Scripture would gladly turn aside. For it seems as if he were compelled to say at the outset, "that St. Paul was mistaken, and that in support of his mistake he could appeal to the words of Christ himself." Nothing can be plainer than the meaning of those words, and yet they seem to be contradicted by the very fact that, after eighteen centuries, the world is as it was. In the words which are attributed, in the Epistle of St. Peter, to the unbelievers of that day, we might truly say that, since the fathers have fallen asleep, all things remain the same from the beginning. Not only do "all things remain the same," but the very belief itself (in the sense in which it was held by the first Christians) has been ready to vanish away.

Why, then, were the traces of such a belief permitted to appear in the New Testament? Some will say, "As a trial of our faith"; others will have recourse to the double senses of prophecy, to divide the past from the future, the seen from the unseen. Others will cite its existence as a proof that the books of Scripture were compiled at a time when such a belief was still living, and this not without, but within, the circle of the Church itself. It may be also regarded as an indication that we were not intended to interpret Scripture apart from the light of experience, or violently to bend life and truth into agreement with isolated texts. Lastly, so far as we can venture to move such a question of our Lord himself, we may observe that his teaching here, as in other places, is on a level with the modes of thought of his age, clothed in figures, as it must necessarily be, to express "the things that eye hath not seen," limited by time, as if to give the sense of reality to what otherwise would be vague and infinite, yet mysterious in this respect too, for of "that hour knoweth no man"; and that however these figures of speech are explained, or these opposite aspects reconciled, their meaning dimly seen has been the stay and hope of the believer in all ages, who knows, nevertheless, that since the Apostles have passed away, all things remain the same from the beginning, and that "the round world is set so fast that it cannot be moved."

The surprise that we naturally feel, when the attention is first called to this singular discrepancy between faith and experience, is greatly lessened by our observing that even the language of Scripture is not free from inconsistency. For the words of our Lord himself are not more in apparent contradiction with the course of experience, than they are with other words which are equally attributed to him by the Evangelists. He who says, "This generation shall not pass away until all these things be fulfilled," is the same as he who tells his disciples, "It is not for you to know the times and the seasons which the Father hath put in his own power," and "Of that hour knoweth no man, no, not the angels of God, nor the Son, but the Father." Is it reverent, or irreverent, to say that Christ knew what he himself declares "that he did not know"? Is it consistent, or inconsistent, with the language of the Gospels, that the Apostle St. Paul should at first have known no more than our Lord had taught his disciples? or that in the course of years only he should have grown up to another and a higher truth, that "to depart and be with Christ was far better"? Is it strange that, from time to time, he should change his tone, seeming by this very change to say, "Whether in the body, or out of the body, I cannot tell"; when our Lord himself at one time speaks of "Jerusalem being encompassed by armies"; at another, gives no answer to the question, "Where, Lord?" but, "Where the carcass is, there will the eagles be gathered together"? Our conception, both of place and time, becomes indistinct as we enter into the unseen world. And does not the Scripture itself acknowledge these necessary limits of its own revelation to man?

But instead of regarding this or any other fact of Scripture as a difficulty to be explained away, it will be more instructive for us to consider the nature of the belief, and its probable effect on the infant communion. Strictly speaking, the expectation of the day of the Lord was not a belief, but a necessity, in the early Church; clinging, as it did, to the thought of Christ, it could not bear to be separated from him: it was his absence, not his presence, that the first believers found it hard to realize. "Yet a little while, and they did not see him; but yet a little while, and they would again see him." Nor was it possible for them at once to lay aside the material images in which the faith of prophets and psalmists had clothed the day of the Lord. We readily admit that they lingered around "the elements of the law"; but we must admit also that the imagery of the prophets had a reality and fact to them which it has not to us, who are taught by time itself that all these things "are a shadow, but the substance is of Christ."

We naturally ask, Why a future life, as distinct from this, was not made a part of the first preaching of the Gospel? Why, in other words, the faith of the first Christians did not exactly coincide with our own? There are many ways in which the answer to this question may be expressed. The philosopher will say that the difference in the modes of thought of that age and our own, rendered it impossible, humanly speaking, that the veil of sense should be altogether removed. The theologian will admit that Providence does not teach men that which they can teach themselves. While there are lessons which it immediately communicates, there is much which it leaves to be drawn forth by time and events. Experience may often enlarge faith, it may also correct it. No one can doubt that the faith and practice of the early Church, respecting the admission of the Gentiles, were greatly altered by the fact that the Gentiles themselves flocked in; "The kingdom of heaven suffered violence, and the violent took it by force." In like manner, the faith respecting the coming of Christ was modified by the continuance of the world itself. Common sense suggests, that those who were in the first ecstasy of conversion, and those who after the lapse of years saw the world unchanged, and the fabric of the Church on earth rising around them, could not regard the day of the Lord with the same feelings. While to the one it seemed near and present, at any moment ready to burst forth, to the other it was a long way off, separated by time, and as it were by place, a world beyond the stars, yet, strangely enough, also having its dwelling in the heart of man, as it were the atmosphere in which he lived, the mental world by which he was surrounded. Not at once, but gradually, did the cloud clear up, and the one mode of faith take the place of the other. Apart from the prophets, though then, beyond them, springing up in a new and living way in the soul of man, corrected by long experience, as the "fathers one by one fell asleep," as the hope of the Jewish race declined, as ecstatic gifts ceased, as a regular hierarchy was established in the Church, the belief in the coming of Christ was transformed from being outward to becoming inward, from being national to becoming individual and universal, from being Jewish to becoming Christian.

It must be admitted as a fact, that the earliest Christians spoke and thought about the coming of Christ in a way different from that which prevails among ourselves. Admitting this fact, we have now to consider some of the many aspects of this belief, and its effect on the lives of believers. It is hard for us to define its exact character, because it is hard to conceive a state of the Church, and of the human mind itself, unlike our own. In its origin it was simple and childlike, the belief of men who saw but a little way into the purposes of Providence, who never dreamed of a vista of futurity. It was not what we should term an article of faith, but natural and necessary; flowing immediately out of the life and state of the earliest believers. It was the feeling of men who looked for the coming of Christ as we might look for the return of a lost friend, many of whom had seen him on earth, and could not believe that he was taken from them for ever. But it was more than this; it was the feeling of men who had an intense sense of the change that had been wrought in themselves, and to whom this change seemed like the beginning of a greater change that was to spread itself over the world. It was the feeling of men who looked back upon the past, of which they knew so little, and discerned in it the workings of the same spirit, one and continuous, which they felt in their own souls; to whom the world within and the world without were reflected upon one another, and the history of the Jewish race was a parable, an "open secret" of the things to come. It was the feeling of men, each moment of whose lives was the meeting-point to them of heaven and earth, who scarcely thought either of the past or future in the eternity of the present.

Let those who think this is an imaginary picture recall to mind, and compare with Scripture, either what they may have read in books or experienced in themselves, as the workings of a mind suddenly converted to the Gospel. Such an one seems to lose his measure of events, and his true relation to the world. While other men are going on with their daily occupations, he only is out of sympathy with nature, and has fears and joys in himself, which he can neither communicate nor explain to his fellows. It is not that he is thinking of the endless ages in which he will partake of heavenly bliss; rather the present consciousness of sin, or the present sense of forgiveness and of peace in Christ, is already a sort of hell or heaven within him, which excludes the future. It is not that he has an increased insight into the original meaning of Scripture; rather he seems to absorb Scripture into himself. Least of all have persons in such a state of mind distinct or accurate conceptions of the world to come. The images in which they express themselves are carnal and visible, often inconsistent with each other, if they are uneducated, wanting in good taste, yet not the less the realization to them of a true and lively faith. The last thing that they desire, or could comprehend, is an intellectual theory of another life. They seem hardly to need either statements of doctrine or the religious ministration of others; their concern is with God only.

Substitute now for an individual a church, a nation, the three thousand who were converted on the day of Pentecost, the multitudes of Jews that believed, zealous for the law; imagine them changed at the same instant by one spirit, and we seem to see on a larger scale the same effects following. Their conversion is an exception to the course of nature; itself a revelation and inspiration, a wonder of which they can give no account to themselves or others, not the least wonderful part of which is their communion with one another. They come into existence as a society, with common hopes and fears, at one with each other, separated from mankind at large. What they feel within spreads itself over the world. The good and evil that they are conscious of in themselves, seem to exist without them in aggravated proportions; a fellowship of the saints on one side, and a mystery of iniquity on the other. They do not read history, or comprehend the sort of imperfect necessity under which men act as creatures of their age. The same guilt which they acknowledge in themselves they attach to other men; the same judgment which would await them is awaiting the world everywhere. In the events around them, in their own sufferings, in their daily life, they see the preparations for the great conflict between good and evil, between Christ and Belial, if, indeed, it be not already begun. The circle of their own life includes in it the destinies of the human race itself, of which it is, as it were, the microcosm, seen by the eye of faith and the light of inward experience. This is what the law and the prophets seemed to them to have meant when they spoke of God's judgments on his enemies, of the Lord coming with ten thousand of his saints. And the signs which were to accompany these things were already seen among them, "not in word only, but in power, and in the Holy Spirit, and in much assurance."

To us the preaching of the Gospel is a new beginning, from which we date all things, beyond which we neither desire nor are able to inquire. To the first believers it was otherwise; not the beginning of a new world, but the end of a former one. They looked back to the past, because the veil of the future was not yet lifted up. They were living in "the latter days," the confluence of all times, the meeting-point of the purposes of God. They read all things in the light of the approaching end of the world. They were not taught, and could not have imagined, that for eighteen centuries servants of God should continue on the earth, waiting, like themselves, for the promise of his coming. They were not taught, and could not have imagined, that after three centuries the Church which they saw poverty-stricken and persecuted should be the mistress of the earth, and that, in another sense than they had hoped, the kingdoms of this world should become the kingdoms of the Lord and of his Christ. Instead of it, they beheld in a figure the heavens opening, and the angels of God ascending and descending; the present outpouring of the Spirit, and the evil and perplexity of the world itself, being the earnest of the things which were shortly to come to pass.

It has been often remarked, that the belief in the coming of Christ stood in the same relation to the Apostolic Church that the expectation of death does to ourselves. Certainly the absence of exhortations based upon the shortness of life, which are not unfrequent in the Old Testament, and are so familiar to our own day, forms a remarkable feature in the writings of the New Testament, and in a measure seems to confirm such an opinion. And yet the similarity is rather apparent than real; or, at any rate, the difference between the two is not less remarkable. For the feeble apprehension which each man entertains of his own mortality can bear no comparison with that living sense of the day of the Lord which was the habitual thought of the first Christians, which was not so much a "coming" as a "presence" to them, as its very name implied (παρουσία). How different also was the event looked for, no less than the anticipation of it! There is nothing terrible in death; it is the repose of wearied nature; it steals men away one by one, while the world goes still on its way. We fear it at a distance, but not near. But the day of the Lord was to be a change, not to the individual only, but to the world; a scene of great fear and great joy at once to the whole Church and to all mankind, which is in its very nature sudden, unexpected, coming "as a thief in the night, and as travail upon a woman with child." Yet it might be said to be expected, too, so strange and contradictory is its nature; for the first disciples were sitting waiting for it, "with their lamps lighted and their loins girded." It was not darkness, nor sleep, nor death, but a day of light and life, in the expectation of which men were to walk as children ot the light, yet fearful by its very suddenness and the vengeance to be poured on the wicked.

Such a belief could not be without its effect on the lives of the first converts, and on the state of the Church. While it increased the awfulness of life, it almost unavoidably withdrew men's thoughts from its ordinary duties. It naturally led to the state described in the Corinthian church, in which spiritual gifts had taken the place of moral duties, and of those very gifts, the less spiritual were preferred to the more spiritual. It took the mind away from the kingdom of God within, to fix it on signs and wonders, "the things spoken of by the prophet Joel," when the sun should be turned into darkness, and the moon into blood. It made men almost ready to act contrary to the decrees of Cæsar, from the sense of what they saw, or seemed to see, in the world around them. The intensity of the spiritual state in which they lived, so far beyond that of our daily life, is itself the explanation of the spiritual disorder which seems so strange to us in men who were ready to hazard their lives for the truth, and which was but the natural reaction against their former state.

It is obvious that such a belief was inconsistent with an established ecclesiastical order. A succession of bishops could have had no meaning in a world that was to vanish away. Episcopacy, it has been truly remarked, was in natural antagonism to Montanism; and in the age of the Apostles as well, there is an opposition, traceable in the Epistles themselves, between the supernatural gifts and the order and discipline of the Church. Ecclesiastical as well as political institutions are not made, but grow. What we are apt to regard as their first idea and design is in reality their after development, what in the fulness of time they become, not what they originally were, the former being faintly, if at all, discernible in the new birth of the Church and of the world.

Nor is it unreasonable to suppose that the meagreness of those historical memorials of the first age which survived it, has been the result of such a belief. What interest would be attached to the events of this world, if they were so soon to be lost in another? or to the lessons of history, when the nations of the earth were in a few years to appear before the judgment-seat of Christ? Even the narrative of the acts and sayings of the Saviour of mankind must have had a different degree of importance to those who expected to see with their eyes the Word of life, and to us, to whom they are the great example, for after ages, of faith and practice. Among many causes which may be assigned for the great historical chasm which separates the life of Christ and his Apostles from after ages, this is not the least probable. The age of the Apostles was an age, not of history, but of prophecy.

THE DEATH OF CHRIST, CONSIDERED AS A SACRIFICE.*

By JAMES FOSTER, D. D.

One of the positive institutions of Christianity is what we commonly call the Lord's Supper. And as in this accordance, the death of Christ is commemorated under the notion of a *sacrifice*, I shall, before I specify the moral uses of it, endeavor briefly to explain and vindicate that representation; which is the more necessary, because nothing in the whole Christian doctrine has been more grossly misrepresented, or given its adversaries, who take their accounts of it from party writers, and not from the New Testament itself, (a method of proceeding that argues great unfairness and prejudice,) a more plausible occasion to triumph. But if the matter be rightly considered, it will appear that the advantages which they think they have against the Christian religion upon this head are but imaginary. For,

1. The New Testament nowhere represents God as a rigorous, inexorable being, who insisted upon *full satisfaction* for the sins of men, before he could be induced to offer terms of reconciliation. It says, indeed, not one word of satisfaction, much less of strict and adequate satisfaction, not a syllable of the infinite evil of sin, of infinite justice, the hypostatical union, or "the Deity's being so united to the man Christ Jesus, as that the two infinitely distinct natures

* From the Defence of the Christian Revelation, in reply to Tindal.

constitute one person," and, "by virtue of this union, giving an infinite value to the sufferings of the human nature, and enabling it to pay a strict equivalent to God's offended vindictive justice." All this, I say, is the invention of more modern ages, (which, by subtle distinctions, and metaphysical obscurities, have deformed true Christianity to such a degree, that scarce any of its original features appear,) and bears not the least similitude to the language of the New Testament; in which the Divine Being is always described as slow to anger, merciful, and condescending to the frailties and infirmities of mankind; and forgiveness of sin represented, not as a thing for which a *price of equal value* was paid, and which might consequently be demanded in strict justice, but as a voluntary act of pure favor, and the effect of free and undeserved goodness. Nay, further,

2. The New Testament never asserts, that God could not have pardoned sin without a sacrifice, nor, consequently, that the death of Christ, considered in that view, was, upon any account, absolutely necessary. If indeed it be proved that this method is of Divine appointment, this will and ought to satisfy us, that there are wise reasons for it, but it cannot be inferred from hence, that it was absolutely necessary, or that the same wise purposes might not have been as effectually answered some other way. Nor,

3. Does the Christian religion anywhere expressly declare, or so much as intimate to us, that natural reason could not discover God to be a propitious being, and ready to be reconciled to his guilty creatures upon their repentance; but, on the contrary, lays down this as the fundamental point of all religion, and consequently as a principle that might be argued with great probability, that "God is a rewarder of them who diligently seek him," Heb. ii. 6, and supposes, that the great goodness, which he has demonstrated in the general constitution of things, and course of providence, was a rational encouragement to the Gentile world to serve and worship him, in hopes of acceptance and mercy.

4. It is of great importance to observe, that the death of

Christ, as appears, would have happened, if it had never been designed as a sacrifice, and consequently was not appointed arbitrarily and solely with a view to that. The true state of the case seems to be this. The wise and merciful God, having compassion on the ignorance and degeneracy of the world, determined, at a certain time fixed by his infinite wisdom, to interpose, and when they had corrupted the religion of nature, and were not likely to recover the right knowledge of it, teach them their duty by an external revelation. The person whom he chose to be his messenger is characterized as his Son, an innocent person, of great dignity and excellence, whom he had before employed in the most important transactions, and who was highly beloved and favored by him; and the principal reason of his employing one so extraordinary as his minister upon this occasion, we are told in the New Testament, was to conciliate greater attention and regard to his doctrine. Matt. xxi. 37; Heb. i. 1, 2; ii. 2, 3. We are to take it, therefore, I think, that the first view of God in sending Christ into the world was, that, as a prophet, he might restore the true religion, and publish the glad tidings of life and immortality, and by this means reform the errors and vices of mankind.

But, as he was sent to preach a most strict and holy doctrine, among a people abominably corrupt and vicious, to recommend a rational and spiritual worship of the Deity to those who were fond of form and ceremony, and resolved the whole of the religion into external rites and traditional superstitions, and assumed the character of their Messiah, or king, when both his circumstances in life, and the religion he taught, contradicted the expectations they had entertained of temporal pomp and grandeur under the Messiah's government, and consequently disappointed all the views of their covetousness and ambition, he gained comparatively but few converts, and was abused and persecuted by the priests and men in power, whom the multitude blindly followed, and at last put to death with great torment and ignominy. From this plain and unquestionably true account of the fact, it appears that his sufferings were the *natural consequence* of attempting to reform the manners of a degenerate age, and opposing the superstition and darling prejudices of the Jewish nation; and could not be avoided, but by such a compliance on his part, as would have been inconsistent with virtue and integrity, or by a miraculous interposition of Providence. And God, who foresaw all this, appointed that the death of Christ, which really happened in the natural course of things, should be considered as a sacrifice.

Let me observe, by the way, that by considering the matter in this light, all objections against the justice of God, in determining that an innocent person should suffer for the guilty, are entirely obviated. For the death of Christ was not appointed absolutely and arbitrarily with this view, but, which is vastly different, and cannot sure have the least appearance of injustice, it fell out just as other events do, in the common course of things; and all that can be immediately attributed to God in the whole affair is, that he sent him into the world, though he foresaw the consequences of it; and ordered that his death, which would have happened without a miracle, if there had been no such design, should be regarded as a sacrifice. Though, I must own, I cannot see, if the matter had been otherwise, how it could be unjust, or tyrannical, to propose even to an innocent person to suffer, with his own free consent, in order to promote so great a good; especially if we suppose, what the Christian revelation expressly teaches in the present case, that he would be gloriously and amply rewarded for it. Having thus removed all the difficulties of any moment that lie against this doctrine, the only thing that remains is to show what wise ends might be served by it.

I shall not inquire into the original of expiatory sacrifices, which were as early in the world as the first accounts of history; whether they were owing to an express appointment of God, as may seem probable from the history of Moses, or had their rise from the fears and superstition of mankind, who, being uneasy under a sense of guilt, confused in their reasonings about the goodness of the Deity, and uncertain whether he would accept them, notwithstanding past offences, upon their repentance and reformation only, (though, I make no doubt, they might have argued this truth, with a good deal of probability, even from the light of nature,) would naturally fly to every little expedient, that their bewildered imaginations suggested might be proper; and so began first with sacrificing brute creation, and afterwards, as their distrust and fears increased, had recourse, in many heathen nations, to the abominable practice of human sacrifices. Which shows plainly, that their reason was more and more perplexed, and corrupted, and darkened to a prodigious degree, with respect to the very fundamental principles of religion and virtue.

If sacrificing was entirely a human invention, it would be hard to give any account of it, more than of innumerable other superstitions, which, in the darkness and extreme depravity of the Pagan world, almost universally prevailed. Human sacrifices are a disgrace to our nature, as well as in the highest degree dishonorable to God. And for others, there is no foundation at all in reason to suppose that they could expiate the guilt of moral offences, or be of the least efficacy towards reinstating the sinner in the Divine favor. On the other hand, if sacrifices were originally of Divine appointment, they could not be designed to propitiate the Deity, because the very institution of them necessarily supposed that he was already propitious. For what end then were they ordained? Was it because the all-wise and merciful Governor of the world delighted in the blood of innocent animals? Or was he fond of being served with great expense and ceremony? These are low and unworthy conceptions of him. All the uses therefore that it was possible, in reason, for sacrifices to serve, or, consequently, that they should be designed to answer, if they were of divine original, may I think be reduced to these two; namely, keeping up a firm belief of God's reconcilableness, and being ready to forgive his guilty creatures upon their repentance, and, at the same time, a strong sense of the evil of sin, and their own demerit upon the account of it. In this view of standing memorials and testimonies to the most important truths, they might be very useful; but proper *expiations* they neither were, nor could be, whether they began from superstition, or immediate revelation.

And now the death of Christ may be very fitly represented as a sacrifice, nay, described in the strongest sacrificial phrases, since it answered completely all the rational purposes that expiatory sacrifices could ever serve. It is a standing memorial of God's being propitious, and inclined, as the Christian revelation assures us, not only to forgive sin in part, but entirely, and not only to remit the whole of the punishment, which the sinner had deserved, but moreover to bestow on him the glorious reward of eternal happiness upon his sincere repentance and reformation, and persevering in a virtuous course. So that it removes the uncertainty of our natural reasonings, and is wisely calculated to maintain in all ages a firm belief of that fundamental principle of *all* religion, which men's superstitious fears had very much corrupted and darkened, and gives the strongest possible encouragement to virtue.

Again, the death of Christ considered under the notion of a sacrifice will be, to the end of the world, a most lively memorial of the evil and demerit of sin. Nay, as God, in his infinite wisdom, has ordered it in such a manner, that nothing less should be considered as the sacrifice for the sins of the world than the death of a person so dear to him and of such transcendent dignity and excellence, he has by this appointment declared much more strongly his displeasure against sin, and what the sinner himself deserved to suffer, and cut off more effectually from wilful and impenitent offenders all ground of presumptuous hope and confidence in his mercy, than it was possible to do by any sacrifices of brute creatures. So that by the way in which he has condescended to pardon us there is the utmost discouragement given to vice, and the greatest care taken that could be by any method whatever to preserve the honor of the Divine government, and the reverence due to the authority of its laws. For, besides what hath been already suggested, a sense of our ill deserts upon account of our transgressions, of which the death of Christ represented as a sacrifice is a most affecting memorial, has a natural tendency to inspire us with the deepest humility, and fill us with shame and remorse for having deviated from the rule of right, and consequently to make us more circumspect and regular in our future behavior; and a sense of God's great goodness in freely forgiving our offences, when we had merited quite the contrary, must, if we have any sentiments of gratitude or honor, make us solicitous to please, and fearful of offending him.

If it be asked, how the death of Christ can answer the purpose of an expiatory sacrifice, when it happened in the natural course of things, and was not appointed directly, and only with that view, I answer, that, such sacrifices being never designed to *propitiate* the Deity, or as proper *expiations*, but memorials, in the manner above explained, there is no difficulty in accounting for it. For, in all other cases, it was God's appointing and accepting the sacrifice only, that made it a proper memorial; otherwise it could have no significancy, but what the fancy and superstition of men suggested. The use of sacrifices, therefore, depending entirely on his institution of them, or at least the use of those which were directly of his ordaining being that, and that only, which he intended, it follows, in the very nature of the thing, that if he is pleased to call the death of Christ a sacrifice, and would have it considered under that character, it must be a fit memorial of all he designed should be represented by it. And, besides, it has been shown, that there are several circumstances which render it a more useful memorial, than any other sacrifices that were ever offered.

Let me add to what has been said concerning the advantages of considering the death of Christ as a sacrifice in general, that by its being described as the one offering which has "perfected for ever them that are sanctified," Heb. x. 14, the Christian religion has guarded, in the most effectual manner, against the use of *all* sacrifices for the future, and particularly against human sacrifices, one of the most monstrous corruptions of anything which has borne the name of religion, that ever appeared in the world. And I would hope, that even its adversaries will allow this to be a great argument in its favor, that it was so wisely suited to the state of the world at that time, and not only abolished sacrificing, but in a way accommodated in some measure to the general conceptions and prejudices of mankind, and consequently the more likely to take, guarded against the revival of a custom afterwards, (preserving however all the rational uses of it,) which had been the source of infinite superstition.

Should it be said, that there is no need of such *memorials* as sacrifices were, and the death of Christ is represented to be, because if the Christian religion had asserted clearly that God is a propitious being, and particularly expressed the terms upon which his guilty creatures might be reconciled to him, — if it had declared absolutely against the use of *all* sacrifices, and condemned especially the barbarity and inhumanity of human sacrifices, — this alone would have been sufficient; I answer, that it might indeed have been sufficient; but how does it appear, which is the point on which the argument wholly turns, that the appointing a memorial of these things, in the sacrifice of Christ, is *useless?* Thus much is undeniable, that these things do not in the least interfere. But, besides, was not the great end in view most likely to be secured by positive declarations, and a standing memorial both, that will naturally give light to and strengthen each other? To which we may add, that the superstition of men will in some circumstances pervert the plainest words; but it is not so easy to evade the design of a *memorial*, especially in that very way, namely, under the notion of a *sacrifice*, to which their superstition would directly tend.

There is nothing, that I can find, advanced by the author of *Christianity as old as the Creation*, upon this head, but what has been fully obviated, or goes upon the common *mistakes* of the Scripture doctrine of Christ's sacrifice. Only, whereas, he says, "that the reasons assigned for it could never influence those who never heard of Christ." * I allow it. But what then? Is it not enough, that they may be of great use to those who have heard of him? Nay, the doctrine of Christ's being a propitiation for the sins of the whole world is not therefore useless, because a great part of the world know nothing of it, since it is of the highest moral advantage to those who enjoy the Christian revelation; as it represents to them the universal goodness of the common Father of mankind, and that "in every nation, he that feareth God, and worketh righteousness, is accepted with him"; and, consequently, encourages universal benevolence, and an esteem of the whole rational creation, however distinguished by external privileges, and restrains that spiritual pride and insolence, which prompt many Christians, to the reproach of our holy religion, (and is indeed too common in all religious sects, who imagine the superiority to be on their side,) to confine the favor of God to themselves, and despise, censure, and condemn all others.

I proceed now to point out a few of the excellences and eminent advantages of that positive institution of Christianity, in which we commemorate the death of Christ, and particularly under the character of a sacrifice. And the moral uses of it are so plain, and withal so various, and exceeding great, that it may be questioned, whether anything of a positive nature can possibly be appointed, that has a stronger tendency to promote the practice of virtue, nay, as will sufficiently appear by just enumerating them, of the most amiable, generous, and heroic virtue.

In general, as we perform this service in honor of Christ, we thereby, as well as by baptism, solemnly profess our belief of his religion, and consequently engage to make it the rule of our behavior. But to mention some of its peculiar advantages. Frequently commemorating the death of Christ, as a sacrifice for sin, must maintain in us a constant, firm

* Christianity, &c., p. 418.

belief of that first principle even of natural religion, that God is ready to forgive all sincere penitents, and "a rewarder of them that diligently seek him"; and, at the same time, as it sets before us our own great demerit, must impress a strong and lively sense of the goodness of God, in freely pardoning our offences, and rewarding so abundantly our sincere though imperfect virtue; the natural consequence of which will be, shame for having done amiss, and affronted the government of so gracious and compassionate a Being, and the highest abhorrence of such an ungenerous conduct for the future. If we reflect, with becoming gratitude, on God's wonderful benevolence and mercy to mankind, it is impossible but this must produce a cheerful obedience to all his commands, and especially a delight in doing good after his most excellent and perfect example. Again, when we remember, that the very design of the death of Christ was "to redeem us from all iniquity," and make us "zealous of good works," Tit. ii. 14, and that upon these terms only we are to expect any advantage from it, nothing can have a more powerful tendency to excite to strict and universal purity.

Further, if we consider our partaking of this ordinance as a communion, "the cup of blessing, which we bless, as the communion of the blood of Christ, and the bread, which we break, as the communion of the body of Christ," 1 Cor. x. 16, by which we acknowledge all sincere Christians, however denominated and distinguished, as our brethren, members together with ourselves of the same spiritual body, or society, entitled to the same privileges, and having the same "hope of their calling"; that "we, being many, are one bread, and one body, because we are all partakers of that one bread," ver. 17;—this must be of excellent use to promote mutual esteem, concord, and harmony; and, if the true intention of it was followed, would make Christians regard one another according to their real merit, and not for the trifling peculiarities of any particular sect, and effectually reconcile all party differences; by which means impositions upon conscience, violent controversies, unscriptural terms of communion, schisms, persecutions, which have been of fatal consequence both to religion and civil society, would be entirely prevented. But lest we should stop here, and confine our benevolence to the household of faith, considering the death of Christ as "a propitiation for the sins of the whole world," 1 John ii. 2, will naturally inspire a universal love of mankind. For there is an irresistible force in the Apostle's argument, "If God so loved us, we," who are dependent upon and obliged to each other, and cannot subsist without a mutual intercourse of good offices, "ought *much more* to love one another." Chap. iv. 11.

Indeed, commemorating the death of Christ in a devout and solemn manner, in its entire design, and with all its circumstances, will suggest the greatest and most generous sentiments, and afford motives to the most extensive and heroic benevolence that mankind can possibly practise. For, besides what has been already hinted, if we consider that God gave his Son to die for us while we were enemies, Rom. v. 10, this must kill all the seeds of malice and revenge in us, and raise such a noble spirit of humanity and compassion as the greatest injuries shall not bear down and extinguish; which will be further strengthened by reflecting on the behavior of Christ, who under the greatest abuses and indignities pitied and prayed for his persecutors. His example, likewise, in choosing to die rather than forfeit his integrity, and to promote the happiness of mankind, will teach us, and accordingly it is thus inculcated by St. John, 1 John iii. 16, to sacrifice all private considerations, nay, life itself, for the public good; and, besides, has a tendency to beget in us an entire submission to Providence under the worst circumstances that may befall us, and an undaunted fortitude, resolution, and constancy of mind, when we are called to suffer in a good cause, and for the advancement of truth and virtue. And all these arguments will receive an additional force, when we reflect that the example we commemorate is that of a friend and generous benefactor, an example that is in itself amiable, and which we should consequently be ambitious to imitate; and from the innocence and dignity of the sufferer.

As therefore it appears that we cannot commemorate the death of Christ in the manner in which Christianity has commanded it, without having our resolutions to practise universal virtue strengthened, and improving in the greatest, most amiable, useful, and godlike dispositions, which this institution has a peculiar and most admirable aptitude to excite and confirm; need I add anything more to prove that it is worthy of God, a being of absolute purity, a being of most perfect and universal goodness? Or that it is becoming the wisdom of his providence, and suitable to the great end he has in view, the rectitude and happiness of the moral creation, to oblige us by a law made on purpose, and the practice of a plain, significant rite, to enter frequently upon such reflections as are of the utmost moral use, and yet, without some institution of this kind, (considering how little inclined the bulk of mankind are to think, unless they are put upon it,) are likely to be omitted, or very much neglected; and, besides, cannot reasonably be expected to have that weight and influence in a slight, cursory, occasional meditation, as they will very probably, when they are considered as a solemn act of devotion, which we perform in obedience to an express Divine command?

THE EPISTLES TO THE CORINTHIANS, IN RELATION TO THE GOSPEL HISTORY.

By ARTHUR P. STANLEY, M. A.,*
CANON OF CANTERBURY.

"Have I not seen Jesus Christ our Lord?" — 1 Cor. ix. 1.

The two Epistles to the Corinthians, as has been already observed, are eminently historical; and in the course of the remarks made upon them it has been my object to draw out as clearly as possible every illustration or testimony which they afford to the history of the early Church. But there is another kindred question, which is so important in itself, that, though partially touched upon in the several passages which bear upon it, it may yet not be out of place at the close of these Epistles to consider it as a whole.

The question which the Apostle asked of his Judaizing opponents, and which his Judaizing opponents asked of him, "Have I not seen Jesus Christ our Lord?" is one which in our days has been often asked in a wider sense than that in which the words were used by the Apostle or his adversaries. "Is the representation of Christ in the Epistles the same as the representation of Christ in the Gospels? — What is the evidence, direct or indirect, furnished by St. Paul to the facts of the Gospel history? If the Gospels had perished, could we from the Epistles form an image of Christ, like to that which the Gospels present? Can we discover between the Epistles and the Gospels any such coincidences and resem-

* From his Commentary on the Epistles of Paul to the Corinthians.

blance as Paley discovered between the Epistles and the Acts? Is the 'Gospel' of the Evangelical Apostle different from the 'Gospel' of the Evangelistic narratives?"

Such an inquiry has been started sometimes in doubt, sometimes in perplexity. It is suggested partly by the nature of the case, by that attitude of separation and independent action which St. Paul took apart from the other Apostles, and which, even irrespectively of his writings, awakened in the minds of his opponents the suspicion that "he had not seen the Lord Jesus," — that he was not truly an "Apostle of Christ," and that therefore "he taught things contrary to Christ's teaching." It is suggested also by the attempts which in later times have been made, both by those without and by those within the outward pale of Christianity, to widen the breach between the teaching of the Epistles and the Gospels; both by those who have been anxious to show that the Christian faith ought to be sought in "not Paul, but Jesus"; and by those who believe and profess that "the Gospel" is contained, not in the Evangelical History, but in the Pauline Epistles.

From many points of view, and to many minds, questions like these will seem superfluous or unimportant. But, touching as they do on various instructive subjects, and awakening in some quarters a peculiar interest, they may well demand a consideration here. The two Epistles to Corinth are those from which an answer may most readily be obtained, both because they contain all, or almost all, of the most important allusions to the subject of the Gospel history, and also because they belong to the earliest, as well as the most undisputed, portion of the Apostolical writings. At the same time, it will not interfere with the precision or unity of the inquiry, if it includes such illustrations as may be furnished by the other Epistles also.

I. The first class of coincidences to which we most naturally turn, are those which relate to isolated sayings of Christ. This (partly for reasons which will be stated hereafter) is the least satisfactory part of the inquiry. It cannot be denied that they are few and scanty, and that, in these few, there is in no case an exact correspondence with the existing narratives.

There are in St. Paul's Epistles only two occasions on which our Lord's authority is directly quoted. In 1 Cor. vii. 10, when speaking of marriage, the Apostle refers to a command of the Lord, as distinct from a command of his own, and as the command he gives the words, "*Let not the wife depart from her husband.*" In 1 Cor. ix. 14, when speaking of the right of the Apostles to receive a maintenance from those whom they taught, he says, "*Even so the Lord 'ordained'* (διέταξεν) *that they which preach the Gospel should live of the Gospel.*" In neither case are the exact words of the existing records quoted; but we can hardly doubt that he refers in one case to the prohibition, "*Whosoever shall put away his wife .... causeth her to commit adultery*" (Matt. v. 32; Mark x. 11; Luke xvi. 18); in the other, to the command to the Twelve and the Seventy, "*Carry neither purse nor scrip nor shoes,....for the laborer is worthy of his hire*" (Luke x. 4, 7; Matt. x. 9, 10).

To these quotations we may add, that in the Acts of the Apostles (xx. 35), in his speech to the Ephesian elders, "*Remember the words of the Lord Jesus, how he said, It is more blessed to give than to receive.*" It is also to be observed, that, in closing the discussion on the conduct of Christian assemblies (1 Cor. xiv. 37), he says, "If any man think himself to be a prophet, or spiritual, let him acknowledge that the things that I write unto you are *commandments of the Lord*" (κυρίου ἐντολαί). The form of expression seems to imply that here, as in vii. 10, he is referring to some distinct regulation of Christ, which he was endeavoring to follow out. But if so, this, like the saying just quoted in Acts xx. 35, is now nowhere to be found.

Four other passages may be mentioned, which, not from any distinct reference on the part of the Apostle, but from their likeness of expression, may seem to have been derived from the circle of our Lord's teaching. (*a.*) "*Being reviled, we bless*" (λοιδορούμενοι εὐλογοῦμεν, 1 Cor. iv. 28), may have some relation to Luke vi. 28, "*Bless them* that curse you" (εὐλογεῖτε τοὺς καταρωμένους). (β.) "*Know ye not that the saints shall judge the world?*" (1 Cor. vi. 2) may refer to Luke xxii. 30 (Matt. xix. 28), "*Ye shall sit on thrones, judging the twelve tribes of Israel.*" (γ.) In the command that the woman is to "*attend on the Lord without distraction*" (εὐπάρεδρον . . . . ἀπερισπάστως, 1 Cor. vii. 35), the two emphatic words are substantially the same as are employed in the narrative containing the commendation of Mary. "Mary *sitting*" (παρακαθίσασα), "Martha *cumbered*" (περιεσπᾶτο, Luke x. 39, 40). (δ.) In 1 Cor. xiii. 2, "*Faith, so that I could remove mountains,*" may be an allusion to Matt. xvii. 20: "If ye have *faith*, ye shall say unto this *mountain, Remove hence.*" These instances, however, are all too doubtful to serve as the foundation of an argument.

With respect to all, however, three remarks may be made, more or less important: First, their want of exact agreement with the words of the Gospel narrative implies (what indeed can hardly be doubted for other reasons), that, at the time when the Epistles to Corinth were written, the Gospels in their present form were not yet in existence. Secondly, this same discrepancy of form, combined with an unquestionable likeness in spirit, agrees with the discrepancies of a similar kind which are actually found between the Gospel narratives; and, when contrasted with the total dissimilarity of such isolated sayings as are ascribed to Christ by Irenæus, show that the atmosphere, so to speak, of the Gospel history extended beyond the limits of its actually existing records, and that within that atmosphere the Apostle was included. The Apostle, to whom we owe the preservation of the saying, "It is more blessed to give than to receive," has thereby become to us truly an "Evangelist." Thirdly, the manner in which the Apostle refers to these sayings proves the undisputed claim which they had already established, not only in his own mind, but in that of the whole Church. He himself still argues and entreats "as the Scribes"; but he quotes the sentence of Christ, as that from which there was to be no appeal, "as of one having authority." "Not I, but the Lord" (1 Cor. vii. 10), is the broad distinction drawn between his own suggestions respecting marriage, and the principle which the Lord had laid down, and which accordingly is incorporated in three out of the four Gospels, and once in the discourse especially designed to furnish the universal code of Christian morality.* So, too, the command that the teachers of the Gospel were "to live of the Gospel" (1 Cor. ix. 14), had received such entire and absolute acceptance, that it was turned by the Judaizing party into a universal and inflexible rule, admitting of no deviation, even for the sake of Christian love. Already the Lord's words had become the law of the Christian society; already they had been subjected to that process by which, as in later times so in this particular instance, the less enlightened disciples have severed the sacred text from the purpose to which it was originally applied, and sacrificed the spirit of the passage to a devout but mistaken observance of the letter.

II. From the particular sayings, we turn to the particular acts of the life of Christ. These, as might be supposed, appear more frequently, though still not so generally as at first sight we should naturally expect.

To the earlier events it may be said that the allusions are next to none. "Born (γενομένου) of the *seed of David* after the flesh" (Rom. i. 3), "born of a *woman*" (γενόμενον ἐκ γυναικός), "born under *the law*" (γενόμενον ὑπὸ νόμον), Gal. iv. 4, are the only distinct references to the Nativity and its accompaniments. So far as they go, they illustrate the stress laid by the Evangelists on the lineage of David (Luke ii. 4, 23, Matt. i. 1), on the announcement and manner of his birth (Luke ii. 4, Matt. i. 23), and on the ritual observances which immediately followed (Luke ii. 21 – 24). But this is all; and perhaps the coincidence of silence between the Apostle and the two Evangelists, who equally with himself omit these earlier events, is more remarkable than his slight

* Matt. v. 32; Mark x. 11; Luke xvi. 18.

confirmation of the two who record them. The likeness to St. Mark and St. John in this respect may, if we so consider it, be regarded as instructive as the unlikeness to St. Luke and St. Matthew.

Neither is there any detailed allusion to the ministry or miracles of Christ. To the miracles, indeed, there is none, unless it be granted that in the expression, "Ye cannot partake of the Lord's table, and the table of *devils*" (δαιμονίων) (1 Cor. x. 21), the peculiar stress laid on that word, not elsewhere used by the Apostle, is deepened by the recollection that He whose table they thus profaned had so long and often cast out the very demons with which they now brought themselves into contact. To the general manner, however, of our Lord's mode of life, there is one strong testimony which agrees perfectly both with the fact and the spirit of the Gospel narrative. 2 Cor. viii. 9, "For your sakes He *became poor*" (ἐπτώχευσε). To this we must add the corresponding, though somewhat more general, expression in Phil. ii. 7. "He took upon Him the form *of a slave*" (μορφὴν δούλου). It is possible, perhaps probable from the context, that in both these passages the Apostle may have meant generally the abnegation of more than earthly wealth and power, the assumption of more than earthly poverty and humiliation. But the context shows, also, that poverty in the one case, and lowliness of life in the other, each in its usual sense, were the special thoughts in the Apostle's mind; and in the case of "poverty," the word (ἐπτώχευσε) can signify nothing less than that He led a life, not only of need and want, but of houseless wandering and distress. It points exactly to that state, implied rather than expressly described in the Gospels, in which "He had not where to lay His head"; and in which He persevered "when He was rich"; that is, when He might have taken the "kingdom of Judæa," "the kingdoms of the world," and "twelve legions of angels" to defend Him.

But it is in the closing scenes of our Lord's life that the Apostle's allusions centre. In this respect, his practice is confirmed by the outward form of the four Gospels, which unite in this portion of the history, and in this portion only. This concentration, however caused, is the same both in the Evangelists and in the Apostle. His "Gospel," it would seem, in his narrative of the events of the Evangelical history, began with the sufferings of Christ. "First of all, I delivered to you how that Christ died for our sins" (1 Cor. xv. 8). And the main subject of his preaching in Corinth and in Galatia was the crucifixion of Christ, not merely the fact of his death, but the horror and shame of the manner of his death. "The *cross* of Christ" (1 Cor. i. 17, 18); "Christ *crucified*" (ib. ii. 23); even vividly, and, if one may so say, graphically portrayed before their eyes; "Jesus Christ was *evidently set forth* ('as in a picture,' προεγράφη) crucified amongst them" (Gal. iii. 1).

The distinct allusions to His sufferings are few, but precise; for the most part entirely agreeing with the Gospel narratives, and implying much more than is actually expressed. There are two not contained in these Epistles, but certainly within the limits of the teaching of the Apostle. One is the allusion to the agony in the garden, in Heb. v. 7: "In the days of his flesh, when he had offered up prayers and supplications and strong crying and tears unto Him that was able to save him from death, and was heard in that he feared." That the account is drawn from a source independent of the four Gospels is clear from the mention of *tears*, which on that occasion nowhere occurs in the Gospel narratives. But the general tendency is precisely similar. The other is the allusion in 1 Tim. vi. 13, to "the good confession" which Christ Jesus "witnessed *before Pontius Pilate*." This is the more remarkable, because, although it may be sufficiently explained by the answer, "Thou sayest," in Matt. xxvii. 11, yet it points much more naturally to the long and solemn interview peculiar to the narrative of St. John. (John xviii. 28 – xix. 12.) But the most definite and exact agreement of the Apostle's writings with the Gospel narratives is that which, in 1 Cor. xi. 23 – 26, contains the earliest written account of the institution of the Lord's Supper. It is needless to point out in detail what has already been shown in the notes on that passage. But it is important to observe how very much it implies as to the Apostle's knowledge of the whole story. Not only are the particulars of this transaction told in almost the same words, — the evening meal, the night of the betrayal, the Paschal loaf, the Paschal cup, the solemn institution, — but the form of words is such as was evidently part of a fixed and regular narrative; the whole history of the Passion must have been known to St. Paul, and by him been told in detail to the Corinthians; and, if so, we may fairly conclude that many other incidents of the sacred story must have been related to them, no less than this which, but for the peculiar confusions of the Corinthian Church, would have remained unrecorded.

The Resurrection, like the Death, of Christ, is the subject of allusions too numerous to be recounted. But here, as in the case of the Death, we have one passage which shows us that not merely the bare fact was stated, but also its accompanying circumstances. This is the almost necessary inference from the enumeration of the various appearances of Christ after his Resurrection, as recorded in 1 Cor. xv. 4 – 7. Here, as in the four Gospel narratives, a distinct prominence is given to the Burial of Christ, here, as there, in connection with the Resurrection rather than the Death; here, as there, the appearances are described as occasional only, not constant or frequent; one of those to which the Apostle refers (that to Peter) is alluded to in the Gospels (Luke xxiv. 34); the appearance to the Twelve is described in Matt. xxviii. 16 (?); Mark xvi. 14; Luke xxiv. 36; John xx. 19. On the other hand, the mention of the appearance to James, and to the five hundred brethren, shows that, although in substance the same narrative, it is different in form; the source is independent; there are still the same lesser discrepancies between the Apostle and the Evangelists, as between the several Evangelists themselves.

It may be observed, in concluding these detailed references to the Gospel history, that they almost all, so far as they refer to one Gospel narrative rather than another, agree with that of St. Luke. The exceptions are the doubtful allusions to the interview recorded by St. John, in 1 Tim. vi. 13; the saying recorded by St. Matthew, in 1 Cor. xiii. 4; and the agreement with St. John and St. Mark, rather than with St. Luke, in omission of distinct references to our Lord's early history. All the rest, even to words and phrases, have a relation to St. Luke's Gospel, so intimate as to require some explanation; and there is no reason why we should not adopt the account anciently received, that the author or compiler of that Gospel was the companion of the Apostle.

These are the main facts which are recorded from the Gospel History. Perhaps they will not seem many; yet, so far as they go, they are not to be despised. From them a story might be constructed, even if we knew no more, which would not be at variance — which, in all essential points, would be in unison — with the Gospel narrative.

III. But the impression of this unison will be much confirmed, if from particular sayings or facts we pass to the general character of Christ, as described in these Epistles.

(1.) It may be convenient, in the first instance, to recall those passages which speak of our Lord in the most general manner, — 1 Cor. i. 30, which tells us that "He was made unto us wisdom, and righteousness, and sanctification, and redemption"; 1 Cor. viii. 6, which speaks of "the one Lord Jesus Christ, by whom are all things, and we by him"; 1 Cor. xv. 45, in which He is called "the second Adam"; 2 Cor. v. 16, 19, in which He is spoken of as the Judge of all men, and that in Him was God, reconciling the world unto himself by Him. Other passages to the same effect might be multiplied, but these will suffice.

We are so familiar with the sound of these words, and so much accustomed to apply them to other purposes, that we rarely think of the vastness and complexity, and at the same time freshness and newness, of the ideas implied in their first application to an actual, individual Man. Let us imagine ourselves hearing them for the first time, — perceiving that they were uttered by one who had the deepest and most sober conviction of their truth, — perceiving, also, that they were spoken, not of some remote or ideal character, but of One who had lived and died during the youth or early manhood of him who so spoke. Should we not ask, like the Psalmists and Prophets of old, "Who is this King of glory? Who is this that cometh, travelling in the greatness of his strength?" With what eagerness should we look for any direct account of the life and death, to which such passages referred, to see whether or not the one corresponded with the other?

Let us (for the sake of illustration) conceive ourselves, in the first instance, turning to the *Apocryphal* Gospels, — the Gospels of the Infancy, of James, of Thomas, and of Nicodemus, from which (it is no imaginary case) was derived the only picture of our Lord's life known to the Arabian and Syrian tribes of the seventh century, in the time of Mahomet; and we should at once feel that with the utterly trivial and childish fables of those narratives the Apostle's representation had no connection whatever. The Koran, wishing to speak with high respect of "Jesus, the Son of Mary," contains a chapter devoted to the subject. The following is the speech which He is represented as uttering, to commend himself to the Jews: "I come to you, accompanied by signs from the Lord. I shall make of clay the figure of a bird; I shall breathe upon it, and, by God's permission, the bird shall fly. I shall heal him that was born blind, and the leper; I shall, by God's permission, raise the dead. I will tell you what you have eaten, and what you have hid in your houses. All these facts shall be as signs to you, if you will believe. I come to confirm the Pentateuch, which you have received before me. I will permit to you the use of certain things which have been forbidden you. I come with signs from your Lord. Fear Him and obey me, — He is my Lord and yours. Adore Him; this is the right path." * It may be that the Arabs to whom this picture of Christ was presented

* Koran iii. 43, 44.

could not have risen at the time to anything higher. But we cannot wonder that such a picture should have produced no deep impression upon them, or have seemed inferior to the prophet who had himself risen up amongst them. And from seeing what *might* have been the image of Christ presented to us, we may form a livelier notion of that which *has* been presented to us.

From these Apocryphal Gospels let us suppose ourselves turning for the first time to those of the New Testament. No one, even though doubting the inferences which the Apostle draws, could doubt that the Christ there exhibited must have been He of whom he spoke. Even if the name were different, we should feel sure that the person must be the same. Here alone in that age, or any age, we should find a life and character which was truly the second beginning of humanity; here, if anywhere, we should recognize God speaking to man. In that life, if in any life, in those words and deeds, if in any words and deeds whatever, we should see the impersonation of wisdom, and righteousness, and holiness, and redemption. As the readers of the Prophets instinctively acknowledged that to Him bare all the Prophets witness, so, if we had up to this time been readers of the Epistles only, and now first become acquainted with the Gospel narratives, we should even thus far be constrained to say, "We have found Him of whom 'Paul in his Epistles wrote,' Jesus of Nazareth, the son of Joseph." *

The Apostle's words, then, thus considered, may be regarded, on the one hand, as a striking testimony to the general truth of the Gospel narrative; on the other hand, as a striking prediction of what has since taken place. On the one hand, they presuppose that a character of extraordinary greatness had appeared in the world; and such a character, whatever else may be thought of it, we actually find in the Gospels. We feel that each justifies the other. The image of Christ in the Gospels will be by all confessed to approach

* John i. 45.

more nearly to the description of the Second Adam, the new Founder of humanity, than any other appearance in human history; and if we ask what effect that life and death produced at the time of its appearance, we are met by these expressions of the Apostle, uttered, not as if by any effort, but as the spontaneous burst of his own heart, within one generation from the date of the events themselves. And as these expressions correspond with the past events to which they refer, so also do they correspond with the future to which they point. If the expression of "the Second Adam" was meant to characterize a great change in the history of the human race, we should expect to find such a change dating and emanating from the time when the Second Adam had appeared. Such a change we do in fact find, of which the beginning is crowned with the life of Christ. It is true that the great division of modern from ancient history does not commence till four centuries later; and it is undeniable that the influx of the Teutonic tribes at that time had a most important influence in moulding the future destinies of the civilized world. But still the new life which survived the overthrow of the Empire had begun from the Christian era. Christianity, with all that it has involved in the religion, the arts, the literature, the morals of Europe, beyond all dispute originated with Christ alone. The very dates which are now in use throughout the world are significant, though trivial, proofs of the justice of the Apostle's declaration, that Christ was the Second Man; that "as in Adam all had died, even so in Christ all were made alive."

(2.) Thus much would be true, even if nothing more precise were recorded. But every shade of this general character is, if one may so say, deepened by the Apostle's more special allusions; and although perhaps, without the help of the Gospel narratives, we might miss the point of his expressions, yet with that help the image of Christ comes out clearly, and we still see it to be no invention of the Apostle's imagination, but the same historical definite character which is set before us in the Gospels.

(a.) "Christ Jesus was made unto us *wisdom*." (1 Cor. i. 30.) "In Him were hid all the treasures of *wisdom and knowledge*." (Col. ii. 3.) "The spirit of *wisdom* is given to us in the *knowledge* of Him." (Eph. i. 17.) These expressions may be merely general phrases of reverence, but how much clearness do they gain when they are compared with the actual display of wisdom stored up in the living instructions of Christ! There is no special reference by the Apostle to any of the parables or discourses of the Gospels. But how completely do those "things new and old," "brought out of his treasure" (Matt. xiii. 52), answer to this general description of His character. "Wisdom" is not the attribute which a zealous convert would necessarily think of applying to the founder of his religion. It is so applied by the Apostle, and we see from the Gospels that his application of it cannot be questioned.

(b.) He frequently speaks of "the *truth* of Christ," and he dwells especially on the certainty and fixedness which characterized all His life. "*In Him was not yea and nay*," but "*yea* and *Amen*." (2 Cor. i. 20.) It is at least a striking illustration of these passages to remember what Christ again and again says of himself in St. John's Gospel, as having come into the world for the purpose of bearing witness to the truth, as being the Truth; * it is more than a mere conjecture to read in the Apostle's words the echo of the solemn asseveration and ratification of truth which runs through all the Gospel discourses, "Verily, verily, *Amen*, *Amen*, I say unto you."

(c.) The Apostle urges on his converts the freedom of the doctrine which he preached, its contrast to the narrowness and mystery and concealment of the Jewish law, and he tells them that they must attain this freedom through "the Spirit of *the Lord*," that is, of Christ, and through contemplation of his likeness. We turn to the Gospels, and we find in their representation of Christ this very freedom of which the Apos-

* John viii. 32; xiv. 6; xviii. 37.

tle speaks exemplified in almost every page; the sacrifice of the letter to the spirit, the encouragement of openness and sincerity, there emphatically urged by precept and example, at once give an edge and a value to the Apostle's argument, which else it would greatly want.

(d.) The Apostle expressly appeals to the history of Christ as an example of surrendering his own will for the sake of the scruples of others. "We that are strong ought to bear the infirmities *of the weak,*" and not to please ourselves, for *even Christ pleased not himself,* but, as it is written, "the reproaches of them that reproached thee fell on me." (Rom. xv. 1, 3.) "Give *none offence* .... even as I please all men..... Be *followers of me,* even as I am *of Christ.*" (1 Cor. x. 32, 33; xi. 1.) Of this consideration for human weakness and narrowness, the direct instances in the Gospel narrative are, perhaps, less striking than the general indication of this peculiar aspect of the true Christ-like character. Yet his constant, though not universal, acquiescence in the forms of the Mosaic law; the limits within which he restrained his own teaching, and that of his disciples; the many things which he withheld, because his disciples were not then able to bear them; the condescension to human weakness which runs through the whole texture of the Gospel history, — fully justify the Apostle's appeal, not the less from the very indirect ness of the application.

(e.) He beseeches his converts not to compel him to say or do anything which shall be inconsistent with "the meekness and gentleness (πραΰτης καὶ ἐπιείκεια) of Christ." (2 Cor. x. 1.) These words are not the mere expressions of ideal adoration; they recall definite traits of a living human person. They describe traits which could not be said to be specially exemplified in the Apostle himself, but which were exemplified to the full in the life and teaching of Him to whom the Apostle ascribes them.

(f.) In many passages the Apostle speaks of Love. In 1 Cor. xiii. 1 – 13, he describes it at length. It is a new virtue. Its name first occurs in his Epistles. Yet he speaks of it as fixed, established, recognized. To what was this owing? To whom does he ascribe it? Emphatically, and repeatedly, he attributes it to Christ. "The love of Christ." "The love of God in Christ." Now in all the Gospels, the self-devoted, self-sacrificing energy for the good of others which the word "Love" (ἀγάπη) denotes, is the prevailing characteristic of the actions of Christ; in the first three, the word itself is not used; but in the fourth, it is used even more emphatically and repeatedly than by St. Paul; and thus, besides its general testimony to the truth of all the Gospel narratives, it specially serves to knit together in one the thoughts and words of St. Paul and St. John.

(g.) On one occasion only the Apostle gives us an instance, not of what he had "received" of Christ as on earth, but of what had been revealed to him concerning Christ by himself. In answer to his entreaty thrice offered up to Christ as to his still present, ever-living friend, there had been borne in upon his soul, how we know not, a distinct message, expressed as at his conversion in articulate words, "My grace is sufficient for thee, my strength is perfected in weakness." In the similar mode of revelation at the time of his conversion, "Why persecutest thou me?" "I am Jesus whom thou persecutest," the spirit of the whole expression is the same as that which in the Gospels represent Christ as merged in the person of the least of his disciples. So these words of Christ, reported by the Apostle himself in his Epistle, are an exact reflex of the union of divine strength with human weakness which pervades the narrative of all the Gospels. There is the same combination of majesty and tenderness, the same tones of mingled rebuke and love, that we know so well in the last conversations * by the Sea of Galilee, the same strength and virtue going forth to heal the troubled spirit, as of old to restore the sick, and comfort the afflicted.†

We have now gone through the enumeration of all the most

* John xxi.

† Luke vi. 19; viii. 46.

important allusions to the facts of the Gospel history which St. Paul's epistles contain, — an enumeration tedious perhaps in itself, and without profit to many. Yet, before we proceed, I would ask those who have followed me thus far to pause for a moment, and reflect on the additional strength or liveliness which this enumeration may have given to their conceptions of the Gospel history. It is not much, but, considering from whom these instances have been taken, — from a source so near the time, from writings whose genuineness has never been questioned by the severest criticism, — it is something if it may suggest to any one a steadier standing-place and a firmer footing, of however narrow limits, amidst the doubts or speculations which surround him. Nor, I trust, can it have been wholly unprofitable to have approached from another than the usual point of view the several features of our Lord's life and character which I have just enumerated, — to dwell on the Apostolic testimony rendered, one by one, to the several acts and words, still more to the several traits, most of all to the collective effect of the character, which we usually gather only from the Gospels. His severe purity of word and deed, — His tender care for even the temporal wants of his disciples, — the institution of that solemn parting pledge of communion with Himself and with each other, — the hope of a better life which He has opened to us, amidst the sorrows and desolations of the world, — His steadfastness and calmness amidst our levity and littleness, — His free and wide sympathy amidst our prejudice and narrowness, — His self-denying poverty, — His gentleness and mildness amidst our readiness to offer and resent injuries, — His love to mankind, — His incommunicable greatness and (so to speak) elevation above the influence of time and fate, — all this, at least in general outline, we should have, even if nothing else were left to us of the New Testament but the passages which have just been quoted.

It may still, however, be said, that these indications of the Apostle's knowledge of the Gospel history are less than we might fairly expect; and we may still be inclined to ask why, when there are so many resemblances, there are not more? why, if he knew so much as these resemblances imply, he yet says so little?

It is perhaps impossible to answer this fully, or, at any rate, to answer as it deserves within the limits here prescribed. But some suggestions may be made, which, even if they do not entirely meet the case, may yet be sufficiently important to deserve consideration.

First, it must be remarked that the representation of the life, and work, and character of Christ, in all probability, belonged to the oral, and not the written, teaching of the Apostle. The Gospels themselves have every appearance of having grown up out of oral communications of this kind; and the word "Gospel," which must have been employed by the Apostle substantially for the same kind of instruction as that to which it is applied in the titles of the histories of our Lord's life, is by him usually, if not always, used in reference, not to what he is actually communicating in his Epistles, but to what he had already communicated to his converts when present. This supposition is confirmed by the fact, that the most express quotation of a distinct saying of Christ occurs, not in a letter of the Apostle, but in the eminently characteristic speech to the Ephesian elders (Acts xx. 18 – 35), and that, in the two passages in the Epistles to the Corinthians where he most clearly refers to what he had "delivered" to them whilst he was with them (1 Cor. xi. 23 – 26; xv. 3 – 7), it is clear that his instructions turned not merely on the general truths of the Christian faith, but on the detailed accounts of the Last Supper, and of the Resurrection. Had other subjects equally appropriate in the Gospel history been required for his special purpose, there seems to be no reason why he should not equally have referred to these also, as communicated by him during his stay at Corinth. His oral teaching — that is to say, his first communication with his converts — would naturally touch on those subjects in which all believers took a common interest. The instances of that teaching, in other words, the everlasting principles of the Gospel, are contained, not in tradition, nor yet (except through these general allusions) in his own writings, but in the four Gospels. His subsequent teaching in the Epistles would naturally relate more to his peculiar mission, — would turn more on special occasions, — would embody more of his own personal and individual mind. "I, not the Lord."* And in ancient times, even more than in our own, in sacred authors no less than classical, we must take into account the effect of the entire absorption of the writer in his immediate subject, to the exclusion of persons and events of the utmost importance immediately beyond. Who would infer from the history of Thucydides the existence of his contemporary Socrates? How different, again, is the Socrates of Xenophon from the Socrates of Plato! Except so far as the great truth of the admission of the Gentiles was, in a certain sense, what he occasionally calls it, "his own" peculiar "Gospel," he had already "preached the Gospel" to his converts before he began his Epistles to them. In the Epistles he was not employed in "laying the foundation" (that was laid once for all in "Jesus Christ," 1 Cor. iii. 10), but in "building up," "strengthening," "exhorting," "settling."

But, over and above this almost inevitable distinction, he was in his Epistles — in his individual dealings with his converts — swayed by a principle which, though implied throughout his writings, is nowhere so strongly expressed as in these two. When called to reply to his Jewish opponents, who prided themselves on their outward connection with Christ, as Hebrews, as Israelites, as Ministers of Christ, as Apostles of Christ, as specially belonging to Christ (2 Cor. v. 12, x. 7, xi. 22, 13), when taunted by them with the very charge which, in a somewhat altered form, we are now considering, that he had "not seen Jesus Christ our Lord" (1 Cor. ix. 1), his reply is to a certain extent a concession of the fact, or rather an assertion of the principle by which he desired to confront any such accusations. With the strongest sense of freedom from all personal and local ties, with the deepest consciousness that from the moment of his conversion all his past

* 1 Cor. vii. 12.

life had vanished far away into the distance, he answers, "Though we have known Christ after the flesh, yet henceforth know we him no more." (2 Cor. v. 10.) Startling as this declaration is, and called forth by a special occasion, it yet involved a general truth. It is, in fact, the same profound instinct or feeling which penetrated, more or less, the whole Apostolical, and even the succeeding age, with regard to our Lord's earthly course. It is the same feeling which appears in the fact, strange if it were not well known, that no authentic or even pretended likeness of Christ should have been handed down from the first century; that the very site of his dwelling-place at Capernaum should have been entirely obliterated from human memory; that the very notion of seeking for relics of his life and death, though afterwards so abundant, first began in the age of Constantine. It is the same feeling which, in the Gospel narratives themselves, is expressed in the almost entire absence of precision as to time and place, — in the emphatic separation of our Lord from his kinsmen after the flesh, even from his mother herself, — in his own solemn warning, "What and if ye shall see the Son of man ascend up where he was before: the words that I speak unto you, they are spirit and they are life. It is the spirit that quickeneth, the flesh profiteth nothing." And this is the more observable when contrasted with the Apocryphal Gospels, which do to a great extent condescend to the natural or Judaic tendency, which the Gospels of the New Testament thus silently rebuke. There we find a "Gospel of the Infancy," filled with the fleshly marvels that delighted afterwards the childish minds of the Bedouin Arabs; there first are mentioned the local traditions of the scene of the Annunciation, of the Nativity, of the abode in Egypt; there is to be found the story, on which so great a superstructure has been built in later ages, of the parents and birth of her whom the Gospel history calls "blessed," but studiously conceals from view.*

The Apostle's reserve no doubt was strengthened by his

* See "Evangelia Apocrypha" (ed. Tischendorf), pp. 1 – 11, 68, 79 – 81, 184, 191 – 201.

antagonism with his Jewish opponents; but the principle on which he acted is applicable to all times. It explains in what sense our Lord's life is an example, and in what sense it is not. That life is not, nor ever could be, an example to be literally and exactly copied. It has been so understood, on the one hand, even by such holy men as Francis of Assisi, who thought that the true "Imitation of Christ" was to reproduce a fac-simile of all its outward circumstances in his own person. It has been so understood, on the other hand, by some in our own day, who have attacked it on the express ground that it could not, without impropriety, be literally re-enacted by any ordinary person in England in the nineteenth century. But it is not an example in detail; and those who try to make it so, whether in defence or in attack, are but neglecting the warning which Bacon so beautifully gives on the story of the rich young man in the Gospels: "Beware how, in making the portraiture, thou breakest the pattern." * In this sense the Christian Church, as well as the Apostle, ought to "know Christ henceforth no more according to the flesh." All such considerations ought to be swallowed up in the overwhelming sense of the moral and spiritual state in which we stand towards Him. In this sense (if we may so say) He is more truly to us the Son of God than He is the Son of man. His life is our example, — not in its outward acts, but in the spirit, the atmosphere which it breathes, — in the ideal which it sets before us, — in the principles, the motives, the object with which it supplies us.

This brings us to yet one more reason why St. Paul's Epistles contain no further details of our Lord's ministry. It was because they were to him, and to his converts, superseded by an evidence to himself, and to them, far more convincing than any particular proofs or facts could have for them, — the evidence of his own life, of his own constant communion with Him in whom he lived, and moved, and had his being. He had, no doubt, his own peculiarities of character, his own especial call to the Gentiles. These gave a turn

* Bacon's Essays, Vol. I. p. 41.

to his life, to his teaching, to his writings. These gave the Epistles a character of their own, which will always distinguish them from the Gospels. But still the spirit which pervaded both alike was (to use his own words, often and often repeated) "of Christ," and "in Christ." "The life that he lived in the flesh, he lived in the *faith of the Son of God*, who died and gave himself for him." And this "faith," on which he dwells with an almost exclusive reverence, is not, it must be remembered, faith in any one part or point of Christ's work, but in the whole. "Faith in his Incarnation," "faith in his merits," "faith in his blood," are expressions which, though employed in later times, and, like other scholastic or theological terms, often justly employed as summaries of the Apostle's statements, yet are, in no instance, his own statements of his own belief or feeling.* Measured by the requirement which demands these precise forms of speech from the lips of all believers, the Apostle no less than the Evangelists will be found wanting. The one grand expression, in which his whole mind finds vent, is simply "the faith of Christ." It is, as it were, his second conscience; and, as men do not minutely analyze the constituent elements of conscience, so neither did he care minutely to describe or bring forward the several elements which made up the character and work of his Master. And though these elements are distinctly set forth in the Gospels, yet the Gospels agree even here with the Epistles, in that they, like the Epistles, put forward not any one part, but the complex whole, as the object of adoration and faith. The language of our Lord in the Gospels, like that of St. Paul regarding him in the Epistles, is (not "Believe in my miracles," "Believe in my death," "Believe in my resurrection," but) "Believe in *me*."

Finally, if it be said that this is an impression too vague and impalpable to be definitely traced, the answer is in the Apostle's character. Much there was doubtless peculiar to himself, much that was peculiar to his own especial mission. But, if in any human character we can discern the effect pro-

* The apparent exception in Rom. iii. 25 is, it need hardly be observed to those acquainted with the original language, only apparent.

duced by contact with another higher and greater than itself, such an effect may be discovered in that of St. Paul: "The love of Christ,"* the love which Christ had shown to man, was, as he himself tells us, his "constraining" motive. That love, with the acts in which it displayed itself, was the great event which rose up behind him as the background of his life; as the single point from which all his thoughts diverged in the past, and to which they converged again in the future. Unless a love, surpassing all love, had been manifested to him, we know not how he could have been so constrained; and, we must also add, unless a freedom from his past prejudices and passions had been effected for him, by the sight of some higher freedom than his own, we know not how he could have been thus emancipated.

Such a love, and such a freedom, we find in St. Paul's Epistles. Such a combination — rarely, if ever, seen before, rarely, alas! seen since — is one of the best proofs of the reality of the original acts in which that combination was first manifested. The Gospel narratives, as we now possess them, were, in all probability, composed long after these Epistles. But the life which they describe must have been anterior. That life is "the glory," of which, as the Apostle himself says, his writings and actions are "the reflection." Whatever other diversities, peculiarities, infirmities, impassably divide the character of the Apostle from that of his Master, in this union of fervor and freedom there was a common likeness which cannot be mistaken. The general impulses of his new life — "the grace of God, by which he was what he was" — could have come from no other source. Whatever may be the force of the particular allusions and passages which have been collected, the general effect of his whole life and writings can hardly leave any other impression than that — whether by "revelation," or by "receiving" from others, whether "in the body, or out of the body,"† we cannot tell — he had indeed seen, and known, and loved, and followed Jesus Christ our Lord.

---

* 2 Cor. v. 14. † Gal. i. 12; 1 Cor. xi. 23 – xv. 3; 2 Cor. xii. 3

APOSTOLICAL WORSHIP.

By Rev. ARTHUR P. STANLEY.

1 Cor. xiv. 26 – 40.

It may be important, at the close of this Section, containing, as it does, the Apostle's final advice on Christian worship, to sum up all that this Epistle, combined with the other notices in the New Testament, has presented to us on this subject.

First. The Christian assemblies of the Apostolical age, unlike those of later times, appear not to have been necessarily controlled by any fixed order of presiding ministers. We hear, indeed, of "presbyters," or "elders," in the churches of Asia Minor,* and of Jerusalem.† And in the church of Thessalonica mention is made of "rulers" (προϊσταμένους ὑμῶν); ‡ and, in the churches of Galatia, of "teachers" (τῷ κατηχοῦντι). § As the object is here only to give the state of the Church at the time of these Epistles to Corinth, no notice need be taken of the allusions in Epistles of a later date. But no allusion is to be found to the connection of these ministers or officers, if so they are to be called, with the worship of the Apostolic Church, and the omission of any such is an almost decisive proof that no such connection was then deemed necessary. Had the Christian society at Corinth been what it was at the time when Clement addressed his Epistle to it, or what that at Ephesus is implied to have been

* Acts xiv. 23.
† Acts xi. 30; xv. 6, 22, 23.
‡ 1 Thess. v. 12.
§ Gal. vi. 6.

in the Ignatian Epistles, it is almost inevitable that some reference should have been made by the Apostle to the presiding government which was to control the ebullitions of sectarian or fanatical enthusiasm; that he should have spoken of the presbyters, whose functions were infringed upon by the prophets and speakers with tongues, or whose authority would naturally moderate and restrain their excesses. Nothing of the kind is to be found. The gifts are to be regulated by mutual accommodation, by general considerations of order and usefulness; and the only rights, against the violation of which any safeguards are imposed, are those of the congregation, lest "he that fills the place of the unlearned" (that is, as we have already seen, "he that has not the gift of speaking with tongues") should be debarred from ratifying by his solemn Amen the thanksgiving of the speaker. The gifts are not, indeed, supposed to be equally distributed, but every one is pronounced capable of having some gift, and it is implied as a possibility that "all" may have the gift of prophesying or of speaking with tongues.

Secondly. Through the gifts thus distributed, the worship was carried on. Four points are specially mentioned: —

(1.) *Prayer.* This, from the manner in which it is spoken of, in connection with the tongues, must have been a free outpouring of individual devotion, and one in which women were accustomed to join, as well as men.*

(2.) What has been said of prayer may be said also of *Praise* or *Song*, ψαλμός.† We may infer from Eph. v. 19, where it is coupled with "hymns and odes" (ὕμνοις καὶ ᾠδαῖς), that it must have been of the nature of metre or rhythm, and is thus the first recognition of Christian poetry. The Apocalypse is the nearest exemplification of it in the New Testament.

(3.) Closely connected with this, both in itself and by the context, is *Thanksgiving.* The "song of the understanding" is specially needed in the giving of thanks.‡ In this passage

* xiv. 13–15; xi. 5. † xiv. 15, 26. ‡ xiv. 16.

we have the earliest intimation of a liturgical form. Although the context even here implies that it must have been a free effusion, yet it is probable that the Apostle is speaking of the Eucharistic thanksgiving for the produce of the earth; such as was from a very early period incorporated in the great Eucharistic hymn used, with a few modifications, through all the liturgical forms of the later Christian Church. And from this passage we learn that the "Amen," or ratification of the whole congregation, afterwards regarded with peculiar solemnity in this part of the service, was deemed essential to the due utterance of the thanksgiving.

(4.) "Prophesying," or "teaching," is regarded (not by the Corinthians, but) by the Apostle as one of the most important objects of their assemblies. The impulse to exercise this gift appears to have been so strong as to render it difficult to be kept under control.* Women, it would seem from the Apostle's allusion to the practice in xi. 5, and prohibition of it in xiv. 34, 35, had felt themselves entitled to speak. The Apostle rests his prohibition on the general ground of the subordination of women to their natural instructors, their husbands.

Thirdly. The Apostolical mode of administering the Eucharist has already been delineated at the close of chap. xi. It is enough here to recapitulate its main features. It was part of the chief daily meal, and, as such, usually in the evening; the bread and wine were brought by the contributors to the meal, and placed on a table; of this meal each one partook himself; the bread was placed on the table as a loaf, and then broken into parts; the wine was given at the conclusion of the meal; a hymn of thanksgiving was offered by one of the congregation, to which the rest responded with the solemn word "Amen."

These points are all that we can clearly discern in the worship of Apostolic times, with the addition perhaps of the fact mentioned in Acts xx. 7, and confirmed by 1 Cor. xvi. 2,

---

* xiv. 32

that the first day of the week was specially devoted to their meetings.

The total dissimilarity between the outward aspects of this worship and of any which now exists, is the first impression which this summary leaves on the mind. It would seem at first sight as if almost every vestige of the Apostolic forms was gone, and as if the present forms had no basis in that age on which to ground themselves. But this impression is relieved by various important considerations. First, when we consider the state of the Apostolic Church as described in the Acts and in this Epistle, it is evident that in outward circumstances it never could be a pattern for future times. The fervor of the individuals who constituted the communities, the smallness of the communities themselves, the variety and power of the gifts, the expectation of the near approach of the end of the world, must have prevented the perpetuation of the Apostolic forms. But if Christianity be, as almost every precept of its Founder and of its chief Apostle presumes it to be, a religion of the spirit, and not of the letter, then this very peculiarity is one of its most characteristic privileges. No existing form of worship can lay claim to universal and eternal obligation, as directly traceable to Apostolic times. The impossibility of perpetuating the primitive forms is the best guarantee for future freedom and progress. Few as are the rules of worship prescribed in the Koran, yet the inconvenience which they present, when transplanted into other than Oriental regions, shows the importance of the omission of such in the New Testament.

But, secondly, there are in the forms themselves, and in the spirit in which the Apostle handles them, principles important for the guidance of Christian worship in all times. Some of these have been already indicated. In this last concluding Section, the whole of this advice is summed up in two simple rules: "Let all things be done unto edifying," and "let all things be done decently and in order."

"*Let all things be done unto edifying.*"

"Edifying" (οἰκοδομή) has, as already noticed in xiv. 3,

the peculiar sense both of building up from first principles to their practical application, and of fitting each member of the society into the proper place which the growth and rise of the whole building require. It is "development," not only in the sense of unfolding new truth, but of unfolding all the resources contained in the existing institution or body. Hence the stress laid on the excellence of "prophesying," as the special gift by which men were led to know themselves (as in xiv. 24, 25, "the secrets of their hearts being made manifest"), and by which (as through the prophets of the older dispensations) higher and more spiritual views of life were gradually revealed. Hence the repeated injunctions that *all* the gifts should have their proper honor;* that those gifts should be most honored by which not a few, but *all*, should benefit;† that *all* who had the gift of prophecy should have the opportunity of exercising that gift;‡ that *all* might have an equal chance of instruction and comfort for their own special cases.

"*Let all things be done decently and in order.*" §

"Decently" (εὐσχημόνως); that is, so as not to interrupt the gravity and dignity of the assemblies. "In order" (κατὰ τάξιν); that is, not by hazard or impulse, but by design and arrangement. The idea is not so much of any beauty or succession of parts in the worship, as of that severe and simple majesty which in the ancient world, whether Pagan or Jewish, seems to have characterized all solemn assemblies, civil or ecclesiastical, as distinct from the frantic or enthusiastic ceremonies which accompanied illicit or extravagant communities. The Roman Senate, the Athenian Areopagus, were examples of the former, as the wild Bacchanalian or Phrygian orgies were of the latter. It is to impress this character on Christian worship, that the Apostle has condemned the rejection by the women of the Greek custom of the veil,‖ the speaking of women in the assemblies,¶ the in-

* xii. 20 – 30. † xiv. 1 – 23. ‡ xiv. 29 – 31.
§ xiv. 40. ‖ xi. 1. – 16. ¶ xix. 34.

discriminate banqueting at the Lord's Supper,* the interruption of the prophets by each other.† "The spirits of prophets are subject to prophets," is a principle of universal application, and condemns every impulse of religious zeal or feeling which is not strictly under the control of those who display it. A world of fanaticism is exploded by this simple axiom; and to those who have witnessed the religious frenzy which attaches itself to the various forms of Eastern worship, this advice of the Apostle, himself of Eastern origin, will appear the more remarkable. The wild gambols, yearly celebrated at Easter by the adherents of the Greek Church round the chapel of the Holy Sepulchre at Jerusalem, show what Eastern Christianity may become; they are living proofs of the need and the wisdom of the Apostolical precept.

To examine how far these two regulations have actually affected the subsequent worship and ritual of Christianity, to measure each Christian liturgy and form of worship by one or other of these two rules, would be an instructive task. But it is sufficient here to notice, that on these two points the Apostle throws the whole weight of his authority; these two, and these only, are the Rubrics of the Primitive Church.

---

* xi. 16 – 34.

† xiv. 30 – 32.

THE EUCHARIST.

By Rev. ARTHUR P. STANLEY.

1 Cor. xi. 16–34.

It has been truly said, though with some exaggeration, that for many centuries the history of the Eucharist might be considered as a history of the Christian Church. And certainly this passage may be regarded as occupying in that history, whether in its narrower or larger sphere, a point of remarkable significance. On the one hand, we may take our stand upon it, and look back through its medium, on some of the institutions and feelings most peculiar to the first commencement of the Apostolic age. We see the most sacred ordinance of the Christian religion as it was celebrated by those in whose minds the earthly and the heavenly, the social and the religious aspect of life were indistinguishably blended. We see the banquet spread in the late evening, after the sun had set behind the western ridge of the hills of Achaia; we see the many torches * blazing, as at Troas, to light up the darkness of the upper room, where, as was their wont, the Christian community assembled; we see the couches laid and the walls hung,† after the manner of the East, as on the night of the betrayal; we see ‡ the sacred loaf, representing, in its compact unity, the harmony of the whole society; we hear the blessing or thanksgiving on the cup § responded to by the joint "Amen," such as even three centuries later is described as like a peal of thunder; we witness the complete realiza-

---

* λαμπάδες ἱκαναί, Acts xx. 8. † ὑπέρῳον ἐστρωμένον, Matt. xxvi.
‡ 1 Cor. x. 17; xi. 29. § x. 31.

tion, in outward form, of the Apostle's words, suggested doubtless by the sight of the meal and the sacrament blended thus together, "*Whether ye eat or drink*, or whatsoever ye do, do all to the glory of God." * "Whatsoever ye do in word or deed, do all in the name of the *Lord Jesus, giving thanks* to God and the Father by him." †

This is one side of the picture; but there is another side, which is exhibited here also, and which imparts to this passage its peculiar interest. Already the difficulties of bringing an ideal and an actual life together make themselves felt. What the falsehoods of Ananias and Sapphira were to the community of property at Jerusalem, that the excesses and disorders of the Corinthian Christians were to the primitive celebration of the Eucharist. The time was come, when the secular and the spiritual had to be disentangled one from the other; the "simplicity" and "gladness" of the first Apostolical communion was gradually to retire before the Apostolical rebuke. The question arose whether the majesty, the tenderness, the awe of the feast should be lost in a senseless orgy, and it is (humanly speaking) by means of this verdict of the Apostle against the Corinthian church, that the *form* of the primitive practice was altered, in order to save the *spirit* of the original institution. It is of the more importance to remember the extent of the danger to which the celebration of the Eucharist was then exposed; because a great part of its subsequent history would seem to be a reaction, in part just, in part exaggerated, against the corruption which then threatened it; a reaction encouraged by the extreme severity with which that corruption is denounced by

---

* Col. iii. 17.

† Perhaps the nearest likeness now existing, to this union of social intercourse with religious worship, is to be found in the services of the Coptic Church. The Eucharist indeed is even more divested of its character of a supper, than in the Western Churches. But there is an air of primitive freedom, and of innocent enjoyment, blended with the prayers of the general service, which, bearing as it does the marks of long antiquity, conveyed to me, on the one occasion on which I witnessed the worship of the Copts in their cathedral at Cairo, a livelier image of the early Christian assemblies than anything else I ever saw.

the Apostle, and which was itself called forth by the greatness of the crisis. This is the last mention of the administration of the Lord's Supper, according to the ancient fashion; the "Supper" itself had ceased to be a supper, as early as the beginning of the first century, as we learn from the Epistles of the younger Pliny; * and was celebrated, if not very early in the morning, at least before the night, although in some Egyptian cities the practice of partaking of it on the *evenings* of Saturday still continued in the fourth century.† The social meal was divided from it under the name of "Agape," or "Love-feast," but still continued to be celebrated within the walls of churches as late as the fifth century, after which it disappears, having been already condemned by councils on account of abuses similar to those here described at Corinth. ‡ Thus the Eucharist became more and more set apart as a distinct sacred ordinance; it withdrew more and more from the possibility of the Corinthian desecration, till at last it was wrapt up in the awful mystery which has attached to it, in the highest degree, in the churches of the East, but in some degree in the churches of the West also, both Protestant and Roman Catholic. Beginning under the simple name of "the breaking of bread," and known from this Epistle by the social and almost festive appellations of "the Communion," and "the Lord's Supper," it first receives in Pliny the name of "Sacramentum," and in Justin Martyr that of "Eucharistia"; both, indeed, indicating ideas of strictly Apostolical origin, though more closely connected with the words, and less with the act, than would have been the case in the first Apostolical times; till in the days of Chrysostom it presents itself to us under the formidable name of the "Dreadful Sacrifice."

These two views of the Lord's Supper have been thus set forth in this place side by side; because, as has been said, they both to a certain extent appear together in this chapter. A careful investigation of the passage will prob-

* X. 97. † Sozomen, A. E. vii. 19.

‡ Bingham's Antiquities, Book XV. ch. 7.

ably lead to the conclusion, that as, on the one hand, the general view of the Apostolical practice, its simplicity, and its festivity, as implied in the Apostle's arguments and in his designation of the ordinance, have been in later times too much underrated; so, on the other hand, the severity of his denunciation against unworthy partakers has been too generally and too rigorously enforced; because the particular object, and the particular need of his rebuke at that time, have not been clearly understood. The Holy Communion can never be again exactly what it was then; and therefore, although his words will always impart to the great ordinance of Christian worship a peculiar solemnity, yet the real lesson which they convey relates now more directly to such general occasions as that out of which his warning grew, than to the ordinance itself. The joy and almost merriment of the first Christian converts after the day of Pentecost could not now be applied to the Eucharist as it was then, without fear of great profaneness and levity. But the record of it implies that with a serious and religious life generally there is nothing incompatible in the freest play of cheerful and innocent gayety. In like manner, although we cannot without superstition imagine that the judgments which the Apostle denounced will fall on a desecration of the Communion different in all its circumstances from that which occurred at Corinth, yet there may still be an irreverence towards sacred things, a want of brotherly kindness, a dulness in discerning the presence of Christ, even in our common meals, which may make us fear "lest we eat and drink condemnation to ourselves." And in the Communion itself the Apostle's words are instructive, as reminding us that "the body of the Lord," to which he looked, was, as elsewhere in his writings, so here, the body which is represented by the whole Christian society. So the Apostle conceives it to be in all times and places, and not least in the institution especially intended to exhibit the unity and community of interests, feelings, and affections, to produce which is always described as one chief purpose of the Death of Christ, shown forth in the Lord's Supper.

UNITY AND VARIETY OF SPIRITUAL GIFTS.

BY REV. ARTHUR P. STANLEY.

1 Cor. ch. xii.

THE historical value of this chapter has been sufficiently set forth in the notes. It is the most detailed contemporary record of the extraordinary powers which manifested themselves in the Christian society during the first century; and which, however they may be explained, confirm the narrative in the Acts of the Apostles, and illustrate that in the four Gospels, especially the statement in Mark xvi. 17 – 20: "They went forth, and preached everywhere, the Lord working with them, and confirming the word with signs following"; that is, "casting out devils, speaking with tongues, taking up serpents, drinking poison without hurt, and laying hands on the sick for their recovery." They resolve themselves into two classes: (1.) Those which relate to healing exactly correspond with the description of the miracles of Peter and John,* and with the allusion in James v. 14, 15: "Is any sick among you? let him call for the elders of the church; and let them pray over him, anointing him with oil in the name of the Lord: and the prayer of faith shall save the sick, and the Lord shall raise him up." (2.) The gifts of teaching which are here classed under the names of "prophets," "teachers," "knowledge," "wisdom," are implied rather than expressly claimed in the authority which the narrative

* Acts iii. 1 – 10; v. 12 – 16; ix. 33 – 42.

of the Acts ascribes to the numerous speeches of the Apostles. But to gifts of this kind allusions are expressly made in the intimations in Matt. x. 20, John xvi. 13, of "the Spirit speaking in the disciples," and "guiding them into all truth." And to the same effect are the passages in Rom. xii. 6–8: "Having then gifts differing according to the grace that is given to us, whether prophecy, let us prophesy according to the proportion of faith; .... or he that teacheth, let him wait on teaching, or he that exhorteth, on exhortation." Eph. iv. 7, 11: "Unto every one of us is given grace..... He gave some, apostles; and some, prophets; and some, evangelists; and some, pastors and teachers." 1 Pet. iv. 10, 11: "As every man hath received the gift, even so minister the same one to another..... If any man speak, as the oracles of God." The Apostle seems to claim this gift for himself, both by implication in all his Epistles, and expressly in 1 Cor. vii. 40: "I think that I also (i. e. as well as others) have the Spirit of God." Of the special gifts of prophesying, and of speaking with tongues, there will be another occasion to speak in considering the fourteenth chapter. It is in the highest development of these various forms of the gift of teaching, that we find the only direct traces of what in modern language is called "inspiration"; and although the limits of such a gift, and the persons in whom it existed, are never clearly defined, the description of it is important, because, unlike the other gifts, its results can still be appreciated. We cannot judge of the gifts of healing; their effects have long since passed away. But we can judge of the gift of teaching by the remains which it has left in the writings of the New Testament; and these remains incontestably prove that there was at that time given to men an extraordinary insight into truth, and an extraordinary power of communicating it.

It is important to observe, that these multiplied allusions imply a state of things in the Apostolical age, which has certainly not been seen since. On particular occasions, indeed, both in the first four centuries, and afterwards in the Middle Ages, miracles are ascribed by contemporary writers to the influence or the relics of particular individuals; but there has been no occasion when they have been so emphatically ascribed to whole societies, so closely mixed up with the ordinary course of life. It is not maintained that every member of the Corinthian church had all or the greater part of those gifts, but it certainly appears that every one had some gift; and this being the case, we are enabled to realize the total difference of the organization of the Apostolical Church from any through which it has passed in its later stages. It was still in a state of fusion. Every part of the new society was instinct with a life of its own. The whole atmosphere which it breathed must have confirmed the belief in the importance and the novelty of the crisis.

But yet more remarkable, both as a proof of the Divine power and wisdom which accompanied this whole manifestation, and also as affording a lesson to after times, is the manner in which the Apostle approaches the subject, and the inference which he draws from it. His object in enumerating these gifts is, not to enlarge on their importance, or to appeal to them as evidences of the Christian faith; it is to urge upon his readers the necessity of co-operation for some useful purpose. Such a thought at such a moment is eminently characteristic of the soberness and calmness which pervade the Apostle's writings, and affords a striking contrast to the fanatical feeling which regards all miracles as ends and not as means; and which despises, as alien and uncongenial, the ideas of co-operation, subordination, and order.

This chapter has a yet further interest. It is the introduction of a new idea into the Sacred Volume. It has been truly observed, that the great glory of the Mosaic covenant was, not so much the revelation of a truth before unknown, as the communication of that truth to a whole people, — the first and only exception which the Eastern world presented to the spirit of caste and exclusion. But even in the chosen people this universal sympathy with each other, and with the common objects of the nation, can hardly be said to have been fulfilled as it was intended.

The idea of a whole community swayed by a common feeling of interest and affection, was not Asiatic, but European. It was Greece, and not Judæa, which first presented the sight of a πόλις or state, in which every citizen had his own political and social duties, and lived, not for himself, but for the state. It was a Roman fable, and not an Eastern parable, which gave to the world the image of a "body politic," in which the welfare of each member depended on the welfare of the rest. And it is precisely this thought which, whether in conscious or unconscious imitation, was suggested to the Apostle, by the sight of the manifold and various gifts of the Christian community.

The image of the Christian Church, which the Apostle here exhibits, is that of a living society in which the various faculties of the various members were to perform their several parts, — not an inert mass of mere learners and subjects, who were to be authoritatively taught and ruled by one small portion of its members. It is a Christianization, not of the Levitical hierarchy, but of the republic of Plato. It has become in after times the basis, not of treatises on church government, but of Butler's Sermons on the general constitution of human nature and of human society. The principle of co-operation, as generally acknowledged in the economical and physical well-being of man, was here to be applied to his moral and spiritual improvement. The peculiar element, which the Apostle blends with this general idea of social and moral union, is that which could only be given by the Christian faith. There would always be the fear lest an object so high and abstract as the promotion of man's moral welfare might seem indistinct, and be lost in the distance. Something nearer and more personal was required to be mixed up with that which was indistinct from its very vastness. The direct object, therefore, of Christian co-operation, according to St. Paul, was to bring Christ into every part of common life, to make human society one living body, closely joined in communion with Christ. And lest this comparison of the Church with the human body might in one respect lead to error, because there resides such a sovereignty in the brain or head, that in comparison of its great activity some of the other members may be called passive; therefore the functions of the head in the Christian Church are by the Apostle assigned exclusively to Christ himself.*

This idea of the Christian community in the Apostolical age was kept up, not only by the universal diffusion of the spiritual gifts, but by all the outward institutions of the Church; by the primitive mode, as already described, of celebrating the Lord's Supper; by the co-operation of the whole community in the expulsion or restoration of offenders; by the absence, as would appear from this chapter, of any definite form of government or constitution; and, in the church of Jerusalem, by the community of property.

Of these institutions most, if not all, even before the termination of the Apostolical age, had been either greatly modified or had ceased to exist; and the gifts, from which the institutions derived their life and spirit, had, as the Apostle himself anticipated, almost, if not altogether, vanished away. But the general truth which their existence suggested to the Apostle is still applicable to the natural gifts which constitute the variety of all civilized society.

If Christ be truly Lord of all, if to him have truly been committed all things both in heaven and on earth, then we may trace his hand, not only in the extraordinary and supernatural, but in the ordinary and natural gifts of men; the earliest form of the Christian society was, as it were, a microcosm of the world at large; what was supplied to it in its first stage by miraculous intervention, is to be sought for now in the various faculties and feelings which it has comprehended within its sphere. And therefore it is truly a part of Christian edification to apply what St. Paul and St. Peter †

* For this whole subject of the idea of the early Church and its relations to the institutions of later times, I cannot forbear to refer to the instructive passages in Arnold's Fragment on the Church, pp. 149, 150.

† Rom. xii. 6-8; 1 Cor. xii. 28; 1 Pet. iv. 10, 11. See Arnold's Sermons, Vol. II. 217; VI. 300.

have said of the diversity and relative importance and final cause of the first extraordinary display of the gifts of the Spirit, to the analogous variety of the gifts of imagination, reasoning powers, thought, activity, means of beneficence. Variety and complexity are the chief characteristics of civilization; and it is one of the many indications of the new birth of the world involved in the introduction of the Gospel, that these very same qualities, by which human society is now carried on in nations and in churches, should thus appear impressed on the face of primitive Christianity.

THE GIFT OF TONGUES AND THE GIFT OF PROPHESYING.

By Rev. ARTHUR P. STANLEY.

1 Cor. xiv. 1 – 40.

The Apostle now arrives at the point to which his argument on the spiritual gifts has throughout been converging, — the special tendency of the Corinthian church to exaggerate the importance of the gift of tongues in comparison of the less extraordinary, but more useful, gift of prophesying. It becomes necessary, therefore, to form some general notion of the nature of these gifts and their relation to each other.

(1.) The gift of "prophesying" or of "the prophets." The word "prophet" (προφήτης) is derived in the first instance from the interpreters of the pagan oracles, who *spoke forth* or expounded the unintelligible answers of the Pythoness of Delphi, or the rustling of the leaves of Dodona. In a metaphorical sense it is used of poets, as interpreters of the Gods or Muses. It was then adopted by the LXX. as the best equivalent of the "nabi" or "seer" of the Old Testament. In the New Testament it is used for a gift which, though in many respects similar to that of the older covenant, was a revival, rather than a continuation, of the ancient prophetical office. According to the common Jewish tradition, prophecy had expired with Malachi; and there is no recorded instance of it between his time and the Christian era. It is true that the application of the name to the Baptist and to Christ, shows that the appearance of a prophet was not a thing unlooked for.* Our Lord speaks as if proverbially of "a prophet having no honor." † Zacharias is said "to prophesy." ‡ Anna is said to be "a prophetess." § But the frequency of the gift, if not its existence, was regarded as a special sign of a new dispensation, and as such its universal diffusion is described at the day of Pentecost. "Your sons and your daughters shall prophesy, ... and on my servants and on my handmaidens I will pour out .... of my Spirit; and they shall prophesy." ‖ In the subsequent narrative of the Acts, prophets and prophetesses are spoken of as everywhere to be found in Christian congregations: "Then came prophets from Jerusalem unto Antioch. .... One of them named Agabus signified by the Spirit that there should be great dearth throughout all the world." ¶ "There were in the church that was at Antioch certain prophets and teachers; as Barnabas, and Simeon that was called Niger, and Lucius of Cyrene, and Manaen, which had been brought up with Herod the tetrarch, and Saul." ** "Judas and Silas being prophets." †† At Cæsarea, Philip the Evangelist had four daughters "which did prophesy." ‡‡ In all the Epistles, the gift of prophecy occupies a conspicuous place in all enumerations of the gifts of the Spirit. The Apocalypse itself is called "a prophecy"; §§ and "the spirit of prophecy," ‖‖ and "the prophets" as "servants of God," and "witnesses," are often mentioned ¶¶ as in the Christian Church. Not only does this wide-spread appearance and variety of prophetical characters agree with the fact of its general diffusion through the whole Corinthian church, but the meaning is substantially the same in all the cases where it occurs. Throughout the New Testament, as throughout the Old, and, it may be added,

* Matt. xiv. 5; xxi. 11 – 46; Mark xi. 32; Luke i. 76; vii. 26, 28, 39; xiii. 33; John iv. 19; ix. 17.

† Matt. xiii. 57. ‡ Luke i. 67. § Luke ii. 36.

‖ Acts ii. 17, 18. ¶ Ibid. xi. 27, 28. ** Ibid. xiii. 1.

†† Ibid. xv. 32. ‡‡ Ibid. xxi. 9. §§ Rev. i. 3; xxii. 7, 10, 18.

‖‖ Ibid. xix. 10.

¶¶ Ibid. xi. 3, 6, 10, 18; xvi. 6; xviii. 20, 24; xxii. 6, 9.

in the use of the Arabic word "nabi" in the Koran, the prominent idea is, not that of prediction, but of delivering inspired messages of warning, exhortation, and instruction: and the general object of the gift, as elsewhere implied, is exactly that here spoken of: building up, exhorting, and comforting"; * "convincing, judging, and making manifest the secrets of the heart." † The ancient classical and Hebrew sense prevails everywhere. Epimenides and Mahomet, on the one hand, Elijah and Paul on the other hand, are called "prophets," not because they foretold the future, but because they enlightened the present.

(2.) We now come to the "gift of tongues," which is a much more difficult subject. The most important passages relating to it are those contained in this chapter, and the allusions to it in xii. 10, 28, as "divers kinds of tongues" (γένη γλωσσῶν), and xiii. 1: "Though I speak with the tongues of men and of angels." To these we must add Mark xvi. 17: "These signs shall follow them that believe..... They shall speak with new tongues" (γλώσσαις λαλήσουσι καιναῖς). There are also the descriptions of the gift at the day of Pentecost, Acts ii. 3–21; at the conversion of the twelve disciples of John the Baptist, Acts xix. 6.

It is nowhere else mentioned by name, though several other passages have been thought to contain allusions to it. Luke xxi. 15: "I will give you a mouth and wisdom, which all your adversaries shall not be able to gainsay." Eph. v. 18: "Be not drunk with wine wherein is excess (compare Acts ii. 13): but be filled with the Spirit; speaking in yourselves (λαλοῦντες ἑαυτοῖς) in psalms and hymns and spiritual songs, singing and making melody in your hearts to the Lord." 1 Thess. v. 19: "Quench not *the Spirit;* despise not prophesyings." 1 Pet. iv. 11: "Each one as he has received a gift..... If any man speak (λαλεῖ), let him speak as the oracles of God."

The only allusion to this gift as still existing after the

* Rev. xiv. 3. † Ibid. xiv. 25.

Apostolic times, is in Irenæus adv. Hær. vi. 6: "We hear many brethren in the Church, having prophetical gifts, and by the Spirit speaking in all kinds of languages." Many speculations occur in the later Fathers on the subject; but their historical testimony to the nature of the gifts may all be summed up in one sentence of Chrysostom, in his comment on this chapter: "This whole place is very obscure; but the obscurity is produced by our ignorance of the facts described, which are such as then used to occur, but now no longer take place."

Such are the data on which we have to proceed. The following conclusions may be attained with tolerable certainty: —

First. The gift in question is always described as something entirely new in the Apostolical age. "They shall speak with *new* tongues." * The effect on the spectators at Pentecost is of universal bewilderment and astonishment.† It is described as the special mark following upon conversion ‡ (whether immediately before baptism, § or immediately after ||). It is, moreover, spoken of as in an especial manner a gift "*of the Spirit*," that is, the new manifestation of God in the hearts of Christians. Hence its appearance at the day of Pentecost: "They were all filled with the Holy Spirit, and began to speak with other tongues as the *Spirit* gave them utterance." ¶ Hence "the speaking with tongues" was the sign that Cornelius had "received the *Holy Spirit*." ** Hence, when Paul placed his hands on the disciples at Ephesus, "the *Holy Spirit* came upon them, and they spake with tongues." †† Hence the very name of "the Spirit" and "spiritual gifts" seems to have been appropriated to this gift, at Corinth and elsewhere. Compare the argument in xii. 1–13, and the particular expressions in xiv. 1, 12, 14, 37; and perhaps 1 Thess. v. 19; Eph. v. 18.

Secondly. It was closely connected with the gift of

---

* Mark xvi. 17.
† Acts ii. 7, 12.
‡ Mark xvi. 17.
§ Acts x. 46.
|| Ibid. xix. 6.
¶ Ibid. ii. 4.
** Ibid. xx. 44, 46, 47.
†† Ibid. xix. 6.

prophesying. This appears not only from these chapters where the two are always compared, as being, though different, yet homogeneous, in xii. 10 – 28, xiii. 1, xiv. 1 – 6, 22 – 25, but from the notices in the Acts. In Acts ii. 17 – 21, Peter, in his justification of himself and the Apostles, describes it under no other name than "prophesying"; and in Acts xix. 6, the converts are described "speaking with tongues and prophesying." To the same effect is the connection in 1 Thess. v. 19, where "quench not the Spirit" is followed by "despise not prophesyings."

Thirdly. Whilst it follows from what has been said, that this gift, like that of prophesying, must have been a possession of the spirit and mind of the speaker by an extraordinary influence, over which he had little or no control, it would seem that its especial distinction from prophesying was, that it consisted not of direct warning, exhortation, or prediction, but of thanksgiving, praise, prayer, singing, and other expressions of devotion: "*pray* with the tongue"; "my spirit *prays*"; "I *sing* in the spirit"; "thou *givest thanks* (εὐλογᾷς) in the Spirit." * "We hear them speaking *the wonderful works of God.*" † "They heard them speaking with tongues, and *magnifying God.*" ‡ And this is illustrated, if not confirmed, by Eph. v. 19: "Speaking .... in psalms and hymns and spiritual songs, singing and making melody .... to the Lord, *giving thanks* always."

Fourthly. It would appear that these expressions of devotion were outpourings of the heart and feelings, rather than of the understanding; so that the actual words and meaning were almost always unintelligible to the by-standers, sometimes to the speakers themselves. "He that speaketh with a tongue speaketh *not to men, but to God;* for no one heareth; and in the Spirit he speaketh mysteries; .... he that speaketh with a tongue edifieth *himself*" [and not the Church]. § "If I come to you speaking with tongues, what shall I profit

* 1 Cor. xiv. 13 – 16.
† Acts ii. 11.
‡ Ibid. x. 46.
§ 1 Cor. xiv. 2, 4.

you?"* "Let him that speaketh with a tongue pray that he may interpret."† "If I pray with a tongue, my spirit prayeth, but my understanding is unfruitful."‡ "If thou givest thanks in the spirit, how shall he that filleth the place of the unlearned say Amen to thy giving of thanks; for he knoweth not what thou sayest."§ "I had rather speak five words with my understanding, that I may instruct others also, than ten thousand words with a tongue."‖ "Making melody *in your hearts.*"¶ To the same effect are the passages which describe the impression produced on by-standers: "If all speak with tongues, and the unlearned or unbelievers come in, will they not say that ye are mad?"** "Others, mocking, said, They are full of new wine"; where, though the words are described as spoken in jest, they are deemed of sufficient importance to be refuted by Peter.†† Compare also Eph. v. 19, where the injunction "to be filled with the Spirit" and to "speak in themselves," is preceded by the prohibition, "be not filled with wine."

Thus far there is no difficulty in combining the several accounts. It is sufficiently clear that it was a trance or ecstasy, which, in moments of great religious fervor, especially at the moment of conversion, seized the early believers; and that this fervor vented itself in expressions of thanksgiving, in fragments of psalmody or hymnody and prayer, which to the speaker himself conveyed an irresistible sense of communion with God, and to the by-stander an impression of some extraordinary manifestation of power, but not necessarily any instruction or teaching, and sometimes even having the appearance of wild excitement, like that of madness or intoxication. It was the most emphatic sign to each individual believer that a power mightier than his own was come into the world; and in those who, like the Apostle Paul, possessed this gift in a high degree, "speaking with tongues

* 1 Cor. xiv. 6. † Ibid. xiv. 13. ‡ Ibid. xiv. 14.
§ Ibid. xiv. 16. ‖ Ibid. xiv. 19. ¶ Eph. v. 19.
** 1 Cor. xiv. 23. †† Acts ii. 13–15.

more than they all,"* it is easy to conceive that, when combined with the other more remarkable gifts which he possessed, it would form a fitting mood for the reception of "God's secrets" (μυστήρια),† and of "unspeakable words, which it is not lawful for man to utter," "being caught into the third heaven," and into "Paradise."‡ And thus the nearest written example of this gift is that exhibited in the abrupt style and the strange visions of the Apocalypse, of which the author describes himself, almost in the words of St. Paul, as "being in the Spirit on the Lord's day," and "hearing a voice as of a trumpet," § and "seeing a door open in heaven," and "a throne set in heaven," ‖ and seeing "the New Jerusalem," "the river of life," and "the tree of life." ¶

But a difficulty arises when we ask, What was the special form which these outpourings of devotion and these prophetic trances assumed? This must be sought in the names by which they were called: (1.) "Speaking with tongues" (λαλεῖν γλώσσαις); ** "speaking with a tongue" (λαλῶν γλώσσῃ).†† (2.) "The tongues" (αἱ γλῶσσαι), ‡‡ "a tongue" (γλῶσσαν), §§ "kinds of tongues" (γένη γλωσσῶν). ‖‖ (3.) "Speaking with other tongues" (λαλεῖν ἑτέραις γλώσσαις), ¶¶ "speaking with new tongues" (γλώσσαις λαλήσουσιν καιναῖς).***

The use of the word "tongue" (γλῶσσα) need not necessarily imply a distinct language of a nation. The only occasions on which it is ever so used in the New Testament are in the poetical language of the Apocalypse; ††† in all which it is used in the phrase "kindreds, and nations, and peoples, and *tongues*," as is the corresponding phrase in Dan. iii. 4, 7, v. 19, vi. 25; Judith iii. 8. In Gen. xi. 7, τὴν γλῶσσαν is

---

* 1 Cor. xiv. 18.
† Ibid. ii. 7; iv. 1; xiv. 2; xv. 51.
‡ 2 Cor. xii. 4 – 6.
§ Rev. i. 9.
‖ Rev. iv. 1.
¶ Rev. xxi. 1; xxii. 1, 2.
** 1 Cor. xiv. 5, 6, 23, 39; Acts x. 46; xix. 6.
†† 1 Cor. xiv. 2, 4, 13, 14, 18. 19, 27.
‡‡ Ibid. xiv. 22.
§§ Ibid. xiv. 26.
‖‖ Ibid. xii. 28.
¶¶ Acts ii. 4.
*** Mark xvi. 17.
††† Rev. v. 9; vii. 9; x. 11; xi. 9; xiii. 7; xiv. 5; xvii. 15.

used in the phrase, "Let us confound their language," as a translation of שָׂפָה, which, however, in all other places in that chapter (verses 1, 7, 9) is translated φωνή or χεῖλος. The word ordinarily used, in sacred as in classical Greek, for "the language of a nation or country" is διάλεκτος, as in Acts i. 19, ii. 6, 8, xxi. 40, xxii. 2, xxvi. 14. We may, therefore, conclude that the word "tongue" (γλῶσσα) was applied to this spiritual gift, partly from the fact that the word in classical Greek was naturally applied to strange, uncommon expressions, as in Aristotle,* partly from the circumstance that, in the use of this gift, "the tongue" was literally the organ employed, the mind, as it were, remaining passive, whilst the tongue gave utterance to words of which the speaker was hardly conscious. That these meanings were both intended to be conveyed, is confirmed by the manner in which kindred expressions are used. When, in xiii. 1, the Apostle says, "Though I speak with the tongues of men and *of angels*" (ταῖς γλώσσαις τῶν ἀνθρώπων λαλῶ καὶ τῶν ἀγγέλων), it is clear from the last word that he was not thinking of languages or dialects, but of every conceivable form of speech or style. And when, in xiv. 9, he says, "So ye, unless ye utter by *the tongue* (διὰ τῆς γλώσσης) "a clear sound," it is clear that he is using the word in reference to the phrase so often repeated in the immediate context, "speaking with a tongue" (λαλῶν γλώσσῃ). It is probable, however, that this peculiarity of style or speech was, if not always, yet occasionally, heightened by the introduction of foreign words or sentences into the utterances thus made. The expressions "kinds of tongues," † "new tongues," ‡ "other tongues," § though they need not of necessity imply anything more than a variety or a novelty of modes of expression, yet become more appropriate if something of a new language, or of different languages, were united with these new or various modes. This is the impression conveyed by the comparison of "the speaker with

* Rhet. III. 3, 4 ; Poet. XXI. 6.

† 1 Cor. xii. 10, 28.

‡ Mark xvi. 17.

§ Acts ii. 4.

tongues" to "a barbarian" (i. e. a foreigner),* and of the sign of tongues generally to the sign of foreign languages, "other tongues and other lips" (ἑτερογλώσσοις καὶ ἐν χείλεσιν ἑτέρων), spoken of in Isaiah, xxviii. 11.† And such certainly must be the meaning of the first recorded appearance of the gift on the day of Pentecost, however it may be explained in detail. The stress laid on the variety of nations there assembled, and the expressions, "every man heard them in *his own language*" (τῇ ἰδίᾳ διαλέκτῳ), ‡ "how hear we every man in *our own language*, wherein we were born?" § "we hear them speak in *our tongues* (ἐν ταῖς ἡμετέραις γλώσσαις) the wonderful works of God," ‖ can hardly be explained on any other supposition than that the writer meant to describe that, at least to the hearers, the sounds spoken seemed to be those of distinct languages and real dialects. If this account is to be taken literally, it would imply that the fervent expressions of thanksgiving which on that occasion, as on others, constituted the essential part of the gift, were so far couched in foreign dialects as to be intelligible to the natives of the several countries. And viewing this passage in connection with the general spirit and object of the Acts, we can hardly avoid seeing, in the emphatic record of this peculiar characteristic of the gift, the design of pointing it out as the natural result and the natural sign of the first powerful and public manifestation of a religion whose especial mission it was to break through the barriers which divide man from man and nation from nation. Such a signification, however suitable to the occasion of the first revelation of a Universal Church, would not be equally appropriate, and is certainly not required, in the more ordinary manifestations of the gift. But it is not difficult to see that the effect described as occurring on the day of Pentecost might grow out of, and form part of the more general nature of "the tongues," as described in the rest of the New Testament. As Xavier is said to have

* 1 Cor. xiv. 11. † Ibid. xiv. 21, 22. ‡ Acts ii. 5.
§ Ibid. ii. 8. ‖ Ibid. ii. 11.

understood and made himself understood by the Indians, without knowing their language, and as, even in ordinary matters, persons in a highly wrought state of feeling are enabled to understand each other, though not speaking the same language, so this gift, which, above all others, lifted the speaker out of himself, might have the same effect. And the peculiar form of language ordinarily used as the vehicle of communication at that time would contribute to the same result. Hellenistic Greek, compounded as it was of Greek, Latin, and Hebrew, and instinct with that peculiar life and energy which we see it assume in the various styles of the New Testament, especially in St. Paul and in the Apocalypse, was almost in itself "a speaking" in divers "kinds of tongues." It has often been remarked, that the spread of this dialect by the conquests of Alexander was a providential preparation for the spread of the Gospel; and there is nothing more strange in the development of this peculiar language into the gift of tongues, than in the development of the natural powers of strength and intellect into the gifts of "ministry," of "wisdom," and of "knowledge." All the various elements of Aramaic and Hellenic speech, latent in the usual language of the time, would be quickened under the power of this gift into a new life, sometimes intelligible, sometimes unintelligible, to those who heard it, but always expressive of the vitality and energy of the Spirit by which it was animated.

It needs hardly to be observed after this comparison of the various passages which speak of this gift, that, even if foreign words were always part of its exercise (of which there is no proof), there is no instance and no probability of its having been ever used as a means of instructing foreign nations, or of superseding the necessity of learning foreign languages. Probably in no age of the world was such a gift less needed. The chief sphere of the Apostles must have been within the Roman Empire, and within that sphere Greek or Latin, but especially Greek, must have been everywhere understood. Even on the day of Pentecost, the speech of Peter, by which the first great conversion was effected, seems to have been in Greek, which probably all the nations assembled would sufficiently understand; and the speaking of foreign dialects is nowhere alluded to by him as any part of the event which he is vindicating and describing. The Epistles, in like manner, were all written in Greek, though many of them are addressed to the very nations whose presence is described in the Acts on that occasion; the people of "Judæa, Cappadocia, Pontus, Asia, Phrygia, and the dwellers at Rome." When the Lycaonians addressed Paul and Barnabas in the speech of Lycaonia,* there is no mention of Paul and Barnabas answering them in that language. According to one of the oldest traditions, Peter is described as employing Mark for an interpreter.† Irenæus, who alone of the early Fathers alludes to the gift of tongues, and that in a manner which seems to imply diversity of language,‡ was himself obliged to learn the Gaulish language. And, lastly, the whole chapter now in question is inconsistent with such a supposition. The church of Corinth is described as full of speakers with tongues, and yet evidently no work of conversion was going on, nor any allusion made to such a work as a possible object for the gift. Yet had such an object been within even its distant scope, the argument almost imperatively demanded that it should be noticed, and that the Apostle should have said, "Why do you waste so great a gift on those who cannot profit by it, when you might go forth beyond the limits of the Empire to preach with it to the Scythian and Indian tribes?"

The subject must not be left without reference to similar manifestations which may serve, either by way of contrast or resemblance, to illustrate its main peculiarities. In the Pagan world the Apostle's words, at the opening of the twelfth chapter, of themselves remind us of the unconscious utterances which accompanied the delivery of the ancient oracles, when the ejaculations of the Pythoness stood to the inter-

* Acts xiv. 11. † Eus. H. E. III. 39. ‡ Adv. Hær. VI. 6.

preters of the oracle in a relation similar to that which existed between the speakers with tongues and the prophets. In the Jewish dispensation we may compare the burst of song and trance, which accompanied the first great display of the prophetical spirit in the time of Samuel, "a company of prophets coming down from the high place with a *psaltery*, and a *tabret*, and a *pipe*, and a *harp* before them," and prophesying; and "the *Spirit* of the Lord" descending upon those who witnessed the spectacle, however unprepared for it before; so that they too caught the inspiration "and prophesied also," and were "turned into other men," and passed days and nights in a state of ecstatic seclusion.* What the "tongues" were to the "prophesyings" at Corinth, the trance of Saul was to the Psalms of David. But it is perhaps in subsequent periods that the nearest outward likenesses to the gift of "tongues" can be found. The wide difference between the character, intellectual, moral, and spiritual, of the early Christian Church, and that of the sects in which such later manifestations have appeared, places a deep gulf between the Apostolical gift and these doubtful copies. Still as the preaching, the teaching, the government, the gifts of knowledge, of wisdom, of ministry, which appear in the Apostolical age, are illustrated by the analogous institutions and faculties of less sacred times, so the excitement and enthusiasm, and the gifts more especially associated with this aspect of the early Church, may be illustrated no less from the expressions of later enthusiasm. Such phenomena, however inferior to the manifestations of the Apostolical times, have their origin in the same mysterious phase of human life and human nature, which was included with so much besides of the most opposite character in the wide range of the spiritual influences of Apostolical Christianity.

The earliest of these manifestations was the alleged ecstatic state of the Montanists at the close of the second century. "There is at present a sister amongst us," says Ter-

* 1 Sam. x. 5, 6, 10; xix. 20 – 24.

tullian, "who has obtained the gift of revelations, which she receives in the congregation or solemn sanctuary by ecstasy in the Spirit, who has converse with angels, sometimes even with the Lord, and sees and hears sacred truths (*sacramenta*), and discerns the hearts of some, and ministers remedies to those who want them. Also, according as the Scriptures are read, or the Psalms sung, or exhortations (*adlocutiones*) uttered, or petitions presented, so from these several sources materials are furnished for her visions. We had happened to be discussing something about the soul, when this sister was in the Spirit. After the conclusion of the service and the dismissal of the congregation, she, after her usual manner of relating her visions (for they are carefully recorded that they may be examined), amongst other remarks, said the soul was shown to me in a bodily form, the spirit appeared, but not of an empty or shapeless quality, but as something which gave hope of being held, tender and bright and of an aerial hue, and altogether of human form."

Another instance was the utterance of strange sounds among the persecuted Protestants of the South of France, at the beginning of the last century, commonly called the "Prophets of Cevennes," of whom full accounts are to be found in the "Histoire des Pasteurs," by Peyrat; of the "Troubles de Cevennes," by Gibelin; and of the "Eglises de Désert," by C. Coquerel. There is also an "Impartial Account of the Prophets," by an eyewitness, in A Letter to a Friend,* on their appearance in England, where they excited much attention and the ridicule of Lord Shaftesbury in his "Characteristics." There is little of detailed interest in these descriptions; but they are remarkable, especially the last named, as bearing testimony to the good character and general sobriety of the persons professing to be inspired.

But the most important of these manifestations, as the one claiming the most direct connection with the Apostolical gifts, was the so-called "gift of tongues" in the followers of Mr.

---

* London: Morphew, 1708.

Irving, about 1831–1833. Of the exercise of this gift, accounts are here subjoined from two eyewitnesses: the first, a believer in its Divine origin at the time he wrote; the second, a believer and actor in the transactions which he describes, but at the time that he wrote rejecting their Divine, though still maintaining their supernatural (though diabolical) origin.

(1.) "As an instance of the extraordinary change in the powers of the human voice when under inspiration, I may here mention the case of an individual whose natural voice was inharmonious, and who besides had no ear for keeping time. Yet even the voice of this person, when singing in the Spirit, could pour forth a rich strain of melody, of which each note was musical, and uttered with a sweetness and power of expression that was truly astonishing, and, what is still more singular, with a gradually increasing velocity into a rapidity, yet distinctness of utterance, which is inconceivable by those who have never witnessed the like; and yet, with all this apparently breathless haste, there was not in reality the slightest agitation of body or of mind. In other instances, the voice is deep and powerfully impressive. I cannot describe it better than by saying that it approaches nearly to what might be considered a perfect state of the voice, passing far beyond the energies of its natural strength, and at times so loud as not only to fill the whole house, but to be heard at a considerable distance; and though often accompanied by an apparently great mental energy and muscular exertion of the whole body, yet in truth there was not the slightest disturbance in either; on the contrary, there was present a tranquillity and composure, both of body and mind, the very opposite to any, even the least degree of excitement.

"Every attempt at describing these manifestations, so as to convey an accurate knowledge of them to others, is sure to fail; since, to have any adequate perception of their power, they must be both seen and felt. Yet, were it otherwise, my conscience would scarcely allow me the liberty of entering into so minute a detail; for the consciousness of the presence of God in these manifestations is fraught with such a holy solemnity of thought and feeling, as leave neither leisure nor inclination for curious observation. In a person alive to the presence of the Holy Ghost, and overwhelmed by his manifestations beside and around him, and deeply conscious that his heart is naked and exposed unto the eye of God, one thought alone fills the soul, one way of utterance is heard, 'God be merciful to me a sinner.' Nor can the eye be diverted from the only sight that is then precious to it, far more precious than life itself: 'The Lamb of God, that taketh away the sin of the world.'" *

(2.) "After one or two of the brethren had read and prayed, Mr. T. was made to speak two or three words very distinctly, and with an energy and depth of tone which seemed to me extraordinary, and it fell upon me as a supernatural utterance which I ascribed to the power of God; the words were in a tongue I did not understand. In a few minutes Miss E. C. broke out in an utterance in English, which, as to matter and manner and the influence it had upon me, I at once bowed to as the utterance of the Spirit of God. Those who have heard the powerful and commanding utterance need no description; but they who have not, may conceive what an unnatural and unaccustomed tone of voice, an intense and riveting power of expression, with the declaration of a cutting rebuke to all who were present, and applicable to my own state of mind in particular, would effect upon me and upon the others who were come together, expecting to hear the voice of the Spirit of God. In the midst of the feeling of awe and reverence which this produced, I was myself seized upon by the power, and in much struggling against it was made to cry out, and myself to give out a confession of my own sin in the matter for which we were rebuked...... There was in me, at the time of the utterance, very great excitement; and yet I was distinctly con-

* A Brief Account of a Visit to some of the Brethren in the West of Scotland. Published by J. Nisbet, London, 1831, pp. 28, 29.

scious of a power, acting upon me beyond the mere power of excitement. So distinct was this power from the excitement, that, in all my trouble and doubt about it, I never could attribute the whole to excitement." * "I read the fourth chapter of Malachi; as I read the power came upon me, and I was made to read in the power. My voice was raised far beyond its natural pitch, with constrained repetitions of parts, and with the same inward uplifting which at the presence of the power I had always before experienced." † "Whilst sitting at home, a mighty power came upon me, but for a considerable time no impulse to utterance; presently, a sentence in French was vividly set before my mind, and, under an impulse to utterance, was spoken. Then, in a little time, sentences in Latin were in like manner uttered; and, with short intervals, sentences in many other languages, judging from the sound and the different exercise of the enunciating organs. My wife, who was with me, declared some of them to be Italian and Spanish; the first she can read and translate, the second she knows but little of. In this case she was not able to interpret nor retain the words as they were uttered. All the time of these utterances I was greatly tried in mind. After the first sentence, an impulse to utterance continued on me, and most painfully I restrained it, my conviction being that, until something was set before me to utter, I ought not to yield my tongue to utterance. Yet I was troubled by the doubt, what could the impulse mean, if I were not to yield to it? Under the trial, I did yield my tongue for a few moments; but the utterance that broke from me seemed so discordant that I concluded the impulse, without words given, was a temptation, and I restrained it, except as words were given me, and then I yielded. Sometimes single words were given me, and sometimes sentences, though I

* Narrative of Facts characterizing the Supernatural Manifestations, in Members of Mr. Irving's Congregation and other Individuals, in England and Scotland, and formerly in the Writer himself, by Robert Baxter. 2d edition, Nisbet, London, 1833, pp. 5 – 7.

† Ibid., p. 12.

could neither recognize the words nor sentences as any language I knew, except those which were French or Latin." * "My persuasion concerning the unknown tongue, as it is called (in which I myself was very little exercised), is, that it is no language whatever, but a mere collection of words and sentences; and in the lengthened discourses is, most of it a jargon of sounds; though I can conceive, when the power is very great, that it will assume much of the form of a connected oration." †

It must again be repeated, that those instances are brought forward, not as examples of the Apostolical gift, but as illustrations of it. But, however inferior they may have been to the appearances of which they were imitations or resemblances, they yet serve to show the possibility of the same combination of voice, and ecstasy, and unknown or foreign words, as has been described in the case of the Apostolic gift; they show also how, even when accompanied by extravagance and fanaticism, such a manifestation could still be, in a high degree, solemn, impressive, and affecting. It was the glory of the Apostolical age, that, instead of dwelling exclusively on this gift, or giving it a prominent place, as has been the case in the sects of later days, the allusions to it are rare and scanty, and (in the chapter now before us, which contains the fullest account of it) even disparaging. The Corinthian Christians, indeed, regarded it as one of the highest manifestations of spiritual influence; but this was the very tendency which the Apostle sought to repress. The object of this Section of the Epistle, as of the whole discussion on spiritual gifts of which it forms a part, is to restrain, moderate, and reduce to its proper subordination, the fervor, the enthusiasm, the eccentricity, so to speak, occasioned by these gifts, and to maintain beyond and above them the eternal superiority of the moral and religious elements which Christianity had sanctioned or introduced.

In this respect, as in many others, the mission of the

---

* Narrative of Facts, &c., pp. 133, 134. † Ibid., pp. 134, 135.

Apostle was analogous to, though at the same time wholly unlike, that of the ancient prophets. There was in the early Christian Church no fear (except from the Jewish party) of an undue development of that ceremonial and hierarchical spirit, against which the Prophets and Psalmists, from Samuel and David downwards, had so constantly lifted up their voices to assert the paramount importance of justice, mercy, and truth; of obedience above sacrifice; of a broken and contrite spirit above burnt-offerings of bulls and goats. It was from an opposite quarter that these great spiritual verities were endangered in the beginning of the Christian Church; but the danger was hardly less formidable. The attractions of miraculous power, of conscious impulses of a Divine presence, of a speech and an ecstatic state which struck all beholders with astonishment, were the temptations which, amongst the primitive Gentile Christians, threatened to withdraw the Church from the truth, the simplicity, and the soberness of Christ and of Paul, as the stately ceremonial of the Jewish worship had, in ancient times, had the like effect in withdrawing the nation of Israel from the example of Abraham and the teaching of Moses. That the gifts were not less necessary to sustain the first faith of the Apostolical Christians, than the Levitical rites were to sustain that of the Jewish people, does but render the illustration more exact. What, therefore, the protests of Isaiah and Amos are against the corruptions of the ancient Jewish priesthood, what the protests of the Apostle himself in the Epistles to the Romans and Galatians are against circumcision and the rites of the Mosaic Law, that this chapter is against all those tendencies of the human mind which delight in displays of Divine power more than in displays of Divine wisdom or goodness, which place the evidence of God's spirit more in sudden and wonderful frames of feeling and devotion, than in acts of usefulness and instruction, which make religion selfish and individual rather than social. Gregory the Great warned Augustine of Canterbury not to rejoice that spirits were subject to him by miraculous power, but that his name was written in the Book of Life through the conversions which he had effected. The attempts of Paley to rest Christianity solely upon its external evidence have, in our own times, been rejected by a higher and more comprehensive philosophy. The great body of the Christian Church has, in all ages, given little heed to the extraordinary displays of power, real or pretended, by particular sects or individuals. In all these cases the warning of the Apostle in this chapter has been at hand, to support the more rational and the more dignified course (if so it may without offence be called), which minds less enlightened, and consciences less alive to the paramount greatness of moral excellence, may have been induced to despise. If the Apostle's declaration, that "he himself spake with tongues" "more than they all," when combined with his other qualities, is a guaranty that the Apostolical gift of tongues was not imposture or fanaticism; yet, on the other hand, his constant language respecting it is a guaranty no less that gifts such as these were the last that he would have brought forward in vindication or support of the Gospel which he preached. The excitable temperament of Eastern, as compared with Western nations, may serve to explain to us, how it was that conditions of mind like that implied in the gift of tongues should have accompanied, without disturbing, a faith so lofty, so sober, so dispassionate, as that of the Apostle. But it also makes that soberness the more remarkable in the Apostle, born and bred in this very Oriental atmosphere where, as is still shown by the exercises of the Mussulman dervishes, nothing is too wild to be incorporated into religious worship; where, as is still shown by the ready acceptance of the legends of Mahomet and the Mussulman saints, nothing is too extravagant to be received as a miracle. He acknowledged the truth, he claimed the possession, of this extraordinary power; and yet he was endowed with the wisdom and the courage to treat it as always subordinate, often even useless and needless.

LOVE, THE GREATEST OF GIFTS.

By Rev. ARTHUR P. STANLEY.

1 Cor. xii. 31 – xiii. 13.

This passage stands alone in the writings of St. Paul, both in its subject and in its style; yet it is the kernel of the whole Epistle. This Epistle finds its climax here, as that to the Romans in the conclusion of the eighth chapter, or that to the Hebrews, in the eleventh. Whatever evil tendencies he had noticed before in the Corinthian church, met their true correction in this one gift. To them, whatever it might be to others, to them, with their factions, their intellectual excitements, their false pretensions, it was all-important. Without this bond of Love he felt that the Christian society of Greece would as surely fall to pieces, as its civil society in former times had appeared to philosophers and statesmen to be destined to dissolution, without the corresponding virtue of *φιλία*, or mutual harmony. Therefore, although in a digression, he rises with the subject into the passionate fervor which in him is only produced by a directly practical object. Unlike the mere rhetorical panegyrics on particular virtues, which are to be found in Philo and similar writers, every word of the description tells with double force, because it is aimed against a real enemy. It is as though, wearied with the long discussions against the sins of the Corinthian church, he had at last found the spell by which they could be overcome, and uttered sentence after sentence with the triumphant cry of "Eureka!"

The particular motive for the introduction of the passage in this place was, as we have seen, the wish to impress upon his readers the subordination of gifts of mere display, such as the gift of tongues, to gifts of practical utility, such as prophecy. And analogously the same truth still needs to be impressed: "To all but one in ten thousand," it has been well said, "Christian speculation is barren of great fruits; to all but one in ten thousand, Christian benevolence is fruitful of great thoughts." Such is the directly practical result of the chapter. But the very style shows that it rises far above any immediate or local occasion. On each side of this chapter the tumult of argument and remonstrance still rages: but within it, all is calm; the sentences move in almost rhythmical melody; the imagery unfolds itself in almost dramatic propriety; the language arranges itself with almost rhetorical accuracy. We can imagine how the Apostle's amanuensis must have paused, to look up on his master's face at the sudden change of the style of his dictation, and seen his countenance lighted up as it had been the face of an angel, as the sublime vision of Divine perfection passed before him. What then, let us ask, is the nature and origin of that new element of goodness, of which this is the earliest detailed description?

In the first place, the word ἀγάπη is, in this sense, altogether peculiar to the New Testament; and in the New Testament, to the writings of Paul, Peter, and John. It is a remarkable fact, that the word, as a substantive, is entirely unknown to classical Greek. The only passage where it is quoted in Stephens's Thesaurus as occurring, is in Plutarch's Symposium; and there it has been subsequently corrected by Reiske from ἀγάπης ὤν to the participle ἀγαπήσων. The verb ἀγαπᾷν, indeed, is used in classical Greek, but in the sense only of acquiescence and contentment, or of esteem and value. It is in the LXX. that we first find it employed, to designate what we call "love"; and it is there introduced (probably from its likeness in sound to the Hebrew words) to represent אָהַב and עָגַב ("ahab" and "agab"), both words expressive of passionate affection, drawn from the idea of panting, aspiring after a desired object. The substantive ἀγάπη only occurs in Cant. ii. 4, v. 6, viii. 6, 7, for sexual love, and is there probably suggested by the Hebrew feminine from אַהֲבָה ("ahabah").* The peculiarity of its use in the New Testament is, that when used simply, and unexplained by anything else, it is equivalent to benevolence based on religious motives. The Old Testament (in the word אָהַב) exhibited the virtues both of conjugal affection and of friendship passing the love of women, as in the case of David; it exhibited also, in the case of David, the same passionate devotion transferred from man to God, as is wonderfully shown throughout the Psalms; it exhibited, lastly, the same feeling emanating from God himself towards his peculiar people, the spouse of his choice, the daughter of Zion. The Greek world also exhibited in a high degree the virtue of personal friendship, which was, indeed, so highly esteemed, as to give its name (φιλία) to affection generally. Domestic and conjugal affection, strictly speaking, there was not. The word (ἔρως), which most nearly approaches to the modern notions of love, expressed either a merely sensual admiration of physical beauty, or, when transferred in the sublime language of Plato to a loftier sphere, an intellectual admiration of ideal beauty. The writers who at Alexandria united the last efforts of Grecian philosophy with the last efforts of Jewish religion, went a step in one sense beyond both the Old Testament and also the Greek literature, though in another sense below them both. Benevolence to man, as man, expressing itself in the word φιλανθρωπία, occupies in the writings of Philo very much the same position as that occupied in the New Testament by ἀγάπη. But whilst it breaks through the narrow limits in which the love of the Hebrew dispensation was confined, it loses its intensity. It becomes an abstraction to be panegyrized, not a powerful motive to be acted upon.

In contradistinction to all these, and yet the complement

* So βάρις, "a boat," is used as the translation of בִּירָה, "a palace."

and completion of all, is the Love, or ἀγάπη, of the New Testament. Whilst it retains all the fervor of the Hebrew aspiration and desire, and of the personal affection of the Greek, it ranges through as wide a sphere as the comprehensive benevolence of Alexandria. Whilst it retains the religious element that raised the affections of the Hebrew Psalmist to the presence of God, it agrees with the classical and Alexandrian feelings in making its chief object the welfare of man. It is not Religion evaporated into Benevolence, but Benevolence taken up into Religion. It is the practical exemplification of the two great characteristics of Christianity, the union of God with man, the union of religion with morality; Love to man for the sake of Love to God; Love to God showing itself in Love to man.

It is, perhaps, vain to ask by what immediate means this new idea was introduced to the Apostle's mind; it may be that this very passage is the expression of his delight at first fully grasping the mighty truth which henceforth was never to pass from him. But the impression left by the words rather is, that he assumes it as something already known; new, indeed, in its application to the wants of the Corinthian church, but recognized as a fundamental part of the Christian revelation. Is it too much to say, that this is one of the ideas derived expressly from what he calls "the revelations of *the Lord*"? that it is from the great example of self-sacrificing love shown in the life and death of Jesus Christ, that the Apostle, and through him the Christian world, has received the truth, that Love to man for the sake of God is the one great end of human existence. "A new commandment he gave unto us, that we should love one another, as he loved us. Greater love hath no man than this, that he lay down his life for another." Until Christ had lived and died, the virtue was impossible. *The fact* of its having come into existence, *the urgency* with which the Apostle dwells upon it, *is itself a proof* that he had lived and died as none had ever lived and died before. And it is further remarkable, that a word and an idea which first appears in the writings of St. Paul should receive its full meaning and development in those of St. John. To the minds of both these great Apostles, amidst all their other diversities, "Love" represented the chief fact and the chief doctrine of Christianity. Has it occupied the same place in Christian theology or Christian practice at any later period?

THE RESURRECTION OF CHRIST.

By Rev. ARTHUR P. STANLEY.

1 Cor. xv. 1 – 11.

The foregoing Section is remarkable in two points of view: —

First. It contains the earliest known specimen of what may be called the Creed of the early Church. In one sense, indeed, it differs from what is properly called a Creed, which was the name applied, not to what new converts were taught, but what they professed on their conversion. Such a profession is naturally to be found only in the Acts of the Apostles; as an impassioned expression of thanksgiving, in Acts iv. 24 – 30; or more frequently as a simple expression of belief, in Acts viii. 37, where (in some manuscripts) the eunuch, in reply to Philip's question, answers, "I believe that Jesus Christ is the Son of God"; and in Acts xvi. 31, xix. 5, where the same, or nearly the same, is implied of the jailer of Philippi and of the converts at Ephesus. But the value of the present passage is, that it gives us a sample of the exact form of the oral teaching of the Apostle. As has been before remarked, it cannot be safely inferred that we have here the whole of what the Apostle means to describe as the foundation of his preaching; partly because of the expression "first of all," partly because, from the nature of the case, he brings forward most prominently what was specially required by the occasion. Still, on the whole, the more formal and solemn introduction of the argument, as in

xi. 23 ("I delivered, I received"), and the conciseness of the phrases ("died," "was buried," and the twice-repeated expression "according to the Scriptures"), imply that at least in the third and fourth verses we have to a certain extent the original formula of the Apostle's teaching. And this is confirmed by its similarity to parts of the Creeds of the first three centuries, especially to that which, under the name of the Apostles' Creed, has been generally adopted in the churches of the West.

Of the details of this primitive formula, enough has been said in the commentary. It is important, besides, to observe its general character. Two points chiefly present themselves, as distinguishing it from later productions of a similar nature: (1.) It is a strictly historical composition. It is what the Apostle himself calls it, not so much a Creed as a "Gospel"; a "Gospel" both in the etymological sense of that word in English as well as in Greek, as a "glad message," and also in the popular sense in which it is applied to the narratives of our Lord's life. It is the announcement, not of a doctrine, or thought, or idea, but of simple matters of fact; of a joyful message, which its bearer was eager to disclose, and its hearers eager to receive. Dim notions of some great changes coming over the face of the world, vague rumors of some wide movement spreading itself from Palestine, had swept along the western shores of the Mediterranean; and it was in answer to the inquiries thus suggested, that Apostle and Evangelist communicated the "things that they had seen or heard." Thus it was that the Apostle's "Gospel" was contained in the brief summary here presented, and such a summary as this became the origin of the "Gospels," and, according to the wants of the readers, was expanded into the detailed narratives which still retained the name of "glad tidings," though, strictly speaking, it belonged only to the original announcement of their contents.

(2.) A point of subordinate interest, but still remarkable as belonging solely to the Apostolical age, is the emphatic connection of the facts announced with the ancient dispensation. Amongst all the forms, some of them of considerable length, which are preserved, of the creeds of the first four centuries, there are only two (that of Tertullian * and of Epiphanius, † from whom, probably, it was derived in the Nicene Creed), which contain the expressions here twice repeated, "according to the Scriptures," and in those two probably imitated from this place. The point, though minute, is of importance, as helping to bring before us the different aspect which the same events wore to the Apostolical age and to the next generations. If, in so compendious an account of his preaching the fundamental facts of the Gospel history, the Apostle thinks it necessary twice over to repeat that they took place in conformity with the ancient prophecies, it is evident that his hearers, Gentiles as in this instance they were to a great extent, must have been not only familiar with the Old Testament, but anxious to have their new faith brought into connection with it. Later ages have delighted in discovering mystical anticipations or argumentative proofs of the New Testament in the Old; but these words, expressing, as they do, the general feeling of the Apostolical writings, carry us back to a time when the events of Christianity required, as it were, not only to be illustrated or confirmed, but to be *justified*, by reference to Judaism. We have in them the sign that, in reading this Epistle, although on the shores of Greece, we are still overshadowed by the hills of Palestine; the older covenant still remains in the eye of the world as the one visible institution of Divine origin; the "Scriptures" of the Old Testament are still appealed to with undivided reverence, as the stay of the very writings which were destined so soon to take a place, if not above, at least beside them, with a paramount and independent authority.

Secondly. This passage contains the earliest extant account of the resurrection of Christ. Thirty years at the most, twenty years at the least, had elapsed, that is to say, about the same period as has intervened between this year

---

* Adv. Prax. c. 2.

† II. p. 122.

(1855) and the French Revolution of 1830; and, as the Apostle observes, most of those to whom he appeals as witnesses were still living; and he himself, though not strictly an eyewitness of the *fact* of the resurrection, yet, in so far as he describes the vision at his conversion, must be considered as bearing unequivocal testimony to the *belief* in it prevailing at that time. It is not, however, the mere assertion of the general fact which gives especial interest to this passage, but the details of the appearances. The belief in the fact is sufficiently implied in other Epistles of the same date, and of genuineness equally incontestable; as in Rom. i. 4; iv. 24, 25; v. 10; vi. 4–10; viii. 11, 34; x. 9; xiv. 9; 2 Cor. iv. 10, 11, 14; v. 15; Gal. i. 1; 1 Thess. i. 10; iv. 14. Indeed, it is almost needless to quote particular passages to prove a conviction which the whole tenor of the Apostle's writings presupposes, and which has hardly ever been doubted. But this Epistle on several occasions not only implies and states general facts, but descends into particular details of the Gospel history. Accordingly, in this passage we have here the account of five appearances after the resurrection, besides the one to himself. The general character of the appearances remarkably agrees with that in the Gospel narratives. They are all spoken of as separate and transient glimpses, rather than a continuous and abiding intercourse. Some of the instances given are certainly identical in both. Such are the appearances to the two collective meetings of the Apostles. The appearances to Peter, to the five hundred, and to James, are distinct from those in the Gospel narrative; and it may be remarked that this variation itself agrees with the discrepancies and obscurities which characterize that portion of the Gospel narrative. The appearance to James in particular, agreeing as it does with the account of a rejected Gospel (that according to the Hebrews), and not with those of the canonical Gospels, indicates an independent source for the Apostle's statement. The appearance to Peter is also to be noticed especially, as an example of an incident to which there is an allusion in the Gospel narrative,* which here only receives its explanation. The appearance to the five hundred is to be observed as exemplifying with regard to the Apostle's relation, with regard to the Gospel narratives, what is often to be observed with regard to his relation to the Acts; namely, that he, writing nearer the time, makes a fuller statement of the miraculous or wonderful than is to be found in the later accounts; the reverse of what is usually supposed to take place in fictitious narratives.

The result, therefore, on the whole, of the comparison of St. Paul's narrative with that of the Gospels, is, —

(1.) That there must already have existed at this time a belief in the main outline of the Gospel story of the Resurrection, much as we have it now.

(2.) That the Gospel to which his statements, as elsewhere so here, bear the closest resemblance, is that of St. Luke, thus confirming the usual tradition of their connection.

(3.) That with regard to the Resurrection in particular, there was, besides the four accounts preserved in the Gospels, a fifth, agreeing with them in its general character, but differing from them as much as they differ from each other, and, whilst it is earlier in time, giving stronger attestations to the event.

---

* Luke xxiv. 34.

THE RESURRECTION OF THE DEAD.

By Rev. ARTHUR P. STANLEY.

1 Cor. xv. 35 – 58.

This passage is important, as exemplifying what may be called the soberness of the Apostle's view of a future life. He enters into no details, he appeals to two arguments only: first, the endless variety of the natural world; secondly, the power of the new life introduced by Christ. These two together furnish him with the hope, that out of God's infinite goodness and power, as shown in nature and in grace, life will spring out of death, and new forms of being wholly unknown to us here will fit us for the spiritual world hereafter. On one point only he professes to have a distinct revelation, and that not with regard to the dead, but to the living. So firmly was the first generation of Christians possessed of the belief that they should live to see the second coming, that it is here assumed as a matter of course; and their fate, as near and immediate, is used to illustrate the darker and more mysterious subject of the fate of those already dead. That vision of "the last man," which now seems so remote as to live only in poetic fiction, was, to the Apostle, an awful reality; but it is brought forward only to express the certainty that, even here, a change must take place; the greatest that imagination can conceive. The last of the human race will have passed away; but in that moment of final dissolution, the only thought that is present to the Apostle's mind is not death, but life and victory. The time was approaching, as it seemed, when, in the language of modern science, "not the individual only, but the species of man, would be transferred to the list of extinct forms," and all the generations of men would be "gone, lost, hushed in the stillness of a mightier death than had hitherto been thought of." To us the end of the world, though now indefinitely postponed, is a familiar idea; then it was new in itself, and its coming was expected to be immediate. As in that trial of his individual faith and patience, mentioned in the Second Epistle,* it was revealed to him that "Christ's grace was sufficient for him"; so also in this trial, which appeared to await the whole existing generation of men, it was (so he seems to tell us) declared to him "in a" revealed "mystery," that in that great change "God would give them the victory" over death and the grave, "through Jesus Christ."

The question, with which the passage opens and which even in later times has often been asked again with elaborate minuteness, "How are the dead raised up, and with what body do they come?" is met with the stern reproof, "Thou fool"; nor is what we call "the resurrection of the body," properly speaking, touched upon in these verses. The difficulties which have been raised respecting the Resurrection in the Apostle's time or in our own, are occasioned by the futile endeavor to form a more distinct conception of another life than in our mortal state is possible. The inquiry which he answers is like that of the Sadducees, "In the resurrection whose wife shall she be of the seven?" and the spirit of his reply is the same as that of our Lord, "In the resurrection they neither marry, nor are given in marriage, but are as the angels of God in heaven. . . . . God is not the God of the dead, but of the living." All that the Apostle directly asserts is, that whatever body there may be after death will be wholly different from the present, and that the infinite variety of nature renders such an expectation not only possible, but probable. His more positive belief or hope on this subject

* 2 Cor. xii. 8, 9.

must be sought, not here, but in 2 Cor. v. 1–6. This much, however, may be inferred from the two passages combined, and from such expressions as Rom. viii. 23, "The redemption of our body"; Rom. viii. 11, "He that raised up Christ from the dead shall also quicken your mortal bodies"; Phil. iii. 21, "Who shall change our vile body, that it may be fashioned like unto his glorious body";—namely, that the Christian idea of a future state is not fully expressed by a mere abstract belief in *the immortality of the soul*, but requires a redemption and restoration of the whole man. According to the ancient creed of Paganism, expressed in the well-known lines at the commencement of the Iliad, the souls of departed heroes did indeed survive death; but these souls were not themselves, they were the mere shades or ghosts of what had been; "themselves" were the bodies left to be devoured by dogs and vultures. The Apostle's teaching, on the other hand, is always that, amidst whatever change, it is the very man himself that is preserved; and, if for the preservation of this identity any outward organization is required, then, although "flesh and blood cannot inherit the kingdom of heaven," God from the infinite treasure-house of the new heavens and new earth will furnish that organization, as he has already furnished it to the several stages of creation in the present order of the world. "If God so clothe the grass of the field, which to-day is and to-morrow is cast into the oven, shall he not much rather clothe you, O ye of little faith?"

THE CREDIBILITY OF MIRACLES.

By THOMAS BROWN, M. D., F. R. S. Ed.,

PROFESSOR OF MORAL PHILOSOPHY IN THE UNIVERSITY OF EDINBURGH.*

The *possibility* of the occasional direct operation of the Power which formed the world, in varying the usual course of its events, it would be in the highest degree unphilosophical to deny: nor can we presume to estimate the degree of its probability; since, in many cases, of the wide bearings of which on human happiness we must be ignorant, it might be the result of the same benevolent motives which we must suppose to have influenced the Divine mind in the original act of creation itself. But the theory of the Divine government, which admits the possibility of such occasional agency, is very different from that which asserts the necessity of the perpetual and uniform operation of the Supreme Being, as the immediate or efficient cause of every phenomenon. The will of the Deity, whether displayed in those obvious variations of events which are termed miracles, or inferred from those supposed secret and invisible changes which are ascribed to his providence, is itself, in all such cases, to be regarded by the affirmer of it as a new physical antecedent, from which, if it really form a part of the series of events, a difference of result may naturally be expected, on the same principle as that on which we expect a change of product from any other new combination of physical circumstances.

---

* From a note to his "Inquiry into the Relation of Cause and Effect."

It is on this view of the Divine will, — as itself, in every case in which it may be supposed to operate directly in the phenomena of the universe, a new circumstance of physical causation, — that every valid answer to the abstract argument of Mr. Hume's Essay on Miracles must, as I conceive, be founded. The great mistake of that argument does not consist, as has been imagined, in a miscalculation of the force of testimony in general: for the principle of the calculation must be conceded to him, that, whatever be the source of our early faith in testimony, the rational credit which we afterwards give to it, in any case, depends on our belief of the less improbability of the facts reported, than of the ignorance or fraud of the reporter. If the probabilities were reversed, — and if it appeared to us less probable that any fact should have happened as stated, than that the reporter of it should have been unacquainted with the real circumstances, or desirous of deceiving us, — it matters little from what principle our faith in testimony may primarily have flowed: for there is surely no one who will contend, that, in such a case, we should be led by any principle of our nature to credit that which appeared to us, at the very time at which we gave it our assent, unworthy of being credited, or, in other words, less likely to be true than to be false.

Whether it be to experience that we owe our belief of testimony in general, or whether we owe to it only our knowledge of the possibilities of error or imposition, which makes us hesitate in admitting any particular testimony, is of no consequence then to our belief, in the years in which we are called to be the judges of the likelihood of any extraordinary event that is related to us. It is enough that we know, as after a very few years of life we cannot fail to know, that it is possible for the reporter to be imperfectly acquainted with the truth of what he states, or capable of wishing to deceive us. Before giving our complete assent to any marvellous tale, we always weigh probability against probability; and if, after weighing these, it appear to us more likely, on the whole, that the information is false, than that the event has really happened, in the manner reported, we should not think ourselves in the slightest degree more bound to admit the accuracy of the narrative, though a thousand arguments were urged, far more convincing than any which have yet been offered, to persuade us, that there is an original tendency in the mind, before experience, to believe whatever is related, without even the slightest feeling of doubt, and consequently without any attempt to form an estimate of its degree of probability.

It is not in any miscalculation, then, of the force of general testimony, whether original or derived, that the error of Mr. Hume's abstract argument consists. It lies far deeper, in the false definition of a miracle, which he has given, as "a violation of the laws of nature"; — a definition which is accordant, indeed, with the definitions that have been usually given of it by theologians, but is not on that account more accurate and precise, as a philosophic expression of the phenomena intended to be expressed by it. To the theologian himself it is, I conceive, peculiarly dangerous; because, while it makes it essential to the reality of a miracle, that the very principle of continued uniformity of sequence should be false, on which our whole belief of causation, and consequently of the Divine Being as an operator, is founded, it gives an air of inconsistency, and almost of absurdity, to the very assertion of a miracle, and at the same time deprives the doctrine of miracles of its principal support against an argument, which, if his definition of them were philosophically a just one, Mr. Hume must be allowed to have urged very powerfully against them.

In mere philosophy, however, the definition, though we were to consider it, without any theological view, simply as the expression of certain phenomena of a very peculiar kind, is far from being just. The laws of nature, surely, are not *violated*, when a new antecedent is followed by a new consequent; they are violated only when, the antecedent being exactly the same, a different consequent is the result: and if such a violation — which, as long as it is a part of our very constitution to be impressed with an irresistible belief of the uniformity of the order of nature, may be said to involve, relatively to this belief, a physical contradiction — were necessarily implied in a miracle, I do not see how the testimony of any number of witnesses, the wisest, and most honorable, and least interested from any personal motive in the truth of what they report, could afford evidence of a miracle that might amount to proof. The concurring statements might, perhaps, be sufficient to justify a suspension of judgment between belief and disbelief; but this suspension is the utmost which the evidence of a fact so monstrous as the sequence of a different consequent when the antecedent had been exactly the same, could reasonably claim. When we have once brought our mind to believe in the violation of the laws of nature, we cannot know what we should either believe or disbelieve, as to the successions of events; since we must, in that case, have abandoned for the time the only principle on which the relation of cause and effect is founded: and, however constant the connection of truth with testimony, in the most favorable circumstances, may be, it cannot be more, though it may be less, constant than the connection of any other physical phenomena, which have been, by supposition, unvaried in their order of sequence, till the very moment of that supposed violation of their order in which the miracle is said to consist.

Let us suppose a witness, of the most honorable character, to state to us a fact, with which he had every opportunity of being perfectly acquainted, and in stating which he could not have any interest to deceive us, but might, on the contrary, subject himself to much injury by the public declaration; — it must be allowed, that it is in the highest degree improbable that his statement should be false. To express this improbability in the strongest possible manner, let us admit that the falsehood of his statement, in such circumstances, would be an absolute miracle, and therefore, according to the definition that is given of a miracle, would be a violation of a law of nature. It would be a miracle, then, if, in opposition to his former veracity and to his own interest in the case supposed, he should wish to deceive us; but if it be a miracle, also, which he asserts to have taken place, we must, equally whether we credit or do not credit his report, believe that a law of nature has been violated, by the sequence of an unaccustomed effect after an accustomed cause; and if we must believe such a change as constitutes an absolute violation of some law of nature, in either case, it is impossible to discover, in the previous equal uniformity of nature in both cases,— without the belief of which regular order of sequence we cannot form the notion of physical probabilities at all,— any ground of preference of one of these violations to the other.

Though we were to admit, then, to testimony in general all the force for which Dr. Campbell and other writers have so laboriously, and, as I conceive, in relation to the present argument, so vainly contended,— and though we were to imagine every possible circumstance favorable to the veracity of the reporter to be combined,— the utmost that can be implied in the admission is, that it would be a violation of a law of nature, if the testimony were false; but if it would not be more so than the alleged violation of a law of nature concerning which the testimony is offered, and if, beyond the uniformity of antecedence and consequence in the events of the universe, we cannot form a notion of any power whatever, a suspension of judgment, and not positive belief, in a case, in which, before we can believe either of the violations, we must have abandoned the very principle on which our whole system of physical belief is founded, is all which the propounder of a miracle, in this view of it, can be supposed reasonably to demand.

It would be vain, in such a case of supposed opposite miracles, to endeavor to multiply the improbabilities on one side, and thus to obtain a preference, by counting the number of separate witnesses, all wise, all possessing the means of accurate information, all honorable men, and all perfectly disinterested, or having personal motives that, if they were less honorable, would lead them rather to refrain from giving evidence; since the only effect of this combination of evidence would be to add to the probability of the statement, which, if once we have admitted the falsehood of it to be miraculous, is already as great as it is possible to be. It is a miracle, that one witness, who has had perfect opportunities of accurate observation, and every motive of personal interest to give a true representation of an event, should yet, in opposition to his own interest, prefer to give a false account of it. That a hundred, or a thousand, or a hundred thousand witnesses, should, in the same circumstances, concur in the same false account, would be a miracle indeed, but it would only be a miracle still. Of probability there are many degrees, from that which is merely possible to that which is almost certain; but the miraculous does not admit of gradation. Nobody thinks that the conversion of water into wine at the marriage-feast in Galilee would have been a greater miracle if the quantity of transmuted water had been doubled; and a commentator would surely render himself a little ridiculous, who, in descanting on the passage of the Israelites through the Red Sea, should speak of the myriads of liquid particles of the mass that were prevented from following their usual course, as rendering more miraculous the passage itself, than if the number of drops had been less by a few scores or hundreds. But if this numerical calculation would be absurd in the one case, when applied to a number of particles of matter, each of which, individually, may be considered as exhibiting the influence of a miraculous interposition of a Power surpassing the ordinary powers of nature, it is surely not less absurd, when applied to a number of minds, in each of which, in like manner, a violation of an accustomed law of nature is supposed. It is a miracle, that one drop of water should become wine: it is a miracle, that a thousand drops of water should be so changed. It is a miracle, that a single witness, with many motives to declare the truth, and not one motive to utter a falsehood, should yet, with great peril to himself, prefer to be an impostor: it is a miracle, that a thousand witnesses, with the same motives, should concur, at the same risk, in the same strange preference. In miracles there are truly, as I have said, no degrees. The Deity either must act or not act, — or, according to the false definition which I am opposing, a law of nature must either be violated or not violated. There may be less than a miracle; but there cannot be more than a miracle.

As long as a miracle is defined to be a violation of the law of nature, it is not wonderful that it should shock our strongest principles of belief; since it must require from us the abandonment, for the time, of the only principle by which we have been led to the belief of any power whatever, either in God himself, or in the things which he has created; — while, at the same time, it is defined to be that which must, by the very terms of the definition, be as improbable as false testimony can be in any circumstances. It may be less, but it cannot be more, worthy of the name of a miracle, that we should be deceived by the testimony of the best and wisest of mankind, as to a fact of which they had means of the most accurate knowledge, than that any other event should have happened, which is admitted by the reporters of it to be a violation of the order of nature, as complete as the falsehood of the testimony which reports it to us, in these or in any circumstances, itself could be.

With Mr. Hume's view of the nature of a miracle, then, — if we rashly give our assent to his definition, — it seems to me not very easy to get the better of his sceptical argument. The very assertion of a violation of a law of nature is, as we have seen, the assertion of something that is inconsistent with every principle of our physical faith: and, after giving all the weight which it is possible to give to the evidence of concurring witnesses, with the best means of knowledge, and no motives of interest that could lead them to wish to deceive, we may perhaps succeed in bringing one miracle against another, — the miracle of their falsehood against the physical miracle reported by them, — but we cannot do more than this: we cannot render it less a violation of a law of nature, — and less inconsistent, therefore, with the principle, which, both speculatively and practically, has guided us in all our views of the sequences of events, — that the reported miracle should have happened, than that the sage, and amiable, and disinterested reporters should knowingly and intentionally have labored to deceive us.

The definition, however, which asserts this apparent inconsistency with our experience, is not a just one. A miracle is *not* a violation of any law of nature. It involves, therefore, primarily, no contradiction, nor physical absurdity. It has nothing in it which is inconsistent with our belief of the most undeviating uniformity of nature: for it is not the sequence of a different event when the preceding circumstances have been the same; it is an effect that is new to our observation, because it is the result of new and peculiar circumstances. The antecedent has been, by supposition, different; and it is not wonderful, therefore, that the consequent also should be different.

While every miracle is to be considered as the result of an extraordinary antecedent, — since it flows directly from a higher power than is accustomed to operate in the common trains of events which come beneath our view, — the sequence which it displays may be regarded, indeed, as out of the common course of nature, but not as contrary to that course, any more than any other new result of new combinations of physical circumstances can be said to be contrary to the course of events, to which, from the absolute novelty of the circumstances, it has truly no relation whatever, either of agreement or disagreement. If we suppose any one, who is absolutely unacquainted with electrical apparatus and the strange phenomena which that apparatus can be made to evolve, to put his hand accidentally near a charged conductor, so as to receive from it a slight shock, though his sensation may be different from any to which he had been accustomed, we do not believe that he will on that account consider it as a proof of a violation of a law of nature, but only as the effect of something which was unknown to him before, and which he will conceive therefore to be of rare occurrence. In a miracle, in like manner, nothing more is to be supposed. It is the Divine will, that, preceding it immediately, is the cause of the extraordinary effect which we term miraculous; and whatever may be the new consequent of the new antecedent, the course of nature is as little violated by it, as it was violated by the electrician who for the first time drew lightning from the clouds, or by the aeronaut who first ascended to a region of the air of more ethereal purity than that which allows the gross substance of a cloud to float in it.

The Highest of all powers, of whose mighty agency the universe which sprung from it affords evidence so magnificent, has surely not ceased to be one of the powers of nature, because every other power is exercised only in delegated and feeble subordination to his omnipotence. He is the greatest of all the powers of nature; but he is still one of the powers of nature, as much as any other power, whose hourly or momentary operation is most familiar to us: — and it must be a very false philosophy indeed, which would exclude his omnipotent will from the number of powers, or assert any extraordinary appearances, that may have flowed from his agency, to be violations of an order, in which the ordinary sequences were different before, because the ordinary antecedents in all former time were different. There may be, or there may not be, reason — for this is a different question — to believe, that the Deity has, for any particular purpose, condescended to reveal himself as the direct producer of phenomena that are out of the usual course of nature; but, since we are wholly unacquainted with any limits to his power, and cannot form any notion, therefore, of events, as more or less fitted to be the physical consequents of his will to produce them, it would evidently be absurd for us to speak of any phenomenon that is said to be consequent on his will, as a violation of the natural order of the phenomena that might be expected to flow from an energy, of the transcendent extent of whose operation we are ignorant, and know only, that it is worthy of a reverent and grateful admiration, far surpassing what our hearts, in the feebleness of their worship, are capable of offering to it.

The shock of an earthquake, and the descent of stones from the sky, are not regarded as violations of any law of nature, though they are phenomena of very rare occurrence, which require a peculiar combination of the circumstances that physically precede them. What these circumstances are, the witnesses of the resulting phenomena may be wholly unable to state; but as they have been witnesses of the great results, they know at least, that the necessary combination, whatever it may have been, must previously have taken place. By the assertors of a miracle, the same necessity is always supposed. They do not contend, that, when the extraordinary event, which they term miraculous, happened, the previous circumstances were the same as at other times, when no such event was consequent; any more than a meteorologist contends, that, when stones fall from the air, the previous circumstances, however much their difference may have been beyond his power of observation, were absolutely the same as in the fall of rain or snow, or in any other phenomenon of the atmosphere that is more familiar to us. On the contrary, they contend that the difference of the effect — as proved by the evidence of their senses, or of indubitable testimony, in the same way as the truth of any other rare phenomenon is established — implies an extraordinary cause: and since all the circumstances of which the mere senses could judge, previously to the miracle, were the same as had frequently existed before, without any such marvellous result, they suppose the difference to have been in something which was beyond the sphere of the perceptive organs, and have recourse to the Divine volition, as a power of which the universe itself marks the existence, and which, in all the circumstances of the case, it seems most reasonable to consider as the antecedent of the extraordinary effect.

That a quantity of gunpowder, apparently as inert as the dust on which we tread, should suddenly turn into a force of the most destructive kind, all the previous circumstances continuing exactly the same, would be indeed contrary to the course of nature, but it would not be contrary to it, if the change were preceded by the application of a spark. It would not be more so, if the antecedent were any other existing power, of equal efficacy; and the physical influence which we ascribe to a single spark, it would surely not be too much to claim for that Being, to whom we have been led by the most convincing evidence to refer the very existence of the explosive mass itself, and of all the surrounding bodies on which it operates, and who has not a less powerful empire over nature now, than he had at the very moment at which it arose, and was what he willed it to be.

To that Almighty Power the kindling of a mass of gunpowder, to which our humble skill is adequate, is not more easy, than any of the wonders which we term miraculous. Whatever he wills to exist, flows naturally from that very will. Events of this kind, therefore, if truly taking place, would be only the operation of one of the acknowledged powers of nature, producing indeed what no other power might be capable of producing, but what would deserve as much to be considered as the natural consequence of the power from which it flows, as any other phenomenon to be regarded as the natural consequence of its particular antecedent. In the assertion of a miracle, therefore, whatever other reasons of doubt there may or may not be in any particular case, there is no longer the primary physical absurdity of a violation of a law of nature to be brought against the physical absurdity of another violation of a law of nature, — or of the asserted agency of a particular power, as marked by a breach of that very order the uniformity of which is all that constitutes our very notion of power itself. Every law of nature continues as it was; for every antecedent has its ordinary effect. We have only physical probabilities to be weighed with physical probabilities, precisely as in any other case in which any very extraordinary event is related to us; and according as the difference of these is greater or less, our doubt or belief or disbelief is to be the result.

The argument of Mr. Hume, in the only part of his Essay that is of importance in the philosophy of general belief, is an abstract one; and it is not the object of the present Note to enter into an historical and logical review of the probability or improbability of any particular miracles, but only to consider that abstract argument, in the universal application which its ingenious author was inclined to make of it, as sufficient, of itself, to preclude the necessity of examining the evidence of any miracle whatever, even in circumstances which, if the event related had been of any other kind, would have been regarded as in the highest degree favorable to the veracity of the reporters.

The assertor of a miracle — according to the view which I have taken of it, and which it seems to me impossible not to take of it, if the phenomenon to which that name is given be minutely analyzed — is not the assertor of a violation of any law of nature. What he asserts is the operation of a power that must be allowed to have existed truly at the moment of the alleged miraculous event, whether we admit or do not admit that particular operation, — the greatest of all existing powers, since it is by it alone that every other power of nature is what it is, — and of which, as of not less irresistible dominion now than it was in the moment of the original Creative will, what we term the laws of nature are nothing more than the continued manifestation.

If, indeed, the assertor of a miracle had to combat with an atheist, it will be allowed that the conditions of the reasoning would be changed, and that it would be impossible for him to obviate the force of the abstract negative argument, till he had previously established the truth of the first principles of theism; — as little possible, as it would be to prove lightning to be an electrical phenomenon to one who persisted in the denial of such a power as electricity. A miracle is stated to be the result of the operation of one of the powers of nature, whose very existence is denied by the atheist; and if the existence of the power itself be denied, the operation of that power in any case must also be denied. To the conception of an atheist, therefore, every miracle would be truly a violation of a law of nature, in the strictest sense of that phrase, and would of course involve all the physical absurdity that is implied in such a violation: the antecedent would seem to him the same, while the consequent was asserted to be different; because in his denial of the existence of any superhuman power is involved the denial of that new antecedent from which the miracle, as itself a new consequent, is supposed physically to flow, like any other physical consequent of any other antecedent.

If, however, the existence of the Deity be admitted, and, with his existence, the possibility of his agency, in circumstances in which it would be more for the advantage of his creatures that he should operate, than that he should abstain from operating, — the possible occurrence of which circumstances can be denied only by those who profess that they are capable of comprehending the infinite relations of events, and thus of ascertaining exactly, in every case, what would be more or less for the happiness of the universe, — then is the evidence of his asserted agency to be regarded in the same manner as the evidence of any other extraordinary event, that is supposed to have resulted from any other new combination of physical circumstances. It is to be met, not with a positive denial, nor with a refusal to examine it, but with a cautious slowness of assent, proportioned to the extraordinariness of the marvellous phenomenon. Strong, and closely bordering on disbelief, as our first feeling of doubt may be, it is still necessary, before we think ourselves authorized to disbelieve, that we should examine what, even though at first it may seem to us little worthy of being credited, may not on that account be positively false; and if, on examination, we find the evidence to be such, that we could not hesitate in admitting it, if it had related to any other species of extraordinary event, the result of any other combination of physical circumstances, so rare as never before to have been recorded by any observer, we surely cannot think ourselves justified in rejecting it altogether, because the physical power to whose agency it is supposed to bear witness, is the greatest of all the powers of nature.

In this discussion, we are never to forget, what I have already frequently repeated, that a miracle, if it truly take place, far from violating any physical law, is, in the peculiar circumstances in which it takes place, the natural result of the operation of a physical power, as much as any other rare phenomenon; and we may, therefore, derive some light, in our inquiry, from the consideration of the frame of mind with which we receive the narrative of any other physical event, so extraordinary as to be altogether new to our experience.

When we first heard of the fall of stones from the sky, there was considerable slowness to admit the fact; and this slowness, in such circumstances, it will be allowed, was accordant with the spirit of sound philosophy. But after the concurring reports of many creditable witnesses, have we remained incredulous, because a meteor so very strange may never have come under our own observation, — though for year after year, in every season and in every seeming variety of heat and light and moisture, we may have been most watchful observers of all the changes of the atmosphere? There is not a philosopher, whatever theory he may have formed of their origin, who is not now convinced that such bodies have truly fallen on the surface of our earth: — and why is he convinced? It is because the extraordinary fact, which has probably never come under his own observation, has been attested by many witnesses, able to form a judgment of it, and having no motive of interest to give a false report. But the power that is capable of working miracles is a power that must be believed to exist, as truly as the power, or combination of powers, in the upper regions of the atmosphere, or above our atmosphere, by which we suppose the aerolite to be produced. The event which we term miraculous, if there truly be such an event, is as natural a result of his operation in particular circumstances, as the aerolite of the rare combination of circumstances in which that peculiar atmospherical phenomenon has its origin. If the testimony of many sage and disinterested witnesses be capable of proving the one, it is equally capable of proving the other. The extraordinariness of the event, in both cases, should indeed, as I before said, make us peculiarly cautious in examining the evidence on which it is asserted; it affords, in the first statement of the fact, a presumptive improbability; and if this strong primary doubt, which, without amounting to disbelief, might in various circumstances approximate to it, were all for which Mr. Hume's argument had contended, there would have been little reason to dissent from his doctrine. But the extraordinariness, though demanding greater caution, does not, of itself, furnish counter-evidence. Above all, it does not entitle us to say at once, that whatever evidence can be offered on the subject is unworthy of our examination. We have still to examine the evidence of the extraordinary physical facts that are termed miracles, as we have to examine the evidence of any other extraordinary physical facts, that are reported to us under any other name.

He who was able to form the universe as it is, and to give life to man and everything which lives, may be presumed, if such be his pleasure, to be capable of giving life to a body that lies before us in death, inert and insensible indeed at present, but not more inert and insensible than the mass which was first animated with a living soul. God exists, then; his power is ever present with us; and it is capable of performing all which we term miraculous. We may be assured, indeed,—for this the regularity of the apparent sequences of phenomena justifies us in believing,—that he will not himself appear as the direct operator of any wonderful change, unless for some gracious purpose, like that which led him originally to the performance of the first miracle that produced everything which exists before us. But, as he operated then, he *may* operate again; from a similar gracious purpose we may infer a similar result of benefit to the world; and it certainly would be a most unwarrantable argument, which, on the acknowledged fact of one great miracle of creation, would found a reason for asserting that no miracle is afterwards to be credited, and from the many provisions for existing happiness infer that He whose beneficence at one time operated in the production of these, cannot be reasonably expected at any other time to do what, by supposition, it would be for the happiness of the world that he should do.

It is essential, indeed, for our belief of any miraculous event, that there should be the appearance of some gracious purpose, which the miracle may be supposed to fulfil; since all which we know of the operation of the Divine power in the universe, indicates some previous purpose of that kind. In our own nature, and in everything that exists around us, and that is capable of affecting us in any way, there is proof of the existence of a Divine operator, and of the connection of a beneficent design with his operation, as much as, in any other physical sequence of events, there is proof of a permanent relation of any other antecedent to any other consequent. The same principle, then, which leads us to expect the light of another day from the rising of the morrow's sun above the horizon, or, in a case more analogous because more extraordinary, the fall of a stone from the sky, if the circumstances should recur which are necessary for the production of that rare meteor, would justify our expectation of the still rarer phenomena which are termed miracles, if we had reason to believe, at any time, that circumstances had occurred, in which the happiness that was in the view of the Divine mind, in the original miracle of creation, would be promoted by a renewal of his mighty agency. It will be acknowledged, indeed, that, from our ignorance of the wide relations of events, we are very ill qualified to judge accurately of such circumstances. But though we may be very likely to be mistaken in determining them, it is not the less true, that such circumstances may exist; and that, in that case, the denial of the probability of a miracle would itself be inconsistent with belief of that very principle of uniformity, from which the experience that is said to be opposed to miracles derives its whole force, — the principle according to which we believe, that, in all similar circumstances, what has been once will be again.

If the creation of man was an act that was worthy of the Divinity, it was worthy on account of its object; and if other miracles tend to the same great object, they surely were not excluded by that primary miracle, with the beneficent purpose of which they are in harmony. Is there any reason which can be urged, *a priori*, to show, that a power which operated once is therefore never to operate again, and that it would be unworthy of Him who surrounded his creatures with so many means of increasing happiness, and endowed them with faculties of progressive advancement in knowledge, to give them, when a portion of that progress was completed, a revelation of truths of a higher order, by which they might become still more wise and happy? And if it would not be unworthy of Him who loved mankind, to favor them with such views of his moral government of the world, and of the futurity that awaits them, as might have this salutary influence, it could not be unworthy of Him to sanction his revelation by displays of extraordinary power, that might be sufficient to mark the high Author from whom it came. GOD exists: that HE has deigned to operate, the whole universe, which is the result of that operation, shows; — and it shows, too, that when he did thus deign to operate in that greatest of all miracles, which the sagest and most cautious deniers of every other miracle admit, the antecedent volition was a will of good to his creatures, in perfect analogy with that antecedent graciousness of will of which the assertors of other miracles suppose them to be the consequents.

If, before stating his abstract argument, Mr. Hume had established any one of the following propositions, — that there is no proof of any power by which the universe was formed, — or that the power which formed the universe, and was the source of all the regularity which we admire in nature, exists no longer, — or that the race of beings for whom, still more than for any other of its various races, our earth appears to have been formed, have now become wholly indifferent to the great Being, who then, by his own immediate agency, provided for them with so much care, — or that it is inconsistent with his wish for the happiness of his creatures, which that early provision for them shows, that he should make to them at any time such a revelation as would greatly increase their happiness, — or that, if we should still suppose him capable of making such a revelation, he could not be expected to sanction it with the authority of such events as those which we term miracles, — then, indeed, when either the Divine power was excluded from the number of the existing powers of nature, or his agency in the particular case was excluded, and when nothing, therefore, was left to be compared but the opposite probabilities or improbabilities of breaches of the familiar sequences of events, the argument on which the Essayist is disposed to found so much, might have been brought forward with irresistible force. But if it be admitted that a Power exists, who wrought the great miracle of creation with a gracious view to the happiness of man, — that there is no reason to believe this happiness to be less an object of Divine benevolence than it was originally, — that a revelation, of which the manifest tendency was to increase this happiness, would not be inconsistent with such benevolence, — and that, if a revelation were deigned to man, a miracle, or series of miracles, might be regarded as a very probable sanction of it; — then, since a miracle would be only the natural result of an existing physical power, in the peculiar and very rare circumstances in which alone its mighty energy is revealed, the evidence of its operation is to be examined, precisely like the evidence of any other extraordinary event. There is no violation of a law of nature, but there is a new consequent of a new antecedent. The extraordinary combination of circumstances, of which a miracle is the physical result, has now taken place; as when an earthquake first shook the hills, or a volcano first poured out its flood of fire, after the earth itself had perhaps existed for many ages, there was that combination of circumstances of a different kind, of which earthquakes and volcanoes are the natural results.

A miracle, I repeat, if it truly take place, is as little contrary to any law of nature, as any other phenomenon. It is only an extraordinary event, the result of extraordinary circumstances; — an effect that indicates a Power of a higher order than the powers which we are accustomed directly to trace in phenomena more familiar to us, but a Power whose continued and ever-present existence it is atheism only that denies. The evidence of a miracle, therefore, being the evidence, not of any violation of a law of nature, but of a fact that is reducible, like every other fact, to the physical operation of one of the powers of nature, does not form a class apart, but is to be considered exactly like the evidence of any other extraordinary phenomenon, that depends on circumstances over which we have no control. It is to be admitted or rejected, therefore, not simply as being evidence of a miracle, but as evidence which is, or is not, of sufficient weight in itself to establish the reality of the extraordinary phenomenon, in support of which it is adduced. It leaves the mind still free to examine, in every particular case, the likelihood or unlikelihood of the mighty agency which is asserted; but in the freedom of a philosophic mind, which knows that there truly exists a Power capable of doing what is asserted to have been done, it will find only such doubt as leads to greater caution of inquiry, and not instant disbelief or unexamining rejection.

I have already said, that it is not the object of this Note to enter into an examination of the credibility of any particular set of miracles: it is only to show that the general abstract argument, with which Mr. Hume would render unavailing the most powerful testimony that can be imagined to be offered in support of asserted facts of this kind, has not the overwhelming force which he conceived it to possess. By correcting the false definition which has been generally given of miracles, with an analysis of them which appears to me more philosophic, I would reduce them to the rank of other physical facts, and in this light would claim for them the same examination which we give to the reports of other phenomena that are wholly new to us, — an examination that may be accompanied with the strongest doubt, and may terminate in disbelief, if the evidence be slight and scanty, but which may terminate also in belief, and be accompanied with doubt progressively fainter and fainter, as the evidence in the course of inquiry appears to be of greater force. This title to be examined, it might, perhaps, be too much to claim for any miracle, if it were asserted to be the actual violation of those laws of nature, on the belief of the uniformity of which our very examination of its probability must proceed. But it is not too much to claim for it, when it is shown not to involve the inconsistency that is implied in a violation of a law of nature, but to be only the physical operation of an existing power, as little opposite to the regularity of nature, in the particular circumstances in which it is said to take place, as any other new phenomena that result from new combinations of physical circumstances. There is not a phenomenon, however familiar now, which had not at one time a beginning; and I may say even, that there is not a phenomenon which was not originally, as flowing from the Creative will, an event of this very class. Everything has once been miraculous, if miraculous mean only that which results from the direct operation of a Divine power; and the most strenuous rejecter of all miracles, therefore, if we trace him to his origin, through the successive generations of mankind, is an exhibiter, in his own person, of indubitable evidence of a miracle.

NOTES.

NOTE A.

(See page xix.)

"THE high antiquity of the account of the agony in the garden," says De Wette, "is attested by Heb. v. 7, and by its internal verisimilitude and beauty, especially as it is given in Matthew. This internal verisimilitude and beauty must not be disturbed by unnatural suppositions, as where some (Thiess, Paulus) suppose a bodily feebleness and enervation, and others (Olshausen) a mystical abandonment by God. The following observations may serve to place the narrative in a proper light. Heroic indifference to suffering, the want of which Celsus and other opposers of Christianity have charged upon Jesus, belongs not to the primitive Christian ideal. The moral strength of the Christian is the Divine element, which is mighty in human weakness. It is a touching and consoling truth, that Jesus felt the full weight of his sufferings, wholly shared with us the weakness of humanity, and went before us in overcoming it through the power of prayer. The ground of his anxiety was fear on account of his sufferings (ver. 39); but not merely on account of his bodily pain. We must also take into view the pain which he felt that the object of his mission could be attained only through rejection, persecution, blood, and death, and thus consider the pain which he felt on account of sins not his own, for which he was to suffer." *

* De Wette on Matt. xxvi. 36.

"Jesus cries out in the language of Ps. xxii. 1, and the question arises, In what sense did he use this verse? Certainly he intended to express something passing within himself, but yet borrowed from, and of course in conformity with, the sense of the passage in its connection with the Psalm. In both connections complaints are made of great suffering, which overpowers human nature and disturbs its harmony with God, — a suffering so great, that he who bears it believes himself bereft of the assistance of God. But we know that a man cannot at any time be literally forsaken by God; since he is omnipresent. Nor can a truly pious man, in his permanent consciousness, believe himself to be forsaken by him; as this would be impious. The thought expressed in the quotation can only be regarded as a transient, momentary obscuration of our Saviour's consciousness of God. So, in the original passage, the tone of complaint is changed at last by the Psalmist into one of confidence and hope. Of all persons Jesus could least be, or believe himself to be, deserted by God; since in him the consciousness of God was most perfect. Yet this consciousness might momentarily be disturbed by the transient ascendency of human weakness. For we must suppose a certain infirmity in Jesus, in accordance with his liability to temptation implied in Matt. ch. iv. Since he made use of the words of Ps. xxii., it is more than probable, that he called up before his mind its whole contents, and of course the change of complaint into comfort. On this supposition, the disturbance of his consciousness of God ceased immediately after his utterance of the words of the first verse, and thus his language has the same import as that which he used in ch. xxvi. 39 would have had, if he had only said, 'If it be possible, let this cup pass from me,' and had not added, 'Nevertheless, not as I will, but as thou wilt.' The suffering which Jesus experienced for a moment was not mere bodily pain, but pain of soul on account of the sins for which he suffered. See on xxvi. 39. But we must not suppose it to have been a suffering which expiated the sins of men, and absolutely sunk itself in them, if we would not darken the sin-conquering strength of Jesus upon the cross. The lovers of the horrible may compare Olshausen, and Ebrard, p. 693, &c." *

On John xii. 27, De Wette also remarks: "After this lofty burst of enthusiasm, human weakness makes itself felt for a moment in Jesus, and with noble openness he gives expression to it in the language, 'Now is my soul troubled, and what shall I say? Father, save me from this hour!' .... But with the expression of submission to the Divine will, in the language, 'Father, glorify thy name!' i. e. cause [through my death] that men shall acknowledge and honor thee as what thou art, as Father! the spirit of Jesus triumphs over the flesh, as in Matt. xxvi. 39, in the words, 'Not as I will, but as thou wilt.'"

Dr. Lücke, in his comments on John xii. 27, 28, remarks: "When Jesus says, 'Now is my soul troubled,' &c., it seems as if he were interrupted in the thoughts which had occupied his mind in ver. 23 – 26, by a strong emotion, so that he was not in a condition to continue them. The excitement of his feelings does not wholly overmaster him. He can think — he can speak; but it is so strong that his utterance becomes abrupt and brief, so that for a moment he knows not what to say; — 'and what shall I say?' What is it that so deeply moves him? What is it which against his will takes possession of his soul? It is the thought of his impending death, which in ver. 23 – 26 presses upon him with so much power. But how? Jesus has spoken of his death with so much clearness as to represent it as necessary for the salvation of his kingdom, and as the principal means of his glorification. In general, death has had for him, the holy one, no sting. No pain even on account of the temporary interruption of his work by death appears in ver. 25 and 26 to have affected his mind. How then are we to explain the fact, that his soul is

* De Wette's Exegetisches Handbuch, Matt. xxvii. 46.

now so much shaken by the thought of his impending death? This would be wholly inexplicable, were it not true that the only-begotten son of God was also the son of man, so that he was subject to the involuntary emotions of the soul, — to the purely human feeling of fear as well as of joy. The strong joy in life which man naturally possesses includes in itself as naturally the fear of death. It is according to a holy law of nature that death has its terrors for men, especially death in youth, in the freshness of life. If we also regard the death of Jesus as the culminating point of his conflict with the sinful world, it acquires even for a holy spirit a dismaying power. A soul so delicately organized as we must conceive that of the Redeemer to have been, must necessarily have been seized by it. But Jesus was seized by it only for a moment. A permanent possession by it such as prevents all thought, all speech, is under any circumstances inconceivable in the spirit of the only-begotten son of God, and especially immediately after what he has said with such clearness and explicitness in verses 23 – 26. As in other cases the virtue of the Redeemer in conflict appears at the same moment in triumph, and as the passive state of his mind suddenly changes into an active one, so also here. Even in the very expression of his dismay, he rises above it. But it is in his prayer to his Father that his divine rest and composure completely return. Yet it is only by degrees that the emotion subsides, and the waves of mental agitation become still. Thus the language of the Redeemer is an actual prayer. 'Father, save me from from this hour!' the hour of death. So vivid is the thought of this, that he sees himself already in the midst of it. He is in conflict, he suffers, now. Hence the words, 'Save me from this hour!' Griesbach and Lachmann read the sentence interrogatively. According to their pointing, the prayer acquires a peculiar character. Jesus asks, as it were, whether he should so pray. Thus in not venturing or resolving so to pray, he manifests a degree of resignation. But De Wette supposes that the language should be understood without the interrogation, as an actual prayer; as in Matt. xxvi. 39. He is right. The prayer naturally expresses the opposition, the conflict, between his fear of death and the spirit of resignation which belonged to the consciousness of his Divine mission. The question, 'What shall I say?' is the expression of this conflict in prayer. But the conflict is victoriously ended, when he says, 'But for this cause came I to this hour.' These words, being the concise expression of strong feeling, are obscure. If we regard it as doubtful whether the phrase, 'to come to this hour,' ἔρχεσθαι εἰς τὴν ὥραν, means to come to an appointed hour with the idea of experiencing it, we may take ἦλθον, 'I came,' in an absolute sense, as denoting the coming of the Redeemer into the world; and εἰς τὴν ὥραν ταύτην, 'to this hour,' as denoting the design of his coming, namely, the suffering of the hour of death. In this case we may refer διὰ τοῦτο, 'for this cause,' to the same, so that as an indefinite expression it becomes more closely defined by εἰς τὴν ὥραν ταύτην, 'for this very hour.' [In this way the rendering will be, "It was for this I came,—for this hour."] But on a comparison of the phraseology with εἰσέρχεσθαι εἰς τὴν ζωήν, 'to enter into life,' in Matt. xix. 17, εἰς τὴν κατάπαυσιν, 'to enter into rest,' in Heb. iii. 11, and εἰς πειρασμόν, 'into temptation,' in Matt. xxvi. 41, the doubt is removed. As in verse 23 the hour for Jesus is said to have come, so he has now come to this hour in the sense of experiencing it. [In this way the rendering of the Common Version is correct, "for this cause came I to this hour."] But what is meant by 'this cause'? It is not definitely expressed. How is it to be understood from the connection? According to De Wette, 'this cause' means either 'to die,' or to fulfil what is expressed in verse 24. But the former is tautological, the latter too remote. Olshausen supposes 'this cause' to denote the redemption of mankind. But this gives only a general view of the meaning, and is not indicated in the connection. Meyer is right in understanding 'this cause,' on account of its connection with what follows, as relating to Christ's glorification. It is, as it were, an abbreviated expression of the words in verse 23, 'Now is the Son of Man glorified,' which floated in the mind of John in the conception of the prayer. In the prayer this is more definitely expressed in the words, 'Father, glorify thy name.' This is the absolute object, in which everything else is included. With this absolute 'for this cause,' our Lord recovers the divine clearness and brightness of his spirit, which he had before his soul was momentarily and involuntarily troubled, as in verse 23. It is the glorification of the Divine name, the New Testament name of Father, in which his own glory as Son was included, for which he prays with full confidence. With the same spirit of submission the similar agitation of his soul in the garden of Gethsemane begins and ends." *

Meyer, on Matt. xxvii. 46, remarks: "Jesus expresses his feeling in the first words of the twenty-second Psalm. It is the feeling of being momentarily overpowered by the severest pain. . . . . By the words, 'Why hast thou forsaken me?' Jesus expressed what he personally felt, his *consciousness* of communion with God having been for a moment interrupted by his sufferings. But this momentary subjective feeling is not to be confounded with an actual objective abandonment by God (against Olsh. and the older commentators), which at least in the case of Jesus would have been a physical and moral impossibility. . . . . To find, with the older dogmatic theologians, the vicarious feeling of Divine wrath in the cry of anguish, 'Why hast thou forsaken me?' is to go beyond the New Testament view of the atoning death of Christ, as also that of the agony in Gethsemane. On the other hand, the opinion of some interpreters, that Jesus, when he quoted the first verse of the Psalm, had in his mind the whole of it, is arbitrary, and brings into his condition of immediate feeling the heterogeneous element of reflection and citation."

Bishop Pearson, than whom no writer of the Church of

* Commentar über das Evang. des Johannes, *ad loc.*

England has greater authority with Episcopalians, remarks on Matt. xxvi. 29: "These words infer no more than that he was bereft of such joys and comforts from the Deity as should assuage and mitigate the acerbity of his present torments." *

The long note of Bleek on Heb. v. 11 is substantially the same as the briefer one of the recent commentator Lünemann: "Who in the days of his flesh, when he had offered up prayers and supplications with strong crying and tears unto Him that was able to save him from death, and who was heard on account of his fear of God." On this Lünemann remarks: "In characterizing God as 'Him that was able to deliver Christ from death,' is implied the subject of Christ's prayer, namely, *deliverance from death.*"

De Wette, in his note on the same passage, maintains that our Saviour's prayer mentioned in it was for preservation from death, even if εἰσακουσθεὶς ἀπὸ τῆς εὐλαβείας should be understood as meaning "and was heard and delivered from his fear." De Wette supposes that "the being heard" may refer not even to the resurrection of Christ, but only to the strength given him to endure his sufferings, which was suggested to the writer by the tradition of the strengthening angel, recorded in Luke xxii. 43.

Ebrard, in his note on the passage, remarks: "Christ was, *in reference to his prayer to be preserved*, heard, and thus saved, ἀπὸ τῆς εὐλαβείας, *from his fear.* But then there is in these very words, ἀπὸ τῆς εὐλαβείας, a limitation of εἰσακουσθείς, *and was heard.* He prayed to be preserved from the death which threatened him, and was *heard* and saved from the fear of death." †

---

* Pearson on the Creed, Art. IV.

† Ebrard on Heb. v. 7.

NOTE B.

(See page xxi.)

All that is to be said in defence of our ancestors in reference to this and other cases of interference with the rights of conscience, or what Roger Williams called soul-freedom, is that they acted up to their principles; which are strongly stated in Norton's Epistle Dedicatory to the General Court, which is prefixed to his Answer to Pynchon: "That licentious and pestilent proposition, The care of religious matters belongs not to the magistrate, is a stratagem of the Old Serpent and Father of lies, to make free passage for the doctrine of devils; an invention not unlike Saul's oath, the trouble of Israel and escape of the enemy; a Satanical device tending to undermine the policy of God; attempting to charm that sword with a fallacy, whose dexterous and vigorous use instrumentally puts away evil from Israel, and turneth every way in its manner to keep the path of the tree of life. The rusting of this sword of Divine execution in the scabbard hath been more destructive unto truth than the drawing of the sword of persecution."

THE END.

Descriptive Catalogue of Books

PUBLISHED BY

WALKER, WISE, & CO.,

FOR THE

AMERICAN UNITARIAN ASSOCIATION,

21 Bromfield Street, Boston, Mass.

THE Books of the Association are stereotyped, and published in a neat and attractive style, and offered at prices considerably less than the usual cost of volumes of corresponding size and quality.

The publishers depend for remuneration upon the co-operation of the friends of Liberal Christianity, in effecting *large sales.*

Additions will be made, from time to time, to the *Theological* and *Devotional Libraries*, as also to the miscellaneous list.

OF THE THEOLOGICAL LIBRARY,

The following volumes are published :—

VOL. I.—SELECTIONS FROM THE WORKS OF WILLIAM E. CHANNING, D. D. A handsome 12mo volume of 480 pages, containing "all the clearest and fullest statements he gave of his views concerning theology and religion." Price, 60 cents.

"Some of the most original and brilliant thoughts that have been contributed by the literature of the age are scattered through these pages."

"No better service can be rendered to a young man who may be sceptical as to the truth of Christianity, than to place this volume in his hands."

VOL. II.—UNITARIAN PRINCIPLES CONFIRMED BY TRINITARIAN TESTIMONIES; being Selections from the Works of eminent Theologians belonging to Orthodox Churches. By JOHN WILSON. This volume has more than 500 pages; and, as it has quotations from over four hundred of the most approved theological writers in all ages, it comprises a whole library in one volume. Its object is to show what concessions have been made by Trinitarian writers to the essential truth of Unitarian views. Second edition. Price, $1.

"By a vast deal of study, and under the guidance of a most conscientious accuracy and candor in selecting and verifying his quotations, the author has gathered from Christian writers who are not Unitarians, admissions, avowals, and emphatic declarations, which fully authenticate the Christian character and the Christian sentiment and principles of those who profess Unitarianism." — *Rev. George E. Ellis, in Christian Examiner.*

VOL. III.—STATEMENT OF REASONS FOR NOT BELIEVING THE DOCTRINES OF TRINITARIANS CONCERNING THE NATURE OF GOD AND THE PERSON OF CHRIST. By ANDREWS NORTON. Second Edition. With a Memoir of the Author, by Rev. Dr. NEWELL of Cambridge. This is the fullest, the ablest, and most conclusive argument that has ever been published on this subject. Price, $1.

"Mr. Norton writes for intelligent men, for those who do not shrink from

examination and patient thought, who are not disgusted at being required to exercise a manly independence, who seek for truth for truth's sake, and are willing to pay the price of its attainment. Such will find, in the work before us, ample materials for study and reflection." — *Christian Examiner.*

VOL. IV. — A COLLECTION OF THEOLOGICAL ESSAYS FROM VARIOUS AUTHORS. With an Introduction by GEORGE R. NOYES, D. D. Price, $1.00.

"A collection of thoughtful and carefully prepared papers on some of the leading topics of theological difference, from such men as Stanley and Jowett, Tholuck and Powell, Guizot, Newcome, Roland Williams, Edward Harwood, and Thomas Brown, could not fail to possess both an immediate interest and a permanent value. Such is the character of the volume before us." — *Professor Huntington's Religious Magazine.*

"So valuable a collection, so interesting, so advanced in thought, so liberal in tone, has never been made before." — *Boston Evening Transcript.*

VOL. V. — STUDIES OF CHRISTIANITY; or, Timely Thoughts for Religious Thinkers. A Series of Papers by JAMES MARTINEAU. Edited by WILLIAM R. ALGER. Price, $1.00.

Those who are acquainted with Mr. Martineau's genius, with the extraordinary value of whatever he writes, will need no exhortation to provide themselves with this fresh and crowded volume, containing, as it does, the larger number of his latest and most important papers. But to others it may be said, that in all the noblest endowments of a theological and religious teacher, — gifts of intellect and imagination, loftiness of character, range of experience, consummate learning and culture, — Mr. Martineau is first among the very foremost living men. And nowhere are his acuteness and comprehensiveness of thought, his vast acquisitions, his matchless splendor of diction, and his commanding catholicity of spirit, more lavishly shown than in these "Studies of Christianity," which ought to be studied by every clergyman and every cultivated layman in our land.

"Take this volume for all in all, it is the product of a bold, independent, and original mind; from the beginning to the end it throbs with life; is suggestive in almost every sentence; opens wide visions of thought on questions that concern the sublimest interests of the soul, and deals with them in a manner worthy of their sublimity; breathes everywhere the humanity of a strong yet gentle nature; arouses the heart of the brave, the generous, the honorable, the heroic; repels with righteous scorn the mean, the maudlin, the effeminate, everything in idea or conduct that is spurious or unmanly; is written in a style of musical variety, as well as soaring and expansive grandeur, and which only errs, when it does err, in an excess of beauty; contains more passages of striking, profound, and inspiring eloquence than we have often before met with in the same number of pages." — *Boston Courier.*

THE DEVOTIONAL LIBRARY.

VOL. I. — THE ALTAR AT HOME. A Collection of Prayers for Private and Social Use, written by Unitarian Ministers in and near Boston. Nine editions of this well-known work have been published. Price, 60 cents.

"It has been prepared in a devout and earnest spirit, in excellent taste, and freedom from sectarian and polemical bias. We commend this work to the favorable attention of the public." — *Boston Atlas.*

"From a careful perusal we have no hesitation in saying that it is a book of uncommon excellence, well adapted to multiply the blessings of private and domestic worship, and ought to find a place in every family." — *Christian Inquirer.*

"They are all written with simplicity and beauty, and some of them are marked by a high degree of solemnity and fervor." — *Puritan Recorder.*

Vol. II. — THE CHRISTIAN DOCTRINE OF PRAYER. By James Freeman Clarke. It discusses the whole subject of the foundation of prayer, objections to it, reasons and preparations for it, its results and bearings upon the spiritual life, in the bold and clear style of its author. Price, 60 cents.

"We can hardly praise this book too highly. It fully meets the questions which it attempts to discuss. We know of no writer who addresses the religious world from precisely such a stand-point as Mr. Clarke. He is eminently free from all sectarian limitations, and therefore speaks to a much larger audience than most writers upon religious or theological questions. He powerfully appeals to the reason, while he continually addresses the spiritual nature." — *Salem Gazette.*

Vol. III. — THE ROD AND THE STAFF. By Rev. Thomas T. Stone. Second Edition. Price, 60 cents.

"This work is not to be placed in the same rank with the small, meagre, sentimental manuals, which religious societies are perpetually issuing as devotional literature, and which pious people dutifully purchase for the torment of their children. It is large, genial, written for all souls, good for everybody. It deserves to rank with Jeremy Taylor. Few can read thoughtfully the chapters of this volume without feeling that an addition has been made to their mental resources." — *Christian Inquirer.*

"It is written in a sweet and earnest spirit, which must commend it to all who seek to nourish the life of Christian piety in their hearts." — *Christian Examiner.*

"The work is written in an excellent spirit, and embraces many valuable ideas." — *Boston Journal.*

"This work is not of a sectarian, nor yet of a doctrinal, but chiefly of a devotional character. It bears the impress of a highly gifted mind, that has no partiality for a beaten track." — *Boston Puritan Recorder.*

Vol. IV. — THE HARP AND THE CROSS. By Rev. S. G. Bulfinch. The work contains between one and two hundred gems of sacred poetry, culled from all the best writers in the English language, by one who has himself added some of the choicest contributions to this department of letters. Price, 60 cents.

Vol. V. — ATHANASIA; or, FOREGLEAMS OF IMMORTALITY. By Rev. E. H. Sears. Third Edition. In this work, the subjects of death and a future life are fully considered; and cheering views are presented, which "turn the shadow of death into the morning." Price, 60 cents.

"'Athanasia' will stand as a lovely classic in sacred literature, and a beautiful inspiration of pure devotional feeling. . . . . . The best test of merit of a book is when we feel that we have been made better by reading it; and while 'Athanasia' widens the field of intellectual vision, and makes solid and substantial the bridge from time to eternity, it quickens the conscience in its sense of duty, and softens the heart with a tenderer and more celestial love." — *New York Christian Inquirer.*

"The American Unitarian Association have never published a work which will reach the core of more souls than this. The other productions of Mr. Sears have been marked by the loftiest moral beauty in the purest and most elegant diction; but this is his *chef d'œuvre* in many respects. . . . . . On the whole, we know no religious work of the age adapted to make a deeper, more practical, and more gladdening impression on thoughtful and lofty minds." — *Boston Christian Register.*

VOL. VI. — STORMY SUNDAYS. Dedicated to those who are kept from church by stormy weather. This is a series of religious services to be read in the quiet of one's home. There are seven sermons, never before printed, written by distinguished divines. Price, 60 cents.

The *London Inquirer* thus concludes a long notice: "The book is full of beauties of the highest order, and does great credit to the taste of the compiler."

☞ *In addition to the foregoing* "LIBRARIES," *we publish the following valuable works:* —

REGENERATION. By E. H. SEARS. Sixth Edition. It describes the necessity and process of the great transformation which the Gospel is designed to make in the individual life, and is written in a style of exceeding freshness and beauty. Price, 44 cents.

THE SUNDAY-SCHOOL LITURGY. This book is free from sectarianism or dogmatism. It was prepared by a pastor, who for years has consecrated scholarly and devout gifts to this interesting department of religious instruction. His manuscripts were examined by several gentlemen, who were requested to add, suppress, or recast portions, or entire parts, according to their judgment and taste. They gave time and care to this revision. Price, 37 cents.

THE DISCIPLINE OF SORROW. By Rev. WILLIAM G. ELIOT, D. D., of St. Louis. Second Edition. Hundreds of bereaved families have expressed their grateful sense of the value of these soothing and hopeful words. Price, 30 cents.

GRAINS OF GOLD. Selections from the Writings of Rev. C. A. BARTOL. A beautiful little gift, containing gems of thought from one of the most gifted writers. Price, 25 cents.

CHANNING'S THOUGHTS. This is another little gift-book, got up in an attractive style. It contains those short, epigrammatic sentences into which Dr. Channing so often condensed his grandest thoughts. Miss Dix, the well-known philanthropist, remarked that she had distributed hundreds of copies, and found few books so well calculated to lead to a larger acquaintance with the writings of this divine. Price, 25 cents.

☞ We propose to keep a *full stock* of **UNITARIAN BOOKS**, whether published in this country or abroad. No pains will be spared to make the assortment complete, so that any work in this department of literature may be had of us, if in print. *Mail orders* will receive prompt attention; *and any work advertised by us will be forwarded by mail* FREE OF EXPENSE, on the receipt of the advertised price, in postage-stamps or bankable money.

A FULL CATALOGUE is in preparation, which will be issued as soon as possible, and may be had on application.

WALKER, WISE, & CO.,

21 Bromfield Street, Boston.

www.ingramcontent.com/pod-product-compliance
Lightning Source LLC
LaVergne TN
LVHW021233110826
845150LV00002B/325
* 9 7 8 1 4 2 5 5 6 2 2 7 4 *